Political Psychology

D0206629

What shapes political behavior more: the situations in which individuals find themselves, or the internal psychological makeup—beliefs, values, and so on—of those individuals? This is perhaps the leading division within the psychological study of politics today. *Political Psychology: Situations, Individuals, and Cases, second edition*, provides a concise, readable, and conceptually organized introduction to the topic of political psychology by examining this very question.

Using this situationism–dispositionism framework—which roughly parallels the concerns of social and cognitive psychology—this book focuses on such key explanatory mechanisms as behaviorism, obedience, personality, groupthink, cognition, affect, emotion, and neuroscience to explore topics ranging from voting behavior and racism to terrorism and international relations. The new edition includes a new chapter on the psychology of the media and communication. Houghton has also updated the text to analyze recent political events such as the 2012 election, and to include up-and-coming research in the areas of neuroscience, behavioral economics, and more.

Houghton's clear and engaging examples directly challenge students to place themselves in both real and hypothetical situations which involve intense moral and political dilemmas. This highly readable text will provide students with the conceptual foundation they need to make sense of the rapidly changing and increasingly important field of political psychology.

David Patrick Houghton is Senior Lecturer in Defence Studies at the Department of Defence Studies at King's College London.

Political Psychology

Situations, Individuals, and Cases

Second Edition

David Patrick Houghton

Routledge
Taylor & Francis Group

NEW YORK AND LONDON

This edition first published 2015
by Routledge
711 Third Avenue, New York, NY 10017

and by Routledge
2 Park Square, Milton Park, Abingdon, Oxon OX14 4RN

Routledge is an imprint of the Taylor & Francis Group, an informa business

© 2015 Taylor & Francis

First edition published by Taylor & Francis in 2008

Trademark notice: Product or corporate names may be trademarks or registered trademarks, and are used only for identification and explanation without intent to infringe.

Library of Congress Cataloging in Publication Data
Houghton, David Patrick.
Political psychology : situations, individuals, and cases / David Patrick Houghton. — Second edition.
    pages cm
 1. Political psychology.   I. Title.
 JA74.5.H68 2014
 320.01′9—dc23
                                                    2013048890

ISBN: 978-0-415-83365-3 (hbk)
ISBN: 978-0-415-83382-0 (pbk)
ISBN: 978-0-203-36262-4 (ebk)

Typeset in Perpetua
by RefineCatch Limited, Bungay, Suffolk, UK

Contents

PART III
Bringing the Two Together   189

Illustrations

Figures

Tables

Preface to the Second Edition

The original version of this book was written out of a sense of frustration, both that of my students and my own: we could not find a book on political psychology that everyone really liked, and which had some overriding organizational framework to make sense of things. The sheer number of theories in political psychology can be bewildering for undergraduates, so I set out to write something that would expose them to the most important ones while fitting these into larger conceptual baskets. This version therefore retains the situationist versus dispositionist emphasis of the original, and makes another distinction used in the first edition—*Homo economicus versus Homo psychologicus*—more explicit and up front than it was.

Political psychology is a fast-moving field, and a number of things have happened to it since this book first appeared five years ago. Most notably, advances in genopolitics, neuropolitics, and our understanding of the role that emotion plays in decision-making have had a significant impact on the topics and materials those of us who focus on this area teach and study. During the last few years, a number of very interesting and important books have also been published which expand on some of the themes covered in this textbook, including John Hibbing et al.'s *Predisposed*, Daniel Kahneman's *Thinking, Fast and Slow*, Jonah Lehrer's *How We Decide*, George Lakoff's *The Political Mind*, Carol Tavris and Elliot Aronson's *Mistakes Were Made (But Not By Me)*, and many, many more. Apart from the opportunity to generally update the book using these fresh sources, changes in this new edition include:

- Chapter 1 has been revised and updated, making the organizing devices used in the new edition more explicit. The existing edition dealt only briefly with the content of *Homo economicus* or the Rational Actor Model (RAM), but this section has been revised and expanded. It also viewed the *Homo psychologicus* model mostly from the perspective of the cognitive psychology of the 1980s and 1990s. In the last few years, however, cognitive science—and neuroscience in particular—has uncovered further ways in which individual decision-makers depart from pure rationality. For instance, it has been discovered that much reasoning is undertaken by the unconscious brain, before we are ever aware of "making" a decision. It has also been found that we don't necessarily know what our own preferences are before making a decision, and that those preferences can be altered by purely presentational factors. This version makes these points more explicitly.

- I have added an entirely new chapter entitled "The Psychology of Political Communication, Persuasion, and the Mass Media," containing a discussion of how and why particular political arguments prove more appealing psychologically than others, as well as a consideration of political communication more generally. Also new to this version is a discussion of the related but separable issues of *agenda setting*, *framing*, *priming*, and *anchoring*, especially the work of Kahneman and Amos Tversky, George Lakoff, Dennis Chong, James Druckman, Ann Crigler, Doris Graber, and Russell Neuman. I had resisted including all of this impressive work in the original edition in order try to avoid overwhelming the reader with too much literature, but I now realize that this objective was achieved only at the cost of leaving out an important and growing topic within political psychology. This has now become Chapter 13, and the existing chapters have been pushed back in number so that there are now 18 in total.

- Chapter 11 has been substantially rewritten and updated to cover recent research in biopolitics, neuropolitics, and genopolitics, developments which were just beginning to have an impact when the original edition appeared but which have increased exponentially in importance during the last few years.

- I have added discussions of one or two classic research projects which were omitted from the first edition and which various scholars of political psychology have told me they would like to see included. The classroom "eye color" experiment of Jane Elliott, for instance, has much to say about the psychology of racial, ethnic, and religious differences, and I have also added Leon Festinger's "Marian Keech" story to the discussion of cognitive consistency. The chapter on race has also been updated.

- Examples have been generally updated throughout to take account of the 2012 presidential election in the United States and developments in the neuroscience of voting.

- The fast pace of change in the field of political psychology has necessitated an updated conclusion—now called "The Future of Political Psychology"—which is Chapter 18 in this new edition. The new conclusion addresses many of the new directions that political psychology has taken and innovations that have occurred since the first edition. In particular, the recognition gained within the field of economics of many of the theories presented in this book is changing that field quite dramatically. A new field of *behavioral economics* has emerged in a discipline long dominated by the Enlightenment view of reason and "Rational Man." The new conclusion will address why no approach called "behavioral politics" has yet emerged, however. While there has long been a recognition of the significance of "bounded rationality" in the study of both foreign policy decision-making and voting behavior, political science as a field has largely failed to integrate these approaches into a concerted attack upon the Rational Actor Model. Why? In part, analysts have clung to the simplifying but non-empirical assumptions that traditional *Homo economicus* provides, allowing political behavior to be modeled in a comforting but ultimately misleading way. The new final chapter argues for a fresh approach to the study of politics based on the integration of the approaches covered in the book into a single "cognitive neuroscience of politics," "behavioral politics," "neuropolitics," or "political neuroscience."

• A list of resources for the teacher and the student has been added at the end of each chapter. For instance, Stanley Milgram's own home-made film *Obedience* is something that in my experience students benefit very greatly from watching, since it brings the topic to life in a way it is hard to do via prose or teaching alone. References to CRM's film *Groupthink* and BBC specials like *Five Steps to Evil* and *The Stanford Experiment* are added here too.

Finally, the author would like to thank Michael Kerns and Darcy Bullock at Routledge for their devotion to this project and great patience while this second edition took shape. As always, I especially thank my father Bernard, mother Deirdre, daughter Isabelle, and son Carlos for their constant love and encouragement, without which none of the writing I've done would have been possible.

Orlando, Florida and Shrivenham, England
November 2013

Introduction

Chapter 1

Two Conceptual Schemes
or Distinctions

What we know (or think we know) about political behavior is changing rapidly, mostly because our understanding of how the brain itself works and how the mind and body affect one another is being transformed. Our popular conception of the supposed "rationality" of human beings—in which our actions are the outcome of conscious thought and deliberation, and where such rational thought trumps (or ought to take precedence over) "wayward" emotions—has been popular at least since the eighteenth century. It has long had an instinctive appeal with philosophers and the person in the street alike. But it is increasingly being challenged by advances in neurobiology and neuroscience, building in a more and more radical way on a critique which began in earnest with the birth of psychology as a field in the nineteenth and twentieth centuries.

As the cognitive linguist George Lakoff points out, this standard view of human decision-making is very much a product of a historical period we commonly term "the Enlightenment." During the eighteenth century, "reason" triumphed over "tradition." In politics, monarchies were increasingly replaced by republics (and later liberal democracies) in the West, and religion was challenged by science and secularism. Although this period of human history certainly represented a great advance on what had gone before, Lakoff suggests, it had one major downside: it saddled us with a way of thinking about human reasoning and decision-making that we now know to be misleading. We implanted a vision of ourselves as highly reasoned and rational, but modern cognitive science and political psychology fundamentally challenge that. "Most of us think we know our own minds. This is because we engage in conscious thought, and it fills much of our waking life," Lakoff notes.

> But what most people are not aware of, and are sometimes shocked to discover, is that most of our thought—an estimated 98 percent—is not conscious. It is below the level of consciousness. It is what our brains are

doing that we cannot see or hear . . . Your brain makes decisions for you that you are not consciously aware of.[1]

We may *feel* as if we are rational beings, but advances in neuroscience are challenging our understanding of ourselves and the extent to which we "know our own minds." In particular, the idea that emotion is not usually a destructive force but actually essential to reasoned decision-making is beginning to take hold in the study of political psychology. As Rose McDermott puts it:

> Most of us are taught from early on that logical, rational calculation forms the basis of sound decisions . . . we assume that emotions can only interfere with this process . . . But what if we were wrong about the general impact of emotion on decision making? What if, most of the time, emotion serves a productive function, providing the foundation for swift and accurate decision making? What if emotion assumed equal, or even primary, status in generating choice?[2]

We will have more to say about this transformation in our understanding of behavior later on, especially when we discuss the topics of emotion and neuroscience in more depth. But for now we should note that this radical critique ultimately calls into question the notion that we are even conscious agents making choices, and challenges the notion that we can somehow divorce feelings and emotions from decision-making. More broadly, this point about how we commonly *assume* that human beings make decisions and how they actually *do* gives rise to the first distinction that we'll use in this book, between what are commonly called *Homo economicus* and *Homo psychologicus*. It is also rather useful, I shall suggest, to distinguish between two more general approaches to understanding political behavior, *situationism* and *dispositionism*; in other words, is our behavior most often a product of the situations in which we find ourselves, or do our basic predispositions about the world fundamentally shape the ways in which we react to it? We'll take each conceptual distinction in turn.

Homo Economicus and Homo Psychologicus (or "Econs" and "Humans")

Traditionally, psychology has provided only one set of approaches to understanding what drives political behavior, for the development of modern political science has been influenced by economics as well. At present, two models of decision-making still dominate our thinking about political behavior,

Table 1.1 A summary of the features of the *Homo economicus* and *Homo psychologicus* models

Homo economicus
- Humans are fully rational actors.
- They possess perfect information.
- Derived from microeconomics.
- Actor maximizes "subjective utility."
- Actor weighs up the costs and benefits of various actions.
- He/she then selects the option that delivers the greatest benefits relative to cost (optimal choice).
- Actors update their beliefs when new information becomes available.

Homo psychologicus
- "Boundedly rational" actor.
- Actors do not possess perfect information.
- There are limits to human beings' processing abilities.
- Derives from social and cognitive psychology, and from neuroscience.
- Actor "satisfices" instead of maximizes utility.
- He/she employs various cognitive short cuts in order to manage "information overload" or a shortage of information.
- Actors fail to update their beliefs, even when new information becomes available.
- Group and broader social pressures may lead the actor to behave in non-rational ways, even contrary to his/her beliefs and values.

one derived from economics, the other derived from psychology. Each is summarized in Table 1.1.

One point of contention between the two views is that while the *Homo economicus* model holds that actors update their views when new information becomes available, *Homo psychologicus* maintains that they very often do not. One classic approach within the latter camp that we'll discuss later in the book is called "cognitive consistency" theory, and it's especially well illustrated by the Marian Keech story, which shows what typically happens "when prophecy fails." During the early 1950s, the psychologist Leon Festinger infiltrated what we would nowadays call a religious cult. Its leader, "Marian Keech"—her name was changed in Festinger's book to protect her identity— was predicting that the world would soon come to a cataclysmic end, and she specifically predicted that this would happen on December 21, 1954. She also prophesied (rather dramatically) that a flying saucer would pick up the "true believers" the day before, thus saving them from the devastation which would befall the "sinners" who remained.

Many members of the group had a lot to lose if Keech's prediction was wrong; they had sold their houses and given up their jobs and their savings in preparation for the coming of the space ship. But for Festinger, this scenario represented a godsend. He knew that the prophecy would fail, and he was thus presented with a golden opportunity to observe how people react psychologically when a prediction in which they ardently believe turns out to be untrue. Unlike them, he knew that the flying saucer would never show up. How would they handle the news, though? What would they do? In the event, when the saucer failed to show, Keech (conveniently) had a new "vision from God" shortly before 5am on the 21st, saying that "everyone was saved." The group members then rationalized away the evidence that they had been wrong all along, and for some the saucer's non-appearance even *strengthened* their belief in the cult! While it would be easy to dismiss the members of the group as mad or unhinged, Festinger's view was that this incident actually illustrates a very common and very normal psychological tendency.[3] While *Homo economicus* suggests that we just update our beliefs when our theories are disconfirmed, Festinger argued that in reality we usually just find a way to ignore or discount dissonant information. We bring things back into balance, in other words, by coming up with some sort of psychologically comforting rationalization or excuse.

Homo economicus—often referred to simply as "rational choice" or the "rational actor" approach—constitutes a somewhat popular approach to the understanding of political behavior. However, it is not (at least in the author's view) properly considered an approach to political psychology. Although there has long been talk of combining the psychological and economistic approaches somehow to construct a single unified theory, no one has so far succeeded in doing so. Certainly, there have been efforts by rational choice theorists in particular to make their assumptions more realistic, but the great strength of *Homo economicus* is arguably that it provides a way of simplifying human behavior in a way designed to make the latter more or less predictable. Many economists use it as a set of simplifying assumptions *in the full knowledge* that these assumptions are not realistic, but utilize them nevertheless in the expectation that they will generate powerful models and predictions. As soon as the complexity and greater realism of *Homo psychologicus* is conceded, however, it becomes clear that much of human behavior is idiosyncratic and unpredictable. In any case, the remainder of this book focuses on the latter model, and though *Homo economicus* will frequently be referred to in what follows, it will mainly be used as a foil to *Homo psychologicus*. Unlike the former, political psychology as a field is highly *empirical*: it is concerned with describing and explaining how political agents actually do behave, and not primarily with how they ought to, or with making simplifying assumptions about reality.[4] As we shall see, however, there is a great deal of disagreement among political psychologists as to what that reality looks like.

It's worth pointing out here that *Homo economicus* is even being challenged within economics *itself*, by a field of that discipline which its advocates call behavioral economics (and increasingly by advocates for "neuroeconomics" too). The term "behavioral" is significant here; it is a reference to the fact that some economists have become disenchanted with making unrealistic assumptions about how people might (or ought to) behave, wishing to focus instead on how they really do behave and drawing on *Homo psychologicus* in doing so. One pioneer of this subfield, Richard Thaler, often distinguishes between what he calls "Econs" and "Humans."[5] "Econs" are logical, consistent, and fully rational; their preferences do not change, and they act in selfish ways to obtain what they know they want. "Humans," on the other hand, are far less rational, often act in selfless (rather than selfish) ways, and are not at all sure what they want or what they will do. Paradoxically, then, there is at least one branch of Economics nowadays which does not follow the teachings of *Homo economicus*.

"My Brain Made Me Do It"

Until very recently, the critique of *Homo economicus* has been inspired mostly by the perspective of the cognitive psychology of the 1970s and 1980s. In recent years, though, that critique has been much further developed—as we have already noted—by discoveries within neuroscience or the study of the human brain. Neuroscience has uncovered further ways in which individual decision-makers depart from pure rationality. For instance, it has been discovered that much reasoning is undertaken by the *unconscious* brain, long before we are ever aware of "making" a decision. Some experiments have been conducted which suggest that a quarterback's unconscious brain "knows" that he is going to throw the ball to the left (or right) side of the field *before he does*, or that the brain of a soccer player taking a penalty knows that he will kick the ball to (say) the right side of the goal, before he is consciously aware of having made that decision. It has also been found that we don't necessarily know what our own preferences are before making a decision, and that those preferences can be altered by purely presentational factors.

These findings actually predate the widespread availability of MRI machines. In the 1980s, Benjamin Libet and his colleagues hooked his subjects up to an EEG machine—a device which measures brain activity—and asked them to simply raise their finger at a time of their own choosing. Using a timer, the subjects were asked to push a button at the exact moment they decided to move. Libet and his colleagues found that there was a slight delay between consciously deciding to move and actually doing it. No surprise there. But they also found something a lot more astonishing: the brain wave patterns of subjects showed that the brain became active more than a second before the subjects became aware of actually making any decision. This experiment has been replicated countless times using slightly different scenarios, but in each case the results have been essentially the same: the brain appears to "know" what we are going to do, even before we become aware of making the choice. Some replications even put the time lag (before we are consciously aware of our decision) at as much as seven seconds. This has sparked a long-running debate about legal responsibility and free will. Can we really be "guilty" of something, if we never made a conscious decision? This remains unresolved at the time of writing, but what is clear about this experiment is that our unconscious brains are up to something long before we are actually aware of it.[6]

Another indication of the power of unconscious thinking is that when we actually do become aware of something—for instance, when we deliberately think about performing an action, like walking downstairs—it actually becomes harder to do than if we did it on auto pilot. Jonah Lehrer refers to this phenomenon as "choking on thought." He gives the example of an otherwise outstanding opera singer, Renee Fleming, who became convinced that she was going to make an error in a passage of Mozart's *The Marriage of Figaro*.[7] Despite having successfully sung that portion hundreds of times before, she became unable to perform it because she could no longer "let go" and simply sing the passage without thinking about it. There is, in other words, such a thing as "thinking too much," and this too may be a reflection of the fact that much of what we do is done unconsciously. We will have more to say about this topic when we discuss the subjects of emotion in Chapter 10 and neuropolitics in Chapter 11.

Situationism and *Dispositionism*

In early 2004, the world was shocked by the publication of revolting images depicting the torture and humiliation of detainees by American soldiers at the now infamous Abu Ghraib prison in Iraq. Ironically, the prison had been used for years to house anyone whom Iraq's former dictator Saddam Hussein considered a potential enemy or threat to his power, and countless Iraqis had undergone agonizing torture and/or summary execution there. And now here were the representatives of the United States, supposedly Iraq's liberator, engaging in human rights abuses, and capturing it on film. More than anything else, perhaps, the pictures did most to undermine America's legitimacy in Iraq early on. After numerous investigations, narrowly confined to the lowest level of the chain of command, seven individuals were eventually put on trial for the abuses committed at Abu Ghraib.

In *The Lucifer Effect*, social psychologist Philip Zimbardo argues that the scandal at Abu Ghraib—in which ordinary, psychologically "normal" prison guards tortured and humiliated Iraqi prisoners—was in large part a result not of the characteristics of the individuals themselves, but of the strong situational forces they faced.[8] As Zimbardo puts it, he was "shocked but not surprised" by the horrors of Abu Ghraib when the scandal erupted in May 2004, as dramatic images of prisoner abuse spread around the world via television and the internet:

> The media and the "person in the street" around the globe asked how such evil deeds could be perpetrated by these seven men and women, whom military leaders had labeled as "rogue soldiers" and "a few bad apples." Instead, I wondered what circumstances in that prison cell block could have tipped the balance and led even good soldiers to do such bad things. To be sure, advancing a situational analysis for such crimes does not excuse them or make them morally acceptable; rather, I needed to find the meaning in this madness. I wanted to understand how it was possible for the characters of these young people to be so transformed in such a short time that they could do these unthinkable deeds.[9]

A famous practitioner in the field of political psychology, Robert Jervis, uses the example of people sitting in a burning building to illustrate situationism in relation to political behavior, and we can readily adapt this for our own purposes.[10] Suppose that a classroom in which you are sitting erupts spontaneously into flame. Or if this is too much of an imaginative stretch, imagine that someone has dropped a lighted cigarette, and the rather cheap, flammable carpeting in the room soon catches fire.[11] It becomes obvious that the whole room will burn to the ground, or that we will all die of smoke inhalation if we remain where we are. We all make speedily for the exit.

Do we need to study individuals and their particular characteristics to explain behavior in this instance? It seems not. The character or structure of the situation itself determines our actions. If we don't run for the exit, we shall meet with a very unpleasant death, most of us long before our time. We hadn't planned on going out this way, and we'll be damned if we sit around and let it happen. This approach to understanding human behavior is sometimes paired with the assumption of *rationality*, which assumes that human behavior is regularized and predictable. Because most of us at a minimum correctly perceive that we have an interest in self-preservation, we will accordingly leave the room before the flames engulf us.

At least some scenarios in human life are like the burning building example, in the sense that they leave relatively little leeway for human choice. Even in this example, though, there is at least some room for variation. For instance, if there are two exits to the room, what psychological characteristics affect the choice of one or the other? More interestingly, some of us may leave in an orderly fashion, while others may literally clamber over their classmates in a mad struggle to get out. Do moral concerns for others disappear in the stampede for the exits, or is this kind of situation one that brings out a basic nobility in some? Some (hopefully the professor, for instance) might adopt a leadership role, trying to organize the departure and maybe looking around for a fire extinguisher. On the other hand, at least one member of the class may be so depressed at his or her prospects of passing the course that he or she actually chooses to remain in the room in order to "end it all." Less flippantly, some people actually do run *into* burning buildings. Many firemen and policemen lost their lives on September 11, 2001, selflessly attempting to rescue others from the burning World Trade Center. If the situation is everything, why does human behavior vary like this?

These are all quibbles in the sense that they don't challenge the fundamental assumption that most of us, most of the time, will move speedily to the exit. There is a more telling objection, though. Most scenarios in politics actually cannot be meaningfully described as "burning buildings," in the sense that they allow far more leeway for choice than the extreme example just given; this is so even in a situation of dire threat to the security of a nation, where everyone agrees that the "building" is in fact on fire. In real-life politics, the choices available are rarely so clear-cut as the issue of whether one exits a room, and the ambiguity of the situation is such that reasonable individuals very often disagree as to the proper course of action. As Jervis suggests, in politics there is often profound disagreement as to whether the room *is even burning at all.*[12]

Zimbardo's handy distinction between "the apple" and "the barrel" provides a useful way of explaining what we mean by the terms *situationism* and *dispositionism*, a distinction which is going to be critical to the rest of the book. Were the appalling events at Abu Ghraib caused by "bad apples," or was the barrel itself turning the apples inside it rotten? In that book, situationism is defined as an approach in which the environment or situation that surrounds the individual—in Zimbardo's terms, "the barrel"—is considered most important in shaping an actor's behavior; dispositionism, on the other hand, is defined as an approach in which the individual actor—his or her beliefs, values, and personality, or "the apple" in Zimbardo's parlance—are considered most significant in this respect. We can think of behavior as driven by *internal* causes (dispositions) or *external* causes (situations), or of course by some combination of both. Within the situational camp there are various forms of external causes that are held to shape behavior, from the position our country occupies within the international system to the immediate social roles we play in our daily lives. Inside the dispositionist approach, a diversity of approaches as to what causes the behaviors of individuals—their neurobiologies, genetic predispositions, knowledge structures, beliefs, personalities, and so on—are present as well. We will use this simple distinction to explain and contrast a variety of psychological theories of relevance to an understanding of politics, and then show how these can be used to explain genocide, voting behavior, racism, nationalism, conflict between states, and a variety of other political behaviors.

The distinction between dispositional and situational factors as forces acting on behavior has long been central to social psychology, and it continues to be utilized by major scholars in that field today.[13] Social psychologists usually come down on the situationist side of the debate. Most of us, on the other hand, are instinctive dispositionists. We like to think that *who* we are—what we believe about the world and the kind of personality we have—exerts a fundamental impact on our behavior. Our political and legal systems largely just assume that this is so, holding us primarily responsible for our actions.[14] We tend to recoil from the view presented by much research in social psychology, which suggests that (for most people, at least) the character of the situation we are facing—*where* we are—matters more than our *own* characters to a greater extent than we could ever imagine. And we like to think that our political behaviors—how we vote, what form our political participation takes, how tolerant we are, and so on—are shaped by who we are as well. But is this true? This is the central question this book poses and the issue around which the organization of the book revolves.

One interesting thing to note is that this kind of distinction between the individual and his or her environment appears in practically every discipline which analyzes social behavior. In political science and especially in the subfield of international relations, a distinction is drawn between "levels of analysis" or "agents" and "structures."[15] International relations theory reflects a division between dispositionists (especially those who study the psychological aspects of foreign policy decision-making) and situationists (including neorealists like Kenneth Waltz and neoliberals like Robert Keohane). In the analysis of foreign policy, situationist theories do exist, but have been drawn mostly from organizational theory rather than social psychology.[16] In economics, there is a common distinction made between macro- and microeconomics (the latter examining the economics of the individual business or firm, the former the workings of the whole economy). In sociology, history, and other disciplines, there has long been a similar debate between those who believe that individuals drive events and those who counter that situational forces are more critical.

A second interesting point is that political psychology has drawn mostly from the dispositionist side of the mother discipline of psychology. As Rose

McDermott notes, much political psychology—at least as conventionally defined as an academic "discipline"—operates at the individual level of analysis,[17] or is dispositionist in the sense that it assumes that individual actors "matter" and that their behavior can be traced to meaningful differences in our beliefs and personalities. Nevertheless, a large body of work within social psychology is far more hospitable to situationism than it is to dispositionism. Research on the ways in which social situations can shape behavior has had less impact on the development of political psychology than have Freudianism and modern cognitive psychology, each of which studies the human mind (though in rather different ways). Moreover, it is not always acknowledged in literature on political psychology that the findings of social psychologists like Stanley Milgram and Philip Zimbardo among others—though profoundly political in their implications—depart significantly from the idea that individual attributes are critical in shaping an individual's behavior. The reasons for this are unclear, but we shall spend a good half of this book looking at prominent situationist arguments that attempt to explain some fundamental aspects of political behavior.

A third interesting thing to note about approaches which argue that individuals do make a difference take two basic but sharply different forms which should be contrasted with one another. One perspective, often but not always rooted in arguments which make use of behavioral genetics or evolutionary psychology, claims that all human beings are born "hard-wired" with inherited dispositions which are essentially *the same*. The well-known classical "realist" Hans Morgenthau, for instance—offering a rather dark view of human nature which drew upon the tradition of Hobbes and Machiavelli—argued that human beings are characterized by what he called the *animus dominandi*, or the desire to accumulate power. The persistence of war throughout human history, he claimed, can be attributed to human nature or the fact that man's basic predispositions never change, and we are essentially stuck with this stubborn trait and have to work with it as best we can.

As we shall see in Chapter 4, Stanley Milgram (in what was mostly a situationist argument) also used this kind of approach to claim that we are born with certain predispositions already built in. He speculated that, via natural selection, obedience to hierarchical authority had conferred evolutionary advantages upon the human race. He thus used an element of dispositionism to try to explain what he saw as the "inherent" human tendency to obey. Similarly, Dominic Johnson's argument about overconfidence in war—something we often term hubris—relies on the claim that overconfidence has conferred similar advantages.[18] According to Johnson, human beings have developed an evolutionary bias towards overconfidence, an enduring trait which he terms "positive illusions." Although it is inappropriate in the modern world—indeed, it can be highly destructive—this bias may have been encouraged initially by natural selection because it offered advantages to our ancestors (maximizing our chances of survival and our fighting abilities, for instance).

It is important to note, however, that many dispositionist approaches explicitly *do not* make this kind of "dispositions-are-the-same-for-everyone" type of argument. Indeed, the notion that all neurobiological approaches to politics (or "biopolitical" perspectives) must inevitably assume that we are all the same or that human beings inherit more-or-less identical genetic traits is one of the biggest mistakes or misconceptions which people have about the field. In their book *Predisposed: Liberals, Conservatives, and the Biology of Political Differences*, John Hibbing, Kevin Smith, and John Alford react sharply against the kind of situationism inherent in the arguments of people like Zimbardo and Milgram, but they also disagree markedly with the claim that we all share the *same* dispositions:

> Predispositions . . . can be thought of as biologically and psychologically instantiated defaults that, absent new information or conscious overriding, govern response to given stimuli . . . a final critical and often misunderstood element of predispositions is that they are not equally present in all people. Just as the content of the predisposition varies from person to person, so too does the degree to which a predisposition is present at all.[19]

Drawing on neuroscientific and biopolitical approaches, they argue that "liberals" and "conservatives"—in the sense that those terms are used in an American political context—quite literally perceive different worlds when they look at the same stimuli or situations, and that these differences can be traced to identifiable neurobiological traits. We will return to this topic in Chapter 11, "Biopolitics, Neuropolitics, and Genopolitics," but for now you should note that both genetic and neurobiological approaches allow for very significant variations in people's dispositions.

Finally, it is important to realize that the distinction between dispositionists and situationists is *not* exactly the same thing as, or directly equivalent to, the rather more familiar "nature versus nature" debate.[20] When the first edition of this textbook came out, some students at my own university instinctively reacted in just this way. "Aha, the nature versus nature debate!" they cried. In fact, though, the situationist–dispositionist dispute is a bit finer grained in the way we will use those terms in this book. The nature versus nurture debate— a very old one in both philosophy and psychology—focuses on the extent to which behavior is *genetically inherited*, or derived from learning, the situation, or the environment. While Plato (for instance) suggested that certain things are inborn or genetically inherited, John Locke on the other side of the debate believed in the *tabula rasa*, which suggests that the mind starts out as a blank slate (a key argument of the behaviorists, as we'll see in Chapter 3). According to this view, everything we believe or do is the result of learned experience (a response to a variety of situations, in other words). But these kind of genetic arguments are only *one* way that one can make a dispositionist argument in political science, and dispositionism is not at all restricted to genetics. It is possible that we start out as blank slates, for instance, and that we develop predispositions early in life which are in some sense a reaction to situations. But then these can be so enduring that once they come about, they can *persist* throughout our lives. In other words, we need not assume that there is anything genetic or inherited about human beings at all, and still end up being a dispositionist. And of course, two individuals can react in an entirely different way to the same situation, which also leads us to focus on the dispositions within us in explaining behavior.

To save confusion, it is most helpful to think of the situationist–dispositionist debate as one which is waged between advocates of *internal* and *external causes*. In other words, this is really a dispute about whether a person's behavior is driven by the external situation or by his or her internal predispositions (which can vary a great deal). Of course, it can be hard to tell in practice (looking from the outside) which drives behavior in a particular case. "If Beth is a mean, aggressive person to others because her sister beat her up as a kid," Fiske and Taylor ask, "is the cause of her current behavior internal or external?"[21] My most astute and thoughtful students eventually come to a realization of this problem when the scheme we will use in this book is presented to them. A pure situationist would argue that *nearly everything* is ultimately situational. In other words, our cognitive structures—the mental categories we use to make sense of the world—are the product of experience. Many if not all of our dispositions are presumably the result of the situations we have been through. To continue Fiske and Taylor's example, there is a sense in which Beth's behavior is situationist in so far as it derives from circumstances she faced in the past. On the other hand, the root of Beth's behavior might be hard-wired, in the sense that aggression might plausibly be rooted in all of us as human beings. Or there might be a great deal of variation between Beth and her friends; perhaps some people are born aggressive, while others are not. These latter arguments are unambiguously dispositionist.

The Ingrained Nature of Political Behavior

This is a book about political behavior, so it makes sense to be very clear at the outset what this term means. Broadly defined, political behavior refers to any type of activity designed to meet some political or broadly strategic end. It encompasses the full range of political activities in which we engage, from extreme behaviors like terrorism and war to more "mundane" behaviors such as the act of voting or joining a local meeting. It includes the study of decision-making—both by voters and by elites in government—but is broader than this. It also encompasses questions as diverse as "why does racism occur?", "why do human beings engage in genocide?", "what determines how people vote?", and "why do states go to war?" As you will see in what follows, there are different ways of answering these questions. Some follow the logic of economics in assuming that human beings are fundamentally rational, weighing up the costs and benefits of various actions available to them, while others are inspired by the social or group focus of sociology. Still others draw on cognitive neuroscience or genetics. Political psychologists, therefore, offer only one set of answers to questions like those posed above. Nevertheless, the purpose of this book is to show how compelling such answers can be.

As Aristotle famously noted, man (and woman) is "a political animal." Hatemi and McDermott put it rather nicely in their edited volume of that name:

> Politics occurs when siblings expect parents to arbitrate fights and when lovers argue. Politics encompass much of what people think of as "gossip" when they talk about who did what to whom and why. And politics are certainly brought to bear when we think about the performance of any coalitional groups, including sports teams, police and fire departments and terrorist cells.[22]

There appears to be something deeply ingrained about politics and political behavior. And there is a growing recognition, as we shall see in this book, that explaining why we do what we do requires an understanding not only of traditional political science, but of history, psychology, sociology, biology, physiology, ethology, and behavioral genetics as well.

Even though politics is something in which humans routinely engage—indeed, we cannot help "being political" much of the time—it is not a *uniquely* human form of activity, for there is a great deal of evidence that our close evolutionary cousins are "political" too. In his path-breaking *Chimpanzee Politics*, for instance, Frans De Waal shows that chimpanzees "strategically manipulate" one another.[23] Their brains, he argues, are sufficiently developed for them to engage in what has been called "Machiavellian intelligence." De Waal argues that:

> when Aristotle referred to man as a *political animal*, he could not know just how near the mark he was. Our political activity seems to be part of

an evolutionary heritage we share with our close relatives . . . the roots of politics are older than humanity.[24]

Just like human beings, they form alliances and coalitions. Building on this insight, later research (such as that of Robin Dunbar) has suggested that the ability to behave strategically depends on the size of an animal's neocortex. Ethologists have found that hyenas, dolphins, and elephants all do politics as well! Spotted hyenas, for instance, have a fairly large neocortex, which allows them to engage in behavior of great complexity relative to animals which have simpler brain structures.[25]

What Determines Our Behavior?

There is an inherent "gray area" between the concepts of dispositionism and situationism. As noted above, almost any theory that does not rely on biology or genetics can be characterized as situationist, since our dispositions are partly shaped by the situations we happen to have experienced throughout our lives. But there are two important points that must be made here: first of all, the reader should note again that when we characterize a theory as "dispositionist," we need only mean that dispositions affect behavior in a proximate or immediate sense. Although our partisan identifications or our attitudes towards the use of military force may have been shaped by situations *originally*, these eventually become lasting dispositions which vary little across elections and wars. Second—and even more importantly—most dispositionist approaches assume that individuals *vary* in their reactions to situations. Barack Obama probably took rather different lessons from the 2003 Iraq war, for instance, than, say, George W. Bush or Dick Cheney. People frequently take differing internal attitudes and beliefs away from precisely the same external situation.

There are different forms of dispositionism, so there are different kinds of situationism as well. Some theories look at direct pressures at the level of the immediate social group, as in the work on groupthink discussed in Chapter 6. Other direct and indirect forms are illustrated by Stanley Milgram's experiments, where social etiquette, the force of authority figures, and other social norms seem to shape behavior (Chapter 4). Other forms of situationism are even more general and subtle in nature, as in Philip Zimbardo's Stanford experiment where widely accepted notions of how guards and prisoners ought to behave seem to have almost insidiously shaped the behavior of his subjects (Chapter 5). The situation may be the immediate social context, a group to which one belongs in the workplace, the wider social groups that shape our identities within society, and the push and pull of the allegiances we develop towards our nation and state. And as we shall see in Chapter 17, what I shall call Kenneth Waltz's "hyper-situationist" perspective—in which states respond almost exclusively to the roles assigned to them by the international system—represents the situational logic writ extremely large.

No attempt will be made in this book to resolve fully the debate between situationism and dispositionism—at least until the concluding chapters—and the reason for this partly has to do with the author's objective in writing a book of this kind. There are essentially two styles of teaching: some instructors exclusively present their conception of the world and expect their students to accept it, at least after they have had the satisfaction of knocking down their views (should they dare to offer them) using skilled and pre-prepared put-downs which they have honed to a fine art over the years. The tone of the previous sentences tells you immediately that the present author is going to at least claim to be a teacher of the second sort: one who presents the student with rival views and then leaves it up to him or her to decide. There are two reasons for that: first of all, the teaching of politics should always be approached with a certain degree of humility. There are no definite answers to many questions in politics, and anyone who claims to have uncovered the "laws" of political behavior should be treated with a heavy dose of skepticism. Second, this book was written by an author young enough to recall being taught using both styles, and he found the first to be exceptionally grating when he was on the receiving end of it (especially where he disagreed with an instructor's all-too-evident world view)!

While we will probably never be able to solve the riddle this book poses for good, one of its central purposes is to encourage you to think deeply about it as you read through chapters which make a case for one position or the other in explaining political behavior. As you will see as you read on, the remaining chapters are organized around the situationist–dispositionist distinction, and later chapters are intended to push you gently in one direction or the other without ever telling you exactly what to think. After reading this book you may determine you are a situationist, or a dispositionist; alternatively, you may adopt a more subtle approach which blends the two according to (say) the area of political behavior we are trying to explain. But that is up to you. As one prominent news organization in the United States likes to put it, "you decide."

The Organization of the Book

Once we accept the idea that individuals *do* matter in politics and that situations do not totally predetermine responses, the next question becomes "how much and when do they matter?" Those influenced by social psychology contend that individual factors matter less than social pressures and the structure of the situation. Those influenced by cognitive psychology and the much older psychoanalytic or psychodynamic tradition, on the other hand, tend to make the opposite argument. Broadly speaking, psychologists examining political questions have tended to favor the first approach, while political scientists have tended to draw on psychological theories which privilege the second.

This basic distinction provides the organizational basis of this book. In Part I, we examine a variety of especially influential approaches derived from social psychology which emphasize the nature of the situation as opposed to individuals and their characteristics. We begin with the ultimate situationist analysis, behaviorism. This is an approach which had an especially powerful influence on political psychology during the 1950s and 1960s, when the focus of both psychology and political science turned away from the study of the mind in favor of an emphasis on the supposedly more "scientific" concept of behavior. Examining the ideas of B.F. Skinner in particular, in Chapter 3 we shall consider Skinner's argument that we would all be better off in a political state that deliberately conditioned its members to engage in "socially desirable" behaviors.

During the early 1960s, Stanley Milgram carried out what are probably the most ingenious (and, some would say, infamous) experiments ever conducted. Milgram's work has had a major impact on the way we understand political obedience within authority structures, but for the moment the reader should note simply that his findings favor the notion that most—though perhaps not all—of us are capable of committing acts that violate our most basic moral precepts and beliefs, provided that the acts are encouraged and sanctioned by the social pressure of an authority we view as legitimate. Milgram's work is used in Chapter 4 to try—in a very preliminary way—to understand the phenomenon of genocide, with a particular but not exclusive focus on the Nazi Holocaust of the 1930s. In the following chapter, Philip Zimbardo's equally fascinating study of the behavior of "prisoners" and "guards"—the famous Stanford experiment—is placed under the microscope. Again, the focus here is on the demands of the situation, and the ways in which socially defined roles shape our behavior. Zimbardo's work is used in Chapter 5 to shed light on the Abu Ghraib scandal.

Chapter 6, the last chapter in this section, examines group behavior, with particular emphasis on the work of Irving Janis and the ways in which individual behavior changes in response to group pressures. In his celebrated book *Groupthink*, Janis argued that even the brightest individuals may "buckle" under social pressures of various kinds in decision-making groups; this often leads, Janis argued, to disastrous courses of action that might not have been pursued had the options been fully considered by individuals acting on their own.[26] Here we will also devote particular attention to the two case studies that Janis himself felt best illustrated the phenomenon of groupthink—the 1961 Bay of Pigs fiasco and the 1965 decisions to "Americanize" the war in Vietnam, as well as criticisms of Janis's approach and more recent perspectives on group decision-making.

Part II, the dispositionist section of the book, looks at individually based psychological theories. Whether justifiably or not, it has to be said that this body of work has had more influence on political psychology to date than the first, perhaps because it takes the idea that individuals matter rather further than the approaches so far discussed.

As we shall see in depth in Chapter 7, psychoanalytical approaches to understanding behavior had an early formative impact on the development of political psychology as a field in its own right. The work of Sigmund Freud and his followers left a strong imprint at the outset, in part because this new field within political science was founded at a time when psycho-dynamic theories were very much in vogue. Naturally, then, the figures instrumental in the movement which led to its development—notably Charles Merriam and Harold Lasswell—imported Freudian-style approaches to the study of politics.

The psychoanalytic imprint on political science spawned a whole tradition which is commonly referred to as psychobiography or psychohistory, and even today those influences continue to be felt. Works like Alexander George and Juliette George's *Woodrow Wilson and Colonel House* and Doris Kearns Goodwin's *Lyndon Johnson and the American Dream* set the standard within this influential subgenre, often arguing that childhood experiences are critical to future personality development and political performance.[27] Taking their cue from their former teacher at the University of Chicago, Harold Lasswell—who saw political behavior in part as the displacement of private or personal conflicts onto public life—George and George, for instance, argued that Woodrow Wilson's inflexibility on issues such as the passage of the League of Nations Treaty stemmed from a need to compensate for Dr. Joseph Wilson's supposed tendency to deny his young son affection and emotional rewards. In Chapter 7 we will examine this and other psychobiographic classics, as well as even more controversial but much newer contributions to this tradition.

The term "personality" is an elusive one which has been used in different ways in the literature on political psychology. It is sometimes utilized as a shorthand term for all of a person's individual characteristics, including his or her beliefs. James David Barber's *The Presidential Character*—a much criticized but endlessly thought-provoking study of presidential personality, and the leading work of comparative psychobiography—has been so influential that no textbook on political psychology could conceivably leave it out.[28] This is examined along with other personality-based theories in Chapter 8, taking account of both the strengths and weaknesses of this kind of analysis. With the passage of time, however, approaches based on the study of leaders' beliefs—most notably, operational code analysis—have partially supplanted the focus on more amorphous concepts like personality, and the evolution of this kind of work is covered in this chapter as well.

Chapter 9 deals with the so-called "cognitive revolution" of the 1980s and 1990s. This movement within psychology has sought to sweep away many of the older Freudian-tinged approaches while still maintaining a basically dispositionist stance, and it has placed a new emphasis on the way that behavior is shaped by knowledge structures present in human memory. Schemas, scripts, analogies, and other knowledge structures are seen as the "building blocks" of the human mind, which then fundamentally influence the ways in which we process information. From this perspective human beings have increasingly come to be thought of as "cognitive misers" who often employ cognitive short cuts and heuristic devices when making decisions. Though this kind of cognitive economy is often necessary in a world in which we are constantly being bombarded with information, it is fraught with perils of various kinds.

Human beings are not just passive receptors and processors of information—what has been termed "cold" cognition—but are also influenced by "hot" processes such as anger, love, sadness, and so on. What was perhaps an overzealous focus on the cold aspects of cognition by political psychologists working in both the elite and mass behavior traditions during the 1980s and 1990s has in turn provoked a compensating emphasis on affect and emotion, and work in this vein is the topic of Chapter 10. Although there are considerable problems involved in the attempt to study emotion in a rigorous way, Chapter 11 examines one potential way forward with an overview of some very new and exciting developments in the study of neuropolitics and genopolitics. These promise the potential development both of new theoretical approaches of relevance to politics as well as novel ways of testing our hypotheses, old and new. For instance, we are beginning to see the development within political psychology of something called "neuropolitics" (the study of the interaction between the brain and politics), as well as a related but logically separable trend towards "genopolitics" (the study of the genetic or evolutionary basis of political attitudes and behavior). Both have been encouraged by the development of advanced techniques such as functional magnetic resonance imaging (fMRI). Advances in such techniques that scientists use to map the human brain are now being used in the study of voting behavior, for instance, to examine the emotions experienced by voters as they look at political stimuli such as campaign ads.

The third and final section (Chapters 12 to 18) is more empirical. It attempts, in a preliminary way, to bring situationism and dispositionism together, and this conceptual device is used here to categorize theories which have tried to explain various empirical areas of political behavior. Chapter 16, for instance, asks to what extent acts of terrorism are typically carried out by psychologically "abnormal" individuals. Many people simply assume that terrorists must be mentally abnormal in some way or even deranged, but recent research on the psychology of terrorist behavior, by John Horgan, Andrew Silke, and others, has largely discounted this widely popular theory. Attempts to uncover a single "terrorist personality" (or to ascribe abnormalities like narcissism to all terrorists) have essentially come to naught, so in many ways we are left with the same conclusion Milgram drew in the case of genocide: namely, that most ordinary men and women are capable of committing acts of extreme violence. This chapter examines the research in this area which ascribes terrorism to situational forces and in particular the dynamics of group behavior. We will also examine theories of nationalism and ethnic conflict, racism and political intolerance, voting behavior, political communication and international security, asking in each case whether dispositionist or situationist approaches best account for the area of behavior in question. Finally, in Chapter 18 we will wrap up our discussion by looking at new directions that the field may be taking, and suggesting ways in which situationism and dispositionism might be integrated with one another.

Having introduced the organizing frameworks that we are going to use in this book, we next need to explain what the study of political psychology involves. What *is* political psychology? When did students of political science first become interested in the application of psychological theory to political behavior? How has political psychology been studied in the past, and which psychological theories have influenced the ways in which we study political phenomena? These are the topics addressed in the next chapter.

Notes

1. George Lakoff, *The Political Mind: A Cognitive Scientist's Guide to Your Brain and Its Politics* (New York: Penguin Books, 2009), p.9.
2. Rose McDermott, "The Feeling of Rationality: The Meaning of Neuroscientific Advances for Political Science," *Perspectives on Politics*, December 2004, p.691.
3. Leon Festinger, Henry Riecken, and Stanley Schachter, *When Prophecy Fails: A Social and Psychological Study of a Modern Group that Predicted the Destruction of the World* (New York: Harper & Row, 1956). See also Carol Tavris and Elliot Aronson, *Mistakes Were Made (But Not By Me): Why We Justify Foolish Beliefs, Bad Decisions, and Hurtful Acts* (New York: Harcourt, 2007).
4. For readers primarily interested in the economistic route to explaining human behavior, I recommend Kenneth Shepsle and Mark Bonchek, *Analyzing*

Politics: Rationality, Behavior, and Institutions (New York: W.W. Norton, 1997). For a wide-ranging critique of this perspective, see Donald Green and Ian Shapiro, *Pathologies of Rational Choice: A Critique of Applications in Political Science* (New Haven, CT: Yale University Press, 1994).

5 This distinction is discussed in Daniel Kahneman's invaluable *Thinking Fast and Slow* (New York: Farrar, Straus, and Giroux, 2011), pp.269–70.

6 For a discussion of Libet's experiment, see for instance David Eagleman, *Incognito: The Secret Lives of the Brain* (New York: Vintage Books, 2012).

7 Jonah Lehrer, *How We Decide* (New York: Houghton Mifflin, 2009), pp.134–36.

8 Philip Zimbardo, *The Lucifer Effect: Understanding How Good People Turn Evil* (New York: Random House, 2007).

9 Ibid., p.19.

10 Robert Jervis, *Perception and Misperception in International Politics* (Princeton, NJ: Princeton University Press, 1976), pp.19–21.

11 If you are sitting in the average university classroom right now, the carpeting probably *is* cheap and flammable.

12 And one could add that perhaps running for the exit is really a dispositionist response as much as a reaction to the situation, since perhaps we have evolved a preprogrammed, self-preservative disposition over thousand of years which serves the useful purpose of preventing the species from dying out.

13 Lee Ross and Richard Nisbett, *The Person and the Situation: Perspectives of Social Psychology* (Philadelphia, PA: Temple University Press, 1991).

14 Ibid., p.320.

15 See for instance Kenneth Waltz, *Man, The State and War: A Theoretical Analysis* (New York: Columbia University Press, 1959); J. David Singer, "The Level-of-Analysis Problem in International Relations," *World Politics*, 14: 77–92, 1961; Alexander Wendt, "The Agent–Structure Problem in International Relations Theory," *International Organization*, 41: 335–70, 1987; Martin Hollis and Steve Smith, *Explaining and Understanding International Relations* (New York: Oxford University Press, 1990).

16 Graham Allison and Philip Zelikow, *Essence of Decision: Explaining the Cuban Missile Crisis*, second edition (New York: Longman, 1999). The major exception is Irving Janis's work on groupthink, which draws on a rich tradition within social psychology. We shall examine this work in Chapter 6.

17 Rose McDermott, *Political Psychology and International Relations* (Ann Arbor, MI: University of Michigan Press, 2004), p.3.

18 Dominic Johnson, *Overconfidence and War: The Havoc and Glory of Positive Illusions* (Cambridge, MA: Harvard University Press, 2004). See also Dominic Johnson and James Fowler, "The Evolution of Overconfidence," *Nature*, 477: 317–20, 2011.

19 John Hibbing, Kevin Smith, and John Alford, *Predisposed: Liberals, Conservatives, and the Biology of Political Differences* (New York: Routledge, 2014), p.24.

20 John Hibbing, "Ten Misconceptions Concerning Neurobiology and Politics," *Perspectives On Politics*, 11: 475–89, 2013.

21 Susan Fiske and Shelley Taylor, *Social Cognition* (Reading, MA: Addison-Wesley, 1984), p.92.

22 Peter Hatemi and Rose McDermott, *Man Is By Nature A Political Animal: Evolution, Biology, and Politics* (Chicago, IL: University of Chicago Press, 2011), pp.1–2.

23 Frans De Waal, *Chimpanzee Politics: Power and Sex Among Apes*, Twenty-fifth Anniversary Edition (Baltimore, MD: The Johns Hopkins University Press, 2007).

24 Ibid., p.207.

25 Sharleen Sakai, Bradley Arsznov, Barbara Lundriga, and Kay Holekamp, "Brain Size and Social Complexity: A Computed Tomography Study in Hyaenidae," *Brain, Behavior, and Evolution*, 77: 91–104, 2011.

26 Irving Janis, *Groupthink: Psychological Studies of Policy Decisions and Fiascoes* (Boston, MA: Houghton Mifflin, 1982), pp.2–13.

27 Alexander George and Juliette George, *Woodrow Wilson and Colonel House: A Personality Study* (New York: Dover, 1956); Doris Kearns Goodwin, *Lyndon Johnson and the American Dream* (New York: Harper & Row, 1976).

28 James David Barber, *The Presidential Character: Predicting Performance in the White House*, fourth edition (New York: Pearson Longman, 2009).

Suggested Further Reading

John Hibbing, Kevin Smith, and John Alford, *Predisposed: Liberals, Conservatives, and the Biology of Political Differences* (New York: Routledge, 2014).

Daniel Kahneman, *Thinking Fast and Slow* (New York: Farrar, Straus, and Giroux, 2011).

Jonah Lehrer, *How We Decide* (New York: Houghton Mifflin, 2009).

Lee Ross and Richard Nisbett, *The Person and the Situation: Perspectives of Social Psychology* (Philadelphia, PA: Temple University Press, 1991).

Films

Ghosts of Abu Ghraib (2007): Excellent documentary featuring the people actually involved at the prison, directed by Rory Kennedy.

Schindler's List (1993): Award-winning recreation of Oskar Schindler's strange heroism during World War II, using Hollywood actors, directed by Stephen Spielberg.

Chapter 2

A Brief History of the Discipline

"Political psychology" can be defined most simply as the study of the interaction between politics and psychology, particularly the impact of psychology on politics. If we can conceive of politics as the master discipline at the center of everything, linking to everything else—a rather contentious move, one must admit, but it was good enough for Aristotle—we can conceive of political science as a kind of Venn diagram with a center circle surrounded by overlapping ones. The intersecting area between economics and politics is called "political economy," between sociology and politics "political sociology," and so on. The intersection of mathematics and politics has developed its own specialized terminology—rational choice, formal theory, or game theory—but it is essentially "mathematical politics."

History, genetics, biology, ethology, philosophy, anthropology, sociology, and many others could be depicted in Figure 2.1 as well, but you get the general idea. Although different social scientists will of course conceive of different "master disciplines" at the center, this kind of scheme will make some sense to most political scientists. We can conceive of political psychology most easily as a bridge between two disciplines. Beyond this simple definition, however, a glance at some past issues of the academic journal dedicated to the intersecting area we are concerned with in this book—entitled, appropriately enough, *Political Psychology*—reveals that there are many different subfields, specialisms, and approaches within it. Consequently, there are many different ways of teaching a course in political psychology.

One distinction within political psychology is that one camp is interested in *mass behavior* such as how people vote, the impact of public opinion on government policies, and so on. The other focuses on *elite behavior* and how elite perceptions shape government policies, the impact of personality on leadership, foreign policy decision-making, and so on. Another important distinction in the field, which we discuss later, is that which exists between explanations of political behavior influenced by social psychology, which

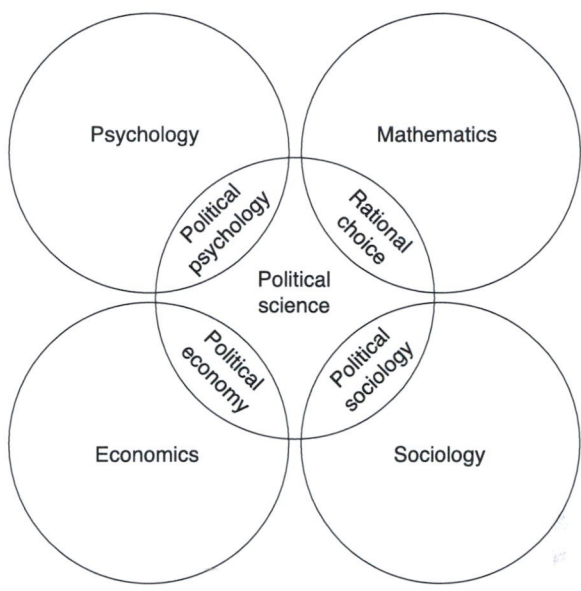

Psychology

Mathematics

Political psychology

Rational choice

Political science

Political economy

Political sociology

Economics

Sociology

Figure 2.1 The relationship between political science and other fields

emphasize the impact of *situations* on behavior, and those influenced by cognitive psychology and the older tradition of abnormal psychology, which stress the importance of *individual* characteristics in shaping the way we behave.

Three observations ought to be made at the very outset about political psychology as a subspecialism within the study of political science. First of all, it is in comparative terms relatively new *as a recognized academic field*. Although pioneers like Harold Lasswell were studying the modern influence of psychology on politics as long ago as the 1920s, not many courses in political psychology were offered until the early 1970s. A *Handbook of Political Psychology*, the first of a subsequent series, appeared in 1973.[1] At the same time a professional apparatus began to be created around the subject. The year 1977 saw the founding of the *International Society for Political Psychology* (ISPP), and the journal *Political Psychology* was founded two years later.

Second, the topic called "political psychology"—in this instance defined as a recognized field taught in universities—is genuinely *international* in focus. While it is especially dominated by U.S. scholars, it is becoming increasingly popular in Europe, Australasia, and other parts of the world as well. The study of political psychology is a genuinely international enterprise today. As noted, political psychology is rather unusual in the sense that its major representative body—the ISPP—is truly global in nature, holding its meetings in places as far apart as Portland, Paris, and Portugal.

Many of the pioneers of the ideas that eventually coalesced into an academic field of study called "political psychology" came from Europe. The Viennese influence of Freud, which is described in a moment, provides an obvious case in point. But in a deeper sense, the topic matter of political psychology is as old as politics itself, for as long as people have reflected on the subject of politics, they have asked themselves the psychological question of why human beings act as they do. One of the first things one discovers in introductory political science classes is that every political world view is ultimately based on a view of human nature (and therefore a view of human psychology). Niccolò Machiavelli obviously had a very dark view of human psychology, and classical conservative thinking is generally more pessimistic on this score than classical liberalism. Furthermore, Thomas Hobbes, John Locke, and Jean-Jacques Rousseau each developed very different conceptions of the "state of nature," a real or hypothesized condition without government, in which the real nature of human beings becomes evident.

In a book which is now sadly out of print, William Stone and Paul Schaffner brilliantly trace the various deeper historical influences that had been brewing for centuries before political psychology emerged as a recognized academic subject in the twentieth century.[2] "The recognition of a strong Germanic impetus to political psychology . . . does not suffice to do full justice to the continental contributions. Contrary to widely held beliefs, the field of political psychology as such originated with conservative authors in Latin countries," they argue. In France, for example, conservative thinkers such as Hippolyte Taine and Gustav Le Bon began to develop "scientific" explanations of human political psychology in the 1800s. And in England—rather ironically given the relative neglect of the topic in U.K. universities—as early as 1908 Graham Wallas, a professor at the London School of Economics and Political Science (LSE), published a book which certainly qualified him as one of the founding fathers of the discipline. In his *Human Nature in Politics*, first published that year, Wallas issued a warning to those who saw every human decision and action as the result of a rational, intellectual process. "When men become conscious of psychological processes of which they have been unconscious or half conscious," Wallas advised, "not only are they on their guard against the exploitation of those processes in themselves and others, but they become better able to control them from within."[3] The greatest contributions, of course, came from Vienna and Frankfurt. Thinkers such as Sigmund Freud and Erich Fromm in particular would have a special impact on the development of the field in the United States, as detailed shortly in this chapter's section on personality studies.

A third important thing to note is that political psychology is rather unusual as a specialism within political science in that much (though by no means all) of it operates at what is usually called the individual level of analysis. The study of international relations in particular commonly distinguishes between three basic kinds of explanation or "levels of analysis": systemic, state, and individual.[4] Are state actions driven by a state's power or position within the international system? Or are the internal characteristics of states critical in shaping their outward behavior? Or is it ultimately the psychology of particular leaders that drives a state's foreign policies?

Many of the theories one encounters within political science tend to operate at levels above that of the individual; in other words, they emphasize the importance of context or the nature of the times rather than the nature of individuals. Neorealist theory—which attributes a great deal of state behavior to a nation's position within the international system (whether it is a super-power, a middle power, a weak power, and so on)—provides a particularly good example.[5] Equally, Marxism tends to discount the role of individuals in history, ascribing to "material" factors a powerful causal effect which over-whelms the significance of particular individuals. Many theories derived from Marxism, such as dependency theory and world-systems theory, make much the same core assumption. Though it stems from a very different tradition, classic pluralism views the state as responsive to the competition between large organized groups, similarly leaving little room for individuals and their psychologies to "matter."

As we have seen already, situational constraints are also emphasized by social psychology, which has had a particular impact on psychologists who turn to political topics. Nevertheless, "political psychology" as studied within political science has always had a particular appeal to those who believe that political actors—their beliefs, past life experiences, personalities, and so on—are at least somewhat significant in determining political outcomes. It has an instinctive appeal to those who believe that individual actors matter; that history is not just the story of how structures and contexts shape behavior, but of how individuals can themselves shape history and politics.

This is one thing most analysts of political psychology have in common. Beyond this, however, there is no real agreement as to which theories are most useful for the purpose of analyzing human behavior and decision-making. As William McGuire has noted in an oft-cited chapter, the nature of what he calls the "poli–psy relationship" has evolved through a number of historical phases during the last eighty years or so.[6] The kind of theories that have been in vogue within the discipline of psychology has changed over time; moreover, since psychology has mostly influenced political science (rather than the other way round), the trends in political psychology have tracked or followed trends within the mother discipline of psychology. McGuire identifies three broad phases in the development of political psychology:

1 the era of *personality studies* in the 1940s and 1950s dominated by psychoanalysis;
2 the era of *political attitudes and voting behavior studies* in the 1960s and 1970s characterized by the popularity of "rational man" assumptions; and
3 an era since the 1980s and 1990s which has focused on *political beliefs, information processing, and decision-making,* and has dealt in particular with international politics.

Personality Studies

Many of the early studies within political psychology—that is, in the 1940s and 1950s—focused on personality, and reflected in particular psychoanalytic theory, then prevalent within psychology. This led to the appearance of many works of what might be called "psychohistory" or "psychobiography." An early and still vibrant approach to studying leadership, these focus on the personality characteristics of political leaders, and on how these characteristics affect their performance in office. Amongst other things, Freudian or psychoanalytic theory analysis is particularly suited to the analysis of personality because it breaks down the drives or motivations that lie, or are alleged to lie, within human beings. Sigmund Freud regarded many of these motivations as *unconscious* in nature, revealing themselves only through dreams and slips of the tongue (the famous "Freudian slips"). According to Freud, we are all born with what he called an *id*, an *ego*, and a *superego*.[7] Freud believed that the id is essentially the child within us. It seeks pleasure and instant gratification. In the case of a baby or a very young child, they seek whatever feels good at the time, with no consideration for the morality of the situation or anything else. The id isn't concerned with external reality or about the needs of anyone else. When the id wants something, nothing else is important. It is operated by what Freud called the "pleasure principle."

Within the next few years, as the child interacts more and more with the world, the second part of its personality develops. Freud called this part the *ego*, which is based on the "reality principle." The ego understands that other people have needs and desires and that sometimes being impulsive or selfish can hurt us in the long run. It's the ego's job to meet the needs of the id, while taking into consideration the reality of the situation. By the age of five, or the end of the phallic stage of development, the child's *superego* develops. The superego is the moral part of us and develops due to the moral and ethical restraints placed on us by our parents or guardians. Many equate the superego with the conscience, as it dictates our belief in what is right or wrong.

In a healthy person, according to Freud, the ego needs to be the strongest of the three components so that it can act as a mediator between the demands of the id and the superego, while still taking external reality into consideration. If the id becomes too strong, self-centered, impulsive behavior rules the individual's life. On the other hand, if the superego becomes too strong, rigid, uncompromising, and moralistic behavior takes over. The ego's task of mediating between these two impulses is far from straightforward and may create various psychological conflicts. The id is a kind of devil on one shoulder, while the superego is the angel on the other; both speak to us simultaneously, creating a kind of motivational tug of war within. We listen to both impulses, take in their differing perspectives and then make a decision. This decision is the ego talking, the one looking for that mediating balance between the two other elements. But because this balancing act is often difficult to do, Freud argued that the ego has certain "defense mechanisms" which help it function. When the ego has a truly difficult time reconciling the impulses of both id and superego, it will employ one or more of these defenses. They include displacement, denial, repression, and transference, all of which (Freud believed) served as insulation mechanisms to protect the ego.

Along with the former American ambassador William Bullitt, Freud himself would venture into the writing of political psychobiography.[8] But his primary impact on the genre came via his influence over others. The role of the unconscious motives, childhood development, and compensatory defense mechanisms would all have a particularly marked impact on the development of political psychobiography during these early years. Most of all, it was Charles Merriam and Harold Lasswell, two of the founding fathers of political psychology, who took Freud's ideas and applied them to the study of politics. Merriam was a primary intellectual influence on Lasswell as his teacher, but because it was the latter who put these ideas down on paper and developed them, Lasswell is often seen as the first American political psychologist and sometimes the first political psychologist per se. Lasswell's book *Psychopathology and Politics*, published originally in 1930, was a landmark in this respect, as was *Power and Personality*, which first appeared in 1948.[9] Unlike many later political psychologists, Lasswell actually took the time to train himself in what were then the latest developments in Freudian psychoanalysis. As a result, he came to argue that what he called the "political personality" results from the displacement of private problems onto public life. His main contention was that "political movements derive their vitality from the displacement of private affect upon public objects."[10] Power may be sought to overcome low self-esteem, for instance, being "expected to overcome low estimates of the self, by changing either the traits of the self or the environment."[11] Individuals who went into politics, in other words, often sought political power as a compensation for something else.

Alexander George and Juliette George's *Woodrow Wilson and Colonel House* is heavily influenced by this kind of approach.[12] In fact, there is an intellectual chain connecting Merriam to Lasswell and the Georges: Merriam taught Lasswell the importance of the psychological aspects of politics, which he then passed on to the Georges at the University of Chicago, which became a kind of intellectual hothouse for the early development of political psychology in America. Though not overtly couched in Freud's language, the text traces much of Woodrow Wilson's adult political behavior to his childhood experiences at the hands of a supposedly stern Presbyterian minister father. Because the father allegedly never showed the son affection or congratulated him on his performance in general, Wilson sought the love of the American people as a kind of compensation. The fame and controversy of *Woodrow Wilson and Colonel House* in turn influenced a whole host of works like Doris Kearns Goodwin's *Lyndon Johnson and the American Dream* and Betty Glad's *Jimmy Carter: In Search of the Great White House*.[13]

Attitudes and Voting Behavior

In the second phase of the history of political psychology, the focus shifted from personality and culture to attitudes and voting behavior. Large-scale survey research, rather than the qualitative analyses of works of psychobiography, became the preferred method of the day. At this point, political psychology also moved from psychoanalysis to an approach more suited to the study of attitudes—cognitive consistency theory—and/or a perspective more suited to the "scientific" study of behavior. Behaviorism is the subject of our next chapter, so we will leave that topic for a moment, but according to cognitive consistency or cognitive balance theories, inconsistencies among a person's attitudes cause an uncomfortable state of tension. Leon Festinger famously referred to this as a state of "cognitive dissonance."[14] Because human beings are unhappy with inconsistencies of this sort, they are motivated to reduce the degree of dissonance in some way. For example, during World War II the United States formed an alliance with the Soviet Union against Nazi Germany. Clearly, this made the most virulent of anti-Communists in the United States decidedly uncomfortable, but these individuals could reduce the degree of dissonance by adding a third statement or belief to the mix: alliances are marriages of convenience, sometimes necessary to achieve moral ends. Robert Jervis's best-known work within international relations draws upon this kind of theorizing.[15]

Angus Campbell and his colleagues developed a model of voting in their book *The American Voter* which was explicitly psychological in its emphasis.[16] While Paul Lazarsfeld and others had begun from the position that social and economic factors directly determine how one votes, Campbell and his colleagues argued that a subjective, psychological variable plays an *intervening* role between objective situationist factors and the vote. In their formative years, voters develop a long-term, enduring attachment to a particular political party.[17] This can take the form of a knee-jerk, almost religious form of loyalty to one party. Campbell and his colleagues believed that these strong psychologically attached blocks of voters were relatively static over time, forming about two-thirds of the voting electorate. It was the one-third of "independent" voters—who for some reason failed to develop this psychological loyalty— who actually decided the results of presidential elections, since they formed a kind of "swing vote" at the center. This model also implicitly drew upon cognitive consistency theory, for it suggested that strong partisans simply screened out or rationalized away unfavorable information about their own party which came to them during the election campaign, and would vote for parties whose views they didn't even agree with on some issues (as Southern Democrats who opposed greater racial integration did for some years after the passage of the civil rights legislation of the mid-1960s). The work of Philip Converse in particular argued that most voters lacked an internally consistent system of attitudes and beliefs, relying instead on long-term party ties in deciding how to vote.[18] Strong partisans would explain away poor economic performance as the product of something other than their party's own policy choices. Faced with the suspicion that Adlai Stevenson was a weak standard bearer for the Democratic Party in 1956, rock-solid Democrats would reduce the dissonance caused by simply downplaying or screening out the information. Rock-solid Republicans could be expected to do the same when their own standard bearer in 1964, Barry Goldwater, appeared extreme in his views and perhaps even dangerous to world peace.

At the same time, rational actor theory or rational choice—a field drawn not from psychology but from mathematics and economics, as we noted earlier— began to exert increasing importance as a model of voting behavior in its own right, forming a rival to the party identification model. This approach argued that voters were in fact more highly informed than the party identification approach had allowed for, assuming that voters actually cast their ballot on the basis of the "fit" between their own attitudes and the issue positions of the parties. Proponents of this approach often assumed, for example, that voters would cast their ballots on the basis of how well their own finances had fared over the previous four years, how well the country had fared, or some combination of the two. Anthony Downs' *An Economic Theory of Democracy* became the foundational text for this new approach.[19] The contrast with the party identification model could not have been more clear: while the latter suggested that voters cast their ballots on the basis of long-term attachments or loyalties, the many proponents of the new approach suggested that electors came pretty close to the idea of "pure rationality" in their voting decisions. These two approaches correspond to two rival models of decision-making which Stephen Ansolabehere and Shanto Iyengar describe as *Homo economicus* and *Homo psychologicus*, which co-exist rather uneasily today, as we will discuss shortly.[20]

Political Beliefs, Information Processing, and Decision-Making

The third phase in the history of political psychology McGuire talks about can be seen coalescing during the second stage. Since the 1980s, cognitive approaches to political psychology—perspectives which emphasize the content of people's knowledge structures in shaping decision-making and behavior in general—have been most influential within political psychology. This is not a single approach, but instead many perspectives; however, if one had to summarize the similarities between these various approaches, we could say that they all start from the assumption that human beings are inherently *limited* creatures. Human individuals, unlike say computers, have a limited capacity to process incoming information, and many cognitive psychologists talk of humans as having a "limited cognitive capacity." What do they mean by this? Well, ideally, to make a fully rational decision, you require *all* the relevant information relating to that decision and you need to consider all the possible alternative courses of action available to you. But in the real world, we know that actual human beings possess neither perfect information nor inexhaustible stamina. The world is an incredibly complex place, and the average individual is constantly bombarded with information which no one brain can actually assimilate.

Suppose that every time you made a decision—of any kind—you had to gather all the information relevant to that decision. Let's say, for instance, you wished to make a fully rational, fully informed decision about where to eat each night. To meet the exacting standards of pure rationality, you would in principle have to read all the menus of all the cafes and restaurants in your town or city. You would have to taste the leading dishes in each dining option that night, comparing taste and quality and price and deciding which represented the optimal choice given your preferences. In that way, you would as economists put it "maximize your utility," selecting the best option relative to its cost. Of course, in reality human beings very rarely behave in this way. Instead, we often process information by means of what are generally called cognitive "short cuts" or heuristics. These are devices for prematurely cutting short the search for information, which allow us to lump for one decision or another far more quickly than we otherwise would. In practice, we often pick the same restaurant or cafe we ate at last week or last month, with the expectation that if the food and/or price was good last time, it probably will be again.

The pioneer in developing this more realistic account of human decision-making behavior was an organizational theorist and political psychologist known as Herbert Simon, who came up with at least two highly significant concepts with which he will always be associated: "bounded rationality" and "satisficing behavior."[21] Human decision-makers are rational, he suggested, but only within the bounds of the information available to them (which is often either limited or too substantial to process). As a consequence, we often "satisfice" instead of "maximize" our utility. In other words, we frequently plump for *the first acceptable option that will "do"* out of a potentially limitless set of choices. So, for example, when you haven't already decided where to eat one evening, you usually don't walk up and down the entire length of the street (and the one adjoining it) looking each place over and comparing prices and quality in minute detail; instead, you generally pick the first place which is satisfactory. And this, on a different scale, is what policy-makers often do, according to the bounded rationality perspective: faced with a potentially limitless range of solutions to a problem, they choose the first available option that is acceptable. So for example, if you have a massive number of options, from A to Z, you will start at A; if that's not OK, you move to B, then on to C, and so on until you find an acceptable solution (say D). You won't go through the whole lot. D may not be the optimal, utility-maximizing choice—the best may actually be L or Q or Y—but you can't consider everything.

Another short cut we shall discuss later in this book is the use of analogical reasoning. This is essentially the use of past situations in order to understand the present and predict the future. Faced with a new or very uncertain situation, decision-makers very often rely on historical analogies to make sense of what's going on. "What does this look like to me?" is the question we consciously (but often subconsciously) ask ourselves. What in my past experience, or my knowledge of history, provides clues as to what is going on here? International relations abound with the use of historical analogies, and the use of schemas, scripts, and analogies as cognitive short cuts has been especially well studied and extensively analyzed in the field of foreign policy analysis.

Neuropolitics and Genopolitics: A Fourth Phase?

In recent years, we have seen the emergence of two interrelated approaches, "neuropolitics" and "genopolitics." We shall examine these in a lot more depth in Chapter 11, but stated simply, the first examines the impact of the brain on politics and the other the impact of our genetic inheritance on politics (as we shall see later, these are closely related but separable approaches). One could contend that this is merely a continuation of the third phase, in the sense that it involves a renewed focus on cognition and decision-making. On the other hand, it is inspired not by the cognitive revolution of the 1970s and 1980s, but by newer approaches which stress the impact of emotion and its integral relationship to cognition, some of which argue that the former approach was not radical enough in its critique of *Homo economicus* and fails to really come to grips with how the human mind actually works. This fourth phase no longer treats human beings as if they were computers, for instance. This phase might also be seen as qualitatively different from the third in the sense that the methodological techniques it employs are entirely novel from a political science perspective, marked by the use of fMRI and EEG techniques from neuroscience and twin studies from behavioral genetics (to take but the two most prominent examples). We will return to this issue in the very final chapter of the book, but for now the reader should note that this is an exciting time to be doing political psychology. The subject was always interdisciplinary, as we have seen already, but one can now credibly argue that it is even *more* interdisciplinary than ever.

So far, we have outlined the differences between two very general approaches to the explanation of political behavior: situationism and dispositionism. We have described the history of political psychology in broad brushstrokes, setting the stage for the more detailed historical account that will follow in later chapters. And we have briefly described the *Homo psychologicus* approach which underpins this book and provides many of its underlying assumptions, as well as a rival perspective which draws upon economics. The next task, then, is to begin to pull apart the situationist and dispositionist perspectives, showing how these broad frameworks encompass a range of more specific theories and approaches. We shall begin this exercise with an example of a situationist theory par excellence: behaviorism, which treats human beings as a "blank slate." Since we are all born without any basic predispositions, the approach contends, it is the social environment around us that essentially shapes our behaviors and, indeed, determines the kind of individuals we turn out to be.

Notes

1 Jeanne Knutson (ed.), *Handbook of Political Psychology* (San Francisco, CA: Jossey-Bass, 1973).
2 William Stone and Paul Schaffner, *The Psychology of Politics*, second edition (New York: Springer-Verlag, 1988). This was incidentally one of the very first textbooks on political psychology (it first came out in 1974).

3 Quoted in Stone and Schaffner, *The Psychology of Politics*, p.17.

4 Kenneth Waltz, *Man, The State and War: A Theoretical Analysis* (New York: Columbia University Press, 1959); J. David Singer, "The Levels-of-Analysis Problem in International Relations," *World Politics*, 14: 77–92, 1961.

5 Kenneth Waltz, *Theory of International Politics* (Reading, MA: Addison-Wesley, 1979).

6 William McGuire, "The Poli–Psy Relationship: Three Phases of a Long Affair," in Shanto Iyengar and William McGuire (eds.), *Explorations in Political Psychology* (Durham, NC: Duke University Press, 1993). Also reprinted in John T. Jost and Jim Sidanius (eds.), *Political Psychology: Key Readings* (New York: Psychology Press, 2004). This chapter draws on many of the insights from McGuire's seminal piece, though it does not attempt to do so with the same breadth or depth.

7 Freud intended these simply as conceptual labels for components of human personality, not physically existing properties of the brain itself.

8 Sigmund Freud and William Bullitt, *Thomas Woodrow Wilson, Twenty-Eighth President of the United States: A Psychological Study* (Boston, MA: Houghton Mifflin, 1967).

9 Harold Lasswell, *Psychopathology and Politics* (Chicago, IL: University of Chicago Press, 1930), especially pp.75–76; Lasswell, *Power and Personality* (New York: W.W. Norton, 1948).

10 Lasswell, *Psychopathology and Politics*, p.183.

11 Lasswell, *Power and Personality*, p.39.

12 Alexander George and Juliette George, *Woodrow Wilson and Colonel House* (New York: Dover, 1956).

13 Doris Kearns Goodwin, *Lyndon Johnson and the American Dream* (New York: Harper & Row, 1976); Betty Glad, *Jimmy Carter: In Search of the Great White House* (New York: W.W. Norton, 1980).

14 Leon Festinger, *Theory of Cognitive Dissonance* (Stanford, CA: Stanford University Press, 1957).

15 Robert Jervis, *Perception and Misperception in International Politics* (Princeton, NJ: Princeton University Press, 1976).

16 Angus Campbell, Philip Converse, Warren Miller, and Donald Stokes, *The American Voter* (New York: Wiley, 1964).

17 This model was imported into the study of British electoral choice by David Butler and his associates. See for instance David Butler and Donald Stokes, *Political Change in Britain: Forces Shaping Electoral Choice* (New York: St. Martin's Press, 1969).

18 Philip Converse, "The Nature of Belief Systems in Mass Publics," in David Apter (ed.), *Ideology and Discontent* (New York: Free Press, 1964).

19 Anthony Downs, *An Economic Theory of Democracy* (New York: Harper & Row, 1957).

20 Stephen Ansolabehere and Shanto Iyengar, "Information and Electoral Attitudes: A Case of Judgment Under Uncertainty," in Shanto Iyengar and William McGuire (eds.), *Explorations in Political Psychology* (Durham, NC: Duke University Press, 1993), pp.322–28.

21 See for instance Herbert Simon, "A Behavioral Model of Rational Choice," in *Models of Man, Social and Rational: Mathematical Essays on Rational Human Behavior in a Social Setting* (New York: Wiley, 1957); Simon, *Reason in Human Affairs* (Stanford, CA: Stanford University Press, 1983).

Suggested Further Reading

Morton Hunt, *The Story of Psychology*, updated and revised edition (New York: Anchor Books, 2007).

Daniel Kahneman, *Thinking Fast and Slow* (New York: Farrar, Straus, and Giroux, 2011).

William McGuire, "The Poli–Psy Relationship: Three Phases of a Long Affair," in Shanto Iyengar and William McGuire (eds.), *Explorations in Political Psychology* (Durham, NC: Duke University Press, 1993). Also reprinted in John T. Jost and Jim Sidanius (eds.), *Political Psychology: Key Readings* (New York: Psychology Press, 2004).

Film

Science Odyssey: In Search of Ourselves (PBS, 1998): A pretty good history of the discipline of psychology and its early development. The second half of the film contains a nice overview of the "Eugenics" versus "Behaviorism" debate, which leads well into the topic of the next chapter.

Part I

The Situation

Chapter 3

Behaviorism and Human Freedom

In order to fully understand behaviorism, it's first necessary to know something about the "Eugenics" movement. Eugenics was first developed in the 1870s by Sir Francis Galton, a cousin of Charles Darwin, who saw himself as extending the latter's teachings to public policy. In essence, eugenics is the belief that governments and other agencies should adopt policies which improve the genetic "quality" of their populations. This involves promoting reproduction of people with desired genetic traits, while simultaneously discouraging the reproduction of people with less-desired traits. As a philosophical approach and political policy, it often led to deportation, enforced sterilization, and to harsh and restrictive anti-immigration policies.

Eugenics was a form of what I like to call "hyper-dispositionism," because it suggested that human behavior was 100 percent determined by biology (nowadays, practically no one makes such a bold claim). Our basic nature, the eugenicists argued, is fixed at birth and unchangeable. Some have charged that Darwin's ideas led directly and inevitably to Hitler and Nazism.[1] This is in my view highly unfair—Darwin never advocated eugenics himself—but eugenicist ideas were certainly co-opted by the Nazis in Germany during the 1930s and used to justify genocide in the name of racial purity, involving the literal eradication of those who did not conform to the Aryan ideal. But eugenicist ideas were popular in the United States before this as well. Many justified strict sterilization and anti-immigration measures in the 1920s on the grounds that immigration from Eastern Europe and elsewhere was supposedly "weakening" the genetic code of America. Some even claimed that the United States was engaging in "race suicide" at the time by continuing to welcome immigrants with supposedly undesirable genetic traits.

Perhaps understandably, there was widespread revulsion against such approaches after World War II, and that revulsion often extended to *all* biological approaches in general. Behaviorism, on the other hand, was much more consonant with the American Dream. The "blank state" notion suggested that we could be what we wanted to be, rejecting all notions of biological determinism. Education in America and Western Europe expanded enormously in the post-World War II era, as young people sought to improve their lot in the world. Behaviorism was a democratic, come-one-come-all doctrine, and it meshed nicely with classical American ideals. It was thus no accident that the field of psychology came to be dominated by stimulus–response (S–R) behaviorism during the 1950s. During the height of behaviorism's popularity, it was widely believed that we could essentially ignore what goes on inside people's heads; this was thought *unmeasurable*, and therefore an inappropriate topic for scientific enquiry. Some behaviorists thought this was one way Freud had gone astray, for he was constantly attempting to uncover mental mechanisms which were largely hidden from view. Therefore, many behaviorists regarded this as plain bad science, since people's "inner states" could not be directly observed. It was asserted instead that we should focus on what is *observable*, namely outward or overt behavior (hence the name "behaviorism"), since this can be measured and tested.

This perspective, like other psychological fashions, had a noticeable impact on political science; for one thing it dovetailed nicely with psychology's aspiration (especially strong at that time) to become a "true science," in the sense of a verified body of well-tested theories that would eventually result in the accumulation of genuine knowledge.[2] In a more specific sense, it also inspired political psychologists in this era. According to McGuire, during the 1950s, one of the major sources of "environmentalistic–theoretical inspiration" for political psychology "was the stimulus–response behaviorism that described how the individual's political personality is conditioned by the stimuli, responses, drives, and reinforcements provided by society's institutions."[3]

The founder of behaviorism was John B. Watson, who in turn influenced other prominent behaviorists such as Edward Thorndike and B.F. Skinner. Behaviorists tended to think of the human mind as a blank slate or *tabula rasa* onto which practically anything could be written using environmental conditioning. "In behaviorism, an infant's talents and abilities didn't matter because there was *no such thing* as a talent or an ability," Steven Pinker notes. "Watson had banned them from psychology, together with other contents of the mind, such as ideas, beliefs, desires and feelings. They were subjective and unmeasurable, he said, and unfit for science, which studies only objective and measurable things."[4] As noted at the end of the previous chapter, this was also an extreme form of situationism: the causes of behavior were to be found in the external environment, not inside the mind itself. During his keynote address to the 1990 American Psychological Association, for instance, B.F. Skinner—in a speech that would turn out to be his last—condemned the study of cognition and the human mind as "the creationism of psychology," a classic statement of the view that we should study the environments that make individuals, not the ways in which individuals supposedly make these environments.

Absolutely central to all forms of behaviorism is the idea of *conditioning*. Most people have heard the famous story of Pavlov's dog, which was trained to salivate at the sound of a bell. The dog was trained with meat powder; every time the experimenter rang the bell, an apparatus would drop a little tasty meat powder on the dog's tongue. Eventually, the dog would salivate (the response) merely at the sound of the bell (the stimulus), since it had come to associate one thing with another. Pavlov's study, conducted in 1927, is an example of what is called *classic conditioning*, which involves learning through reflex. Salivating is an involuntary reflex, but B.F. Skinner—while heavily influenced by Pavlov—was more interested in what became known as *operant conditioning*, in which voluntary behavior is modified. We learn something because it is immediately followed by a pleasant effect known as *reinforcement*. This was Skinner's own contribution to behaviorism, and it led to his argument that human beings could be trained through conditioning to engage in socially responsible behaviors and refrain from irresponsible ones, a position he outlined in his novel *Walden Two*.[5]

Frazier, the hero of *Walden Two* and a thinly disguised version of Skinner himself, derides politics and government as impotent to the task of improving people's lives, though Skinner does not manage to abolish politics altogether; he creates an imaginary community ruled by "planner managers," who call to mind Plato's "philosopher kings."[6] Although overtly anti-political, Skinner imagined a society in which the contentiousness of politics had been done away with and replaced by science and reason. Professor of Psychology Professor Burris and his philosopher friend Castle are outsiders who visit the Utopian community of "Walden Two." Although they find its inhabitants rather passionless and unusual, they discover that this is a happy community free from social problems like crime and drunkenness. For the first hundred pages or so of the novel, the reason for this being only partially clear, the focus is on the small, rather mundane ways in which the society has been reorganized (such as altering the temperatures in the cribs of babies). Later it becomes clear that Frazier has actively (and successfully) conditioned out human "imperfections" such as jealousy from the members of Walden Two. "As to emotions—we aren't free of them all, nor should we like to be," Frazier says. "But the meaner and more annoying—the emotions which breed unhappiness—are almost unknown here, like unhappiness itself. We don't need them any longer in our struggle for existence, and it's easier on our circulatory system, and certainly pleasanter, to dispense with them."[7]

Although the novel was intended as what a novel is—fiction—it was also meant to suggest to its readers the possibility of creating such a society. For devotees of the behaviorist perspective, this approach held obvious social-engineering implications. "If we turned society into a big Skinner box and controlled behavior deliberately rather than haphazardly, we could eliminate aggression, overpopulation, crowding, pollution, and inequality, and thereby attain utopia," Skinner claimed.[8] The radical political aspects of his thinking gained him a notoriety that has persisted long after his death; some even consider him "evil" today, although he was certainly well intentioned.[9]

In the film *A Clockwork Orange* and in Anthony Burgess's book of the same name, the ultraviolent young thug Alex is subjected to this kind of social experiment. Captured by the state and taken into the care of a psychologist called Dr. Brodsky (who is obviously a follower of Watson and Skinner), Alex's eyelids are forcibly held open. He is conditioned through watching horrific films to associate seeing acts of violence with becoming physically ill. As he watches acts of violence on the screen, he is given drugs that cause him to vomit. He is thus forcibly pacified, a process which Burgess calls the "Ludovico technique" in the novel.

Burgess himself gained a dose of undeserved notoriety when his book was made into a violent and disturbing film by the director Stanley Kubrick in the early 1970s. The point of his book was not to glorify violence, however, but to make a philosophical point about humanity and choice which runs directly counter to behaviorism's aspirations to change society. As Burgess himself later put it, the novel was intended as "a vindication of free will."[10] In one scene in the book, Dr. Brodsky displays the reformed Alex in front of an audience, presumably a class lecture of some sort. "Our subject is, you see, impelled toward the good, by, paradoxically, being impelled towards evil," Brodsky tells his audience. "The intention to act violently is accompanied by strong feelings of physical distress. To counter these, the subject has to switch to a diametrically opposed attitude." One questioner protests, though, that Alex now "has no real choice, has he? . . . He ceases to be a wrongdoer. He ceases also to be a creature capable of moral choice." Brodsky dismisses these points as "subtleties," saying that we aren't concerned with the ethical side of things, just with cutting down on crime.[11] But the questioner's point is that the ability to choose between right and wrong is what makes us human; take that away, and we cease, in a way, to *be* a human being. The broader political implication, of course, is that the government has in a way done something more terrible to Alex than the crimes he has committed.

On the other hand, it is easy to see the social benefits of such techniques if they could be made to work. B.F. Skinner died some years ago, but he would probably respond to Anthony Burgess's critique with something like the following. We are all *already* conditioned by the circumstances in which we live, as he often stressed. At present, this occurs randomly and in a haphazard way. But what if psychologists and psychiatrists, with the backing of the government of course, were allowed to condition the general population to behave in socially desirable ways, or at least not to behave in violent or antisocial ways? We would only be bringing order to a conditioning process that occurs naturally in any case. Take the example of the crime of rape. Though it is hard to measure this, many males in advanced industrial societies would probably not engage in rape even if society allowed them to do so. But we know from societies in which the gross mistreatment of women is common (for instance, Afghanistan under the Taliban) that a substantial number of men will in fact abuse women in various ways if the surrounding society allows or encourages this. But what if all males within a given population could be conditioned from a relatively young age (say, in their early teens) to find rape and other violent crimes abhorrent and barbaric? What if they could be taught to find these acts so disgusting that they became almost literally unthinkable? Would this not be a price worth paying? After all, freedom has to have limits, and we already recognize these limits by accepting various rules, laws, and forms of authority. While free will is obviously a desirable thing to preserve, few would defend the criminal's right to rape, torture, or kill. Isn't society better off, in the end, if Alex and his Droogs lose their right to make moral choices?

But, who gets to decide which behaviors are to be encouraged and which not? We can all agree that rape is undesirable, but how about reading pornography? What about the use of cocaine? Should all members of a society be conditioned to find drug use unthinkable? Should we be conditioned not to smoke tobacco or drink alcohol? The point here is that someone has to draw a line, and that line is socially determined and therefore politically contentious. To take a few famous examples, marijuana use is legal in licensed cafes in Holland but can land you a couple of nights in jail and a hefty fine not far away in London, England. Prostitution is legal in parts of Nevada but not in Ohio. In most places in the United States, you can own a gun when you are eighteen but cannot legally order a beer in a bar, while one can drink in a bar at eighteen— and sometimes rather earlier—in most of Western Europe but will have a hard time legally purchasing a firearm. Ironically, it is illegal to drink the bourbon whiskey Jack Daniels in the area where it is manufactured (which is a dry county), while revelers can sup it in an open container along Bourbon Street, New Orleans. Women can be stoned to death for adultery in Iran, while the same transgression (by men or women) is merely frowned upon nowadays in the United States. There are endless other examples one could give, but the central point is that different societies (and even different parts of the same country) view questions of right and wrong very differently. This becomes especially apparent in a federal system like that of the United States, which has a patchwork quilt of laws that can confuse and perplex visitors to its shores.

Skinner himself was well aware of this problem. "Who is to construct the controlling environment and to what end?" he asked. "Autonomous man presumably controls himself in accordance with a built-in set of values; he works for what he finds good. But what will the putative controller find good, and will it be good for those he controls? Answers to questions of this sort are said, of course, to call for value judgments."[12] Skinner was also more than well aware of the argument that a conditioned human being ceases to be capable of making moral choices. Long before Burgess's critique appeared, Skinner has the character called Castle criticize Frazier in *Walden Two* on the grounds that he has "taken the mainspring out of the watch";[13] in other words, he has taken from his subjects the things that make them human. Later Frazier directly addresses the free will question by suggesting that the notion is illusory in a society which is already randomly and haphazardly conditioned:

> Our friend Castle is worried about the conflict between long-range dictatorship and freedom. Doesn't he know he's merely raising the old question of predestination and free will? All that happens is contained in an original plan, yet at every stage the individual seems to be making choices and determining the outcome. The same is true of Walden Two. Our members are practically always doing what they want to do—what they "choose" to do—but we see to it that they will want to do precisely the things which are best for themselves and the community. Their behavior is determined, yet they're free.[14]

At another point, Frazier suggests that this philosophical point is just an unimportant quibble. "We don't puzzle our little minds over the outcome of Love versus Duty," he opines. "We simply arrange a world in which serious conflicts occur as seldom as possible or, with a little luck, not at all."[15]

In a song they composed in the sixties, The Rolling Stones sang "I'm free to do what I want, any old time." But Skinner questioned this kind of (very commonplace) notion that we are free simply because we get to do what we wish. In questioning the widespread notion that human beings make free and independent choices, Skinner suggested that concepts like human freedom and dignity are in fact largely illusory; we want what we want because we have been conditioned to want that thing through positive reinforcers (rewards) and/or negative reinforcers (punishments). And in proposing that the state take control of the conditioning process, he seemed not only to raise the dangerous specter of totalitarianism, but to advocate it. In an era when Westerners had fought off the threat of fascism and were preoccupied with the challenge posed by global Communism, this set off alarm bells among a variety of critics. This is the dark side of Skinner's thought, and it is what gained him the notoriety that persists long after his death, among students and scholars who know relatively little about his work.

In the end, this debate—powerful though the issues are—may be a moot one, in the sense that most psychologists today question the capacity of conditioning to change people's basic behaviors. In both the book and the film *A Clockwork Orange*, the conditioning actually works. If the Ludovico technique seems far-fetched as a device, consider the real-life uses to which behaviorism was (and sometimes still is) put. Steven Pinker uses the example of religious groups who have tried to treat the "disease" of homosexuality. "Many techniques have been foisted on [gay men]," Pinker notes, "psychoanalysis, guilt mongering, and conditioning techniques that use impeccable fire-together-wire-together logic (for example, having them look at Playboy centerfolds while sexually aroused). The techniques are all failures."[16] Oddly, those who espouse such techniques rarely consider that the reverse procedure is equally unlikely to work. If Pat Robertson—who has condemned homosexuality as "a kind of bestiality"—stared at a gay magazine for long enough while sexually aroused, could such a technique make him a homosexual? Feel free to ponder this possibility yourself for a minute or two, but it seems doubtful that the well-known televangelist would be successful, in the unlikely event that he should choose to cultivate what would for him (one assumes) be a rather radical change of lifestyle. Again, the problem with expecting such conditioning to work as Pinker sees it is that we are not "blank slates" inscribed with whatever is in the surrounding culture and environment. Our genetic hardware and neural networks—our dispositions, in the terms we have been using in this book—play a critical role as well.

It would be wrong to assert that conditioning never works—far from it. In general, however, behaviorist techniques seem to work best when only peripheral changes in behavior (as opposed to fundamental changes in lifestyle) are sought. Fear of flying, generalized anxiety, or panic disorders, for instance, are sometimes successfully treated using conditioning. Those suffering from panic attacks in social situations, for instance, are sometimes asked to confront their fears repeatedly in "safe" or simulated situations and may successfully learn not to feel anxiety when around people they don't know. Most young lecturers confronting a class of two hundred students for the first time feel quite nervous when they first experience this—as the author himself did some years ago—but in a sense one becomes "conditioned" by repeated exposure to this activity not to experience fear or discomfort.

Equally, it is clear that there are profound limits to behavioral modification via deliberate conditioning. The Irish soccer player George Best, for example, fought a long battle with alcoholism. Best was an extraordinarily gifted athlete who spent the height of his career with the English team Manchester United during the late 1960s and 1970s. He later finished his career in the United States in the now defunct North American Soccer League (NASL). He led a very active and well-publicized social life, often being photographed in London nightclubs hoisting bottles of champagne with attractive models.

Like many alcoholics, Best became extremely unreliable over the course of his highly abbreviated career, and eventually wouldn't even bother to turn up for matches. After retiring from the game, he continued to drink and party heavily. At one point, doctors implanted a device in Best designed to make him vomit when he drank alcohol—a kind of classical conditioning, à la Pavlov's dog—and the hope was that he would eventually come to associate the taste of alcohol with becoming physically sick. This didn't work, and Best went back to the bottle even after receiving a liver transplant. He eventually died in 2005 at the age of only fifty-nine.[17] Apart from Brazil's Pelé and perhaps Argentina's Maradona, many consider him to have been the most skillful player ever, and certainly one of the most gifted and entertaining.

The political radicalism of Skinner's vision can hardly be questioned. In arguing that we do not really make choices out of our own free will, he undermines—among other things—the whole idea on which the Western legal system is based. Stated in its most simple form, that system assumes that if we do bad things, we deserve to be punished; our choices have consequences, and we are responsible for them. But once we accept the counterargument that human beings do not make autonomous choices, we take a wrecking ball not only to the idea that "bad" actions should be punished, but also to the notion that "good" achievements deserve to be praised and rewarded. The environment surrounding us becomes a kind of puppeteer. In the traditional vision of things, Skinner notes, "a person is responsible for his behavior. Not only in the sense that he may be justly blamed or punished when he behaves badly, but also in the sense that he is to be given credit and admired for his achievements." On the other hand, "scientific analysis shifts the credit as well as the blame to the environment, and traditional practices can then no longer be justified. These are sweeping changes, and those who are committed to traditional theories and practices naturally resist them."[18]

In a somewhat weaker form, we will see again how this kind of situationism challenges the notion of individual legal responsibility in Chapter 5, which deals with the Stanford experiment, the Abu Ghraib scandal, and Philip Zimbardo's attempt to show that one defendant in that trial was only partially responsible for his actions. As we noted in Chapter 1, the idea that situations might determine our behavior presents a formidable challenge to Western notions of legal responsibility, which are essentially premised on the assumption that if you are the actor who performed an act, you are legally responsible for that act (a partial exception is the notion of unintended killing or manslaughter, which still nevertheless carries penalties in most legal systems: proving insanity is of course another way in which legal responsibility for an act may be avoided).

On the other hand, Skinner's vision of the world is in some ways quite democratic. It dovetails nicely with the American Dream, for instance, and it is easy to see why it held a particular appeal during the especially hopeful era of the 1950s and 1960s. Though this cultural viewpoint is easy to caricature, Americans have long believed that individuals are essentially free to pursue the careers and lifestyles they desire as long as they work hard and "play by the rules." In short, you can be what you want to be, and your life path is not predetermined. Behaviorism is quite compatible with this vision in the sense that it holds out precisely the same possibility. For Watson and Skinner, our dispositions are not fixed but entirely malleable, and our achievements in life are simply a matter of the type of social conditioning to which we have been exposed. An individual conditioned to believe that he or she is able to achieve great things in the world is liable to go out and attempt to do so, just as a person who has learned that he or she is trapped by his or her social situation is less likely to try to break out of that situation.

Assessing Behaviorism

Clearly, there are powerful arguments both for and against behaviorism, both as an account of political behavior and as a prescription for political practice. Some of these arguments are summarized in Table 3.1.

Table 3.1 A summary of the arguments for and against behaviorism

For
- Science has the answers that politicians don't.
- We are conditioned *already*, but haphazardly.
- We should condition people not to commit acts of violence (and we could even prevent war).
- The social benefits of conditioning greatly outweigh the costs.
- "Choice" is illusory anyway.
- Behaviorism is in some ways quite democratic.

Against
- The *Clockwork Orange* critique: what makes us human is the right to choose.
- Who is to decide what should be conditioned in or out?
- Behaviorism may be the road to fascism ("who will guard the guardians?").
- Conditioning often doesn't work anyway.

Conclusion

It is up to you to decide which of these arguments you find most convincing. It is odd, perhaps, that so few political psychology textbooks today deal with the political implications of behaviorism, since this is an area in which psychology merges in a very direct way with the concerns of both political theory and practice. This topic also fits rather neatly into our conceptual distinction between situationism and dispositionism, since behaviorism represents an especially radical example of the former. Even if you remain unconvinced by this rather stark form of situationism, there are alternative approaches available within this general camp which may be found to be more appealing. These are discussed in the chapters which follow, beginning with Stanley Milgram's surprising findings about the nature and extent of our obedience to authority. Milgram's approach is largely situationist in character, though as we shall see in Chapter 4, there are dispositionist elements to his theory of obedience as well.

Notes

1 See Richard Weikart, *From Darwin to Hitler: Evolutionary Ethics, Eugenics, and Racism in Germany* (New York: Palgrave Macmillan, 2004) for an argument to this effect.
2 Heinz Eulau, *The Behavioral Persuasion in Politics* (New York: Random House, 1963).
3 William McGuire, "The Poli–Psy Relationship: Three Phases of a Long Affair," in Shanto Iyengar and William McGuire (eds.), *Explorations in Political Psychology* (Durham, NC: Duke University Press, 1993), pp.12–13.
4 Steven Pinker, *The Blank Slate: The Modern Denial of Human Nature* (New York: Penguin, 2002), p.19.
5 B.F. Skinner, *Walden Two* (Indianapolis, IN: Hackett Publishing, 2005). This novel first appeared in 1948.
6 Ibid. The book is in many ways a parody of Plato's *Republic*.
7 Ibid., p.92.
8 Pinker, *The Blank Slate*, p.20.
9 Lauren Slater, *Opening Skinner's Box: Great Psychological Experiments of the Twentieth Century* (New York: W.W. Norton, 2004), p.7.
10 Anthony Burgess, *You've Had Your Time* (New York: Penguin, 1990), p.245.
11 Anthony Burgess, *A Clockwork Orange*, restored version (New York: W.W. Norton, 1986), p.126. The book originally came out in 1962. This scene also appears in Kubrick's film, where a priest plays the role of the questioner.
12 B.F. Skinner, *Beyond Freedom and Dignity* (Indianapolis, IN: Hackett Publishing, 2002), p.22. The book was first published in 1971.
13 Skinner, *Walden Two*, p.103.
14 Ibid., p.279.
15 Ibid., p.149.

16 Pinker, *The Blank Slate*, p.94.
17 A particular problem with this technique as applied to alcoholics is that many are highly accustomed to vomiting at the end of the night or early the next day anyway. Trying to condition someone with a punishment they *already* regularly inflict upon themselves seems unlikely to produce changes in behavior!
18 Skinner, *Beyond Freedom and Dignity*, p.21.

Suggested Further Reading

Anthony Burgess, *A Clockwork Orange* (New York: W.W. Norton, 1986).
Steven Pinker, *The Blank Slate: The Modern Denial of Human Nature* (New York: Penguin, 2002).
B.F. Skinner, *Walden Two* (Indianapolis, IN: Hackett Publishing, 1995).
Lauren Slater, *Opening Skinner's Box: Great Psychological Experiments of the Twentieth Century* (New York: W.W. Norton, 2004). Also especially good on Milgram and Festinger.

Film

A Clockwork Orange (1971): Based on the futuristic novel by Anthony Burgess, this version is a bit violent and sexually charged, but I usually edit it down to show only the conditioning process. Directed by Stanley Kubrick.

Chapter 4

The Psychology of Obedience

The late Stanley Milgram is usually thought of as a social psychologist rather than a *political* one, not least perhaps because he spent his career in departments of psychology rather than political science; the term "political psychology," as noted earlier, is used almost exclusively in the latter discipline. But in spite of the differing labels that practitioners of different fields attach to their work, Milgram could justifiably claim to be one of the most important political psychologists of his time. In fact, Milgram began his initial foray into the world of academia as a political science student, and remained interested in the psychological dimensions of political questions for the rest of his (tragically short) life. And although he made many contributions to our understanding of human behavior, which have implications for politics, he will always be best remembered for his work on political obedience. For instance, Milgram asked, why do individuals so readily obey some "higher" authority such as the state, even when the demands of that authority come violently into conflict with the moral and ethical values most of us like to think we cherish? Through addressing this question, Milgram played an instrumental role in overturning (or at least reducing the appeal of) dispositionist accounts, particularly those which followed in the wake of the Nazi Holocaust and blamed that cataclysmic event upon the supposed "peculiarities" of the German people.

The "Authoritarian Personality"

In order to understand the true impact that Stanley Milgram's work had on our understanding of both political obedience and the practice of genocide, we first need to understand the nature of the times in which he was working. The context for Milgram's experiments was a then widely accepted (though always controversial) dispositionist theory known as the *authoritarian personality*. In the 1940s and 1950s, social scientists from a variety of fields tried to come to grips with the horror of what had happened at concentration camps like Auschwitz and Dachau. Understandably, "why the Holocaust?" became one of the most frequently posed enquiries in social science after 1945.

One popular answer to that question at the time suggested that there was something *unusual* or exceptional about the German people, something which made the Nazi genocide almost inevitable in retrospect. The nature of Germans themselves, and more particularly authoritarian child-rearing practices in the homes within which they had grown up, was directly responsible for the creation of intolerant, conservative thinking, according to the authors of the book *The Authoritarian Personality*. First published in 1950 and authored by Theodore Adorno and his colleagues, the book argued that the roots of fascism are to be found in parental repression and authoritarianism.[1] As James Waller notes, the book was heavily influenced by the Freudian psychoanalytic theories dominant at the time. It argued that:

> The origins of this personality were in the innate, and socially unacceptable, drives of sex and aggression. When the restraints against the expression of these drives are unusually harsh, the individual becomes anxious, insecure, and unusually attuned to external authority sources for behavior guidance. This reverence for authority goes far beyond the normal, balanced, and realistic respect for valid authority that most of us have; it reflects an exaggerated, emotional need to submit.[2]

The harsh child-rearing practices of the parent also generate repressed fear and hostility, which eventually need some outlet. This outlet comes in the form of displacement, often taking the form of hostility towards minority groups and more generally those who are "different." Adorno and his colleagues also developed a scale—known commonly today simply as the "F scale"—which correlated a variety of personality traits with the susceptibility to believe antidemocratic or fascist propaganda.

Milgram's Experiments

Stanley Milgram was very much a *situationist*, and as such he was suspicious of theories like the one above which attribute behavior solely to people's dispositions. As a follower of the social psychologist Solomon Asch, he intuitively believed that if you place people in a powerful enough situation, they will go against their dispositions: their beliefs, their values, even their own eyesight. In the 1950s Asch had conducted what became a very famous series of experiments, in which he asked people to estimate the

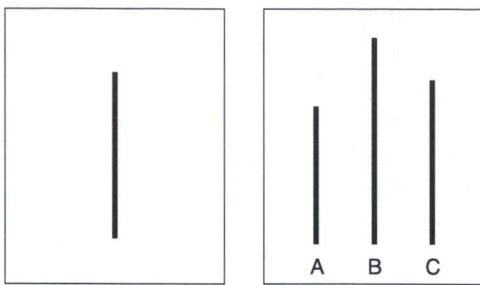

Figure 4.1 The cards used in Solomon Asch's experiments on social pressure

lengths of a series of simple lines. For instance, let's say that you are shown three lines on the right, labeled A, B, and C, as seen in Figure 4.1, and then asked which of the three lines is closest in length to the line presented on the left.

Asch found, as expected, that practically everyone gets the answer right when asked such questions. This was not an earth-shattering result, since the questions were so easy that a child of four or five could have answered them correctly. But this was just a baseline condition, in which people were asked to figure out the correct answers *on their own*. The real purpose of the experiment was to investigate what came next, when he placed his subjects *into groups* and again asked them to perform the same simple task. But there was an interesting piece of deception involved this time. In one variation, he had a "real" subject placed in a room with six others who were in effect actors pretending to be fellow subjects. While for the sake of believability these fake subjects sometimes got the answers right, Asch rigged the experiment so that the six individuals would sometimes collectively give the same wrong answer to a question, and then another, and another, leaving the real subject with a difficult dilemma. For instance, they might claim that option B on the right was closest in length to the line on the left.

Suppose that you are in this situation yourself. What would you do? Would you stand up and tell the other six "you're all wrong, and I'm right. Can't you see that the option you've selected is obviously the wrong answer?" Or would you feel embarrassed and go along with the majority, even though you know they are giving the wrong answer? Would you feel uncomfortable questioning the judgment and intelligence of six strangers? Would you start to question your *own* judgment and intelligence? Or would you start to think that you might well need to visit an optometrist? Asch found that the latter scenarios were by far the most common; in other words, the vast majority of subjects simply went along with the group's faulty judgment, even though they knew (or suspected) that their assessment was simply wrong.[3] Seventy-five percent of his subjects in a series of trials went against their own judgment at least once when the group collectively gave a wrong answer.

Milgram was very much interested in how social pressures like these can affect the judgment of individuals, and after a great deal of thought he came up with a highly inventive research design—like Asch's, involving a clever piece of deception—which would gain him a measure of fame but also a reputation for controversy which would dog him for the rest of his life. He wanted to see how far people would go in following the commands of a "legitimate" authority when those commands became increasingly harsh and inhumane. He created an experiment in which a man in a laboratory coat told subjects to administer increasingly harsh "electrical shocks" to a help-less victim.[4] This was justified to the subjects as part of a supposedly scientific experiment on how people learn in response to punishment. In one classical condition, the "victim" could be heard but not seen behind a thin wall, though Milgram repeated the same experiment in a number of ways, each time varying the degree of proximity between the subject being told to administer the shocks and the "victim," or varying some other aspect of the basic design. The subjects administered the shocks using what were supposedly higher and higher levels of electricity on a generator.

In reality, the "victim" was an actor (an associate of Milgram) and was not actually receiving electrical shocks at all. Also, the generator was fake, but the experiment was set up in such a convincing way that the "teacher" (as the real subjects were termed) genuinely *believed* that he or she was shocking the "learner" (the actor). Prior to his experiment, Milgram conducted a poll of psychiatrists and psychologists. They predicted that less than 1 percent of subjects would go all the way on the "generator," to the maximum charge of 450 volts.[5] Amazingly, though, in the classic condition described above, 65 percent of subjects did this; in fact, they went all the way to a position labeled "danger" and then simply "XXX." This was so, despite the fact that when a certain level of shock was reached, the "victim" would cry out in pain and beg to be allowed to leave the experiment. Nor did the results change (as many people intuitively expect) when Milgram used women as subjects; average obedience remained 65 percent. This is surprising perhaps, since women could be seen either as less obedient (considered more compassionate) or more obedient (considered more passive). Interestingly, though, Milgram found that gender made very little difference, if any.

This was far from all Milgram found, however. He observed a number of interesting reactions in "obedient" subjects as they went about performing their tasks. All, with varying degrees of visibility, experienced strain and discomfort. Some laughed or cried; those who laughed, however, did so not out of sadism or cruelty but as a nervous reaction to stress, Milgram argued. The subjects also became preoccupied with narrow, technical aspects of the job at hand, and afterwards saw themselves as not responsible for their own actions. Here there are potentially interesting parallels with what happens to pilots who are asked to bomb civilian areas. In the Oscar-winning documentary film *Hearts and Minds*, for instance, one bomber pilot who had conducted numerous sorties in Vietnam said that he would become very preoccupied with the task itself when conducting bombing raids, and would not even think about the people he was dropping the bombs on. He relates that he felt like "an opera singer, conducting an aria."[6]

Milgram also varied the form of the experiment in theoretically interesting ways. He wanted to see what effects, for instance, changing (a) the way orders were given, (b) the location of the experiment, and (c) distance between subject and actor would have. One of the most interesting findings related to proximity or distance between the teacher and learner. As proximity between them increased, obedience decreased (although it did not disappear altogether). This was especially true when the subject and victim were placed in the same room. In the "touch–proximity" condition—in which the subjects were required to force the victim's hand down onto the shock plate—it fell to just below 18 percent, and in the "proximity" scenario (where subject and victim were merely in the same room) it was only slightly increased to 20 percent. It is noticeable, though, that even in this condition, obedience was still somewhat high.

The larger point of the experiment was simply this, however: Milgram had selected (by means of an ad in a local paper) ordinary, everyday, law-abiding members of the community of New Haven, Connecticut, obtaining a representative sample of the population across various socioeconomic, religious, and other characteristics. He had also weeded out anyone who seemed psychologically "abnormal"—especially anyone who showed overt signs of a sadistic personality—so that the actions of his subjects could not easily be attributed to their dispositions later on.[7] He had then placed them in a situation in which their dispositions—especially their avowed moral or ethical beliefs—seemed to fall out of the picture. The heavy implication is that we are *all* capable of violating our most cherished principles and values when placed in a situation in which an authority perceived as "legitimate" urges us to obey. Approaches such as the authoritarian personality, on the other hand, are simply wrong, Milgram suggested, since they fail to take account of the ways in which social forces can be more powerful than dispositions in shaping behavior. They make the fatal error of assuming that "evil acts" must be the work of "evil people."

The Banality of Evil

In his book *Obedience: An Experimental View*, Milgram draws parallels between his own work and Hannah Arendt's analysis of Adolf Eichmann in her book *Eichmann in Jerusalem*.[8] As a top Nazi official responsible for deporting Jews to the gas chambers during the Holocaust, but who had escaped Germany after the war, Eichmann had long been a target of Israeli intelligence. In 1960 he was discovered living under an assumed identity in Argentina, and was kidnapped by Israeli agents to face trial for his crimes. He was found guilty in Jerusalem and later executed. Arendt covered Eichmann's trial at the time, but what surprised her most was how ordinary he seemed. The whole trial was televised live in Israel. But rather than the sadistic monster that most Israelis were expecting when they tuned in, they saw instead a rather dull and ordinary man standing in front of the court, a Nazi pen-pusher whose main job had been processing files and making sure that the trains deporting Jews ran on time.

Arendt was strongly criticized for making this observation at the time for reasons that are perhaps understandable, but she coined a phrase to describe Eichmann and those like him which has since become famous: "the banality of evil." Her point was not that Eichmann should be absolved of responsibility for his actions—far from it. It was, rather, that evil is often the end result of a chain of actions for which no one individual bears sole responsibility, and that individual links in that chain can be (and frequently are) composed of the actions of what the historian Christopher Browning more recently referred to as "ordinary men."[9] Similarly, Milgram found that when responsibility for testing and punishing the "victim" was divided among a number of individuals, obedience increases still further. The potential political significance of this is evident, since political decision-making tasks of all kinds are often parceled out like this. Milgram calls this "socially organized evil," where no one person has sole or exclusive responsibility for an act.

Considered together, the independent observations of Arendt and Milgram—the first anecdotal, the second experimental—carry a weight which many find convincing as an explanation of something which almost seems inexplicable, the systematic slaughter of the Jews in supposedly "civilized" countries at the very heart of Europe. Moreover, many of their observations make a good deal of sense when applied to both the Holocaust and more recent genocides. In the case of Nazi Germany, it is clear that the slaughter of the Jews simply could not have been accomplished on the scale that it was had not ordinary, everyday members of German society—people who considered themselves otherwise decent, moral, and law-abiding—been willing to participate (in some cases, very directly) in a process whose objective was the extermination of other human beings whose only crime was being ethnically different from

Adolf Hitler's vision of what was "ideal." We can also observe how thin the line is between what we conventionally call "good" and "evil"—and how easy that line is to cross—in the notorious case of the Rwandan genocide of 1994, in which neighbor killed neighbor on the basis of relatively short-lived racial "differences" which had in many ways been created by Western colonizers to suit their own purposes.

Why We Obey: The Drift Towards Dispositionism

Human beings, Milgram notes, live in hierarchical structures (family, school, college, business, military). This appears to be the result of evolutionary bias (hierarchy works), breeding a built-in potential to obey authority. Interestingly, this argument is the very antithesis of a rigid situationist approach such as S–R behaviorism, which treats the human brain as a "blank slate." Milgram suggests that humans are born with a basic *disposition* to obey, an essentially dispositionist argument of the "dispositions-exist-at-birth" variety. Beyond this, however, his explanation is more situationist in nature. This evolutional tendency, he argues, interacts with social structures and specific circumstances to produce specific cases of obedience.[10] Certain factors made the subjects likely to obey before they even got to the experiment (such as the fact that we are socialized to obey "higher units" in a hierarchical structure), and these then interacted with the specific circumstances designed in the experiment to elicit obedience. As individuals obeyed, they shifted into what Milgram calls the "agentic state"—a psychological condition in which the individuals no longer see themselves as responsible for their own actions.[11]

Milgram's 35 (Or 50) Percent

A complicating factor for Milgram's (mainly situational) paradigm is that there is evidence of *cultural variation* in the degree to which members of different societies obey authority. David Mantell, who repeated Milgram's study in Munich, Germany in the early 1970s, found an obedience rate of 85 percent in the "classic" version of the experiment, a full 20 percent higher than the obedience rate in New Haven.[12] Anecdotally, there is some interesting evidence that Rwandans may also be especially prone to obey authority. Asked why so many ordinary Rwandans in 1994 killed people who were in many cases their neighbors, Francois Xavier Nkurunziza, a lawyer from Kigali with a Hutu father and Tutsi mother, said:

> Conformity is very deep, very developed. In Rwandan history, everyone obeys authority. People revere power, and there isn't enough education.

You take a poor, ignorant population, and give them arms, and say, "It's yours. Kill." They'll obey. The peasants, who were paid or forced to kill, were looking up to people of higher socio-economic standing to see how to behave. So the people of influence . . . are often the big men in the genocide. They may think that they didn't kill because they didn't take life with their own hands, but the people were looking to them for their orders. And, in Rwanda, an order can be given very quietly.[13]

If true, this is ultimately quite compatible with Milgram's approach. His theory of why people obey must leave *some* room for cultural differences in the propensity to obey, since humans are obviously socialized within different authority structures. And in the Rwandan case, there is ample evidence that authority figures of all kinds—mayors, businessmen, even clergy—condoned or encouraged what occurred in Rwanda in 1994. It was the fastest genocide of the twentieth century.

More problematically, situationism arguably falls down in its inability to explain why a significant minority of individuals—fully 35 percent when the actor cannot even be heard crying out in the next room, a not insubstantial figure—refuse to obey authority when it violates conscience or values. And the figure goes up to as much as 50 percent when the actor can be heard, which leads Hibbing and his colleagues to question whether this should really have been a dispositionist analysis rather than a sitautionist one; if as many people disobey as obey, is the situation really driving behavior, or are differing predispositions?[14] Milgram devoted less attention to the analysis of why some people disobeyed, but it is clear that for many of them their own personal experiences and values—their dispositions, in other words—mattered so much that they never felt that they "had no choice." Out of those who refused to shock the victim, one had been brought up in Nazi Germany (a medical technician given the name Gretchen Brandt in Milgram's book). She clearly recognized the similarities between that very vivid series of events and what she was being asked to do. Another disobedient subject was a professor of the Old Testament, and we know that others simply refused to go along on the grounds that "this is wrong." All of this suggests that *dispositions matter* for the 35 percent. The situation, moreover, was insufficiently powerful to shape the behavior of 80 percent of the subjects when forced to shock a victim sitting directly in front of them. Moreover, the fact that Milgram's subjects were told that their actions would result in no damage to the health of the fake "subject" is at the very least a complicating factor, since it is plainly obvious to those who participate in genocides that they are doing real damage, of the very worst possible kind.

There were many who refused to participate in the extermination of the Jews, and even a large number who actively worked against what the Nazis were doing. Oskar Schindler, the German industrialist who risked everything to protect hundreds of Jews, is perhaps the best known, but there were many others who risked even more than Schindler for complete strangers. Raoul Wallenberg and Per Anger, both Swedish diplomats, are together estimated to have saved as many as 100,000 Hungarian Jews from the gas chambers by using their diplomatic immunity to issue fake Swedish passports; German pastor Dietrich Bonhoeffer preached against the Nazi regime in his church, and was eventually executed for his "crimes"; and in the Rwandan case, the Hutu businessman Paul Rusesabagina—made famous by the film *Hotel Rwanda*—saved over a thousand Rwandans (most of them Tutsis) by sheltering them in his hotel and bribing local officials with whiskey, money, and other goods.[15] As the authors of *The Altruistic Personality* suggest, it is clear that we can only explain the heroic acts of these "rescuers" by examining their dispositions.[16]

In addition, it is clear that Milgram's paradigm on its own cannot fully explain all aspects of genocide, though it does illuminate many of the psychological forces which drag ordinary people along in its wake. One thing that is absent from Milgram's experimental design but present in practically all genocides—as we shall see in Chapter 14—is the systematic *dehumanization* of victims. As James Waller notes:

> regarding victims as outside our universe of moral obligation and, therefore, not deserving of compassionate treatment removes normal moral restraints against aggression. The body of a dehumanized victim possesses no meaning. It is waste, and its removal is a matter of sanitation. There is no moral or empathetic context through which the perpetrator can relate to the victim.[17]

The dehumanization of Jews in Europe is but the most obvious form of this. Philip Gourevitch has chillingly described the ways in which Tutsis became dehumanized in the eyes of Hutus over many years prior to the Rwandan genocide of 1994. In the years before the genocide, he notes, "Tutsis were known in Rwanda as *inyenzi*, which means cockroaches."[18] Following a history of being discriminated against, the Hutus took power in the revolution of 1959; Tutsi guerrillas who periodically fought against the new order were the first to be described as "cockroaches."[19] The term would be invoked repeatedly on Rwandan radio after the death of Hutu President Habyarimana, as broadcasters urged Hutus to kill Tutsis. There can be few more demeaning or dehumanizing ways to consider another human being than to compare him or her to an insect.

Interestingly, the subjects in Milgram's experiment did sometimes dehumanize the "learner" *themselves*—one obedient subject famously justified his actions afterwards by claiming that "he was so dumb he deserved it"—but this aspect was mostly absent from Milgram's design. Another factor absent from Milgram's experiment were the powerful emotional forces which attend genocidal acts. Apart from the obvious absence of ethnic hatred, there is no sense of *humiliation* on the part of those doing the "shocking" in Milgram's laboratory. As Adam Jones notes, "it is difficult to find a historical or contemporary case of genocide in which humiliation is not a central motivating force."[20] An obvious example is the sense of outrage which Germans felt after the imposition of the punitive Versailles Treaty in 1919. Combined with the hyperinflation of the 1920s and the Great Depression, many Germans looked around for a scapegoat upon whom blame for the various disasters could be heaped.[21] Similarly, in Rwanda, Belgian colonizers and other Westerners had deliberately discriminated against Hutus and in favor of Tutsis, treating the latter as a privileged elite (and inevitably creating resentment amongst the former).[22] In general, certain socioeconomic circumstances seem to give rise to genocide, or at least provide the enabling conditions for genocide to take place.[23]

While Milgram's research convincingly illustrates the mechanisms which make it possible for normal, everyday people to commit atrocities, it could be argued that it cannot by itself serve as a fully comprehensive account of why genocide occurs. Milgram should not, of course, be held accountable for failing to reproduce all of the conditions typically associated with genocide in his laboratory—there are obvious practical and ethical limits to the things one can do in that kind of environment—and his work on obedience is hence only a starting point in our understanding of why genocides occur. On the other hand, Milgram often noted that he was able to elicit a quite extraordinary level of conformity in his subjects in the absence of *any* of the factors—ethnic hatred, dehumanization, humiliation, and economic distress—we have mentioned above. As Milgram put it at the end of his book:

> The results, as seen and felt in the laboratory, are to this author disturbing. They raise the possibility that human nature, or—more specifically— the kind of character produced in American democratic society, cannot be counted on to insulate its citizens from brutality and inhumane treatment at the direction of malevolent authority. A substantial proportion of people do what they are told to do, irrespective of the content of the act and without limitations of conscience, as long as they perceive that the command comes from a legitimate authority.[24]

Assessing Milgram's Obedience Paradigm

As we did in the previous chapter with behaviorism, it seems appropriate to end with a look at the major strengths and weaknesses of Milgram's approach. In Table 4.1 we summarize the main ones discussed in this chapter. While not exhaustive, they should help you decide for yourself where you stand on the utility (or otherwise) of Milgram's experiments as an explanation for genocide and extreme political behaviors in general.

So far, we have analyzed two explanations of political behavior which emphasize the determining power of the social environment in shaping how we act: Skinner's behaviorism and Milgram's obedience paradigm. We began this book, the reader may recall, with a description of the Abu Ghraib scandal, which did a great deal of damage to the validity of America's invasion of Iraq—and the general image of the United States—in the eyes of the world. In the next chapter, we examine another situationist perspective which may throw some light on the events at Abu Ghraib. Was the highly unethical behavior in which many of the prison guards engaged the product of mental abnormalities, the product of "a few bad apples," as George W. Bush and other members of his administration insisted? Were their psychological dispositions to blame, in other words? Or was their behavior encouraged by

Table 4.1 A summary of some of the arguments for and against Milgram's obedience paradigm

For
- Milgram convinced the vast majority of his subjects (65%) to go against their own dispositions (the power of the situation).
- He used quite *minimal* inducements to produce the high level of obedience observed (e.g. the "authority" was a man in a gray lab coat).
- His findings are supported by other related research in social psychology, such as that of Solomon Asch.
- His findings match the less systematic but interesting observations of others, such as Hannah Arendt.
- His finding that the level of obedience varies with proximity to the victim is borne out by the lessons of modern warfare.

Against
- Milgram cannot explain the dispositionally driven behavior of the 35% who rebelled.
- There seem to be cultural differences in the propensity to obey, presumably related to differing dispositions between nations.
- Milgram himself offers a theory of obedience which is partly based on dispositions inherited through an evolutionary process.
- Many of the causal factors associated with genocides are absent from his experimental design.

a set of situational inducements which might well have been repeated had an entirely different set of individuals played the same roles? This is the question to which we turn next.

Notes

1 Theodore Adorno, Else Frenkel-Brunswik, Daniel Levinson, and Nevitt Sanford, *The Authoritarian Personality* (New York: Harper, 1950).

2 James Waller, *Becoming Evil: How Ordinary People Commit Genocide and Mass Killing* (New York: Oxford University Press, 2002), p.77.

3 As we shall see in Chapter 6, this research also had a profound impact on another situationist, Irving Janis.

4 Stanley Milgram, *Obedience to Authority: An Experimental View* (New York: Harper & Row, 1974).

5 Milgram might not be that famous today if this poll had been accurate in its prediction. Research that merely confirms the conventional wisdom rarely captures much attention!

6 Peter Davis (director), *Hearts and Minds* (BBS Productions, 1974).

7 Milgram, *Obedience to Authority*, p.15.

8 Ibid., p.5; Hannah Arendt, *Eichmann in Jerusalem: A Report On The Banality of Evil* (New York: Viking Press, 1963).

9 Christopher Browning, *Ordinary Men: Reserve Police Battalion 101 and the Final Solution in Poland* (New York: HarperCollins, 1992).

10 Milgram, *Obedience to Authority*, pp.123–34.

11 Ibid., pp.132–34.

12 David Mantell, "The Potential For Violence In Germany," *Journal of Social Issues*, 27: 101–12, 1971.

13 Quoted in Philip Gourevitch, *We Wish To Inform You That Tomorrow We Will Be Killed With Our Families: Stories From Rwanda* (New York: Picador, 1998), p.23.

14 John Hibbing, Kevin Smith, and John Alford, *Predisposed: Liberals, Conservatives, and the Biology of Political Differences* (New York: Routledge, 2014).

15 See Adam Jones, *Genocide: A Comprehensive Introduction* (New York: Routledge, 2006), pp.275–81.

16 Samuel Oliner and Pearl Oliner, *The Altruistic Personality: Rescuers of Jews in Nazi Europe* (New York: Free Press, 1988).

17 Waller, *Becoming Evil*, p.245.

18 Gourevitch, *We Wish To Inform You That Tomorrow We Will Be Killed With Our Families*, p.32.

19 Ibid., p.64.

20 Jones, *Genocide*, p.268.

21 Ibid., p.269.

22 Gourevitch, *We Wish To Inform You That Tomorrow We Will Be Killed With Our Families*, pp.47–62.

23 See Kristen Monroe, "Review Essay: The Psychology of Genocide," *Ethics & International Affairs*, 9: 215–39, 1995.

24 Milgram, *Obedience to Authority*, p.189.

Suggested Further Reading

Hannah Arendt, *Eichmann in Jerusalem: A Report on the Banality of Evil* (New York: Viking Press, 1963).

Thomas Blass, *The Man Who Shocked the World: The Life and Legacy of Stanley Milgram* (New York: Basic Books, 2009).

Stanley Milgram, *Obedience to Authority: An Experimental View* (New York: Harper & Row, 1974).

Films

Obedience (1965): Released by Penn State University Press. Milgram was a pretty good amateur film maker, and this one shows the original experiments themselves in striking and dramatic detail that many people find both amusing and "shocking." It can be hard to find and even harder to purchase, but it's absolutely essential viewing for all students if you can get a copy.

The Human Behavior Experiments (2006): ABC documentary which re-creates the Milgram experiment thirty years later—with some restrictions—coming to very similar results.

Chapter 5

Creating a "Bad Barrel"

We saw in the previous chapter that behaviorism is far from the only perspective that emphasizes the role of situational determinants in shaping political behavior. We now turn to another situationist perspective which is in some ways even more radical in its conclusions than Milgram's perspective. The latter, as we have noted, contains dispositionist elements, but the research we'll examine in this chapter is more purely situationist in its implications. Working in 1971, Philip Zimbardo—then a young professor of psychology at Stanford University in California—was interested in studying the effects of prison roles on behavior. From a situationist perspective, it ought to be possible to place individuals randomly in well-understood roles, and then watch how the expectations associated with these roles affect behavior. This is, in essence, what Zimbardo did. And as we shall see, his findings have possible implications for the explanation of prison scandals such as those that erupted at Guantanamo Bay and Abu Ghraib in 2003 and 2004 respectively, an argument that Zimbardo himself has made in numerous media interviews and which he also made as an expert witness in the trial of Chip Frederick, one of those involved in the abuses at Abu Ghraib.

Zimbardo has recently related the basic philosophical viewpoint behind his famous experiment.[1] We are accustomed to thinking of "good" and "evil" in highly dichotomous terms. Some people are assumed to be naturally "evil" or become that way, while others are basically "good." This is such a popular way of thinking about the philosophy of right and wrong that it hardly requires much deliberation or thought to understand. Theologians of all religious stripes tend to view the world this way, and Western legal systems are based on this notion, as we have seen already. Hollywood movies, moreover, typically portray the victory of intrinsic good over intrinsic evil, providing satisfying endings where virtue triumphs over bad.

But if we do think about this perspective more deeply, we can see that it is basically a *dispositionist* approach. We can either choose good or evil, this argument assumes, and we are fully responsible for the choices we make. On the other hand, Zimbardo suggests that it is rather unhelpful to think of the world this way. Using M.C. Escher's painting *Circle Limit IV*—a visually ambiguous work reproduced in Figure 5.1, which can be seen as portraying either angels or devils depending on one's perspective—Zimbardo suggests that there is an exceptionally thin line between good and evil. "First, the world is filled with both good and evil—was, is, will always be," Zimbardo notes. This is a relatively uncontroversial proposition, to which most theologians and philosophers would probably subscribe. But his next points are more radical. "Second, the barrier between good and evil is permeable and nebulous. And third, it is possible for angels to become devils and, perhaps more difficult to conceive, for devils to become angels," Zimbardo argues.[2]

Figure 5.1 M.C. Escher's *Circle Limit IV*

Like Milgram, Zimbardo is concerned with the ways in which normal, everyday people come to commit acts which societal mores—and even their own internalized values—suggest are "evil." This implies a perspective in which the line between good and evil is "permeable" or part of a continuum, instead of being composed of two hermetically sealed categories. It also implies the radical conclusion that we are *all* capable of committing acts of evil, or at least the great majority of us are. Most of us like to see ourselves as "good" people, in part because it is more comfortable to think this way than it is to consider the alternatives. But given the right situational inducements and conditions, Zimbardo suggests, most of us are capable of behaving in ways we rarely dream of. To see how Zimbardo has come to this radical conclusion after a lifetime of research in social psychology, we need to go back to the summer of 1971 and the experiment which made him famous.

The Stanford Experiment

In 1971, Zimbardo wanted to examine the psychological effects of prison life: what effects does it have on normal, healthy individuals when they become a prisoner or a prison guard? To do this, he put an advertisement in the local paper seeking to recruit subjects for an experiment. A simulated prison— actually part of the basement of the Stanford Psychology Department—was created. Like Milgram, Zimbardo wanted psychologically "normal" individuals so that he could not later be attacked on the grounds that the dispositional characteristics of his subjects had driven their behavior. He therefore screened his pool of applications down to twenty-four. He focused on recruiting young men, though he did not confine himself to Stanford students.

Personality tests were conducted to ensure that guards and prisoners generally would not differ in potentially significant ways. Having ensured that he had a relatively normal bunch of people—he screened out any obvious sadists or "oddballs"—he randomly divided his subjects into prisoners and guards. To make things seem more real, he had the local Palo Alto police conduct public but mock arrests of the prisoners. They were even "charged" with fake crimes. On arrival at the "prison," they were made to strip, deloused, and forced to wear specially designed smocks.

At first things went relatively well, and both "prisoners" and "guards" appeared to recognize the false or constructed nature of what was happening. However, within two days the behavior of both groups deteriorated as the situation began to seem "real" to both. Some guards became sadistic, removing various rights from the prisoners and developing innovative ways of punishing them when they failed to obey orders (they had not been allowed to use physical violence). One guard—whom the prisoners quickly nicknamed

"John Wayne"—was especially adept at devising humiliating punishments, including sexual games in which he "forced" prisoners to simulate acts of sodomy. Some prisoners rebelled, others reacted passively, and some quickly had what appeared to be emotional breakdowns. In short, things deteriorated very rapidly, to the point where the experiment had to be stopped after only six days. It had originally been designed to last two weeks, but Zimbardo decided to halt the experiment after his graduate assistant Christina Maslach— a woman he later married—insisted that it would be immoral to continue. While Zimbardo initially resisted this advice, he quickly came to see that she was right and closed the whole thing down before further damage was done.

In a classic situationist statement, Zimbardo later came to describe his explanation for what he had observed in the Stanford experiment as the "bad barrel" theory. Put ordinary, healthy young men in an extreme situation—"in a bad place," as he often puts it—and the situation can take over. In effect, both "prisoners" and "guards" had quickly fallen into the social roles they were expected to perform, and a structure of authority that condoned or permitted abuses helped to create an environment that allowed conditions to rapidly deteriorate. A vicious cycle was created in which the authorities (the barrel-makers) fashioned a barrel or situation which turned the apples inside it bad. Zimbardo's basic approach is depicted in Figure 5.2.

The situation in which Zimbardo placed his subjects is sometimes referred to as the "Lord of The Flies effect." In the classic novel of that name by William Golding, a group of English schoolboys is marooned on a tropical island without an authority figure.[3] Although the circumstances are not fully explained by Golding, the story appears to take place after a nuclear war, and the boys are left to organize themselves without adult supervision. This scenario gives Golding the opportunity to place his characters in what Thomas Hobbes

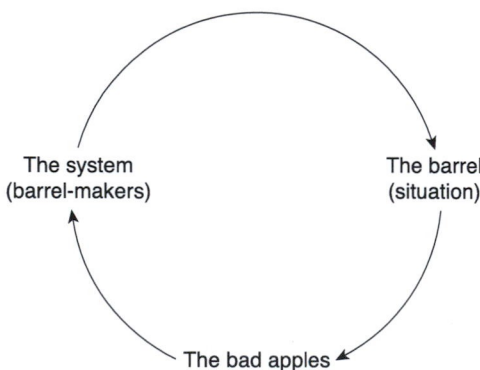

Figure 5.2 Zimbardo's interpretation of the Stanford experiment

and others referred to as a "state of nature," a real or hypothesized condition in which there is no recognized authority system to regulate behavior. And like Hobbes, Golding's vision of what would happen in such a situation is famously stark and uncompromising. The behavior of the boys becomes increasingly savage as they divest themselves of the trappings of modern society, and a "war of all against all"—again, similar to that envisioned by Hobbes—takes place.

The comparison between *The Lord of The Flies* and Stanford may not be apt, perhaps, since there *was* an authority structure in the experiment (albeit of a loose and permissive kind). Moreover, the point being made by Hobbes— that life in a state of nature would be "nasty, brutish and short" in the absence of some overarching authority to provide law and order—was that human beings are in a sense inherently "evil," or at least self-interested or "egoistic" to the point that their own self-preservation would effectively be their only concern in a state of nature. Similarly, Golding adopted a very dark view of human nature, which appeared in virtually all his published works. Both Hobbes and Golding were essentially dispositionists, in other words, who adopted a rather fixed view of human nature. Zimbardo's point is situationist and exactly the opposite: we are not inherently "bad" or "evil," but we can be induced to behave in immoral ways if we are forced to confront a certain type of situation.

This point became clear, for instance, in an interview that Zimbardo conducted with Jon Stewart on *The Daily Show* in 2007, after the appearance of the former's book *The Lucifer Effect*. In the interview it became fairly clear that Stewart had not read the book, or at least had not understood its central message. Stewart suggested to Zimbardo that the message of the book is that "people are much more evil than they would appear to be on the outside." Zimbardo replied forcefully that this is *not at all* what he's saying:

> The Stanford prison experiment that I detail at great length in *The Lucifer Effect* really describes the gradual transformation of a group of good boys, twenty-four college students who volunteered to be in the experiment. We picked only the normal healthy ones, randomly assigned by coin to be guard or prisoner. But we see how quickly the good boys— and that's important, they *start off* good—become brutal guards, and the normal kids become pathological prisoners.[4]

More importantly perhaps, critics have noted that it is not clear exactly what Zimbardo found, since he did not organize his experiment in the rigorous ways that Milgram did. Some even doubt that it deserves the title of an "experiment" for this reason. Partly because the exercise had to be ended prematurely, there was not much variation in circumstances or subtlety to his research design. What if the guards were not in uniform, for instance? What if the roles had later been reversed, or the personnel completely changed? What if the location of the experiment had been altered? What if the guard nicknamed "John Wayne"—the most inventive in his use of sadistic control mechanisms—had not been there? Was his leadership critical? And so on. Consequently, there remains doubt today as to the exact psychological mechanisms involved in Zimbardo's scenario. Is the key finding that anyone placed in a certain role is bound to behave this way, or is the key lesson that the absence of clear authority per se leads people to behave this way?

There are also other concerns which might be highlighted. First of all, the guards did not behave as a monolithic group; there were "good guards" and "bad guards," as Zimbardo admits, and only about one-third of the guards behaved in sadistic ways. There was also variation in the behavior of the prisoners. Some rebelled against authority, while others complied (one prisoner—nicknamed "Sarge"—was especially passive). This suggests that it was their dispositions, not the general situation, that had the greatest impact on their behavior. Second, Zimbardo asked the guards to wear silver mirroring glasses, a style consciously modeled on a sadistic but fictional guard portrayed in the film *Cool Hand Luke*.[5] The film, which starred Paul Newman, was released in November 1967, and was well known at the time (by 1971, it would of course have been shown on network television both in the United States and overseas, and we know that at least some of the subjects had seen the film). What, though, if the film had never been made? There is a possibility that some of the guards and/or prisoners were simply acting out the roles they had seen in the film, or assumed that Zimbardo *wanted them* to behave in such a manner (the mirror glasses could be taken as a "hint" that this was what was expected). Last, the subjects were in a sense self-selected rather than random—they knew that they would be taking part in an experiment on prison life—and perhaps some stayed in the experiment simply because they needed the money (Zimbardo was of course paying them for their time).

Zimbardo himself freely admits that he made errors in the design of the experiment. Unlike Milgram's exercise—where the principal investigator had taken great pains to remove himself from the experiment itself, though not its aftermath—Zimbardo played the part of prison superintendent. It is unclear, therefore, whether his presence influenced the results. And of course, Zimbardo came under heavy criticism on ethical grounds after the findings were published. The ethical or moral dilemma is very close to the one that we observed in the Milgram case. On one hand, there was obvious harm done to the students, so that one could certainly say that the experiment was unethical in an *absolute* sense. Both prisoners and guards suffered, and Zimbardo allowed it all to go on too long. On the other hand, we should also consider *relative ethics*, weighing this against the self-knowledge gained (*pain versus gain*) as few had any idea of what they were in for. As in the Milgram case, however, the participants legally consented to what occurred, and were psychologically debriefed afterwards. Some used the knowledge they gained from the experiment *to better themselves* and others. Doug, who had the first breakdown, is today a clinical psychologist in the prison system, and he credits the experiment with changing his life, but the debate about social benefits versus harm to subjects is obviously one you need to resolve for yourself (if, indeed, you feel that you *can* resolve it).

In a documentary film called the *Human Behavior Experiments*, Zimbardo relates that Milgram actually thanked him personally for, as he put it, "taking some of the ethical heat off me." The Stanford controversy, Milgram thought, had finally distracted the world from the debate still raging around his own work. Here, at last, was an experiment whose ethical pros and cons vied with and perhaps exceeded those of Milgram's electric shock experiments. Regardless of the ethics of what he did, however, Zimbardo's actual findings— that psychologically normal boys can be induced by role expectations and the situation to behave in sadistic ways—remain deeply intriguing. Moreover, they have been given a new impetus by the 2004 events at the Abu Ghraib prison in Iraq.

The Abu Ghraib Scandal: Changing Your "Whole Mind Frame"

The story of Abu Ghraib became public in 2004, producing instantaneous shock and incomprehension both in the United States and around the world. Distributed via the internet and widely broadcast on television, the pictures showed U.S. servicemen and servicewomen torturing detainees— mostly through appalling acts of sexual degradation and sensory deprivation— inside what had been the most feared prison of Saddam Hussein's Iraq. The disgust that the photographs provoked soon led to the arrest of the individuals involved, and numerous investigations were conducted into what had "gone wrong" at the prison.

One problem with the pictures that were publicized—not all of them were released, since some were considered too graphic—is that they depict actions committed by a variety of different individuals and in different contexts. For instance, while the majority of the photos featured U.S. soldiers gloating over naked Iraqi prisoners, the most famous picture of the collection— the well-known "hooded man" photo seen in Figure 5.3—depicts a form of torture which was almost certainly not dreamt up by the bunch of raw recruits

Figure 5.3 One of the photos released in 2004 showing U.S. servicemen torturing detainees at Abu Ghraib prison

Credit: © Associated Press

who took the sexual abuse photos. As Mark Danner has noted, this is a very distinctive and specialized form of torture developed by Brazilian intelligence called "the Vietnam," and it is unclear who arranged the individual depicted in the photograph in this position.

Rory Kennedy's thought-provoking film *Ghosts of Abu Ghraib* begins with scenes from Milgram's documentary *Obedience*, overlain with a haunting soundtrack. Although the film never explicitly spells out the relevance of Milgram's paradigm, the obvious inference is that those who committed the abuses at the prison were following the orders of their superiors. Certainly, this provides one way of applying the insights of political psychology to those disturbing events, and it may well be the best way. However, it has to be said that the events at Abu Ghraib bear an even more striking similarity to the Stanford experiments. "There are stunning parallels between the Stanford Prison Experiment and what happened at Abu Ghraib," Zimbardo argued not long after the events at Abu Ghraib became public knowledge. "Some of the visual scenes that we have seen include guards stripping prisoners naked, putting bags over heads, putting them in chains, and having them engage in sexually degrading acts. And in both prisons the worst abuses came on the night shift." Of course, Zimbardo concedes that there are differences as well.

"Our guards committed very little physical abuse . . . I continually told them that they could not use physical abuse. But then they resorted entirely to psychological controls and psychological domination."

Various similarities between Stanford and Abu Ghraib are immediately apparent:

- Bags placed on heads (dehumanization and deindividuation)
- Prisoners stripped naked (deindividuation)
- Sexual humiliation used by the guards (prisoners forced to simulate sodomy)
- Guards not trained at all or not trained well
- Sheer boredom on the part of guards
- The worst abuses happened on the night shift
- Escalation in nature of acts
- Emergence of a "John Wayne" figure[6]
- Vague chain of command licensing inappropriate behavior.

There are also differences, as we might expect:

- CIA or other higher authorities weren't telling students to "soften up" prisoners in 1971
- No physical violence used in 1971
- "Trophy pictures" not taken in 1971
- No one had demonized the 1971 "prisoners" and 1971 students were not a "real" enemy
- No racial differences in 1971
- No stress of war
- No need for information/intelligence.

Since no two situations are ever identical, of course, the salient question is not "are there differences?" but "how meaningful are those differences that exist?" For Zimbardo, the key to understanding Abu Ghraib is the same as the process he used to understand his Stanford findings. In *The Lucifer Effect*, he compares the two events at great length, arguing that a barrel-maker (in this case a chain of command extending to the White House and the Pentagon) had fashioned an environment or situation (barrel) that "turned good apples bad." Many of those who actually committed the abuses at Abu Ghraib had signed up for the Army willingly after 9/11 out of a sense of burning patriotism, determined that the United States would never again be struck by a deadly terrorist attack of this sort. And yet they found themselves in Abu Ghraib doing things they can hardly have imagined in their wildest dreams. "That place turned me into a monster," former military police officer Javal Davis says. "I was very angry. You know, this Abu Ghraib, it would change your whole mind frame. You know you can go from being a docile, jolly guy . . . And you go to Abu Ghraib for a while, you become a robot."[7]

For Zimbardo, President George W. Bush, Vice President Dick Cheney, and Secretary of Defense Donald Rumsfeld created a system of authority that implicitly or explicitly encouraged acts of torture, and in early 2002 the Bush administration decided that the Geneva Conventions (signed by the United States in 1949) did not apply in this situation. Feeding down the chain of command, military intelligence and private contractors encouraged the amateur guards at Abu Ghraib to "soften up" the prisoners for interrogation. It was the barrel they made, then, that turned basically good people bad. On the other hand, the Bush administration blamed the dispositions of the individuals themselves. "A new Iraq will also need a humane, well-supervised prison system. Under the dictator, prisons like Abu Ghraib were symbols of death and torture," Bush argued. "That same prison became a symbol of disgraceful conduct by a few American troops who dishonored our country and disregarded our values."

We have repeatedly noted that situationism presents a challenge to the Western legal system and its basic notion that individuals are responsible for their own choices and actions. In *The Lucifer Effect*, Zimbardo relates the problems this created when he tried to help the defense of Sergeant Ivan "Chip" Frederick, one of the soldiers who was photographed grinning beside a pyramid of naked Iraqi prisoners. Although Zimbardo had mixed feelings about becoming involved in defending Frederick, he agreed to testify in his trial via videoconference. In Frederick's defense, Zimbardo argued that Frederick was a psychologically normal (if insecure and indecisive) individual who found himself in a highly abnormal situation. While Zimbardo did not attempt to *excuse* Frederick, he did seek to better understand his actions and perhaps to get situational factors considered in the defendant's sentencing. Someone like Frederick, he argued, could actually have been a hero if he'd been in a "better barrel," but he was in many ways in the wrong place at the wrong time. Predictably, this argument was rejected by the judge, who adopted a more traditional dispositionist view: Frederick, he said, had chosen his actions of his own free will, and no one had coerced him to act in unethical ways.

Again, it is for the reader to decide himself or herself who is right. To what extent did the barrel rot the apples, or were the apples rotten from the start? This issue, as we've seen repeatedly, lies at the very heart of the situationist–dispositionist debate. Whatever you conclude, however, it is worth noting that there are those for whom the situation does not take over, individuals whose basic moral sense is more difficult to bypass. In the Stanford case, Christina Maslach—despite powerful situational pressures to conform (Zimbardo was her dissertation supervisor)—tells him that "what you are doing to those boys is wrong." In the Abu Ghraib case, the "hero" role was played by Officer Joseph Darby, a young guard who took the trophy photos depicting acts of prisoner abuse to the military authorities. Initially meeting bureaucratic resistance and incompetence, he insisted that the whistle must be blown on what happened at Abu Ghraib. It is in large part thanks to Darby and one or two others—individuals driven by their *dispositions*, not the power of the situation—that the world found out about Abu Ghraib; it is also due to people like Joseph Darby that the shameful practices being followed there were discontinued. The young serviceman paid a high price for his act of heroism, however, and has been targeted as a traitor by some.

To reiterate the dynamics of Zimbardo's approach, Table 5.1 summarizes the arguments for and against his case.

Table 5.1 A summary of the arguments for and against Zimbardo's "bad barrel" approach

For
- The parallels between the Stanford experiment and the Abu Ghraib situation are quite striking.
- It is remarkable how real the Stanford situation appeared to both "guards" and "prisoners" and how quickly the situation took over.
- Generally speaking, the subjects quickly fell into the social roles expected of them.
- The subjects were psychologically "normal"—as were the guards at Abu Ghraib—but their behaviors were not (this is what happens when we "put good people in a bad place," as Zimbardo would have it).

Against
- There are enough differences between Stanford and Abu Ghraib to make the parallel at least open to question.
- The variation in prisoner and guard behavior in both cases suggests the importance of dispositions, not situations.
- There were few or no control mechanisms used in the Stanford experiment, so that we don't know whether changing some of its features would have altered the result.
- Perhaps both Stanford and Abu Ghraib reveal more about man's basic inhumanity or a disposition toward evil (the Hobbesian or "Lord of the Flies" effect) than they do about the power of situations.
- Perhaps the subjects in Zimbardo's experiment were simply playing out the roles they thought the experimenter *wanted* to see played out.

Conclusion

We begin the next chapter by discussing the case of Roger Boisjoly, a technical adviser at a company working with NASA on the space shuttle. In 1986, NASA was under enormous pressure to launch the shuttle *Challenger* into space. The weather in central Florida was unseasonably cold that year, and this factor—combined with various mechanical difficulties—had led to repeated launches being canceled or "scrubbed," as officials put it behind the scenes. In a conference call between Roger's company Morton-Thiokol and NASA officials—a meeting which included some of the brightest minds in each organization—the decision was made to launch. Boisjoly (as well as one or two others) had repeatedly warned that the O-rings—the seals which connect the shuttle to its solid rocket booster—might not hold up in such low temperatures; the rings might even shatter altogether, potentially causing a catastrophic explosion. The vast majority of the decision-makers within both organizations dismissed Roger's concerns, however; and given a final opportunity to speak and to condemn the decision that the majority was making, Boisjoly fell mysteriously silent, and tragically, the very disaster he had predicted occurred shortly afterwards.

Why *do* smart people often make such poor decisions in groups? And why do equally intelligent individuals who know or feel that the decision being made is the wrong one so often remain silent? Why do people often hold back from saying what they are really thinking in groups? These are questions which fascinated social psychologist Irving Janis, and we shall try to answer them in the next chapter.

Notes

1 Philip Zimbardo, *The Lucifer Effect: Understanding How Good People Turn Evil* (New York: Random House, 2007).
2 Ibid., p.3.
3 William Golding, *The Lord of The Flies* (London: Faber & Faber, 1954).
4 You can view this interview at http://www.comedycentral.com/motherload/index.jhtml?ml_video=84518.
5 Zimbardo, *The Lucifer Effect*, p.52.
6 In the Iraq case, this role was played by Charles Graner.
7 Quoted in Rory Kennedy (director), *Ghosts of Abu Ghraib* (Moxie Firecracker Films, 2007).

Suggested Further Reading

Philip Zimbardo, *The Lucifer Effect: Understanding How Good People Turn Evil* (New York: Random House, 2007).

Films

The Stanford Prison Experiment (2002): High-quality BBC documentary on Zimbardo's experiment, and my favorite visual account. Can be hard to find, but usually available via the website at YouTube or www.Disclose.tv.

Quiet Rage: The Stanford Prison Experiment (2004). Zimbardo's own account of the experiment on film.

The Experiment (2010). Very loose Hollywood "re-creation" of the Zimbardo's experiment using actors, but later parts of the film take a lot of artistic license with the story and "spice it up" for dramatic effect.

Chapter 6

Group Decision-Making

On January 28, 1986, the space shuttle *Challenger* took off from Cape Canaveral in Florida after many delays. Successive launches had been scrapped due to technical issues, and people at NASA were anxious to get going. But the shuttle exploded in the air only seventy-three seconds after takeoff, to the great horror of those watching on the ground and around the world. All seven astronauts on board died.

Few students today remember the explosion personally—you have to be about the author's age to remember seeing it live on TV—but many of you will have seen documentaries about it or viewed the terrible footage on YouTube. A stunned television audience looked on in horror as the shuttle blew up in the sky. The crew were not killed instantly, but were probably unconscious as what was left of the shuttle plummeted into the Atlantic Ocean. It was an absolutely devastating day for many people, especially of course for those who had given the go ahead for the shuttle to fly, but few of the decision-makers at NASA and Morton-Thiokol can have felt as bad as Roger Boisjoly did when a subsequent commission found that the explosion was caused by the disintegration of an "O-ring" in the shuttle's right solid rocket booster. This was the very calamity he had predicted and had repeatedly tried to warn his colleagues about.

At the time, Boisjoly was an engineer who worked for Morton-Thiokol, then a sub-contractor to NASA. He was an expert on O-rings, the seals that connected the space shuttle to the solid rocket booster which was used to propel the shuttle into space. Before the launch, Boisjoly was a deeply worried man. The weather was unseasonably cold for the time of year in Florida, and he knew that the O-rings had not been tested at the kind of low temperatures the shuttle would likely face that day. So he had done what most people would do. He had urged his colleagues to wait until temperatures at Cape Canaveral climbed. He warned his boss of what he thought would happen, but the latter waved Boisjoly's objections away. He thought Roger worried too much about

O-rings because that's what he happened to work with. "Look at the bigger picture," the boss told him. Boisjoly tried to warn others at the company, but most reacted the same way, saying the scientific data about temperatures were inconclusive. One even compared Boisjoly to the fictional children's character "Chicken Little," forever hollering that "the sky is falling."

There was a final conference-call meeting before the launch, between Morton-Thiokol and NASA officials. The latter were keen to go ahead with the launch, and so were the vast majority of the people around the conference table in Boisjoly's own company. But he was still gravely worried about the O-rings and the potential for catastrophe. One by one, the chair of the meeting asked the chief participants for their views—should we go ahead?—and one by one each participant answered in the affirmative. Then the chair asked "is there anyone here who feels that we should *not* go ahead?" Everyone in his own company knew full well that Boisjoly had strong reservations, and all eyes turn warily and impatiently towards him. But then something remarkable happened: he said *nothing*. He didn't press the issue of the O-rings, even though everyone expected him to "harp on" about it yet again. By his silence, he implicitly gave his consent to something that he felt to be wrong. A combination of factors held him back from saying what he really thought. Foremost among them was the pressure of the group bearing down on him.

Why Groups Have an Impact on Us

When we think about the decisions made by our government, we typically imagine a single individual—usually a president or prime minister—sitting at a desk and reviewing various options. We often also imagine decisions being made in an idealized fashion, in the manner envisioned by the *Homo economicus* approach. After suitable deliberation, the leader then selects the option that seems most likely to meet whatever political and policy objective has been set. And on some occasions, this scenario does at least resemble how decisions are made at the highest levels. When Ronald Reagan was president, for instance, he reportedly liked to be handed a single sheet of paper with a list of alternatives on it. He would then tick the box next to his preferred option. Reagan rarely delved down into the lower levels of his administration or read lengthy memoranda. Though he had a far greater appetite for information than Reagan did, President Richard Nixon would also reportedly make decisions largely in isolation from others, hunkering down in the Oval Office away from most of his Cabinet colleagues. His "loner" personality led him to select a system of White House management that reinforced his solitude, a factor which many believe contributed to his ultimate downfall.

There are other times, however, when even chief executives like Reagan and Nixon find it useful to make decisions in groups. Indeed, group decision-making seems to be more typical than its unilateral variation. There are a number of reasons for this.[1] First, working collectively gives the eventual decision reached greater *legitimacy* than if a decision were reached in unilateral fashion, after minimum consultation with others. Second, this provides leaders with a measure of *political cover*; if others have "signed onto" a decision, it becomes harder for them to go public with criticism after the fact if the policy leads to significant failure. Third, group decision-making ensures (at least in principle) that the leading decision-maker is exposed to a variety of differing and possibly dissenting opinions, minimizing the possibility that a leader takes a decision without considering all available facts. As Yaacov Vertzberger notes:

> Decisionmakers operating in a group are likely to be exposed to new information and interpretations more rapidly than if they were operating alone and to arguments they might not have been aware of as independent decisionmakers; both exposure and arguments improve the quality of group members' problem solving and learning . . . argumentation in the process of group decision-making clarifies ambiguities and inconsistencies by disseminating information and alternative perspectives and can illuminate weaknesses in the logical structure of accumulated knowledge and beliefs.[2]

Fourth, some leaders may prefer to work in groups where they are *not well informed* about the policy area concerned. LBJ, for instance, knew relatively little about foreign policy issues coming into the presidency, and relied heavily on what he called his "Harvards" (trusted policy advisers like Robert McNamara and Dean Rusk). Group decision-making also has the added benefit of *reducing psychological strain* on leaders who are uncomfortable with a given policy question or area. Last, making decisions in groups may actually be *mandated* by the legislature under some circumstances, as is the case with the National Security Act of 1948 in the United States.[3]

However, it doesn't necessarily follow that groups make *better* decisions than individuals working alone. As Vertzberger notes, the potential benefits of group decision-making can sometimes be outweighed by other processes, "pathologies of the group [which] act to narrow the scope and complexity of information processing operations and encourage parochialism and conformity."[4] There is an old joke that "a camel is a racehorse designed by a committee." The serious point behind this witticism is that in groups where power is dispersed—that is, where power is widely shared among a number of its members—compromises have to be made in order to reach a consensus position. Suppose that racehorses did not exist and that we gave such a group the task of designing one. One member might propose making it sleek and aerodynamic, with no humps. Another might disagree, saying that a single hump would give the rider something to hang onto during the race. "Why not give it three humps, so that several people can ride it?" another might say. Eventually, they might only be able to agree on an animal with two humps, something that resembles a camel, but which looks rather odd and dysfunctional. A classic example in the legislative sphere is the North American Free Trade Agreement (NAFTA), which was ratified by the United States Senate in 1993. In order to pass, the legislation transferring it into U.S. law had to be backed up with so many exemptions—added on by various lobbying groups, such as orange-growers in Florida, sugar-growers in Louisiana, and environmental lobbyists—that it only partially resembled the original treaty.

In their book *Essence of Decision*, Graham Allison and Philip Zelikow develop a famous model of decision-making—the governmental politics approach or Model III—in which power is dispersed in precisely this way, and decision outcomes are the product of bargaining and compromise. Each member holds sufficient power to thwart the wishes of other members, so whatever decision they come up with will by necessity have to involve a process of give-and-take. If this is so, however, an interesting possibility arises: the eventual decision they reach may reflect no one's real preferences. Any decision arrived at may simply reflect the "least common denominator," that thing which they can all agree upon. But that may not actually be something which anyone wanted, at least not as their first choice.[5]

This is just one way in which groups can actually produce dysfunctional or sub-optimal outcomes, decisions that might well be *inferior* to those taken by an informed individual acting alone. For most of this chapter, however, we will examine another well-known theoretical approach which deals with group decision-making: Irving Janis's "groupthink" theory. As we shall discover, this approach also departs from the rational actor or *Homo economicus* approach in significant ways, and it does so by highlighting the fact that individual decision-makers often behave differently—that is, differ in the extent to which they openly express their views and preferences—when acting singly from the way they do when they form part of a larger group. The premise here is that our behavior changes in subtle ways in groups, so that people behave differently in them from how they would when acting on their own. Again—in keeping with the theme of this section of the book—the power of "the situation" is so great in some circumstances that it effectively overrides the power of the individual.

How might this occur? To start with, consider again Solomon Asch's interesting findings about group conformity. In Chapter 4 we saw that majority influence can exert a powerful impact on the judgments of the minority; when subjects were placed in a room on their own and asked to match the lengths of lines, they generally did so accurately. But they made mistakes 75 percent of the time when placed in a room full of associates of the experimenter who deliberately gave the wrong answers. What was interesting about this experiment, of course, is that people were prepared to suspend their own judgments—even judgments that they knew to be objectively correct—in order to fall in line with the collective views of the group. This and other research on group conformity was the starting point not just for Stanley Milgram's work on obedience to authority, but for Irving Janis's fascinating work on group decision-making in American foreign policy.

The Perils of Groupthink: Smart Guys Making Dumb Decisions

In his path-breaking 1972 book *Victims of Groupthink*—revised ten years later simply as *Groupthink*—social psychologist Irving Janis defined the groupthink phenomenon as a process through which a group reaches a hasty or premature consensus and the group then becomes closed to outside ideas.[6] In Janis's own words, groupthink is "a mode of thinking that people engage in when they are deeply involved in a cohesive in-group, when the members' strivings for unanimity override their motivation to realistically appraise alternative courses of action."[7] High group cohesion can develop, for instance, where the members have known each other for many years and/or think very much alike. While such a group *can* make effective decisions—group cohesion is a necessary but not sufficient condition for groupthink to occur—it can become prey to this pathology where members of the group come to prize "concurrence-seeking"—in other words, unanimity and agreement—over the full and rational consideration of all available courses of action. He contrasts this with vigilant decision-making—in which decision-makers do rigorously and thoroughly appraise all available options—and holds up the Cuban missile crisis as a notable instance of a case in which this kind of superior process occurred.[8]

According to Janis, groupthink has a number of elements (or "antecedent conditions"), in addition to high group cohesiveness:

- Insulation of the group from outside advice—the group does not seek or permit outsiders to offer their own opinions.
- Aggressive and opinionated leadership—the leader makes his or her own opinions so evident at the outset or during the debate about options that meaningful discussion is stifled.

- A lack of norms requiring methodical procedures—there is no tradition within the group of encouraging the full consideration of options in a methodical way.
- Homogeneity of members' backgrounds/ideology—most members of the group come from a similar social and educational background and/or think too much alike.
- High levels of stress—the group is challenged by a problem that induces stress in its members, such as the need to reach a decision quickly.
- Temporary low self-esteem.[9]

How do we know when groupthink is present? Janis identifies eight symptoms which can be used as diagnostic criteria:

- An illusion of invulnerability—the group develops excessive optimism which then encourages risk-taking.
- Collective rationalization—members discount warnings and fail to reconsider their core assumptions.
- A belief in the inherent morality of the group—members come to believe in the "moral rightness" of their cause and become blind to the ethical consequences of their decisions.
- Stereotyped views of outgroups—the group develops an excessively simplified and negative view of the "enemy."
- Direct pressure is exerted on dissenters—members come under pressure not to dissent from the group's opinions.
- Self-censorship—members fail to express their own doubts and deviations from the perceived group consensus.
- An illusion of unanimity—the majority view is assumed to be unanimous, but in reality some members may harbor personal doubts about it.
- Self-appointed "mindguards"—members emerge who take it upon themselves to protect the group and its leader from dissenting views and information that might challenge the group's assumed consensus.[10]

As always, it is easier to see how a theoretical process operates by seeing it in action in a real-life historical case. Here we will provide two illustrations of examples where groupthink has been argued to have played a major role in the decision-making: the 1961 Bay of Pigs fiasco and the 1965 escalation of the Vietnam War. Janis gives these two cases pride of place in his book, arguing that both represent classic examples of the "groupthink syndrome." New evidence since Janis wrote has emerged in recent years that challenges his interpretation of both cases, however, and we will highlight both the empirical and theoretical challenges that have been leveled at his theory.

We will conclude the chapter by examining another, newer approach—
newgroup syndrome—which also emphasizes the pathologies of decision-making
in groups.

Example 1: The Bay of Pigs

By 1961, Communist-controlled Cuba, led at that time by a young revolutionary named Fidel Castro, had become a perceived thorn in the side of any
U.S. administration. Although not considered a security threat in its own
right, the arrival of a pro-Soviet regime in Cuba was troubling to American
presidents for at least two reasons. First of all, it was politically embarrassing
to have a former ally turn to Communism in "Uncle Sam's backyard," only
150 kilometers from the southernmost shores of Florida. More worrying
at the time, though, was the prospect that Cuba's conversion would be only
the first step in a process in which Communism spread rapidly through all
of Latin America. President Dwight D. Eisenhower had formulated the
famous "domino theory," whereby the fall of a single domino would lead
the others to topple in swift succession, and other U.S. presidents—including
Eisenhower's successor, John F. Kennedy—became ardent believers in this
powerful psychological metaphor as well (dubious though the theory now
seems in hindsight).

During the last year of the Eisenhower administration, a secret plan was
hatched by the CIA to invade Cuba and depose Castro, using Cuban exiles as
a front for direct U.S. involvement. This plan was implemented by the new
Kennedy administration, which gave the go-ahead for an invasion of Cuba at
the Bay of Pigs (known on the island as Bahía de Cochinos or Playa Girón) in
early 1961. The whole venture was a miserable failure, however, not least
because Castro's forces fully expected the invasion and were waiting for the
exile forces. One hundred and fourteen of the exiles were killed, and nearly
1,200 men were captured. According to one authoritative report, around
1,800 deaths resulted from the invasion when Cuban civilian casualties are
included.[11] Embarrassingly, the Kennedy administration was also later forced
to pay a ransom to Castro in order to get the prisoners back.

Janis opens his discussion of John Kennedy's decision to approve the plan
by quoting Kennedy himself. "How could I have been so stupid?" the president
is said to have asked his brother Robert and others when the invasion plan
failed spectacularly.[12] This was a huge military and political embarrassment
for an administration which was only a few months old, and Janis is especially
keen to understand why this particular government could have made such
a colossal error. After all, Kennedy's administration was filled with young,
well-schooled, confident individuals, men whom JFK had carefully and very

deliberately selected because he wanted the best talent in America from academia and business.

In retrospect, Kennedy and his colleagues made six major errors, Janis argues.[13] First of all, they reasoned that most ordinary people—both inside and outside the United States—would believe the CIA's cover story that this was entirely a "Cuban exile operation." The invasion plan called for the landing of an exile brigade, which would then link up with anti-Castro dissident groups within Cuba and storm Havana, deposing Castro in the process. It seemed unlikely that the hand of the United States could be disguised even at the time, however, since the details of the plan had not only leaked, but had even been published in *The New York Times* ahead of the invasion! Second, Kennedy and his advisers reasoned that the Cuban Air Force was wholly ineffective, and third, that this force could easily be knocked out by the elderly aircraft that the CIA had given to the invading exile brigade. Neither of these assumptions turned out to be accurate. JFK had canceled a U.S. air strike against the Cuban forces, largely out of a fear that this would make the participation of the United States in the invasion far too obvious, and this undercut the ability of the exile forces to immobilize Cuban air defenses. Fourth, they assumed that Castro's army was simply so weak that the exile brigade would be able to establish a well-protected beachhead at their landing point. Fifth, they assumed that morale was so high among the invading force of 1,400 Cuban exiles that they would not need the support of U.S. land troops. Both of these expectations were problematic as well: morale was actually so low among some of the exiles that they had rebelled against their CIA handlers.

Finally, the president and his colleagues made the critically flawed assumption that an invasion would somehow "instantaneously" spark a popular uprising. This was perhaps the most dubious assumption of all, since—having got wind of the invasion plans—Castro had time to round up and imprison anyone he thought likely to join up with the invasion force. If the spontaneous uprising did not happen, JFK and his advisers reasoned that the forces could always retreat to the Escambray mountains and join anti-Castro guerrillas there. Apparently, no one had told the president that the original landing site had been moved, making any escape impossible if the assumption of an instantaneous uprising proved unfounded (as, in fact, turned out to be the case). In order to escape, the invaders would now have had to wade through hundreds of miles of swampland, but none of JFK's advisers seems to have thought to look at a map. The result, Janis says, was "a perfect failure."[14]

How and why did Kennedy and his advisers convince themselves that such a flawed operation would succeed? As in the Vietnam case discussed below, Janis traces this fiasco to a deeply flawed decision-making process. Applying the theory to the case, he argues that the following symptoms manifested themselves:

- Illusion of invulnerability: as Janis sees it, the "New Frontier" people (a term used to describe Kennedy's officials) thought that they "couldn't fail." Several of JFK's advisers appear to have felt as if they possessed what Ted Sorensen has called "the magic touch." Certainly Kennedy himself was unaccustomed to losing anything in his life, as was the case with most if not all of his key advisers.
- Illusion of unanimity: no one raised doubts about the invasion plan in the many formal meetings that were held to discuss it.
- Suppression of personal doubts: some said afterwards that they harbored significant doubts which they failed to voice at the time, most notably Arthur Schlesinger.
- Self-appointed mindguards: Robert Kennedy and Dean Rusk in particular seem to have acted as the mindguards in this case. Robert Kennedy is said to have told Schlesinger not to voice his doubts in meetings, since the president had "already decided" to go ahead with the plan.
- Docility fostered by suave leadership: John Kennedy himself may have encouraged a sense of complacency and docility by allowing the CIA to dominate the discussion and failing to encourage his advisers to ask the tough questions that might have exposed the plan's flaws.
- Taboo against antagonizing new members: CIA Director Allen Dulles and his Chief of Plans Richard Bissell were both strongly in favor of the plan—which had been formulated by the previous administration—and were held in high esteem by the group. Janis argues that in such a situation, it becomes socially difficult to challenge the wisdom of those who appear to know what they are doing.[15]

Example 2: Escalation of the Vietnam War

Irving Janis argues that the decision to Americanize the war in Vietnam in 1965, made by Lyndon Johnson and his advisers, represents one of the clearest examples of the groupthink phenomenon at work. U.S. land troops went ashore that year, and would remain in Vietnam for the next eight years. The war would end with the collapse of Saigon in 1975, as the last Americans fled the U.S. embassy there by helicopter. In the meantime, more bombs were dropped on North Vietnam than had been dropped in all of World War II. Over 58,000 Americans lost their lives, and millions of Vietnamese: all in the vain attempt to stave off an outcome that could have been prevented back in 1945 if the United States had supported Ho Chi Minh's declaration of independence from the French. Both on that occasion and at various points along the way, there had been various "lost opportunities" which could have been taken to avoid war.[16]

One such opportunity came in the immediate aftermath of World War II. During the war, Ho's Communist forces had allied themselves with the United States against Japan, and his organization (known as the Viet Minh) had actually assisted in the recovery of downed American pilots over Vietnam, Cambodia, and Laos. In 1945 the British returned control of Vietnam to its French colonizers, but Ho unilaterally chose to declare Vietnam's independence. As he did so, members of the American OSS—the predecessor of today's CIA—looked on in approval, and Ho even began his declaration using the first few sentences of the *American* Declaration of Independence. Tragically, however, the decision was made in Washington to side with the French; many in the State Department reasoned that the U.S. should support France in its efforts to regain control of its former colonies, since failing to do so might jeopardize French support for NATO in Europe. At that time, moreover, Europe was considered a far more significant theater of interest than southeast Asia.

Janis does not look at the war in this broader context, but instead chooses to examine Johnson's discrete decision to commit land troops to the war.[17] What was so interesting to Janis as a social psychologist was that Johnson and his advisers showed the same kinds of conformist behaviors in groups as those shown in numerous laboratory experiments. But these were the individuals whom David Halberstam called "the best and the brightest," experienced and highly regarded men Johnson had inherited from his predecessor John Kennedy. And yet the vast majority of these individuals wholeheartedly supported the escalation of a war that ultimately proved disastrous for the country.

The primary forum for Johnson's Vietnam decision-making, Janis argues, was the "Tuesday Lunch Group." This was a small, highly cohesive but informal collection of individuals whose judgment Johnson trusted the most, men like Secretary of State Dean Rusk and Secretary of Defense Robert McNamara. Within this group, Janis observes the presence of a number of tell-tale symptoms that can lead to the emergence of groupthink:

- A small, cohesive group of like-minded decision-makers who valued unity
- Over-optimism and a sense of invulnerability
- Homogenization of views within the "inner circle" of advisers
- Avoidance of potentially useful outside advice (e.g. that of Senator William Fulbright, Senator Mike Mansfield)
- Emergence of mindguards (e.g. National Security Adviser Walt Rostow) and the suppression of personal doubts by group members

- Gradual exclusion of those who threatened the group consensus
- The "domestification" or exclusion of dissenters.

Even within Johnson's inner circle, there was a handful of dissenters. Most notably, Undersecretary of State George Ball harbored significant doubts about Americanizing the war, and repeatedly expressed these doubts in meetings. However, Janis argues that the group defused Ball's dissent by referring to him as a "devil's advocate." This term originates from the Catholic faith and refers to the cardinal within the Vatican who is traditionally chosen to argue against the beatification of a saint, in effect taking the "Devil's side." The other cardinals know that the advocate is not seriously converting to this position, but (much like a lawyer who must defend a notorious criminal in a court trial) he is *required* to take this position. Similarly, many of those who favored escalating the war maintained that Ball was not serious in his dissent, but was merely arguing against the majority position in order to ensure that all positions were heard in the debate.

For the rest of their lives, many of Johnson's decision-makers on Vietnam—Assistant Secretary of State for East Asian Affairs William Bundy is a good example—would continue to maintain that Ball had been a devil's advocate, but this was simply untrue. Ball harbored very real and heartfelt disagreements with the others. But dismissing or "domesticating" the dissenter in this way is exactly what one would expect if groupthink were present, Janis's analysis suggests. Similarly, Lyndon Johnson himself would defuse the criticism of Press Secretary Bill Moyers by announcing "here comes Mr. Stop the Bombing!" whenever Moyers walked into the room, thus blunting anything Moyers might say against the war before he even uttered a comment.[18] And when one of the original architects of the war, Robert McNamara, began to have doubts about the wisdom of the war and began to express these outside the group, Johnson compared him to a son who had let slip to prospective buyers of a house that there are cracks in the basement.[19] "He is just short of cracking up," Johnson is reputed to have told advisers in 1967 when McNamara was not present.

Criticisms of Janis's Perspective

The groupthink approach has been criticized from a variety of perspectives. Attempts to test the model more rigorously than Janis himself did have been met with mixed results.[20] More generally, some have critiqued the theoretical coherence of the model Janis developed, while others have used more recently declassified materials to undermine the empirical arguments he made. As Philip Tetlock and his colleagues note, four broad criticisms have been raised against Janis's work on the theoretical side: first of all, Janis relied on qualitative case studies, a method which frequently tempts the researcher to emphasize evidence which "fits" a theory and discard information which does not; second, there is a "suspiciously perfect correlation" between the presence of groupthink and flawed decision-making in Janis's book, even though he himself concedes that process is not everything and that it is possible (by sheer luck) for a good decision to emerge from flawed procedures. Third, there is a suspicious "all-or-nothing" quality to the way that Janis's cases fit so neatly into the categories of groupthink or vigilant decision-making; and last, there are various conceptual problems with the model itself, especially those having to do with distinguishing the causes from the consequences of groupthink.[21] In their classic critique, for instance, Longley and Pruitt question (amongst other things) the inclusion of "a belief in the inherent morality of the group" and "stereotyped views of out-groups" in the list of the symptoms of groupthink, since unlike the other factors these appear to have little to do with consensus formation or concurrence-seeking.[22] In short, one does not need to hold a simplistic view of one's enemy or an exalted view of one's own moral position to engage in hasty or premature decision-making that excludes minority views.

On the empirical side, David Barrett has notably challenged the idea that Lyndon Johnson didn't receive competing advice on Vietnam. *Most* of his advisers did argue for escalation, but a significant minority did not, Barrett notes. Six advisers in particular argued against escalation. There was George Ball as we know already, but Senator William Fulbright, Vice President Hubert Humphrey, Senator Mike Mansfield, Senator Richard Russell, and presidential adviser Clark Clifford all expressed their feelings against the war directly to Johnson as well.[23] The picture of a president stubbornly ignoring outside advice and relying exclusively upon a tiny group of like-minded individuals therefore does not really fit what actually occurred, Barrett suggests. Of course, we have long known that it was not just Ball who expressed reservations about escalation; many in the CIA, Defense, and State Departments also harbored strong doubts, though it tended to be those lower down the hierarchy who felt this way. Even more significant, perhaps, is the evidence we now have that Johnson himself *agonized* over the decision to escalate quite extensively. Johnson secretly taped a large number of his phone calls, and the declassification of many of these calls since the late 1990s has shown a Johnson who was almost always pessimistic about the chances of success, rather than exhibiting any "illusion of invulnerability." We now know that Johnson and his colleagues were, as Barrett puts it, "uncertain warriors."[24]

With regard to the Bay of Pigs, Robert McNamara has stated that the common emotion among Kennedy's advisers when they initially took office was not one of omnipotence or "the magic touch," as Janis's account suggests, but a strongly *defensive* feeling. Domestically, JFK had won by the narrowest margin in electoral history at the 1960 presidential election, but even more importantly in foreign policy terms the dominant feeling was one of being on the defense against an ever-expanding Communist threat.[25] Roderick Kramer argues that Janis's interpretation of Vietnam and the Bay of Pigs sits poorly with what we now know about both case studies:

> When making a case for the argument that Kennedy and his advisors displayed symptoms of overconfidence and an "illusion of invulnerability" when deciding to proceed with implementation of the CIA operation, Janis did not have access, of course, to the classified records of top secret briefings and meetings. This evidence, now available to scholars, indicates that Kennedy's assessments were undoubtedly influenced not only by deliberately misleading intelligence assessments provided by the CIA, but also by disingenuous, and politically motivated comments made by President Eisenhower to the new president during private, top-secret briefings.[26]

Rather than being influenced by group processes, Kramer suggests, Kennedy may simply have had great difficulty believing that Dwight Eisenhower, "the organizational genius behind the largest, most complex, and most successful amphibious military invasion in U.S. history," would have supported a much smaller and less ambitious amphibiously based invasion that had little chance of success.[27] In both the Vietnam and Bay of Pigs cases, moreover, the decisions each president reached may have had more to do with individual-level *analogical reasoning* processes (see Chapter 9 of this book) as opposed to group-level ones. For instance, the confidence that Kennedy and his advisers had in the CIA may have stemmed from the agency's success in an apparently very similar case, the overthrow of Jacobo Arbenz in Guatemala in 1954. JFK and his advisers seem to have expected that Castro would flee the country when presented with a U.S. plan for his overthrow, just as Arbenz had done seven years earlier.

Newgroup Syndrome

A number of recent scholars have noted—probably with a fair amount of justification—that there has been *too much* attention devoted in research and textbooks to groupthink. No chapter on group decision-making would be complete without devoting a good deal of space to groupthink, as this one has; Janis's theory is always the elephant in the room, a perspective we simply cannot ignore whenever political groups are discussed. Equally, however, empirical and theoretical criticisms of the groupthink approach, such as the ones noted above, have prompted many analysts of foreign policy decision-making to look "beyond groupthink," re-examining the wider literature on group behaviors within social psychology for clues as to how other theoretical frameworks might be developed.[28] One such approach has become known as the *newgroup syndrome*.[29] Eric Stern and Bengt Sundelius, the theory's major advocates, have proposed this approach "to capture a hypothesized pathological conformity dynamic liable to occur in newly formed policy groups . . . in ad hoc or newly institutionalized groups, that is, those in the forming stage."[30] As they further explain, in such groups:

> A common group subculture and well-developed procedural norms tend to be lacking. This vacuum creates uncertainty among the members who are likely to be anxious, tentative, dependent, and, therefore, particularly inclined to take direction from a leader or other assertive group members within the group. These conditions create incentives for both compliance and internalization on the part of the individual member, which in turn results in a tendency toward conformity in the group as a whole.[31]

Drawing in particular on the work of Bruce Tuckman, Stern and Sundelius hypothesize that groups go through a number of developmental stages during the lifetime of their existence—from their initial formation to the point where they formally "adjourn"—and that a differing kind of dynamic operates at each. Stern and Sundelius are especially interested in the beginning of a group's life, however, where a new administration comes to power or a significant turnover in membership (through resignations, hirings, and firings) in effect creates a new group dynamic. While dysfunctional decision-making is not inevitable at this early stage—it all depends on the kind of norms that the group leader encourages at the outset—there is a tendency towards caution and *conformity* (and a corresponding lack of open, critical thinking) at this point.

Stern applies this approach to the Bay of Pigs case study, and we may usefully contrast his own approach with that of Janis. Like Janis, he argues that conformity was a particular problem in the decision-making, but he traces this to the fact that Kennedy—having swept away Eisenhower's decision-making structures and a foreign policy apparatus which is now highly regarded by many scholars[32]—operated in a way that was too informal and ad hoc. The major players did not know one another well and were only beginning to find their feet in their jobs. Moreover, the president himself had little management or executive-level experience, having been a member of Congress and then a senator. "Given Kennedy's relatively laissez-faire management style, he did not attempt to guide consciously and clarify the group decision culture in order to reduce uncertainty and promote critical interaction," Stern concludes.

> He appears to have been unaware of the effect of his person and the weight of his office upon his colleagues. Similarly, the evidence suggests that he was insufficiently conscious of the emergent group norms (unwittingly reinforced by his own conduct) of deference to the president and to "experts."[33]

The Individual in a Group Setting

The group-level form of situationism suggests that groups are more than the sum total of the individuals who compose them: once policy-makers form a group, the resultant body can in a sense "overwhelm" its members and take on a life of its own. As Stern puts it, Kennedy does not appear to have appreciated this possibility at the outset. "He placed a premium on talent, believing that this quality was the key to achieving policy and political success," Stern argues. "In other words, he believed that it was enough to assemble a number of talented people, throw them in a room together, and wait for good things to happen."[34] This kind of perspective is akin to a belief in a kind of narrow dispositionism; in other words, Kennedy's initial view ignored the group dynamic that occurs when we bring individuals together, and situationists like Janis would contend that these dynamics are not always positive in their effects (as we saw in the Bay of Pigs and Vietnam cases). By the time of the October 1962 Cuban missile crisis, however, JFK clearly recognized the effects that group norms and other factors can have on decision-making, taking various steps to ensure that his own presence (for instance) did not preordain the decisions reached. Fortunately for us, he seems to have been a quick learner.

Conclusion

We have seen how situationist arguments can take a number of different forms, though all of the main approaches we have discussed—Skinner's behaviorism, Milgram's obedience paradigm, Zimbardo "bad barrel" theory, and the groupthink approach of Janis—share in common the belief that our dispositions are less critical in shaping our behavior than the situation in which we find ourselves. Most of us, though not perhaps everyone, can reliably be expected to behave in predictable ways when placed in a certain situation. But there is, as we have occasionally noted in the criticism of various situationist approaches, another (rival) way of looking at the underpinnings of political behavior: dispositionism. Dispositionist approaches dispute the notion that human beings generally behave similarly when placed in the same kind of situation; as we saw in Chapter 1, dispositionists believe in the immense *variability* of human beings—their differing beliefs, attitudes, mindsets, and so on—and cite examples that highlight the variation in political behavior which results from these differences. Our next task, then, is to discuss various perspectives that take a dispositionist approach, and we begin that job in the next chapter with an examination of the oldest approach to political psychology, psychobiography. As we shall see, this is a body of work which inherently assumes that individuals and their peculiarities "matter."

Notes

1 See Fritz Gaenslen, "Decision-Making Groups," in Eric Singer and Valerie Hudson (eds.), *Political Psychology and Foreign Policy* (Boulder, CO: Westview Press, 1992).
2 Yaacov Vertzberger, *The World In Their Minds: Information Processing, Cognition and Perception in Foreign Policy Decisionmaking* (Stanford, CA: Stanford University Press, 1990), p.223.
3 Alexander George, *Presidential Decisionmaking in Foreign Policy: The Effective Use of Information and Advice* (Boulder, CO: Westview Press, 1980), p.81.
4 Vertzberger, *The World In Their Minds*, p.224.
5 Graham Allison and Philip Zelikow, *Essence of Decision: Explaining the Cuban Missile Crisis* (New York: Longman, 1999).
6 Irving Janis, *Victims of Groupthink: A Psychological Study of Foreign-Policy Decisions and Fiascoes* (Boston, MA: Houghton Mifflin, 1972); Janis, *Groupthink: Psychological Studies of Policy Decisions and Fiascoes* (Boston, MA: Houghton Mifflin, 1982).
7 Janis, *Groupthink*, p.9.
8 Ibid., pp.132–58.
9 Ibid., pp.176–77.
10 Ibid., pp.174–75.
11 Peter Kornbluh (ed.), *Bay of Pigs Declassified: The Secret CIA Report on the Invasion of Cuba* (New York: W.W. Norton, 1998), pp.2–3.
12 Janis, *Groupthink*, p.16.
13 Ibid., pp.19–27.
14 Ibid., p.14.
15 Ibid., pp.35–47.
16 See Robert McNamara, James Blight, and Robert Brigham, *Argument Without End: In Search of Answers To The Vietnam Tragedy* (New York: Public Affairs, 1999).
17 Janis, *Groupthink*, pp.97–130.
18 Ibid., p.115.
19 Ibid., p.118.
20 See for instance Philip Tetlock, Randall Peterson, Charles McGuire, Shi-Jie Chang, and Peter Field, "Assessing Political Group Dynamics: A Test of the Groupthink Model," *Journal of Personality and Social Psychology*, 63: 403–25, 1992.
21 Ibid., p.404.

22 Jeanne Longley and Dean Pruitt, "Groupthink: A Critique of Janis's Theory," in Ladd Wheeler (ed.), *Review of Personality and Social Psychology* (Beverly Hills, CA: Sage Publications, 1980), p.91.

23 David Barrett, "The Mythology Surrounding Lyndon Johnson, His Advisers, and the 1965 Decision To Escalate the Vietnam War," *Political Science Quarterly*, 103: 637–63, 1988.

24 David Barrett, *Uncertain Warriors: Lyndon Johnson and His Vietnam Advisers* (Lawrence, KS: University Press of Kansas, 1993). For transcripts of many of the relevant phone calls, see Michael Beschloss's two edited volumes, *Taking Charge: The Johnson White House Tapes, 1963–1964* (New York: Simon & Schuster, 1997) and *Reaching For Glory: Lyndon Johnson's Secret White House Tapes, 1964–1965* (New York: Simon & Schuster, 2001).

25 McNamara, Blight, and Brigham, *Argument Without End*, pp.25–31.

26 Roderick Kramer, "Revisiting the Bay of Pigs and Vietnam Decisions 25 Years Later: How Well Has the Groupthink Hypothesis Stood the Test of Time?" *Organizational Behavior and Human Decision Processes*, 73: 236–71, 1998, p.245.

27 Ibid.

28 Paul t'Hart, Eric Stern, and Bengt Sundelius (eds.), *Beyond Groupthink: Political Group Dynamics and Foreign Policy-Making* (Ann Arbor, MI: The University of Michigan Press, 1997).

29 Eric Stern and Bengt Sundelius, "The Essence of Groupthink," *Mershon International Studies Review*, 1: 101–8, 1994; Eric Stern, "Probing the Plausibility of Newgroup Syndrome: Kennedy and the Bay of Pigs," in t'Hart, Stern, and Sundelius (eds.), *Beyond Groupthink*.

30 Quoted in Stern, "Probing the Plausibility of Newgroup Syndrome," p.165.

31 Ibid.

32 See for instance John Burke and Fred Greenstein, *How Presidents Test Reality: Decisions on Vietnam, 1954 and 1965* (New York: Russell Sage Foundation, 1989).

33 Stern, "Probing the Plausibility of Newgroup Syndrome," p.182.

34 Ibid., p.177.

Suggested Further Reading

Irving Janis, *Groupthink: Psychological Studies of Policy Decisions and Fiascoes* (Boston, MA: Houghton Mifflin, 1982).

Film

Groupthink (1991): Fairly short but very useful training video from CRM films which examines the concept of groupthink, using actors to recreate the Challenger decision-making (amusingly, Boisjoly is played by Peter Boyle, best known today for his part in the TV show *Everybody Loves Raymond*). Very expensive to buy, but should be available in many university libraries.

Part II

The Individual

Chapter 7

Psychobiography

Dr. Justin Frank's *Bush On The Couch: Inside the Mind of the President* caused a minor storm when it came out in 2004:

> If one of my patients frequently said one thing and did another, I would want to know why. If I found that he often used words that hid their true meaning and affected a persona that obscured the nature of his actions, I would grow more concerned. If he presented an inflexible worldview characterized by an oversimplified distinction between right and wrong, good and evil, allies and enemies, I would question his ability to grasp reality. And if his actions revealed an unacknowledged—even sadistic—indifference to human suffering, wrapped in pious claims of compassion, I would worry about the safety of the people whose lives he touched. For the past three years, I have observed with increasing alarm the inconsistencies and denials of such an individual. But he is not one of my patients. He is our president.[1]

Drawing on the uncompromising psychoanalytic theories of Melanie Klein, Frank argues that the formation of Bush's personality in early childhood provides the critical key to understanding his later actions. His early development, Frank suggests, was hampered by the treatment he received from both parents: George H.W. Bush was an absentee father, often away in Washington D.C., while Barbara Bush was a cold, unfeeling, and authoritarian mother. In response to this upbringing, Bush developed a Manichaean view of the world characterized by black and white thinking. He also developed delusions of megalomania and omnipotence. His actions as president, Frank maintains, reflect "the drive of an under nurtured and emotionally hobbled infant." Using Bush's history of alcoholism as one example, he lists Bush's failure to draw upon recognized treatment options like Alcoholics Anonymous as evidence of "multiple, serious and untreated symptoms." Removal from office is the only "treatment option," both for Bush's sake and for ours, Frank contends.

In truth, Frank's argument is merely one of the latest additions to what is perhaps the oldest tradition of all within the field of political psychology. Usually termed "psychobiography" or "psychohistory," this approach assumes that individuals are important in the sense that their psychological characteristics are held to have a meaningful impact on real-world events and outcomes (sometimes termed the "hero in history" model). All psychobiography has this factor in common. Another point of similarity is that all work in this area either explicitly or implicitly uses some psychological theory or other to make sense of a person's life history and choices.

It is worth pointing out at the outset that such approaches are nowhere near as fashionable as they once were, probably reflecting the decline of psychoanalytical approaches in general. It is easy to dismiss such arguments as "psychobabble" or unscientific armchair analysis, as many critics do. Others—usually psychiatrists or psychologists nowadays, rather than political scientists—continue to do work within this tradition, and maintain that such an approach is essential to understanding adult behavior, including the behavior of major politicians. On the question of whether such work is ultimately valuable, this chapter will make no presumption either way; that question is left to the reader to work out for him- or herself. But we shall suggest that whatever the advantages and disadvantages of psychobiography may be, these approaches are at the very least worth considering and are often rather intriguing.

The Formative Influence of Sigmund Freud

Many psychobiographies have been influenced, both in the past and today, by psychoanalysis and the arguments of its creator, Sigmund Freud. Freud's claim that events in childhood exert a powerful impact on later development has had an especially strong influence on this type of work. The reader will recall from our earlier discussion that according to Freud, human beings are motivated by only two things: aggression and the sexual impulse (together known as the "pleasure principle"). He saw the mind as composed of what he called the *id*, the *ego*, and the *superego*. Most critically in terms of his impact on the development of psychobiography, Freud hypothesized that childhood experiences do not simply fade in significance as time goes on, but often exert a fundamental impact upon our adult behavior. He pointed out the importance of unconscious processes, which as Butler and McManus note:

> include unconscious and socially "unacceptable" wishes. These are inferred,
> for example, from dreams, slips of the tongue, and mannerisms . . . in

particular, unconscious conflicts are hypothesized to be a prime cause of psychological distress, which psychoanalysts can help to relieve by assisting in their expression, and by using psychodynamic theories based on Freud's work to interpret patients' behaviors.[2]

Freud believed that dreams, for instance, contain expressions of our hidden desires and secrets, and that a skillful psychoanalyst could decode these dreams to reveal the unconscious conflicts within. When conflicts occur between different aspects of the personality, this creates anxiety in the ego; when this anxiety becomes unmanageable, we resort to various unconscious *defense mechanisms* such as repression, rationalization, denial, displacement, and projection.

Freud's legacy has been mixed.[3] As the psychologist Drew Westen notes, Freud virtually invented the concept of the unconscious, the notion that we may act from motives and reasons that are unknown even to ourselves. "Before him, nobody realized that our conscious mind is the tip of the mental iceberg," Westen argues. Today, however, we take the idea of the unconscious pretty much for granted. Also taken for granted is the notion that childhood development may exert a fundamental impact on adult behavior (in Freud's time a radical proposition). Westen adds that Freud was also correct about denial. "The research is crystal-clear that we look the other way not to see what makes us uncomfortable," Westen notes. Some of Freud's ideas are so widely accepted that they have become dissociated from Freud himself, Westen suggests.[4] On the other hand, Freud's reduction of our motives to simply sex and aggression is nowadays viewed almost universally as far too simplistic, and his methods have frequently been attacked as unscientific.

Freud wrote several psychobiographies himself. The best known is probably his study of Leonardo da Vinci, in which he concluded—largely on the basis of a dream reported by the artist and the anatomically detailed drawings of his male subjects—that da Vinci was a homosexual.[5] Of more political relevance, Freud was also supposedly the co-author (with William Bullitt) of a psychobiography of Woodrow Wilson, apparently written in the 1930s but published only in 1967.[6] Nevertheless, his influence upon political psychology was mostly indirect, and it was left to others who had been influenced by Freud's body of work to tease out its larger political applications and implications.

The Formative Influence of Harold Lasswell

Harold Lasswell's path-breaking book *Psychopathology and Politics* was first published in 1930.[7] Lasswell was heavily influenced by Charles Merriam, who inspired Lasswell to explore the relationship between psychology and politics. Unusually for a political scientist, Lasswell took the time to train himself in the psychological theories of the day. Since psychology at the time was heavily influenced by Freudian psychoanalysis, it is natural that his work came to bear the imprint of this body of theory. Simply put, Lasswell's core argument was that what he called the "political personality" results from the displacement of private problems onto public life. A person denied love at home may seek the love of the American people, for instance. Here the Freudian theme of defense or compensation mechanisms comes out strongly, especially the mechanism of displacement. Political ambition and the search for power often serve as compensatory factors to overcome low self-esteem, he thought. As Lasswell himself put it, his argument was that "political movements derive their vitality from the displacement of private affect upon public objects."[8] As a Freudian, Lasswell also viewed sex and aggression as the dominant motivators of human beings and subscribed to the id/ego/superego distinction. The repression of unconscious motives plays a major role in his work. His *Psychopathology and Politics* and later *Power and Personality*— which pursued the idea that politicians often displace private needs such as self-esteem onto the public world—influenced a whole generation of younger scholars, and provided a key intellectual linkage between Freud and the ideas of figures like Alexander George, whose work we shall discuss next.[9]

The Dysfunctional Childhood of Woodrow Wilson?

Alexander and Juliette George's *Woodrow Wilson and Colonel House* is one of the most famous and often-discussed examples of the psychobiographical genre, and as protégés of Lasswell their theories about Woodrow Wilson bore the strong imprint of their former teacher and his ideas.[10] As in Lasswell's work, George and George start from the position that political power in their subject's case was really a compensation for chronic low self-esteem. Like Lasswell before them, they also rely on the notion of unconscious motives lurking below the surface of things and the psychoanalytic emphasis on childhood development. The central claim made in *Woodrow Wilson and Colonel House* is that Woodrow Wilson harbored an unconscious anger towards his father for the treatment he had received during his childhood years. The stern and unyielding Dr. Joseph Wilson, a Presbyterian minister, supposedly pushed his son (who had learning difficulties early on in his life) relentlessly, but would rarely reward his son's achievements with affection. He was allegedly never satisfied with his son's performance, and treated him with cold indifference. He would often tease young Woodrow, George and George argue, leaving him with a sense of inadequacy and making him feel "stupid, ugly, worthless and unlovable."[11] He was "perpetually dissatisfied with himself," they note, striving all his life to achieve great deeds in compensation.[12]

One of the leading characteristics of Wilson's personality was his inflexibility, they note, and this characteristic is also traced to his childhood upbringing. The teasing of his father made Woodrow insecure, rigid, and unwilling to compromise in later life, and this childhood propelled him into a lifelong series of conflicts with "father figures" such as Dean West at Princeton University and later Senator Henry Cabot Lodge. Ironically, Wilson was only too well aware of the importance of negotiation and bargaining within the American political system, but his refusal to compromise over the League of Nations Treaty led to his ultimate downfall. The treaty was in many ways Wilson's own brainchild, but George and George argue that the U.S. Senate would have approved the League of Nations if only Wilson had been willing to make a few compromises. This characteristic inflexibility inevitably led to the rejection of the treaty as well as other self-created policy disasters stemming from his basic inflexibility.

In their original book, George and George hedged this argument with a great deal of tentative words like "perhaps" and "one may speculate that." Perhaps an early reviewer of the book (or one or both authors) insisted on this, for the reader can readily appreciate how untestable a claim of this sort is. They also deny that they are attempting to explain Wilson's behavior solely through his personality.[13] Since we cannot know what is present in our unconscious—otherwise, the phrase "unconscious" would have no meaning—it is well nigh impossible to test George and George's claim. Perhaps surprisingly, given the centrality of Wilson's childhood to their argument, they devote only a few pages of discussion to this topic.

Much of their book is given over to showing how stubborn and inflexible Woodrow could be (that is, to showing that the same patterns recurred through his life), but it does not necessarily follow that the explanation for this lies in the kind of psychological explanation being offered here. One either accepts it on faith, having read their interpretation of his life, or one looks for other explanations. Edwin Weinstein and his colleagues did the latter, arguing that the root of Wilson's inflexibility was physiological.[14] It is well known in medical circles that strokes can lead to mood-changing behavior, and we know that Wilson suffered a series of strokes, the most serious of which occurred in October 1919. This argument probably enjoys wider acceptance today than George and George's—tellingly, a recent PBS film biography of Woodrow Wilson's life makes no mention of the George and George thesis[15]—but it provoked an intemperate debate between Weinstein, Anderson, and Link, and the Georges at the time, a disagreement which is still interesting today because it illustrates how difficult it is to make these kind of arguments "stick."

The Complexity of Lyndon Johnson

Lyndon Johnson presents us with an object case in the complexity of a leader's personality and the corresponding difficulties that arise when dealing with a leader whose personality exhibits so many competing facets. LBJ has variously been described as an active–negative, a narcissist, a presidential paranoid, a manic–depressive, and as the victim of a harsh maternal upbringing. The earliest and best psychological analysis of Johnson came from the presidential historian and former confidante of LBJ, Doris Kearns Goodwin. In her *Lyndon Johnson and the American Dream*,[16] first published in 1976 just three years after LBJ's death, Goodwin applies a psychoanalytic approach to Johnson. Goodwin suggests that his early upbringing—especially his relationship with his mother—shaped his future interactions with his staff and others in the political world. Johnson's rather intellectual and ambitious mother felt robbed of a promising career by Sam Johnson (Lyndon's father), by all accounts a boorish man who was often drunk. She compensated for this by using her son as a substitute for her own ambitions, Goodwin argues, withdrawing her love when Lyndon didn't live up to her high expectations.

"How children dance," Rainer Maria Rilke wrote, "to the unlived lives of their parents" . . . The image of Rebekah Baines Johnson that emerges in these stories is that of a drastically unhappy woman, cut off from all the things that had once given her pleasure in life, stranded in a cabin on a muddy stream with a man she considered vulgar and brutish, a frustrated woman with a host of throttled ambitions, trying, through her first-born son, to find a substitute for a dead father, an unsuccessful marriage, and a failed career. She seemed under a compulsion to renew on her son's behalf all the plans and projects she had given up for herself. The son would fulfill the wishful dreams she had never carried out, he would become the important person she had failed to be.[17]

Johnson recalled that:

> my mother soon discovered that my daddy was not a man to discuss higher things. To her mind his life was vulgar and ignorant. His idea of pleasure was to sit up half the night with his friends, drinking beer, telling stories, and playing dominoes. She felt very much alone. The first year of her marriage was the worst year of her life. Then I came along and suddenly everything was all right again. I could do all the things she never did.[18]

Rebekah fostered Johnson's enormous ego; in LBJ's words, she "made me feel big and important. It made me believe I could do anything in the whole world." And yet her love and affection ebbed and flowed, and could often be withdrawn when (say) the young Lyndon brought home a bad grade report from school. "When he failed to satisfy her desires," Goodwin argues,

> he experienced not simply criticism but a complete withdrawal of affection. "For days after I quit those lessons she walked around the house pretending I was dead. And then to make it worse, I had to watch her being especially warm and nice to my father and sisters."

The same experience was repeated later when Johnson refused to go to college and Rebekah closed him out for weeks, refusing to speak or even to look at him.[19]

Goodwin argues that a striking link is apparent between the way his mother alternately extended and withdrew love and the manner in which Johnson himself treated his own staff and indeed "nearly all his adult relationships." LBJ was capable of incredible warmth and generosity towards his friends, colleagues, and subordinates, but they uniformly recall how swiftly this warmth could turn to anger and hostility when they failed to live up to the high standards he set for them. Johnson:

> demanded a measure of gratitude and loyalty so high that disappointment was inevitable. And when the disappointment came, Johnson tended to withdraw his affection and concern—the "Johnson freezeout"— hurting others in much the same way as his mother had hurt him years before.[20]

Another distinguished presidential historian, Robert Dallek, views Johnson as a textbook case of political paranoia. While in no sense a fully fledged psychobiography, Dallek's *Flawed Giant* argues that "at times, Johnson came frighteningly close to clinical paranoia."[21]

> Plaguing Johnson . . . was an irrational conviction that his domestic opponents were subversives intent on undermining national institutions. Johnson's paranoia raises questions about his judgment and capacity to make rational life and death decisions. I do not raise this matter casually. It is a frighteningly difficult issue, which the country has never seriously addressed.[22]

Dallek confirms Bill Moyers' view, previously attributed to him by Richard Goodwin, that Johnson suffered from spells of intense paranoia and quotes Moyers' belief that Lady Bird Johnson was more concerned about her husband's paranoia than anyone else.[23] He also offers evidence that Secretary of State Dean Rusk was worried. Like his successor Nixon, Johnson saw conspiracies everywhere, both from the left and the right. But the beliefs Johnson expressed about his enemies, though sincerely held, were unfounded, no more than "cranky nonsense" in Dallek's words.[24]

The most forceful advocate of the Johnson paranoia position amongst those who actually worked with him has been Richard Goodwin, Johnson's former speechwriter and Doris Kearns Goodwin's husband. His memoir *Remembering America* created a minor storm when it was first released in 1988, largely due to what its author had to say about Johnson's increasingly strange behavior at the time of the key decisions about Vietnam.[25] Goodwin recalled that:

> During 1965, and especially in the period which enveloped the crucial midsummer decision that transformed Vietnam into an American war, I became convinced that the president's always large eccentricities had taken a huge leap into unreason. Not on every subject, and certainly not all the time . . . There is no question in my mind that both the atmosphere of the White House and the decisions taken until 1965 (the only period I personally observed) were affected by the periodic disruptions of Lyndon Johnson's mind and spirit.[26]

Based on several years of observing Johnson at first hand, Goodwin concludes that LBJ "experienced certain episodes of what I believe to have been paranoid behavior" and that this observation "was shared by others who also had close and frequent contact with the president."[27] In 1965 both Goodwin and Press Secretary Bill Moyers began—independently and without each other's knowledge—consulting psychiatrists about the president and reading psychology textbooks in an effort to make sense of the mental deterioration they observed.

How are we to make sense of an individual as psychologically complex as Johnson? In addition to clues from his childhood and his "Jekyll and Hyde" personality as well as strong hints of paranoia, there is some evidence of narcissism on Johnson's part. On a visit to the Vatican in 1966, Johnson famously presented the Pope with a bust of himself. Everyone in the family was called "LBJ," almost as if he considered himself of such importance historically that he aimed for a kind of vicarious immortality. He has also rather controversially been diagnosed at a distance as a manic–depressive by the psychiatrist Dr. Jablow Hershman.[28] Even figures who appear relatively easy to understand, such as George W. Bush, may actually be the product of psychological experiences we can only dimly comprehend, as Frank's book suggests.

Comparative Psychobiography

No chapter on this topic would be complete without an examination of what is undoubtedly the major work of comparative psychobiography: James David Barber's book *The Presidential Character*.[29] As Paul Kowert notes, individual works of psychobiography are "idiosyncratic, focus on unique sets of variables, and thus offer little basis for comparative analysis."[30] Barber's book was one of the first to analyze American presidents in a comparative way, and the first to come up with a generalizable framework that could be applied to all presidents, no matter what their background, beliefs, or *modus operandi*. He was interested above all in explaining why some presidents succeed while others fail, and in predicting who is likely to succeed or fail before it actually happens. In fact, you can easily guess that by looking at the subtitle of the book, which is *Predicting Performance in the White House*. How does he do that? In essence, he argues first of all that success or failure is largely a function of what kind of personality the president possesses, and he goes on to describe two different dimensions within the notion of presidential character: the active–passive dimension and the positive–negative dimension.

Active versus passive refers to the amount of energy a president puts into the job. Active presidents are movers and shakers, if you like; they are driven individuals who have vast amounts of energy, and they throw themselves enthusiastically into the job. Conversely, passive presidents are far less involved in details, do not work so hard and prefer to steer an even course in policy-making rather than stirring up policy conflicts or challenging the status quo. The *positive versus negative* dimension, on the other hand, refers to the degree of satisfaction that the president gets out of doing his job (his level of contentment, in other words). Although practically all presidents start off wanting to do the job, some find that they don't actually enjoy the position once they're there. Clearly, the responsibilities of the office—and consequently the strains and burdens placed on the incumbent—are massive, and this can lead one to actively dislike being president. Barber suggests that some individuals are negative in the sense that they feel bound by duty or responsibility to hold power, even though they hate exercising power or dislike the demands that go with it. Other presidents are positive about the job, in the sense that they greatly enjoy holding the position and derive immense satisfaction from it.

Barber says that of all the things you can be, it's best by far to be an *active–positive*. Active–positives are balanced individuals who are contented with life, respect themselves, are open to new ideas, and willing to learn from experience. These people are healthy, energetic, "can do" presidents who tend to perform well in presidential office. Presidents FDR, Truman, Kennedy, Ford, Carter, George H.W. Bush, and Clinton are all deemed to fall under this category. Harry Truman, for instance, was able to actively reshape the whole tone of American foreign policy: he introduced NATO, the Marshall Plan, he intervened in Korea, and—most importantly—it was under his presidency that America adopted the long-established policy of containment, which was to remain the key plank of U.S. foreign policy right up until halfway through the Bush administration. Barber would argue that it was Truman's "can do" personality, his energy, and decisive nature that led directly to these actions. Jimmy Carter is another example: although he accomplished far less, Carter was intensively involved in the governmental process and enjoyed being president more than anything else in his life. Indeed, his performance since he left office shows that he liked it so much he's still acting as if he's the current president!

The least desirable thing to be, on the other hand, is an *active–negative*, Barber thinks. These presidents are said to be dangerous because they have a tendency towards compulsiveness and aggression, and they tend to be stubborn and inflexible to the point of bringing disaster on themselves and the country. They often retreat into themselves, hunkering down in the face of opposition. Of recent presidents, Barber claims that Richard Nixon and Lyndon Johnson were both active–negatives who stubbornly pursued courses of action that led to their respective downfalls (Johnson with Vietnam, Nixon with Watergate). Nixon decided to widen the war in Vietnam by invading Cambodia in 1970, thus falling into the trap of sticking to (and indeed, expanding) a line of policy that had essentially failed, and like the paranoid LBJ he saw conspiracies and enemies everywhere. Both ended their presidencies in extreme isolation.

Less undesirable, but not nearly as good as being active–positive, are the passive–positives and passive–negatives. *Passive–positives*, Barber claims, seek love and affection by being pleasant and cooperative instead of confrontational. They are optimistic, friendly, and compliant; but while passive–positives enjoy being president and derive satisfaction from the job to some extent, they don't try to achieve much and don't feel that much is required of them. Ronald Reagan is given as the only recent example of this; again, Barber makes this claim because he thinks Reagan was a very agreeable and personable individual who preferred not to engage in strenuous work. He would often articulate what he wanted in general terms, but would leave it to his advisers to decide how to *implement* these general principles and put them into practice. In other words he was an inactive macro-manager in contrast to the micro-managing Jimmy Carter, who got heavily involved in the day-to-day details of policy-making.

Last, there are the *passive–negatives*. These individuals would rather be almost anything but president, but they feel a sense of duty to do the job anyway. They are in politics, in essence, because they feel they ought to be. This kind of leader derives very little satisfaction from the job and also makes little effort to get things achieved. Barber argues that Dwight Eisenhower fits into this category:

Table 7.1 Barber's characterization of modern presidents

	Positive	Negative
Active	FDR	Woodrow Wilson
	Harry Truman	Herbert Hoover
	John Kennedy	Lyndon Johnson
	Gerald Ford	Richard Nixon
	George H.W. Bush	
	Bill Clinton	
	Jimmy Carter	
	Barack Obama?	
Passive	William Taft	Calvin Coolidge
	Warren Harding	Dwight Eisenhower
	Ronald Reagan	
	George W. Bush?	

Source: Adapted from Barber, *The Presidential Character*, pp.8–11

Eisenhower did not press for any dramatic changes during his terms in office, and appeared to take the job with extreme reluctance. Arguably, he was drafted into the Republican nomination in 1952, and seemed not to want the job. Eisenhower, Barber says, "did not feel a duty to save the world or become a great hero, but simply to contribute what he could the best he was able."[31]

When we put the two dimensions—active versus passive and positive versus negative—together, we obtain a two-by-two table like the one reproduced as Table 7.1.

Barber's theory has been controversial with political scientists ever since it was originally published back in 1972, and it has become one of the most quoted and discussed books in American political science. At worst, it reminds us that presidential performance is the result of a complex mix of factors, rather than just personality, and at best, it may even provide us with what it claims to provide us; that is, a reliable scheme for predicting success or failure in office. Nevertheless, the critics have highlighted a number of problems with the theory that have led to a decline in its fashionability in recent years. And of the criticisms that have been directed at Barber's framework, at least *three* seem especially worthy of note here:

1   It may oversimplify the world in a way that is ultimately misleading. One could claim that there are literally dozens of categories into which presidential personalities might fit, if not hundreds. Creating such a simple framework leads Barber to underestimate the differences between presidents who seem similar on the face of things. Arguably, employing

such catch-all categories does not allow Barber to do what he is attempting to do, which is to distinguish between success or failure. Do Truman and Carter really belong in the same box? Do FDR and Gerald Ford?

2   It is difficult to fit particular presidents into particular "pigeonholes." There is always room for disagreement as to whether a president is active or passive, and most of all as to whether he is negative or positive about the job. Lyndon Johnson is classed here as an active–negative, meaning that he worked hard but derived little satisfaction from the job. But Johnson actually seemed to enjoy being president at the beginning of his tenure; it was only when America got bogged down in Vietnam that he began to hate being president, and even then he found it hard to do what he eventually did do—which was to leave the presidency prematurely by voluntarily deciding not to run again. Or take Bill Clinton as another example: did Clinton really enjoy being president? Some evidence suggests that he did. On the other hand, Elizabeth Drew, in her book *On The Edge: The Clinton Presidency*, recounts various stories which reveal that Clinton was often frustrated by the job and regularly flew into rages and tantrums when things didn't go his way.[32] So in other words, assessing this kind of thing requires us to engage in a certain amount of speculation, and—some would say—mind reading. Examples like this, a critic might say, make Barber's framework seem too subjective and unscientific.

3   Probably the most telling criticism that has been raised against Barber's theory, though, is the argument that presidential performance in office is more a function of *events and circumstances* than it is the result of personality or character (the now familiar situationist critique). The surrounding circumstances—particularly the economic situation—often seem to have the most impact in determining presidential success or failure, regardless of who the incumbent happens to be. Gerald Ford and Jimmy Carter, for instance, were unlucky enough to take office at a time when the global economy was stuck in recession, while Ronald Reagan after 1982 presided over an upturn in the fortunes of the world economy. Some presidential "success" seems to be the product of plain dumb luck, or the lack of it: FDR took office at a time when Herbert Hoover's Republicans had been discredited by the Great Depression and was able to expand presidential power in the wake of World War II.

Presidential power and the opportunities for greatness are usually greatest during times of profound crisis, and FDR was lucky enough to have two during his years in office: the Depression and World War II. Lyndon Johnson, conversely, was unlucky to come into office at a time when tough decisions about Vietnam had to be made. In previous years, Eisenhower and Kennedy had both prevaricated on the question of whether American troops ought to be sent in to protect South Vietnam from the Communist North. By 1965, a year and a half after LBJ had acceded to the presidency, that decision could be put off no longer. Johnson decided to escalate U.S. involvement in the war, but one might argue that *any* president would have done this when faced with this objective set of circumstances. The reality was that South Vietnam would fall without heavy American military assistance, and Johnson was unlucky in the sense that he was the one who had to make that hard decision. And as we have known for some years, it was a decision that ultimately destroyed his presidency.

The Decline of Psychobiography?

In recent years, it has to be said that the quality of some of the psychobiographies that have emerged has not matched the style or sophistication of, say, George and George's analysis of Wilson or Betty Glad's work on Jimmy Carter. There has in particular been a tendency to *politicize* the analysis of individual leaders. We have already cited *Bush on The Couch*, which even many on the left regard as a somewhat dubious piece of work. We will finish this chapter with a psychological analysis of Bill Clinton which most political psychologists never took very seriously when it first appeared during the 1990s. Examining this analysis will be valuable, however, because it will highlight—hopefully in very clear fashion—some of the pitfalls to which this tradition has sometimes succumbed.

The mid-1990s were a time of huge political travails for Bill Clinton. Besieged by allegations that he had lied about numerous extramarital affairs and rumors of financial wrongdoing in the Whitewater affair, Clinton's presidency was on the ropes before his political comeback at the 1996 presidential election. Writing in 1995—a decade before Frank published his book on Bush but written in a strikingly similar style—the clinical psychologist Paul Fick observed President Bill Clinton's political difficulties from afar. Like Frank, Fick had not personally examined the president himself, but he also noticed striking similarities between the president's behavior and a personality disorder he was accustomed to treating in his own practice. Clinton's behavior, Fick argued, is characteristic of many individuals who have been raised by one or more alcoholic parents:

> Here was a president who developed his own chaos . . . and yet thrived on the very chaos he had created. He openly distorted the truth, denied that he distorted the truth, yet epitomized sincerity at all times . . .

> His behaviors went beyond the typical political maneuvering; this behavior was at the core of his character. The realization struck me that instead of becoming the next president of the United States, William Jefferson Clinton could just as well have been any of the hundreds of adult children of alcoholics (ACOA) I have treated in hospital or in my outpatient office.[33]

Fick diagnoses "adult children of alcoholics" syndrome at a distance. Those who have been brought up in alcoholic families, he says, often lie, are indecisive and become self-destructive in their adult life in a way that is strikingly reminiscent of Bill Clinton's behavior both before and during his presidency. Clinton's stepfather, Roger Clinton, was a violent alcoholic who would sometimes beat Bill's mother. The future president's response, as in many cases Fick says he has treated, was to assume the "hero role": typically, one child will step up and effectively play the father or mother role (depending on which parent is absent or unreliable). But this incurs psychic costs for the hero figure; he or she harbors an underlying resentment. Moreover, children of alcoholics recreate the chaotic world they grew up in and may even thrive in it.

Problems With Psychobiographic Approaches in General

There are many objections to psychobiographical works like these, some of which may well have occurred to you as you read this chapter. One difficulty has to do with what social scientists call *falsificationism*. One of the most prominent philosophers of science who has discussed this subject is the late Karl Popper. In his book *The Poverty of Historicism* and other works, Popper railed against theories which cannot be "falsified."[34] The argument goes like this. A non-falsifiable theory is a theory which is so vague and general in nature that it is consistent with absolutely any outcome that might conceivably occur. It is often said that "a theory which explains everything explains nothing." Some students find this confusing: surely if you have a theory which can explain any outcome, you have a pretty good theory! Unfortunately, though, this is often not the case. Consider the example we are interested in here, Freudianism. Popper argued that a major problem with Freud's theories was that he regarded them as accurate regardless of whatever evidence he came across. Similarly, one objection to the aforementioned works on Clinton and Bush is that their authors seem so determined to prove the accuracy of their theories that virtually any empirical evidence "will do" to verify them. When Clinton lied, this was regarded as prime evidence for

Fick's theory, but when he appeared sincere, he was "hiding the truth from himself." Similarly, Bush's tendency to lie is attributed to his upbringing, but don't all politicians lie to some degree?

Second, there is the *problem of confirmation bias*. Just as individuals looking at a potential candidate may see what they want to see in that person and disregard his or her failings (or good points), so a researcher looking for evidence in a case study of a particular leader is prone to discard evidence that does not fit the psychological theory being proposed and retain evidence that does. In other words, there is always the temptation to *fit* evidence to a theory, rather than letting the evidence inform (and possibly invalidate) that theory. This problem is certainly not unique to psychobiography—and nor is the falsification problem—but it is a relevant concern.

Third, there is the *problem of access*. Few of us are qualified to put a president "on the couch," and no president is likely to submit to such a treatment by a political psychologist, trained or otherwise. Leaders who are not in perfect mental health are highly unlikely to admit to this shortcoming, and there is a taboo in most countries among candidates for national office against openly discussing their psychological problems. In 1972, Thomas Eagleton was forced to withdraw as George McGovern's running mate on the Democratic ticket when it became known that he had consulted a psychiatrist in the past and undergone electric shock treatments. In the absence of this kind of access, then, we are forced to examine presidents and other leaders at a distance, a practice to which all of the works discussed in this chapter—with the possible exception of that of Doris Kearns Goodwin, who had remarkably close access to Lyndon Johnson after he left office—were compelled to resort. But there are obvious problems with this. The evidence we have regarding the thoughts that were going through a leader's head at some point in the past is bound to be fragmentary, and may sometimes be unreliable or even non-existent. Perhaps no one can truly "see inside the head" of another individual, and even declassified documents may not reveal a leader's true thinking.

Last, there is the *problem of reductionism*.[35] The first part of this book highlighted the degree to which individual behavior may derive from the character of the situation the individual faces (that is, from the external rather than the inner world). Most psychobiography, on the other hand, is basically dispositionist; it takes the view that our values and beliefs directly determine behavior, or that some aspect of what is going on inside our own minds drives that behavior. But can we reduce our explanations to purely psychological variables? Doesn't the political context in which a leader is operating matter just as much as his or her own psychological characteristics? As we have seen already, this is potentially a major difficulty with approaches like that of James David Barber in his book *Presidential Character*. Simple explanations offer a psychologically comforting way of making sense of the world around us, but a theory can also be too simplistic. This may be a particular problem for all of the works discussed here that highlight the importance of childhood development in explaining later behavior. There is a good deal of research that suggests that childhood events are not nearly as important as we generally think in shaping later behavior. "Early deprivation may increase the chances of becoming a troubled adult, but it by no means guarantees it," Sally Patel notes. "In fact, social scientists find even significant maltreatment does not influence a child's development in a systematic or predictable way."[36]

Conclusion

For all of these failings—some of them more important than others, perhaps—there remains something intuitively appealing about this genre. As James William Anderson notes:

> even the harshest critics of psychological biography concede that the application of psychology to biography makes sense. Since comprehensive biographical studies inevitably include an analysis of the subject's personality, it is reasonable to carry out such analysis systematically and with psychological sophistication.[37]

Perhaps the answer (as this quote suggests) lies in developing more rigorous and generally accepted techniques for analyzing the mindsets of particular leaders or in setting aside the psychoanalytic bias that has always characterized this subfield of political psychology. Or perhaps we need to make a greater effort to dispense with the more polemical aspects of some work in this area (both Fick and Frank, from opposite ends of the political spectrum, clearly dislike their subjects intensely and each obviously has a political axe to grind). But it is surely impossible to explain the actions of leaders without some sort of analysis of their psychological characteristics, and this means that psychobiography or psychohistory is almost certainly with us to stay. You may also have asked yourself whether there are alternative ways of studying the personalities of leaders, and as it turns out, there are. The next chapter examines the ways in which some political psychologists have attempted to study the role of personality in politics more systematically.

Notes

1 Justin Frank, *Bush on the Couch: Inside The Mind of the President* (New York: HarperCollins, 2004), p.xi.

2 Gillian Butler and Freda McManus, *Psychology: A Very Short Introduction* (New York: Oxford University Press, 1998), p.5.

3 Marilyn Elias, "Freud: So Wrong and Yet So Right," *USA Today*, May 4, 2006.

4 Westen, quoted in Elias.

5 Sigmund Freud, *Leonardo da Vinci: A Memory of His Childhood* (London: Routledge, 1999). This work first appeared in 1910.

6 Sigmund Freud and William Bullitt, *Thomas Woodrow Wilson* (Boston, MA: Houghton Mifflin, 1967). The authenticity of this work has been disputed by the psychoanalyst Eric Erikson, among others.

7 Harold Lasswell, *Psychopathology and Politics* (Chicago, IL: University of Chicago Press, 1930).

8 Ibid., p.183.

9 Harold Lasswell, *Power and Personality* (New York: W.W. Norton, 1948).

10 Alexander George and Juliette George, *Woodrow Wilson and Colonel House: A Personality Study* (New York: Dover Publications, 1964). The book first appeared in 1956.

11 Ibid., p.8.

12 Ibid., p.3.

13 Ibid., p.xxii.

14 See Edwin Weinstein, James William Anderson, and Arthur Link, "Woodrow Wilson's Political Personality: A Reappraisal," *Political Science Quarterly*, 93: 585–98, 1978 and Juliette George and Alexander George, "*Woodrow Wilson and Colonel House*: A Reply to Weinstein, Anderson, and Link," *Political Science Quarterly*, 96: 641–65, 1981–82.

15 PBS American Experience, *Woodrow Wilson*. See http://www.pbs.org/wgbh/amex/wilson.

16 Doris Kearns Goodwin, *Lyndon Johnson and the American Dream* (New York: St. Martin's Press, 1976).

17 Ibid., pp.22–24.

18 Ibid., p.22.

19 Ibid., p.25.

20 Ibid.

21 Robert Dallek, *Flawed Giant: Lyndon Johnson and His Times 1961–1973* (New York: Oxford University Press, 1998), p.x.

22 Ibid., p.627.

23 Ibid., p.283.

24 Ibid., p.627.

25 Richard Goodwin, *Remembering America: A Voice From The Sixties* (New York: Perennial Books, 1989).

26 Ibid., p.393.

27 Ibid., p.394.

28 Dr. Jablow Hershman, *Power Beyond Reason: The Mental Collapse of Lyndon Johnson* (Fort Lee, NJ: Barricade Books, 2002).

29 James David Barber, *The Presidential Character: Predicting Performance in the White House*, fourth edition (New York: Pearson Longman, 2009).

30 Paul Kowert, "Where *Does* The Buck Stop? Assessing the Impact of Presidential Personality," *Political Psychology*, 17: 421–52, 1996.

31 Barber, *The Presidential Character*, p.182.

32 Elizabeth Drew, *On The Edge: The Clinton Presidency* (New York: Simon and Schuster, 1994), p.86.

33 Paul Fick, *The Dysfunctional President: Inside the Mind of Bill Clinton* (New York: Birch Lane Press, 1995), pp.11–12.

34 Karl Popper, *The Poverty of Historicism, second edition* (New York: Routledge Classics, 2002).

35 James William Anderson, "The Methodology of Psychological Biography," *Journal of Interdisciplinary History*, 11: 455–75, 1981.

36 Sally Patel, "The Perils of Putting National Leaders on the Couch," *New York Times*, June 29, 2004.

37 Anderson, "The Methodology of Psychological Biography," p.455, pp.456–60.

Suggested Further Reading

Alexander George and Juliette George, *Woodrow Wilson and Colonel House* (New York: Dover Publications, 1964).

Doris Kearns Goodwin, *Lyndon Johnson and the American Dream* (New York: Harper & Row, 1976).

Films

Woodrow Wilson (PBS American Experience): See http://www.pbs.org/wgbh/amex/wilson.

LBJ (PBS American Experience): See http://www.pbs.org/wgbh/americanexperience/films/lbj/. Particularly excellent documentary about Lyndon Johnson's life, and contains portions of interviews with Robert Dallek and Doris Kearns Goodwin. Many of the interviewees attest to LBJ's remarkable personality.

Chapter 8

Personality and Beliefs

Analyzing Personality

Even if one rejects the subjectivity of psychobiography as an approach to studying personality, we cannot leave things at that, not least because there are other ways of approaching the topic. Clearly, personality does not matter in all circumstances, and political psychologists who focus on personality factors nowadays are generally cautious in the kind of claims that they make. A leading advocate of personality-based approaches to politics, Fred Greenstein, provides us with a classic distinction which formalizes in a rather neat fashion some ideas that may have occurred to you already. In assessing whether individual leaders "matter"—in our terms, whether dispositions make a difference in shaping behavior—Greenstein distinguishes between what he calls *actor dispensability* and *action dispensability*.[1] This is a handy way of thinking about the forces that shape politics and history.

Suppose that a given actor—let's make him George W. Bush in the example—has made a decision, and let's further suppose that the decision is to invade Iraq. In order to make a difference to historical events, it is clear that the actor in question (Bush) must not be dispensable; in this case, this is another way of saying that if Bush had not been president—say if Al Gore or John Kerry had been in the Oval Office instead—the decision to invade Iraq might not have been taken (if *anyone* would have taken this decision, then the actor is dispensable). But there is a further test that must be passed if the individual is to have a material impact on history: the decision itself must matter as well. This is what Greenstein calls action dispensability. If the action (the invasion of Iraq) had no real impact on the path of history, then the action is dispensable. Most people would probably come to the opposite conclusion, though: the invasion of Iraq does seem to have had an enormous impact on a variety of outcomes, including the welfare of ordinary Iraqis, domestic politics in the United States, regional stability in the Middle East,

U.S.–European relations, and other things. If an individual leader passes both tests—actor and action dispensability—then he or she has had a material impact on events.

Though psychobiography may no longer be in vogue, the tradition of studying personality within political psychology remains a vibrant one. In the previous chapter we noted the problem of access: political leaders, whether past or present, are difficult to put "on the couch." David Winter argues that we can reliably and objectively measure the personality attributes of leaders "at a distance," however.[2] We can do this by content analysis of speeches, for instance, or by asking experts who know (or have written) about a given individual to fill out personality questionnaires as if they were the individual in question. Paul Kowert, for instance, used the "Q-sort" technique to reach a general view of the personality traits of a number of American presidents.[3] The experts he used included people who had personally known the presidents involved and those who had written about them from a historical, social scientific, or journalistic perspective.[4] This technique has the obvious benefit of generating more consensual or "intersubjective" portraits of leaders across a large range of individuals, rather than relying on a single author's psychobiographical interpretations.

Performing content analyses of the public utterances and/or writings of political leaders also allows us to rate a number of different personality attributes, such as a leader's cognitive style. Some political psychologists examine what they term a leader's *integrative complexity*, for instance.[5] Suedfeld and Tetlock explain what this term means:

> At the simple end of the continuum, decisions are characterized by anchoring around a few salient reference points; the perception of only one side of an argument or problem; the ignoring of subtle differences or similarities among other points of view; the perceiving of other participants, courses of action, and possible courses of action as being totally good or totally bad; and a search for rapid and absolute solutions in order to achieve minimization of uncertainty and ambiguity. At the complex end, we find flexible and open information processing; the use of many dimensions in an integrated, combinatorial fashion; continued search for novelty and for further information; and the ability to consider multiple points of view simultaneously, to integrate them, and then to respond flexibly to them.[6]

When one compares George W. Bush with JFK, for example, "Kennedy scored higher in integrative complexity, and had a coherent verbal manner of expression, laced with irony and wit. Bush's language, in contrast, is awkward and saturated with the earnest rhetoric of conventional morality," David Winter notes.[7]

Much of David Winter's work uses content analysis to rate political leaders according to their *motives*, with a particular emphasis on a recurring set of personality dimensions: the extent to which they seek power, affiliate themselves with others, try to achieve great things, and seek to control events. Winter and Stewart, for instance, find that the need for power and the need for affiliation are particularly important motivations for U.S. presidents.[8] As Winter notes, personality is a complex matter, and he defines it to include not only motives (how much power a leader seeks, for instance) but character *traits* as well (for instance, how introverted or extroverted a leader is). While the latter are relatively fixed, the former can vary over time, making the measurement of personality additionally tricky. Less conventionally, Winter also defines personality to include both *cognitions or beliefs* (what a leader thinks about abortion, for instance) as well as the *social or political context* in which a leader is operating ("the situation," in our terms).

Along with Winter, Margaret Hermann is perhaps the scholar who has done most to place personality at the forefront of political psychology. Although there are many of her studies we could discuss here, one of the best known is her 1980 study of forty-five political leaders.[9] Based on earlier research, Hermann notes that "aggressive leaders are high in need for power, low in conceptual complexity, distrustful of others, nationalistic, and likely to believe that they have some control over the events in which they are involved." On the other hand, the same research suggests that "conciliatory leaders are high in need for affiliation, high in conceptual complexity, trusting of others, low in nationalism, and likely to exhibit little belief in their own ability to control the events in which they are involved."[10] Hermann later built upon this earlier work to develop *leadership trait analysis*, in which personality is treated as a combination of seven traits: belief in one's ability to control events, conceptual complexity, need for power, distrust of others, ingroup bias, self-confidence, and task orientation. Like Winter's framework, this approach utilizes at-a-distance content analysis of public speeches.[11]

Stephen Dyson has also recently applied this approach to the personality of former British Prime Minister Tony Blair.[12] Examining Blair's responses to parliamentary questions on the Iraq War, Dyson investigates the role played by Blair's personality in shaping British decision-making on that issue. Utilizing Hermann's framework, "Blair has a high belief in his ability to control events, a low conceptual complexity, and a high need for power," Dyson argues.

> In the Iraq decisions, the evidence indicates broad support for the expectations as to Blair's preferences and behavior derived from his personality

profile. He demonstrated a proactive policy orientation, internal locus of control in terms of shaping events, a binary information processing and framing style, and a preference to work through tightly held processes in policy making.[13]

According to Margaret Hermann and Thomas Preston, a survey of the literature shows that five factors in particular have shaped the study of leadership style, namely "involvement in the policy-making process, willingness to tolerate conflict, a president's motivation or reason for leading, preferred strategies for managing information, and preferred strategies for resolving conflict."[14] They relate these factors to the kind of advisory system preferred by various American presidents. Preston subsequently broadened some of these insights into a more general framework for categorizing leadership style along two dimensions: the need for power and involvement in the decision-making process on the one hand, and cognitive complexity or sensitivity to context on the other. Along the first dimension, for instance, some leaders exhibit both a high need for control and also a high degree of interest and experience in the policy process. Preston terms these "directors." Others have a low need for control and a low interest ("delegators"). It is also possible to combine a high need for power with low interest ("magistrates") or a low need for power with high interest ("administrators").[15]

Preston also classifies presidents according to their degree of cognitive complexity—where complexity is treated as a relatively fixed personality characteristic—and interest in foreign policy. Here he divides leaders into "navigators," "observers," "sentinels," and "mavericks." Navigators, for instance, have a high degree of interest in foreign policy with a high need for information and a high degree of cognitive complexity. Sentinels have a high degree of interest but a low need for information and a low degree of complexity, and so on. Putting these two categorizations together then allows us to fit presidents (and potentially any kind of leader) into a richer, more detailed, and more reliable kind of "master scheme" than that devised by, say, James David Barber. Preston characterizes Bill Clinton, for instance, as a "delegator–observer"; in other words, he is a delegator along the first dimension—meaning, as the name suggests, that he relied on subordinates and experts a great deal—and an observer along the second (although his cognitive complexity was high, he had limited interest in foreign policy). George W. Bush, on the other hand, best fits Preston's "delegator–maverick" category; although similar to Clinton along the first dimension, he exhibited a low need for information and a low degree of cognitive complexity.[16]

Analyzing Belief Systems

Some students have difficulty initially conceptualizing the difference between personality and *beliefs*, and some scholars (Winter provides a prominent example) actually treat beliefs as one aspect of personality. For the sake of analytical clarity, we will treat them separately in this chapter, however. One useful way of thinking about this distinction in a way that hopefully makes it crystal clear is to contrast a pair of individuals with a similar belief system but differing personalities, or a pair with essentially the same personality traits but differing beliefs. In the first category, former British Prime Minister Gordon Brown and his predecessor provide a useful contrast. Both Blair and Brown were leading members of what became in Britain the "New Labour" movement within the British Labour Party. After suffering defeat after defeat at the polls in successive U.K. elections, "New Labour" members began to feel that the party should move to the center and even the right on many political issues. Both Blair and Brown were political moderates within the party who strongly favored this strategy. In 1994 Blair became leader of the Labour Party, continuing a policy of moving to the center that had been initiated by his predecessor, and in 1997 the party finally won the general election after eighteen years in opposition. "New Labour" won two more elections under Tony Blair until he stepped down in 2007 and was replaced by Brown as both Labour Party leader and U.K. prime minister.

What is especially interesting about this example is that while Blair and Brown shared a very similar ideological belief system, they appeared to exhibit strikingly different personalities. At the time of writing we do not have a systematic comparison of Brown's personality with that of Blair along various trait dimensions, but there is already a consensus of sorts regarding some of the differences. While Blair was outgoing and more "political" in the way that his friend Bill Clinton was, Brown seemed more quiet and reserved. While Brown projected an image of cautiousness and seemed rather "donnish," Blair was more inclined to take political risks, most notably when he went against his own political party and a substantial majority of British public opinion by backing George W. Bush's decision to invade Iraq. While Blair and Bush had enjoyed an apparently warm personal relationship, Brown made it clear from the start that he would not have the same sort of relationship with the American president.

Dissatisfaction with the somewhat vague and imprecise nature of personality itself—and the difficulties involved in tracing the processes by which particular personality attributes produce particular decisions—has led a growing number of political psychologists to turn to the content of people's beliefs or cognitions, which seem more directly related to leader decisions. Although as we have seen in the situationist part of this book there are some major exceptions to this, it seems obvious that our behavior in many situations is frequently shaped by what we believe. This is especially the case when a domestically popular leader is operating under relatively few situational constraints.

The belief system seems like a relatively simple psychological concept to deal with, because it is a term commonly used in colloquial English. Beliefs are among the most basic and central of the mental constructs we use, and yet there is little agreement as to what they are, how they should be defined, or how they should be measured. Some analysts prefer alternative labels, such as attitudes, opinions, or ideologies. Here, though, we shall adopt the definition employed by Yaacov Vertzberger in his book *The World in Their Minds*. According to Vertzberger, "the individual's belief set represents all the hypotheses and theories that he is convinced are valid at a given moment."[17] We can also distinguish between *normative* beliefs (beliefs about what ought to be) and *positive* beliefs (beliefs about what is), *central* and *peripheral* beliefs (beliefs which are unshakeable and beliefs which are less central), and *open* and *closed* belief systems (belief systems which are or are not open to change in general). As we shall discuss in a moment, we can also distinguish between what Alexander George terms *philosophical* and *instrumental* beliefs.

In politics as in other spheres of life, beliefs help determine what we see; they help us define the nature of the situation we are facing (diagnosis), as well as the kind of options or solutions we find appropriate (prognosis). From a cognitive psychological perspective, beliefs can be considered a kind of mental "short cut"; individuals develop beliefs in order to help them make sense of the world. Beliefs are one way of sorting through signals and information that would otherwise be overwhelming to our senses. In the remainder of this chapter we will look at two classic attempts to study rigorously the role beliefs play in international relations: Ole Holsti's "Belief Systems and National Images" article from 1962 and the "operational code" approach associated with Alexander George, Stephen Walker, Mark Schafer, Scott Crichlow, Stephen Dyson, and others.

Ole Holsti, Belief Systems, and National Images

One of the earliest and most famous attempts to study the belief system of a foreign policy decision-maker was Ole Holsti's analysis of John Foster Dulles.[18] Dulles was President Eisenhower's secretary of state during much of the 1950s, and he was famous for adopting an especially strident and uncompromising approach towards the Soviet Union. He would often focus on the totalitarian and atheistic aspects of Communism, frequently labeling it "Godless." According to Holsti, Dulles had a fixed or "closed" belief system, meaning that his beliefs were held so strongly that they were not susceptible to change. Holsti analyzes Dulles' speeches about the Soviet Union during the 1950s, and finds that this closed belief system had a critical effect on his perceptions of Soviet intentions. When the Soviets showed evidence of wanting a thaw in Cold War relations, Dulles interpreted this as a sign of weakness rather than a genuine overture towards peace.

Dulles subscribed to what Holsti calls "the inherent bad faith model." For instance, when the Soviets implemented a troop reduction of 1.2 million men, Dulles saw this as nothing more than a sign of Soviet decline, not a desire for détente or genuine change. Cognitive consistency theory underlies this approach, though Holsti never explicitly mentions this. As previously discussed, this theory—sometimes termed the theory of cognitive dissonance—suggests that when we are confronted with information that runs counter to our beliefs, we experience psychological discomfort and become motivated to bring our beliefs back into harmony with one another. In Dulles' case, this involved rationalizing away evidence that the Soviets desired détente or compromise. The belief that the Communists could not be trusted became problematic when Dulles was confronted with signs of Soviet "good faith," and so the secretary of state reestablished balance by asserting that any overtures revealed nothing but the erosion of the Soviet system from within.

There are potentially a few problems with Holsti's analysis. One is *methodological*. Because Dulles was deceased at the time Holsti wrote, he had no direct access to the former secretary of state and might well have been denied a personal interview in any case. To measure the content of Dulles' beliefs, then, Holsti was forced to analyze his public speeches. But are these a good measure of a leader's true beliefs? Some speeches are genuinely intended to send signals to an adversary, while others are intended primarily for a domestic audience. For instance, in June 2007 Russian President Vladimir Putin threatened in a public speech to target Western Europe with nuclear missiles if the United States went ahead with plans for a national missile defense (NMD). Was this a genuine threat stemming from a real sense of insecurity? Or was it just "saber rattling," designed to please a domestic audience that still views Russia as a major world power, deserving of respect? A second potential objection is more *theoretical*: do beliefs shape behavior, or is it the other way round? Psychologist Daryl Bem, who developed self-perception theory, argues that we often act without knowing why we are doing so, in the absence of specific beliefs. When this happens, we often construct beliefs *after the fact* in order to justify what we have done. If Bem is correct, then perhaps beliefs do not shape our behavior nearly as much as we think.

In truth, neither this second objection nor the first is very telling in this particular case; Dulles' strident speeches are widely accepted as reflecting his true views, and he almost certainly did not construct these views after the fact. More importantly, however, there are *empirical* objections nowadays that we could level at Holsti's analysis. At the time Holsti wrote, it was widely assumed that Dwight D. Eisenhower was a "do nothing" president who spent most of his time on the golf course, delegating domestic policy to his White House Chief of Staff Sherman Adams and foreign policy to Dulles. In recent years, however, revisionist research has largely debunked this unflattering image of the Eisenhower presidency. Thanks to Fred Greenstein's pioneering work in *The Hidden-Hand Presidency*, for instance, we now know that Eisenhower and not Dulles was the real architect of the administration's foreign policies. Eisenhower, he argues convincingly, deliberately gave the appearance of not playing a policy role because he wished to preserve the popularity which comes from the symbolic side of the presidency; knowing that it was his national "father figure" status that underlay his broad popularity—and that getting your hands dirty with the political side of the presidency inevitably erodes that popularity—Eisenhower deliberately cultivated the perception that he was not involved in policy-making, letting Dulles and Adams take the political heat for unpopular decisions; behind the scenes, however, he quietly orchestrated the activities of his administration using what Greenstein calls "hidden-hand" techniques.[19]

Nevertheless, there are parallels between Holsti's analysis and the observations that are often made about George H.W. Bush's relations with the Soviet Union as the Cold War came to an end. Against all expectations, Ronald Reagan had developed warm personal relations with Mikhail Gorbachev as the Cold War drew to a close, but several members of the succeeding Bush administration were suspicious of Soviet intentions, maintaining an "inherent bad faith" model similar to that of Dulles. As secretary of defense, Dick Cheney was especially skeptical about Gorbachev's intentions, as was the president himself.

Operational Code Analysis

One especially prominent approach that political psychologists have used to study political beliefs is called *operational code analysis*.[20] Nathan Leites created the basis for this approach in the early 1950s when he investigated the political beliefs of Lenin, Trotsky, and Stalin. In a classic 1969 article, Alexander George reformulated Leites' observations into two sets of questions or fundamental categories: *philosophical* beliefs and *instrumental* beliefs. The operational code, George argued, provides a "set of general beliefs about fundamental issues of history as central questions as these bear, in turn, on the problem of action":[21]

1 Philosophical Beliefs

- What is the "essential" nature of political life? Is the political universe essentially one of harmony or conflict? What is the fundamental character of one's political opponents?
- What are the prospects for the eventual realization of one's fundamental political values and aspirations? Can one be optimistic, or must one be pessimistic on this score?
- Is the political future predictable? In what sense and to what extent?
- How much control or mastery can one have over historical development?
- What is one's role in moving and shaping history in the desired direction?
- What is the role of "chance" in human affairs?

2 Instrumental Beliefs

- What is the best approach for selecting goals or objectives for political action?
- How are the goals of action pursued most effectively?
- How are the risks of political action calculated, controlled, and accepted?
- What is the best "timing" of action to advance one's interests?
- What is the utility and role of different means for advancing one's interests?

The first set of beliefs has to do with one's general philosophy about the nature of political life, while the second deals with more "practical" questions such as how one goes about implementing one's chosen political objectives. As you can probably see from a brief perusal of the questions, a leader's philosophical beliefs have to do with the answers which animated the classic political thinkers such as Thomas Hobbes and John Locke. While Hobbes had an exceptionally dark view of human nature, Locke held a rather more optimistic view. While Locke saw the world as a harmonious place, Hobbes famously held the opinion that if man were freed from the order-providing shackles of government, life would be "solitary, poor, nasty, brutish and short." Contrasting with these fundamental "*what* is the political world like?" questions, on the other hand, are questions having to do with "*how* should we achieve our goals?" These are our instrumental beliefs.

As Scott Crichlow suggests, the operational code approach is fundamentally dispositionist in the sense that it stresses the ways in which leaders *differ* in their reactions to the *same* political environment. If situation were everything, we would not need to bother studying a leader's beliefs, because these would not add anything much to the explanation (they would be *epiphenomenal*, to use the social scientific phrase). But as Crichlow notes, "operational code analysis provides a means of testing a leader's fundamental predispositions toward political action," and hence of understanding the sources of the differing behaviors of leaders when placed in similar situations.[22] George stresses that there are some circumstances where situation or environment would in effect "force a leader's hand," but in general he maintains that dispositional beliefs could be expected to shape behavior in many circumstances.[23]

Let's consider Lyndon Johnson and how he handled the problem of Vietnam as one example of some philosophical and instrumental beliefs. Addressing just a few of the questions above, one can reliably say that:

- Johnson had little foreign policy experience, so regarding Vietnam he relied on some simple but fundamental beliefs.
- For LBJ the essential nature of political life was conflictual, a war of good versus evil (Hobbesian view).
- Johnson believed that he could control events in Vietnam.
- Domestically and internationally, he steered a "middle course" that was enough to assuage hawks at home but not enough to provoke China into intervening in the war.
- His graduated bombing strategy allowed him to monitor (and to some extent control) risks.
- Instrumentally, he believed in bargaining backed up by threats (this had served him well in the U.S. Senate, but tragically the technique did not work well with his Communist adversary, Ho Chi Minh).[24]

Having laid out the basic form of operational code analysis, George did not conduct many actual operational code analyses himself, but left it to his followers to apply the theory empirically. One of the most prolific of these has been Stephen Walker, who has probably conducted more of these analyses than anyone else during their academic career. One of the best known of his articles is an operational code analysis of former National Security Adviser and Secretary of State Henry Kissinger. Examining Kissinger's work as a political scientist prior to joining the Nixon administration in 1969, Walker demonstrates a strong correlation—with only a couple of deviations—between Kissinger's writings as an academic and his actual behavior in office, albeit on one important issue (policy-making with regard to Vietnam between 1969 and 1973). Walker concludes:

> In spite of the exigencies of bureaucratic politics and alliance diplomacy, plus the personal intervention of President Nixon at key points, Kissinger dominated the conduct of the American foreign policy that terminated

U.S. involvement in the Vietnam War. He acted according to the instrumental principles of his operational code.[25]

Operational code analyses have now been published for a huge variety of leaders since the 1970s, and a new generation of scholars has adopted sophisticated computational techniques designed to tease out the ways in which a particular individual would answer the questions posed by the code. Recent work, moreover, has taken operational code analysis in new and interesting directions. Scott Crichlow, for instance, has used this approach to examine the ways in which leadership beliefs change over time.[26] Charting the operational codes of Israeli leaders Yitzhak Rabin and Shimon Peres, he shows how the basic philosophical views of both leaders became less conflictual between the 1970s and 1990s. Both men shared a similar view of their political environment in the 1970s, and these views changed in a similar direction over time. Crichlow finds that:

> both leaders diagnosed their political universe in the 1990s differently than they had in the 1970s. In the earlier decade they saw a conflictual environment in which they had little chance of achieving their basic political goals. In the 1990s they saw a more unpredictable political universe, balanced between cooperative and conflictual forces.[27]

On the other hand, the analysis shows that in both periods Rabin "was clearly predisposed to acting in a cooperative manner."[28] Crichlow also adds to George's original conception of the operational code by producing a typology of typical codes, ranging from out-and-out idealists to pragmatists to realists, with various categories in between.[29]

In a comparative analysis of the operational codes of Tony Blair and Bill Clinton, Mark Schafer and Stephen Walker examine whether beliefs in the democratic peace—the popular thesis that democracies do not fight one another, but may be especially prone to go to war with non-democracies—vary across political leaders within democracies. The theory is usually proposed on a purely *cultural* level, suggesting that all politicians within a democracy simply internalize the democratic peace and thus that we can expect few if any meaningful differences among individuals *within* a democratic state.[30] But is this the case? Schafer and Walker find that in some ways there are. For instance, they discover that while both Blair and Clinton hold highly positive views of democracies and negative views of non-democracies, they vary in the extent to which they believe that they can control the latter; Clinton scores high on control while Blair does not.[31] On the instrumental side, Clinton's tactics towards non-democracies are also more cooperative than Blair's. Blair has a stronger belief than Clinton in his own ability to control historical events, and when dealing with non-democracies "Blair is less cooperative, both strategically and tactically, than Clinton, having a propensity to use more threats in this domain," Schafer and Walker find.[32]

Stephen Dyson has made especially fruitful use of this approach as well, illustrating the value of operational code analysis as a predictive device.[33] He argues that operational code analysis is especially useful for understanding "new actors" about whom we know little, "an executive or other important figure who has recently come to our attention, without the kind of long-standing and visible record of decision-making and public behavior which would in most circumstances form the basis for a profile."[34] As Dyson puts it in his analysis of Soviet President Vladmir Putin:

> Putin's Operational Code suggests he will, chameleon-like, imitate his environment. One could not expect Putin to act in a norm-bound manner when those with which he is engaged do not. Putin is unlikely to "stick to the rules" in the face of deviation by another . . . Overall, the policy-maker can feel confident that carefully constructed initiatives will not be dismissed out of hand, and that Putin is unlikely to make rash, impulsive or emotional gestures . . . However, the policymaker can feel warned that Putin will reciprocate "bad" as well as "good" behavior, and that a breakdown in cooperation will likely be quite bitter and long-lived.[35]

Prediction is one of the things that political scientists do *least* well, but Dyson's remarks—published originally in 2001—seem quite prescient in the light of the recent deterioration in U.S.–Russian relations over issues like national missile defense and NATO expansion.

One potential weakness of the operational code approach is its frequent reliance on *speeches* and other public communications. While memoirs and other sources have been used to construct operational codes as well (for instance in the Kissinger study noted earlier), there are obvious problems with relying on public utterances as "data," since these do not simply reflect the beliefs of the communicator but may be constructed with certain domestic and/or international audiences in mind, as already noted. In 2007, for instance, Iran's President Ahmadinejad made a series of belligerent-sounding speeches, including one in which he directly threatened Israel. Were these genuinely intended for U.S. or Western consumption, or were they intended to shore up what many believed was the Iranian leader's declining support at home? Speeches are also infrequently penned by leaders themselves. Nevertheless, as Crichlow notes, although there may be instances where a speech is obviously tailored to some audience or another, it is rare indeed for a speech to depart markedly from a leader's core convictions, and equally rare for a speechwriter to pen material which runs counter to a leader's beliefs.[36] The dangers of using pre-prepared speeches can also be ameliorated by using only a leader's "off the cuff" remarks. Mark Shafer and Scott Crichlow discover some differences between the content of Bill Clinton's prepared and unprepared remarks, for instance, and they suggest that the latter might be most reliable for operational code analyses.[37]

Conclusion

Another weakness may be that operational code analysis developed before the "cognitive revolution" in psychology—a development we shall discuss in the next chapter—and thus was originally informed by theories (such as cognitive consistency theory) that have fallen somewhat out of vogue.[38] The operational code framework consequently tells us little about the cognitive sources of beliefs, for instance. Again, however, this may not be a genuine weakness in the sense that today's operational code scholars—trained during or after the period in which cognitive and affective theories became popular in political psychology—do self-consciously integrate this older body of theorizing with newer developments in the field. Walker, for instance, explicitly views modern operational code analysis as incorporating insights from cognitive and affective theories.[39] This is also true of the work of Shafer, Crichlow, and Dyson already cited. Of course, we have not yet given the reader a sense of what we mean by "cognitive and affective theories"; that will be the task of Chapter 9.

Notes

1 Fred Greenstein, "The Impact of Personality on Politics: An Attempt to Clear Away The Underbrush," *American Political Science Review*, 61: 629–41, 1967.

2 David Winter, "Things I've Learned About Personality From Studying Political Leaders At A Distance," *Journal of Personality*, 73: 557–84, 2005. See also Mark Schafer, "Issues in Assessing Psychological Characteristics at a Distance," *Political Psychology*, 21: 511–27, 2000.

3 Paul Kowert, "Where *Does* The Buck Stop? Assessing the Impact of Presidential Personality," *Political Psychology*, 17: 421–52, 1996.

4 Ibid., pp.424–27. The Q-sort approach is so called because it requires experts, or "judges" as Kowert terms them, to sort through a pack of cards. Each card has a personality trait on it, and the expert selects the cards that best describe the personality of the individual leader in question.

5 Peter Suedfeld and Philip Tetlock, "Integrative Complexity of Communications in International Crises," *Journal of Conflict Resolution*, 21: 169–84, 1977. Suedfeld's work on this topic since the 1960s is vast, but of his more recent applications of

the concept see for instance "President Clinton's Policy Dilemmas: A Cognitive Analysis," *Political Psychology*, 15: 337–49, 1994.

6 Ibid., p.172. Cognitive complexity has also been linked to the sophistication and kind of historical analogies used by leaders. See Stephen Dyson and Thomas Preston, "Individual Characteristics of Political Leaders and the Use of Analogy in Foreign Policy Decision Making," *Political Psychology*, 27: 265–88, 2006.

7 Winter, "Things I've Learned About Personality From Studying Political Leaders At A Distance," p.570.

8 David Winter and Abigail Stewart, "Content Analysis as a Method of Studying Political Leaders," in Margaret Hermann (ed.), *A Psychological Examination of Political Leaders* (New York: Free Press, 1977).

9 Margaret Hermann, "Explaining Foreign Policy Behavior Using the Personal Characteristics of Political Leaders," *International Studies Quarterly*, 24: 7–46, 1980.

10 Ibid., p.8.

11 Margaret Hermann, "Assessing Leadership Style: Trait Analysis," in Jerrold Post (ed.), *The Psychological Assessment of Political Leaders* (Ann Arbor, MI: University of Michigan Press, 2003).

12 Stephen Dyson, "Personality and Foreign Policy: Tony Blair's Iraq Decisions," *Foreign Policy Analysis*, 2: 289–306, 2006.

13 Ibid., p.303.

14 Margaret Hermann and Thomas Preston, "Presidents, Advisers, and Foreign Policy: The Effect of Leadership Style on Executive Arrangements," *Political Psychology*, 15: 75–96, 1994, p.81.

15 Thomas Preston, *The President and His Inner Circle: Leadership Style and the Advisory Process in Foreign Affairs* (New York: Columbia University Press, 2001), pp.16–17.

16 Ibid., pp.22–23.

17 Yaacov Vertzberger, *The World in Their Minds: Information Processing, Cognition, and Perception in Foreign Policy Decisionmaking* (Stanford, CA: Stanford University Press, 1990), p.114.

18 This article, originally published in *The Journal of Conflict Resolution* in 1962, was republished as Ole Holsti, "The Belief System and National Images: A Case Study," in James Rosenau (ed.), *International Politics and Foreign Policy*, second edition (New York: Free Press, 1969).

19 Fred Greenstein, *The Hidden-Hand Presidency: Eisenhower As Leader* (New York: Basic Books, 1982).

20 For an excellent edited volume on this topic featuring many of the scholars who utilize this technique, see Mark Schafer and Stephen Walker (eds.), *Beliefs and Leadership in World Politics: Methods and Applications of Operational Code Analysis* (New York: Palgrave, 2006).

21 Alexander George, "The 'Operational Code': A Neglected Approach to the Study of Political Leaders and Decision Making," *International Studies Quarterly*, 13: 190–222, 1969, p.191. See also, for instance, Alexander George, "The Causal Nexus Between Cognitive Beliefs and Decision Making Behavior: The 'Operational Code' Belief System," in Lawrence Falkowski (ed.), *Psychological Models in International Politics* (Boulder, CO: Westview Press, 1979).

22 Scott Crichlow, "Idealism or Pragmatism? An Operational Code Analysis of Yitzhak Rabin and Shimon Peres," *Political Psychology*, 19: 683–706, 1998, p.684.

23 George, "The Causal Nexus Between Cognitive Beliefs and Decision Making Behavior," p.104. On this point see also Stephen Walker, "The Evolution of Operational Code Analysis," *Political Psychology*, 11: 403–18, 1990, pp.408–9.

24 Vertzberger, *The World In Their Minds*, pp.114–15. See also Stephen Walker and Mark Schafer, "The Political Universe of Lyndon B. Johnson and His Advisors: Diagnostic and Strategic Propensities in Their Operational Codes," *Political Psychology*, 21: 529–43, 2000.

25 Stephen Walker, "The Interface Between Beliefs and Behavior: Henry Kissinger's Operational Code and the Vietnam War," *Journal of Conflict Resolution*, 21: 129–68, 1977, p.147.

26 Crichlow, "Idealism or Pragmatism?"

27 Ibid., p.695.

28 Ibid., p.698.

29 Ibid., p.701.

30 Mark Schafer and Stephen Walker, "Democratic Leaders and the Democratic Peace: The Operational Codes of Tony Blair and Bill Clinton," *International Studies Quarterly*, 50: 561–83, 2006.

31 Ibid., p.573.

32 Ibid., p.575.

33 Stephen Dyson, "Drawing Policy Implications from the 'Operational Code' of a 'New' Political Actor: Russian President Vladimir Putin," *Policy Sciences*, 34: 329–46, 2001.

34 Ibid., p.329.

35 Ibid., p.344.

36 Crichlow "Idealism or pragmatism?", pp.689–90.

37 Mark Shafer and Scott Crichlow, "Bill Clinton's Operational Code: Assessing Source Material Bias," *Political Psychology*, 21: 559–71, 2000.

38 Walker, "The Evolution of Operational Code Analysis," p.412.

39 Ibid., p.416.

Suggested Further Reading

Stephen Dyson, *The Blair Identity: Leadership and Foreign Policy* (Manchester: Manchester University Press, 2009).

Alexander George, "The 'Operational Code': A Neglected Approach to the Study of Political Leaders and Decision Making," *International Studies Quarterly*, 13: 190–222, 1969.

Ole Holsti, "The Belief System and National Images: A Case Study," in James Rosenau (ed.), *International Politics and Foreign Policy*, second edition (New York: Free Press, 1969).

Film

Blair: The Inside Story (BBC, 2007). Three-part documentary available on YouTube.

Chapter 9

Cognition

It should be fairly apparent to the reader why personality- and belief-based theories "fit" under the general heading of dispositionism rather than situationism; if all individuals tend to behave the same way when placed in the same objective situation, there would be little point in studying the mindsets of particular individuals. If the situationists are correct, then there is little to be gained by looking "inside people's heads." According to them, we can get all the necessary information about people's behavior by specifying the nature of the situation the individual faces, not by considering his or her dispositions. Again, however, dispositionists assume that individuals *vary* in their responses to situations, and they ask what specific factors seem to produce this variation. Since the 1980s, moreover, political psychologists working in fields as diverse as foreign policy decision-making and voting behavior have increasingly sought to explain these individual differences by examining the knowledge structures or cognitive architecture inside our heads.

During the 1970s, psychology underwent what is often referred to as the "cognitive revolution." The study of cognition (which loosely means thought processes or knowledge, from the Latin term *cognoscere*, "to know") has come to dominate the discipline ever since. How do we make decisions? How do we solve problems? What mental processes shape our reasoning? How do we process information? How do we acquire knowledge? How do we access that knowledge when it is required? What factors shape our perceptions of the world? How do we learn? The study of questions like these involves an analysis of cognitive processes and an appreciation of the ways in which the human mind works. While modern psychology has retained Freud's idea that many of our mental processes are unconscious ones—as we shall see later on in this chapter, we often use various cognitive "short cuts" almost without knowing we are doing so—today's cognitive psychology represents a far cry from the psychoanalytic ideas we began with. And since political psychology borrows heavily from its mother discipline, this has meant that many of the former's proponents have become preoccupied with *political* cognition, the ways in which we think and reason politically.[1]

Many of the assumptions of the model we described in Chapter 1 as *Homo psychologicus* are directly derived from cognitive psychology and the broader field of what has become known as cognitive science. This is broader in the sense that while it essentially covers the same topic matter as cognitive psychology, it draws upon linguistics, computer science, neuroscience, philosophy, and other disciplines as well. David Green and his colleagues define cognitive science as:

> the interdisciplinary scientific study of the mind . . . it seeks to understand how the mind works in terms of processes operating on representations. Mind, and hence the basis of intelligent action in the world, is viewed in terms of computations or information-processes.[2]

The human mind is an incredible tool, and the study of artificial intelligence (AI) has not yet come close to creating computer programs that replicate the range of tasks it performs. As Steven Pinker notes, computers and robots lack what humans call intuition or "common sense." While the human mind is usually able to capture this faculty with ease, that attribute is exceptionally difficult (if not impossible) to program into the "mind" of a computer. The following example illustrates the flavor of the difficulty. Suppose that a female friend of yours has just moved into town. She is throwing a housewarming party and is unattached, but she has a problem: the only people she knows here are other ladies, so she asks you to invite some bachelors to the party. You are really busy at work, so you give your robot "Robbie" the task of inviting the male guests. At the workshop Robbie was programmed with the standard information that a bachelor is an adult male who is not married, and he uses this definition to send out invitations from a list of your known friends and acquaintances. To your jaw-dropping surprise, you discover at the party that Robbie has invited the following:

Guest #1:	Arthur, who has been living happily with Alice for the last five years. They have a two-year-old daughter but have never officially married.
Guest #2:	Charlie is seventeen years old. He lives at home with his parents and is still in high school.
Guests #3 and #4:	Eli and Edgar are homosexual lovers who have been living together for many years.
Guest #5:	Faisal is allowed by the law of his native Abu Dhabi to have three wives. He currently has two and is interested in meeting another potential wife.

Guest #6:   Father Gregory is the bishop of the Catholic Cathedral at Groton Upon Thames.[3]

Computers, of course, do some things far better than we do—given the limitations of human memory, computers are generally far better at data storage and retrieval, for instance. But another example that (indirectly) suggests the comparative brilliance of the human mind is John Searle's Chinese Room thought experiment, which directly challenges the notion that computers can "think" like humans do.[4] Searle's argument is designed to debunk *computationalism*, or the view proposed by some hard-line advocates of AI—popularized in movies like *2001: A Space Odyssey* and *Demon Seed*—that computers are capable of attaining genuine understanding or developing what we often call "consciousness."

Searle asks us to imagine a computer that looks as if it understands Chinese. When a native Chinese speaker inputs a question into the computer, it answers back correctly in Chinese. In fact, it is so good that it seems to our Chinese speaker that he or she is actually talking to another Chinese person. Searle asks us to imagine, however, that we ourselves are inside the computer or "Chinese Room." I personally don't speak a word of Chinese, and probably most of you don't either (if you do, just imagine that the computer is speaking another language instead that you *don't* know). However, what I do when I receive a question in Chinese is simply to consult a rule book. That tells me that when I get a certain set of Chinese characters, I should respond with another set. And so I mindlessly produce this string of characters in response. I have no idea what they mean, just as a computer has no idea what the English symbols being keyed into it mean. But to the Chinese person on the outside, it still looks just like the computer understands Chinese and is genuinely conversing as a human being would. Searle's broader point is of course that computers simply produce sets of rules and syntactic symbols with which we have programmed them, but they are not capable of genuine understanding. No matter how good or how convincing our attempts to mimic human behavior in artificial form, computers or robots will probably never be able to do the things that the human mind is capable of.

Given the sheer complexity of the human brain—and the fact that our study of it is still in its infancy—there are naturally plenty of differences in the ways that cognitive scientists approach the questions about information-processing posed at the beginning of this chapter. Here, however, we shall focus on two theories that have had a particular impact on political psychology in recent years: *attribution theory* (the "naive scientist") and *schema theory* (the "cognitive miser"), after first setting the context with a discussion of cognitive consistency theory. Finally, we will conclude this chapter by examining the related topic of analogical reasoning. As we shall see, the topics of attributions, schemas, scripts, and analogies are so closely related or interconnected that theories based upon them are far more complementary than they are competitive.

Cognitive Consistency Theory

Nowadays, the kind of behaviorism discussed in Chapter 3 has lost most of its adherents within mainstream psychology. This is largely a result of failures like the one noted above, but it is also the product of a turn towards cognition and the inner workings of the mind which reasserted itself at about the same time. Cognitive consistency theory (mentioned in Chapter 2, where we told the story of "Marion Keech") became especially popular in the 1950s and 1960s. When people act in ways contrary to their own beliefs, for instance, this theory suggests that they experience a state of psychological discomfort, as long as the mismatch between behavior and beliefs is perceived. The assumption here is that people do not like to act in ways that violate their own beliefs, dislike holding beliefs that are incompatible with one another, and avoid information or situations that cause such incompatibilities to become clear. Leon Festinger called this mismatch a state of *cognitive dissonance*.[5] A somewhat similar theory of cognitive "balance" was previously developed by Fritz Heider.[6] Strong party identifiers, for instance, may find themselves at odds with their party on a key issue such as abortion or civil rights, or may disapprove of the presidential or vice-presidential candidate their party has nominated. The theory assumes that in the face of such dissonance, the voter becomes strongly motivated to bring things back into balance (what Festinger called "consonance"). This could be done by rationalizing away the issue disagreement or candidate choice as unimportant ("the Civil Rights Act won't change things around here," "Joe Biden will never be president anyway") or perhaps by adding some extra belief which reduces the dissonance. Finally, one could switch one's party allegiance altogether and so bring one's voting behavior more into line with one's choice of party, though many models of voting suggest that this is unlikely for strong party identifiers.

Why did the cognitive consistency theory gradually fall out of favor? Susan Fiske and Shelley Taylor offer some reasons:

> Consistency theories ceased to dominate the field, ironically, as they pro-
> liferated, partly because the variants on a theme became indistinguishable.
> Moreover, it was difficult to predict what a person would perceive as
> inconsistent and to what degree, and which route to resolving incon-
> sistency a person would take. Finally, people do in fact tolerate a fair

amount of inconsistency, so the motivation to avoid it—as an overriding principle—was called into doubt.[7]

In these approaches, cognition was also subservient to motivational processes; people would change their beliefs or behavior only when motivated to do so by powerful negative emotional states. As noted above, advocates of this approach conceded that it was difficult to say in advance precisely how a given individual would seek to reduce dissonance, though in politics many individuals seemed to have a high tolerance for inconsistent beliefs. When deciding how to vote, for instance, advocates of the *party identification model* (examined in Chapter 12—in which voting is regarded as an almost automatic or "kneejerk" process, based on long-term party loyalties rather than consideration of the issues or candidates) argued that most voters simply ignored or downplayed manifest differences between their own issue positions and those of their party. In 2008, for instance, the neoconservative voters and members of the Christian Right disapproved of the past issue positions taken by their own party's nominee, John McCain; he had dismissed some members of the neoconservative movement as "agents of intolerance," for instance. Faced with this kind of scenario, however, the party identification approach predicted that most conservative Republicans would simply "hold their noses" in the voting booth and vote for McCain anyway, ignoring the presence of cognitive dissonance. The same thing happened in 2012, when conservatives took a long time to warm to their presidential candidate Mitt Romney, not least because he had been a relatively "liberal" Governor of Massachusetts some years before and had even pushed through a prototypical version of "Obamacare" there. But if dissonance is such a powerful force, why do people so seldom change their beliefs or electoral behavior?

As a result of growing dissatisfaction with the cognitive consistency model, during the 1970s both cognitive and social psychologists increasingly began to turn to two newer approaches in particular: *attribution theory* and *schema theory*.

Attribution Theory

Rather than viewing human beings as "consistency seekers," attribution theory sees individuals as "naive scientists" or problem-solvers. Instead of being motivated to constantly restore balance in their own beliefs or between those beliefs and their own behavior, attribution theory suggests that human beings are mainly concerned to *uncover the causes* of their own behavior and that of others. People are constantly looking for causes and effects—"why did this happen?"—albeit in a far less sophisticated manner than a scientist working in a laboratory would. They are continually looking to make sense of the world around them, and they draw upon a range of assumptions about themselves and others in doing so. Harold Kelley, Richard Nisbett, and Lee Ross have all been especially influential in developing this approach to cognition.[8]

Attribution theory becomes particularly interesting to us in terms of the distinction we have been drawing between situationism and dispositionism, in part because it is advocates of that theory who have popularized the distinction. According to this approach, we sometimes attribute the causes of someone's behavior to the situation they are in, while at other times we attribute that behavior to the person's internal dispositions. Unfortunately, we frequently make quite substantial errors and mistakes when we try to do this. As Fiske and Taylor note, people are not always very careful when they make attributions. "On an everyday basis, people often make attributions in a relatively thoughtless fashion. The cognitive system is limited in capacity, so people take short cuts."[9]

One particularly notable kind of error with potentially major political consequences is called *the fundamental attribution error*. When we are explaining our own actions, we very often use situational attributions, and in fact we often overestimate the extent to which our actions are the result of the situation. On the other hand, when asked to explain why someone else acted as they did, we often make the opposite kind of mistake: we underestimate the extent to which the situation mattered (and hence overestimate the importance of that person's dispositions). How might this be of interest to students of politics? As the political psychologist and expert on foreign policy decision-making Deborah Welch Larson puts it in her classic study of the birth of Cold War containment:

> Policymakers tend to infer that the actions of their own state were compelled by circumstances, even while they attribute the behavior of other states to the fundamental "character" of the nation or its leaders. Applied to the problem of explaining the change in U.S. foreign policymakers' orientation toward the Soviet Union, attribution theory would suggest that Washington officials were too willing to impute ideological, expansionist motives to Soviet actions that could just as plausibly reflect security calculations similar to those that prompted analogous policies pursued by the United States.[10]

That some policy-makers fall into the trap of making such false attributions does not mean that we are all condemned to do so. During the Cuban missile crisis, for instance, attribution judgments became a matter of life and death.

"Why have the Soviets placed missiles in Cuba?" members of the ExComm asked themselves almost immediately in those first, tense meetings. "What are their intentions?" Air Force General Curtis LeMay appears to have attributed dark dispositionist motives to the Soviet leadership, while others like Robert McNamara, Ambassador Tommy Thompson, and President Kennedy seem to have been more attuned to the possibility that Khrushchev's actions might have been compelled or encouraged by situationist forces. Both the Americans and the Soviets recognized the possibility, moreover, that situationist forces might take over the process and cause the outbreak of an inadvertent war. The exercise of empathy—placing ourselves in the shoes of our adversary—is a useful antidote to the kind of attributional errors that naive scientists often make in international relations, but there are dangers and biases attached to this as well. As Yaacov Vertzberger notes, we may also have a special tendency to invoke dispositionist attributions in others when we have a strongly negative attitude towards them. "Dislike tends to evoke dispositional explanations for undesirable actions by others, while empathy biases explanations of such behavior toward situational attribution," Vertzberger points out.[11]

Supporters of attribution theory argue that two short cuts or heuristic devices are especially important in human decision-making and reasoning: the *representativeness heuristic* and the *availability heuristic*. As Samuel Popkin notes, "representativeness is a heuristic, a rule of thumb, for judging the likelihood that a person will be of a particular kind by how similar he is to the stereotype of that kind of person."[12] Popkin argues that this is how we make assessments of candidates in presidential primaries, about whom most of us know little at first. This heuristic is also used to estimate the likelihood of something occurring by assessing whether it "fits" a particular category. Perceived similarity is what matters here, but one major problem—what makes the science "naive"—is that people usually ignore base information or *statistical* probabilities when making these kind of assessments. When asked to estimate the likelihood that Saddam Hussein is "another Hitler," for instance, most people attempt to match apparent similarities between the two (each was an expansionist, repressive domestically, and so on). What most people fail to do is to look at the statistical probability that "Hussein is a Hitler" (as a scientist presumably would). Arguably, there have been very few genuinely Hitler-like leaders in recent history, but this is not how most people estimate probability.

When people use the *availability* heuristic, on the other hand, they estimate the likelihood of something based on how cognitively available it is to them. Often something is available in our memories simply because it happened recently or because it constituted a very vivid experience that we're unlikely to forget. World War II and Vietnam are especially vivid for makers of U.S. foreign policy, and new situations tend to be compared disproportionately to these two events. This too is clearly "unscientific" because it ignores statistical likelihood. Viewing something as likely to happen simply because something similar happened recently or you were especially influenced by some vividly memorable event is obviously a poor way of estimating probability.

Schema Theory

As John Sullivan and his colleagues note, the actual term "schema" has gone somewhat out of fashion within political psychology since the 1990s, especially in the study of mass behavior. This is in part due to the claims made by some political psychologists that it added little to their understanding of existing political concepts,[13] but it is probably more a product of the fact that most scholars have accepted the basic idea that we have such knowledge structures in our heads and have now become more interested in *how* these affect political behavior. "While schema theory itself may be out of vogue, the ideas that were once packaged together under that appellation are still alive and well, only refashioned in more innocuous terminology such as 'cognitive representations' or cognitive 'categories' or stereotypes," Rahn, Sullivan, and Rudolph point out.[14] Cognitive psychologists also use the term "schema" less than they did, usually preferring nowadays to talk of "associationist networks" or "the computational theory of the mind." But this is really a matter of labels rather than substance. The term "schema" is broadly familiar to most political psychologists, and we will use the label here because it neatly ties together a large amount of work that has been done in a variety of areas across the elite–mass divide. Indeed, this is probably the one theory (or rather body of theories) that has brought together under a single tent those who study international relations from a cognitive perspective and those who focus on mass behaviors such as voting.[15]

In common with the attribution theory, schema theory assumes that human beings possess limited cognitive capacities, and is in many ways compatible with the former. We are bombarded every day with information. Rather than assuming that individuals search for cause and effect patterns or resemble naive scientists, schema theory treats human beings as categorizers or labelers. To cope with information overload, we engage in mental economics; we are "cognitive misers." Rather than treating each piece of new information *sui generis* or on its own merits, we assimilate knowledge into pre-existing categories (usually known as schemas or scripts). This is cognitively efficient, and relatively easy to do.[16]

The term "schema" is often used rather more loosely than it should be, and it has been given a variety of definitions. As defined here, though, a schema is essentially a kind of stereotype stored in memory that provides information on the *typical* features of an object, event, or person. Schemas are *generic* collections of knowledge; general concepts, rules, lessons, and stereotypes stored in memory. They go beyond any one example to provide information on what is *usually* the case, and we use such schemas both to categorize newly encountered information and to make inferences that go beyond the information given. We can also think of a schema as a mental box containing typical or "default values" associated with a thing we are familiar with. Suppose I were to present you with the following very simple puzzle: I'm thinking of "a thing." This thing has fur. It has a tail. It has paws. You take it for walks.

Once we are given the last piece of information, the thing I am talking about becomes obvious. But *why* is it obvious? I still haven't told you what the thing is, but we all somehow know I am talking about a dog. When you think about it, that's a rather amazing feat of collective cognitive activity, and schema theory would explain it this way. First of all, you absorbed each piece of information ("the thing has fur," and so on). Then you compared these attributes to the default values stored in your memory that correspond to various schemas. You then matched these to the generic category "dog" and made a conclusion about what I was thinking of. In other words, you used the information both to *categorize* and to *go beyond* the information actually given. Notice, though, that the use of schemas is fraught with potential error, precisely because it does involve making inferences that exceed the data you have been given. Until I mentioned the last attribute—"you take it for walks"—I *could* have been talking about a cat, but no one in their right mind takes the family cat for a walk. Without that last piece of information, you could easily have erroneously slotted the attributes not only into the schema for a cat, but the schemas for any number of our furry friends.

As with false attributions, this does not mean that we are necessarily "trapped" by schemas or bound to make errors when we use them, but that is the drawback inherent in any cognitive short cut. Nor are we bound to ignore the differences between a prototypical example and an actual one. Julian Hochberg, for instance, argues that "any individual object is recognized first by identifying its schema, and then by noting a small number of features that identify the object more specifically and set it off from other examples of the schema to which it belongs."[17] But the fact that schemas are devices of mental economy does mean that they can mislead us on occasion, and in politics this can have serious consequences.

How *is* all of this relevant to politics? It is relevant because elite decision-makers (and voters too) must almost always make decisions with only incomplete information about the situation at hand. Political actors can and do make incorrect inferences by fitting individuals or events into the *wrong* categories or schemas based on purely superficial similarities. Again, Deborah Welch Larson provides us with a classic example. Thomas Pendergast was Harry Truman's old party boss and mentor in Missouri. In those days, the party bosses essentially ran the political system, especially at the local level, and to rise to prominence at the national level you first had to move through various levels of patronage. Truman never forgot the impact Pendergast had had on his career, and he became a powerful role model for the future president. It was from Pendergast that Truman learned the importance of keeping one's word, and what he called the "code of the politician": if you make a promise, always keep your word.[18]

It just so happened that the Soviet leader Joseph Stalin resembled Pendergast and reminded Truman very much of his old mentor. Because of this superficial resemblance, moreover, Truman initially reacted warmly towards the Soviet leader. In 1946 the two men met for the first time, and Truman was greatly impressed by Stalin:

> His meeting with Stalin reinforced Truman's belief that the Russian dictator was like Boss Pendergast. Truman remarked admiringly to an aide: "Stalin is as near like Tom Pendergast as any man I know." Truman went beyond Stalin's superficial resemblance to Pendergast to infer that the Russian shared personality characteristics with the Missouri boss. Truman told his staff that "Stalin was one, who, if he said something one time, would say the same thing the next time . . . he could be depended upon." Truman inferred that Stalin, like Pendergast, could be trusted to keep his word. "I got the impression Stalin would stand by his agreements and also that he had a Politburo on his hands like the 80th Congress," Truman recalled.[19]

While this cognitive error had no effects over the longer term once Stalin had proved that he could not be trusted to deliver on his promises, in the short term it led Truman astray by causing him to trust the Soviet leader far more than he should have, and Truman even continued to view Stalin somewhat positively after he realized that the latter had betrayed him.[20]

Even more commonplace examples can be drawn from voting behavior. We will deal with this topic in more detail in Chapter 12, but for now we will merely note that Wendy Rahn's argument that many people rely on party or ideological identification as a kind of cognitive short cut captures a perspective that has proven very popular among scholars of electoral choice.

When people have specific information about a candidate at an election, they are perfectly capable of attending to that information and weighing its value in shaping their vote, Rahn finds. However, when voters have *both* particular information and party stereotypes at their disposal:

> they prefer to rely on heuristic-based processing. They neglect policy information in reaching evaluations; they use the label rather than policy attributes in drawing inferences; and they are perceptually less responsive to inconsistent information. Not even extreme party-issue inconsistency prompted individuals entirely to forsake theory-driven processing.[21]

Also consider for a moment how we make decisions about candidates for office we know little about. As we have seen before, party identification is a frequently used cognitive short cut, especially when voters know little or nothing about a candidate other than his or her party. But this is far from being the only economical mental device that voters employ. How, for instance, do we make decisions during the presidential primary season, when *all* the candidates come from our preferred party? Samuel Popkin has developed a theory of candidate appeal in primaries that draws on schema-type notions.[22] We often know very little about the candidates who run for their parties' presidential nomination. Many are governors of states we know little about or senators we may never have heard of. During the 2008 primary season, for instance, how many people knew what Barack Obama's voting record in the Senate was, or what his specific policy proposals were? How many people actually knew who Sam Brownback or Bill Richardson was? With the exception of "big guns" like John McCain and Hillary Clinton, most of the candidates lacked any known national profile.

How, then, do we choose between various unknowns? Popkin argues that we base our decisions on only a few pieces of observable "data." We then use these to fill in missing information about the candidate (default values) and we reach a conclusion of how representative a candidate is of some ideal (or non-ideal) stereotype. This is another way of saying that we fit candidates, however imperfectly and imprecisely, into schemas we already have stored in our heads. Like the dog schema example earlier, we use a few knowns to fill in the unknowns, in order to come to a more general conclusion or assessment. As Popkin puts it:

> voters will decide what kind of governor Jimmy Carter was and what kind of president he will be not on the basis of knowledge about his performance as governor of Georgia but on their assessment of how likely it is that Jimmy Carter, as a person, was a good governor.[23]

Popkin borrows not just from schema theory here but from attribution theory, since he argues that fitting candidates into one stereotype or another involves judgments about representativeness.

Scripts can be thought of as "event schemas," a particular kind of schema which provides typical default values for an event of some kind, such as climbing the stairs, or going to the cinema or a restaurant. How is it that human beings can climb a staircase they have never seen before, even the rather exotic spiral version? This may seem like a silly question to ask, but the reason it seems silly is that we all have a script or schema stored in our heads that deals with climbing stairs. It tells us how to approach the staircase, to place a single foot first on the initial stair, follow that with the next foot on the higher step, and so on. Equally, we have no problem watching a movie at a cinema we have never visited; we simply use our default values to guide our behavior. By the same token, if I tell you that I actually went to see a movie in town last night, you can easily use the same default values you keep in your head for typical visits to the cinema to guess how my evening probably went. I probably bought a ticket first, then gave my ticket to the attendant. Like most people, I probably bought a Coke and some popcorn. I sat down in the movie theater showing the film I'd selected and I watched it until the end. When it was over, I left and did something else.

Again, however, scripts can mislead. Suppose I really did go to the cinema last night. However, professorial salaries where I work in Florida are miserly, and I decided to slip past the ticket attendant without paying when her attention was distracted. I'm on a diet, so I rejected the soda and popcorn they try to sell you before you go in. I found the movie so boring that I fell asleep in it. I was awoken by an angry lady behind me who objected to my snoring, and I stumbled out into the daylight, regretting that I'd wasted my time on another overly hyped Hollywood movie (even though I hadn't bothered to pay). In this case, your default values have led you astray, and again the reason partly relates to our cognitive miserliness. We make assumptions based on the typical or prototypical behaviors which may be entirely misleading or incorrect.

The use of historical scripts is very common in international politics. The *Munich script*, for instance, tells us a story about what happens when a ruthless, expansionist leader is appeased, suggesting that if you don't confront a threat early on, you will most assuredly have to face it later. World War I had had a devastating effect on Europe, and British Prime Minister Neville Chamberlain (as well as other European leaders) not unnaturally wanted to avoid another war of perhaps even greater devastation. In 1938 a peace conference was convened in Munich at which Hitler agreed to restrain his aggressive ambitions in return for part of what was then Czechoslovakia.

Chamberlain famously emerged from the conference waving the agreement that had been reached and promising "peace in our time." This policy of course was a terrible failure, and the word "appeasement" became a dirty word in international relations, ruining the political careers of those who (like then Ambassador Joseph Kennedy in the United States) had advocated it. Hitler violated the terms of the Munich agreement the following year, invading one European state after another and eventually leading the United States to intervene on behalf of the beleaguered and financially ruined Allies. This same script was later evoked on numerous occasions during the Cold War, and most famously by George H.W. Bush after Saddam Hussein invaded Kuwait in 1990; Bush argued that if Hussein's aggression was not confronted early on—if Hussein were appeased, in effect—the rest of the Middle East would soon fall to his expansionist designs.

Analogical Reasoning

Another (very similar) way of thinking about historical events and scripts is through what has become known as analogical reasoning. When we reason by analogy, we compare a new situation to something similar we have faced in the past (or rather, something that *appears* to be similar). We very often use historical analogies when discussing international affairs and foreign policy; indeed, according to former Secretary of State Alexander Haig, "international politics attracts analogies the way honey attracts bears."[24] Since the 1970s, the debate over American foreign policy has often seemed like a war between two historical analogies: Munich/World War II and Vietnam. The first—derived from the unpopularity and ultimate failure of the policy to appease Adolf Hitler—stresses the need to confront an enemy both early and head on, using massive military force; the second—informed by America's inability to defeat the Communist North Vietnam despite its overwhelming conventional superiority—suggests the dangers of doing the first. Phrases like "bogged down," "body bags," and "exit strategy" date from this period of American foreign policy history, suggesting the profound dangers of using military force, at least without very careful planning about precise objectives and the nature of the enemy faced.

There is a now well-established literature on the subject of analogical reasoning in the disciplines of cognitive and social psychology, and a number of significant discoveries about human problem-solving are especially noteworthy. Foremost among these is the fact that analogical reasoning is a cognitive mechanism that tends to be used under conditions of high uncertainty or ambiguity, such as when an individual is confronted by novel or unusual circumstances or a highly stressful situation. Eysenck and Keane note that much of the existing psychological research on human problem-solving examines how people deal with familiar, routine, and recurring situations, but "people can also solve unfamiliar or novel problems. Sometimes we can produce creative solutions when we have no directly applicable knowledge about the problem situation."[25] We can do this by finding something in our experience that seems, to us at least, to resemble the task at hand.

A second central finding—which relates primarily to the processes through which analogical reasoning occurs—is that analogizing involves what several authors have referred to as a "mapping" process. As Eysenck and Keane put it, "various theorists have characterized this analogical thinking as being the result of processes that map the conceptual structure of one set of ideas (called the base domain) into another set of ideas (called a target domain)."[26] The innovators in developing this mapping theory have been Dedre Gentner, Paul Thagard, Mary Gick, and Keith Holyoak. According to Gick and Holyoak, for instance, "the essence of analogical thinking is the transfer of knowledge from one situation to another by a process of *mapping*—finding a set of one-on-one correspondences (often incomplete) between aspects of one body of information and aspects of another."[27] In analogizing, "isomorphic" relationships are discovered between one event, situation, or object and another.

A third, closely related point to note is that analogical reasoning is a *structural* process. An analogy, Dedre Gentner finds, is not simply a statement that something is like something else; rather, it is a comparison in which the subject assumes that the perceived similarities are "structural" (or causally significant) as opposed to merely "superficial."[28] In practice, of course, individuals *do* often draw analogies between things or events that exhibit only a superficial similarity. In the laboratory psychologists can usually set up experiments where it is easy to tell the difference, but in the complex world of foreign policy decision-making, things are rarely so cut-and-dried. The appeal of the Korean analogy to Lyndon Johnson and Dean Rusk during the 1965 debate about escalation in Vietnam was probably enhanced by the fact that Vietnam and Korea are both in Asia.[29] In policy-making, surface similarities are usually easy to confuse with underlying structural ones. Plausible causal or higher order relations must be mapped between the base (that is, the original situation from the past to which the analogy refers) and the target (the new situation being confronted in the present) in order for the analogy to be useful for predictive purposes, but this is relatively easy to do in political decision-making. Reliance on superficial similarity naturally leads to errors and biases, however, not least because analogical reasoning usually involves drawing conclusions from a single case—a practice which any good methodology student knows to be fraught with potential error.

The first political psychologist to reflect extensively upon the use of analogies was Robert Jervis, who devotes a chapter of his *Perception and Misperception in International Politics* to the use of history by decision-makers, and almost all recent work in the field of analogizing has taken its inspiration from him.[30] Jervis's analysis stresses the origin of analogical reasoning in the past personal experiences of decision-makers, showing how analogies can lead the policy-maker to misperceive the character of situations and/or to arrive at policy choices poorly suited to the task at hand. Later work by supporters of the cognitive approach to decision-making has sought to apply Jervis's observations to various case studies, drawn almost exclusively from the United States.

Yuen Foong Khong's book *Analogies at War* is by far the most sustained and in-depth analysis of analogizing in foreign policy to appear to date. Khong examines the decisions by the Johnson administration to escalate U.S. involvement in the Vietnam War in 1965, and finds that analogies played a prominent part in the reasoning processes of both those who opposed the escalation and those who supported it. Under-Secretary of State George Ball, for instance, argued that increased American involvement there would soon lead to "another Dien Bien Phu," a repeat of the disastrous French experience in Indochina in which the French increasingly proved unable to defeat Communist and nationalist insurgents in a guerrilla war and were eventually forced to relinquish their former colony. For President Johnson and many of his other advisers (such as Dean Rusk), however, Korea was the analogy of choice. "To be sure, Johnson was informed by many lessons of many pasts," Khong argues,

> but Korea preoccupied him . . . Whatever it was that attracted Johnson to the Korean precedent, a major lesson he drew from it was that the United States made a mistake in leaving Korea in June 1949; the withdrawal emboldened the Communists, forcing the United States to return to Korea one year later to save the South. Johnson was not predisposed toward repeating the same mistake in Vietnam.[31]

Others, like McGeorge Bundy and Henry Cabot Lodge, drew on the perceived lessons of the Munich–World War II experience in predicting the scenarios they believed would occur if the United States did *not* intervene.[32]

Khong argues that we can think of analogies as "diagnostic devices" that assist policy-makers in performing six crucial functions: they "(1) help define the nature of the situation confronting the policymaker, (2) help assess the stakes, and (3) provide prescriptions. They help evaluate alternative options by (4) predicting the chances of success, (5) evaluating their moral rightness, and (6) warning about dangers associated with the options."[33] He develops what he calls the "AE (analogical explanation) framework," essentially a short-hand term for the belief that analogies are genuine cognitive devices which perform the tasks specified above. The primary research purpose of Khong's book is to argue against the view that analogies are used solely to "prop up one's prejudices" or to justify decisions that have already been decided upon using some other rationale, and he finds that the Johnson people tended to use historical analogies which drew upon recent events such as the missile crisis, the Berlin crises, Korea, Pearl Harbor, and Munich. Khong also shows rather convincingly that in choosing a historical analogy which seemed to "make sense" of Vietnam, Johnson's advisers picked a historical example on the basis of its superficial or surface similarities to the case in hand.[34]

In similar vein, it has been argued that many aspects of the Iran hostage crisis of 1979–81—especially the decisions taken by both Iranian radicals and officials in the Carter administration—can be explained using analogical reasoning.[35] In November 1979 radical Iranian students clambered over the walls of the U.S. embassy in Tehran, initially taking sixty-six Americans captive. When Iran's de facto leader at the time, the Ayatollah Khomeini, refused to return the hostages to America, this sparked a major crisis that dragged on for 444 days and helped destroy the presidency of Jimmy Carter. In 1953, the American and British intelligence services had helped to overthrow Iran's elected leader, Mohammed Mossadegh, and the hostage-takers' main motive seems to have been the suspicion that the CIA was about to depose the Ayatollah in similar fashion. Initially, Carter tried to get the hostages out by diplomatic means. Drawing on his experience of the Pueblo hostage crisis of 1968—in which a similar crisis precipitated by the North Koreans had eventually been resolved through negotiation—Secretary of State Cyrus Vance argued that this strategy would work again if Carter was willing to show suffi-cient patience. Others, notably National Security Adviser Zbigniew Brzezinski, were unwilling to wait, however. Brzezinski in particular drew on an analogy with the Entebbe raid, a highly successful military rescue operation launched by the Israelis in 1976.[36] In early 1980 the president ordered a mission to rescue the hostages in Tehran. The operation was a miserable failure, but it was in part the cognitive image of successfully pulling off "another Entebbe" that proved irresistible to Carter and his colleagues. There were many differences between the two situations which made the Tehran operation much more difficult in a military sense, but analogies can seduce and mislead decision-makers into ignoring or disregarding these.

It is important to reiterate, however, that decision-makers reason not just by using case-based forms of reasoning like analogies, but by drawing on more general, abstract, or rule-based reasoning as well (schema-type reasoning).

Despite the obvious prevalence of analogical reasoning in the making of foreign policy decisions, it may not be as prevalent as other cognitive processes. Marijke Breuning, for instance, points out that more attention should be paid to forms of reasoning other than the analogical variety:

> Abstract reasoning entails the application of general rules or principles. Rather than comparing two or more cases, the problem solver examines the problem to determine whether it has certain structural properties and, hence, belongs to a certain class of problems. It has a more deductive flavor than case-based reasoning. One form of abstract reasoning is explanation-based reasoning, which relies on causal assertions and "if . . ., then . . ." statements.[37]

Examining the U.S. Senate debate on foreign aid in 1950, Breuning finds that abstract reasoning was more prevalent in the deliberations of the senators than its analogical cousin. This concurs with the conclusion of Donald Sylvan and his colleagues that "reasoning in the area of foreign policy seems to be slightly more explanation based."[38]

Conclusion: A Variety of Complementary Concepts

How are attributions, schemas, scripts, and analogies related to one another? The basic answer to this depends on who you ask. Cognitive science is still in its infancy, and there is not yet a consensus on which concepts and labels are best to use. Some cognitive scientists see analogical reasoning as so central to the way humans think that they generally dispense with talk about other organizing categories. Most political psychologists—including the present author—are eclectic on this issue, however, and see these concepts as so closely related that they refer to pretty much the same cognitive processes. It probably makes little difference whether we say that "the president used a historical script," "the president used an event schema," or "the president used an analogy," for instance, since what we are really interested in is the cognitive process by which a decision was reached, and all of these are saying the same thing using a different label.

The analogical reasoning approach is also probably intimately connected to schemas in at least two ways. First of all, the use of schemas involves the same "matching" mechanisms used in analogical reasoning; when you used the dog schema, for instance, you matched the attributes given to you about fur, tails, walks, and so on to the general category for a canine (this also involved the use of the representativeness heuristic, because the example required you to assess how representative the nameless "thing" was of various categories or concepts). Second, analogical reasoning appears to play a key role in schema formation, because it seems to aid the construction of general rules for solving a particular category of problem. Analogical reasoning is seen by many psychologists and cognitive scientists as closely related to schematic processing in this sense. According to Gick and Holyoak, for instance, when an individual has solved a problem successfully in the same way on two or more occasions, he or she will eventually form a general "problem schema," a set of abstract principles for dealing with that problem type which derives from particular analogical cases but which acquires an independent identity of its own.[39] In this way general rules may be formed which derive from—and yet go beyond—any particular case, abstract beliefs for which analogies supply examples and provide concrete support. The statement that "aggression must be stopped early" is a schematic rule divorced from any particular case, but the statement that "Saddam Hussein is another Hitler" is an analogy or specific comparison between two cases. Nevertheless, the two are obviously related. Our general aggression schema might be composed of various individual cases or analogies involving Hitler, Mussolini, Hussein, and others.

Most political psychologists do not treat attribution theory and analogical reasoning as opposing theories either. Many scholars in the field of foreign policy analysis, for instance, mix and match concepts drawn from attribution theory, schema theory, and analogical reasoning, as do (more informally) scholars of electoral choice. Khong, for instance, argues that the availability heuristic explains George Ball's use of the Dien Bien Phu analogy: Ball had worked as a lawyer for the French during the last years of France's colonial control of Indochina, and so the Dien Bien Phu experience was personal to him in a way that it wasn't for most of President Johnson's advisers. The representativeness heuristic, Khong argues, also affected LBJ's reasoning since he was impressed by the superficial similarities between Korea and Vietnam. Similarly, the events of 1979 seemed to most Iranians representative of those of 1953, the Pueblo analogy was cognitively available to Cyrus Vance because he had been sent to South Korea as a presidential envoy during that crisis, and Entebbe was especially available to Brzezinski because he happened to be in Israel as the operation was being planned, and had discussed the idea of a rescue mission with Israeli officials at the time. In short, attribution theory, schema theory, and analogical reasoning are far more complementary as approaches than they are competitive.

One key difference between attribution and schema theory is worth noting especially in the context of this book, however. Schema theory is essentially dispositionist, in the sense that different people carry different "mental baggage" with them. People use different analogies in response to the same objective situation, for instance, depending in part on the varied experiences to which they have been exposed. Individuals therefore vary in their attitudes. Similarly, as we shall see when we look at how schema theory explains the use of racial stereotypes, individuals vary in the extent to which they both develop and activate different mental categories. Attribution theory, on the other hand, is at least partly situationist in nature, in the sense that it allows for *both* situationism and dispositionism: although I have included the discussion of attribution theory under the dispositionist section for the sake of analytical convenience, the fundamental attribution error allows for the fact that the behavior of *others* may be situationally determined, while allowing that our *own* behavior may sometimes be influenced most heavily by our dispositions. We will return to this point in the final chapter of the book, however, and so will defer further discussion of this issue until then.

Notes

1 Two books in particular ushered in the new cognitive phase in political psychology during the 1980s: Susan Fiske and Shelley Taylor, *Social Cognition* (Reading, MA: Addison-Wesley, 1984) and Richard Lau and David Sears, *Political Cognition* (Hillsdale, NJ: Lawrence Erlbaum, 1986).

2 David Green and others, *Cognitive Science: An Introduction* (Cambridge, MA: Basil Blackwell, 1996), p.5.

3 The guest examples are taken from Steven Pinker, *How The Mind Works* (New York: W.W. Norton, 1997), p.13, but originally come from the computer scientist Terry Winograd.

4 John Searle, "Minds, Brains and Programs," *Behavioral and Brain Sciences*, 3: 417–57, 1980. Searle's argument has produced a huge debate in cognitive science and AI which continues to this day, and has even featured in novels. See, for instance, David Lodge's brilliant *Thinks . . .* (New York: Viking Press, 2001).

5 Leon Festinger, *A Theory of Cognitive Dissonance* (Stanford, CA: Stanford University Press, 1957).

6 Fritz Heider, "Attitudes and Cognitive Organization," *Journal of Psychology*, 21: 107–22, 1946; Heider, *The Psychology of Interpersonal Relations* (New York: Wiley, 1958).

7 Fiske and Taylor, *Social Cognition*, p.10.

8 See for instance David Jones, Edward Kanhouse, Harold Kelley, Richard Nisbett, Stuart Valins, and Bernard Weiner (eds.), *Attribution: Perceiving the Causes of Behavior* (Morristown, NJ; General Learning Press, 1972) and Richard Nisbett and Lee Ross, *Human Inference: Strategies and Shortcomings of Social Judgment* (Englewood Cliffs, NJ: Prentice-Hall, 1980).

9 Fiske and Taylor, *Social Cognition*, p.11.

10 Deborah Welch Larson, *Origins of Containment: A Psychological Explanation* (Princeton, NJ: Princeton University Press, 1985), p.38.

11 Yaacov Vertzberger, *The World In Their Minds: Information Processing, Cognition and Perception in Foreign Policy Decisionmaking* (Stanford, CA: Stanford University Press, 1990), pp.162–63.

12 Samuel Popkin, "Decision Making in Presidential Primaries," in Shanto Iyengar and William McGuire (eds.), *Explorations in Political Psychology* (Durham, NC: Duke University Press, 1993), p.363.

13 See for instance James Kuklinski, Robert Luskin, and John Bolland, "Where's the Schema? Going Beyond the 'S' Word in Political Psychology," *American Political Science Review*, 85: 1341–56, 1991.

14 Wendy Rahn, John Sullivan, and Thomas Rudolph, "Political Psychology and Political Science," in James Kuklinski (ed.), *Thinking About Political Psychology* (New York: Cambridge University Press, 2002), p.171.

15 Deborah Welch Larson, "The Role of Belief Systems and Schemas in Foreign Policy Decision-Making," *Political Psychology*, 15: 17–33, 1994.

16 Susan Fiske and Philip Linville, "What Does the Schema Concept Buy Us?," *Personality and Social Psychology Bulletin*, 6: 543–57, 1980.

17 Julian Hochberg, *Perception*, second edition (Englewood Cliffs, NJ: Prentice-Hall, 1978), p.190.

18 Larson, *Origins of Containment*, p.132.

19 Ibid., p.197.

20 Ibid., p.197.

21 Wendy Rahn, "The Role of Partisan Stereotypes in Information Processing about Political Candidates," *American Journal of Political Science*, 37: 472–96, 2003, p.492.

22 Popkin, "Decision Making in Presidential Primaries."

23 Ibid., p.365.

24 See in particular Ernest May, *Lessons of the Past* (New York: Oxford University Press, 1973); Robert Jervis, *Perception and Misperception in International Politics* (Princeton, NJ: Princeton University Press, 1976), pp.217–87; Richard Neustadt and Ernest May, *Thinking in Time: The Uses of History for Decision Makers* (New York: Freedom Press, 1986).

25 Michael Eysenck and Mark Keane, *Cognitive Psychology: A Student's Handbook* (Hove: Lawrence Erlbaum, 1990), p.399.

26 Ibid., p.401.

27 Mary Gick and Keith Holyoak, "Schema Induction and Analogical Transfer," *Cognitive Psychology*, 15: 1–38, 1983, p.2.

28 Dedre Gentner, "Structure Mapping: A Theoretical Framework For Analogy," *Cognitive Science*, 7: 155–70, 1983.

29 Yuen Foong Khong, *Analogies At War: Korea, Munich, Dien Bien Phu, and the Vietnam Decisions of 1965* (Princeton, NJ: Princeton University Press, 1992).

30 Alex Hybel, *How Leaders Reason: U.S. Intervention in the Caribbean Basin and Latin America* (Cambridge, MA: Basil Blackwell, 1990); Khong, *Analogies At War*; David Patrick Houghton, "The Role of Analogical Reasoning in Novel Foreign-Policy Situations," *British Journal of Political Science*, 25: 523–52, 1996; Christopher Hemmer, *Which Lessons Matter? American Foreign Policy Decision Making in the Middle East, 1979–1987* (Albany, NY: State University of New York Press, 2000); Houghton, *U.S. Foreign Policy and the Iran Hostage Crisis* (New York: Cambridge University Press, 2001).

31 Khong, *Analogies At War*, pp.110–11.
32 Ibid., p.134.
33 Ibid., p.10.
34 Ibid., pp.217–18.
35 Houghton, *U.S. Foreign Policy and the Iran Hostage Crisis*.
36 The Entebbe raid was famous in the 1970s and has been depicted in movies a number of times, the most recent being *The Last King of Scotland*.
37 Marijke Breuning, "The Role of Analogies and Abstract Reasoning in Decision-Making," *International Studies Quarterly*, 47: 229–45, 2003.
38 Donald Sylvan, Thomas Ostrom, and Katherine Gannon, "Case-Based, Model-Based, and Explanation-Based Styles of Reasoning in Foreign Policy," *International Studies Quarterly*, 38: 61–90, 1994, p.88.
39 Gick and Holyoak, "Schema Induction and Analogical Transfer," p.32.

Suggested Further Reading

Yuen Foong Khong, *Analogies At War: Korea, Munich, Dien Bien Phu, and the Vietnam Decisions of 1965* (Princeton, NJ: Princeton University Press, 1992).

Alex Mintz and Karl DeRouen, *Understanding Foreign Policy Decision Making* (New York: Cambridge University Press, 2010).

Steven Pinker, *How The Mind Works* (New York: W.W. Norton, 1997).

Yaacov Vertzberger, *The World In Their Minds: Information Processing, Cognition and Perception in Foreign Policy Decisionmaking* (Stanford, CA: Stanford University Press, 1990).

Chapter 10

Affect and Emotion

It is clear that no account of the psychology of politics would be remotely complete without an account of the role that *emotion*—or "affect" as it is sometimes called—plays within it. Many phenomena in politics involve emotion and feelings rather than just the "cold" kind of information-processing we examined in the previous chapter; virtually all political concepts are charged with emotion, either positive or negative, something that many psychologists refer to as "hot cognitions."[1] Political stimuli often provoke strong emotions, feelings such as liking, dislike, happiness, sadness, anger, guilt, gratitude, disgust, revenge, joy, insecurity, fear, anxiety, and so on.

We do not look at politics neutrally, as some kind of super-advanced, artificially intelligent computer might. Very few people can look at a photograph of George W. Bush or Hillary Clinton, for instance, or a picture of an airplane slamming into the World Trade Center on September 11, 2001, without *feeling* something. Few Americans can look at a picture of the late Osama Bin Laden and not feel anger, contempt, or some other negative emotion, just as many radical Islamists in the Middle East look at the same picture and feel pride, admiration, and other positive responses. And this phenomenon is not confined to politics, of course. As the psychologist Robert Zajonc notes:

> one cannot be introduced to a person without experiencing some immediate feeling of attraction or repulsion and without gauging such feelings on the part of the other. We evaluate each other constantly, we evaluate each other's behavior, and we evaluate the motives and consequences of their behavior.

Setting aside social situations, moreover, "there are probably very few perceptions and cognitions in everyday life that do not have a significant affective component, that aren't hot, or in the very least tepid."[2]

Advocates of most cognitive perspectives tend to treat people as pure processors of information. This is not true of the cognitive consistency approach of Leon Festinger, in which the emotion of psychological discomfort (dissonance) motivates people to adapt their beliefs, but it is true of most applications of schema theory, for instance. As Yuen Foong Khong notes, "the information-processing theories of the 1970s and 1980s—including schema theory—consciously shied away from 'hot' cognitions, in part because cognitive psychology's model of the mind was informed by the computer analogy."[3] For some years after cognitive concepts like schemas became popular, it was true to say that the topic of emotion in politics was somewhat neglected. As David Redlawsk has pointed out, rational choice theorists—supporters of the *Homo economicus* approach—have always given emotion short shrift, but advocates of the cognitive theories examined in Chapter 9 have traditionally downplayed this potent force as well:

> Perhaps because accurately measuring emotional response to political stimuli is very difficult, even political psychologists not necessarily working in the rational choice tradition turned first to the tools of cognitive psychology to understand how people process political information. The cognitive revolution of the past decades led to a great deal of focus (much quite successful) on the cognitive underpinnings of political behavior. Yet a long line of psychological research . . . posits that cognition is not unbiased; that people have various cognitive *and* emotional motivations to see the world in particularistic ways. Yet somehow this recognition that emotions matter a lot did not find its way very far into political psychology. Instead a distinctly cognitive information processing approach developed that talked of "schemas" and "heuristics" and "rational" decision-making. But it did not talk much about motivation and emotion.[4]

While this was certainly true until fairly recently, it is fortunately no longer the case, especially in the field of mass political behavior. A flood of books about emotion and voting behavior has come onto the market in recent years, for instance, and the work of George Marcus and his colleagues has been especially important in this regard.[5]

Politics is as much about "feeling" as it is about "thinking."[6] In order to understand political emotions better, though, it helps to categorize the different kinds of political feelings possible, and what we colloquially term "emotion" should really be distinguished in various ways.[7] For one thing, feelings that are *object-specific* (in other words, that derive from a reaction to a specific thing or person) differ from those that are *diffuse* (that is, they are not associated with a specific person or thing). We can label this kind of emotional feeling "mood."

Former British Prime Minister Winston Churchill, for instance, suffered from depression for most of his life, a condition he often referred to as his "black dog." One of the distinguishing features of such moods is that the sufferer is often unable to attribute the dark feelings that come with them to any specific object or cause.[8] Alternatively, we have all had the experience of waking up in a "sunny" mood, and this too is non-specific in nature. "Emotional responses," on the other hand, may be as transitory and fleeting as this kind of good mood, but they are reactions provoked by a particular person or event, and we can thus attribute some sort of "cause" to them. Ronald Reagan once made a rather inappropriate joke—at a time when the Cold War was still going on—about bombing the Soviet Union, for instance. Some reacted to this with anger, others with annoyance, and still others with laughter.

Some emotions differ from both moods and emotional responses in the sense that they are much more long-lasting than either of these. "Evaluations" refer to longer-term attitudes towards (for instance) a particular politician or party, attitudes which rarely change overnight. Both George W. Bush and Hillary Clinton inspire particularly strong affective evaluations among American voters, just as John Howard and Tony Blair did in Australia and Great Britain respectively. It is possible, of course, that we evaluate political leaders using solely "cold" cognitive processes such as schemas or the degree to which the values of a politician fit our own, but this is unlikely because all politicians appear to evoke emotional reactions in people (strong "like" or "dislike," or merely indifference).

Are Emotions "Irrational"?

For a long time, emotions have been treated as something visceral, something which comes "from the gut" rather than the mind. This mode of thinking has ancient roots. In the Western tradition of political thought, it is still very common to contrast "reason" with "emotion"; on the one hand stands ordered, rational reason (something to be aspired to and admired), on the other the pull of irrational, emotional impulses (something to be avoided). This is implicit in Freud's distinction between the id and the superego, for instance. We are very much accustomed to thinking of emotion as something detrimental to informed, factually based decision-making.

This way of approaching the operations of the human mind is clearly present in popular culture and dates back hundreds if not thousands of years, right back to the ancient Greeks. Anyone who has ever watched an episode of *Star Trek* or one of its many movie spin-offs, for instance, knows that the relationship between Captain James Kirk and his assistant Mr. Spock turns on their different ways of approaching the worlds around them. While as a human being Kirk is often passionate and emotional, he is just as often berated by Spock for departing from the dictates of pure reason. When Kirk is led to an emotional response, Spock frequently responds with the cold admonition "that is illogical, Captain." Half-human and half-Vulcan, however, Spock himself constantly experiences an internal psychological struggle between his reasoning, logical Vulcan half and his emotional human half.

This approach may be seriously misleading, however, and there is a very different (and increasingly popular) view within political psychology that challenges the view that emotional processes are inherently irrational or noncognitive in nature.[9] It is certainly true to say that hot cognitions often compete with cold ones. Anyone who has tried to lose weight knows that going on a diet is like warring with oneself, logic telling us that we should avoid purchasing chocolate bars and ice cream, appetite (or perhaps plain greed) dictating the opposite. As Steven Pinker points out, "mental life often feels like a parliament within. Thoughts and feelings vie for control as if each were an agent with strategies for taking over the whole person, you."[10] We are all familiar with the damage that unbridled emotion—especially highly negative affect states such as anger—can do. Nevertheless, emotions are *not necessarily* something which should be regarded as detrimental, he argues. Combining a modern cognitive approach with a Darwinian evolutionary approach, Pinker contends that we have emotions because they have proven useful in propagating the species. We feel love and solidarity with those closest to us, for instance, because we are motivated to ensure the survival of our own genes (a rather unromantic view, he concedes, but very few of us regard such love as "irrational"). Certain cultures are often regarded as more "emotional" than others—take for instance the common stereotype of the "hot-headed Latin" or the "unemotional German"—but Pinker argues that cultures vary only in the ways that their members *display* emotions, not in the extent that they *feel* them. We are all preprogrammed by evolution to feel essentially the same range of emotions, he contends. We do not all feel the same emotions in response to events—differing reactions across the globe to being presented with a picture of Bin Laden again provide a good example here—but we have all developed the same capacity to feel a very similar range of different emotions.

Emotional responses are probably also essential as *motivating* forces. Emotions help supply us with our goals and objectives in life. When somebody pursues a goal doggedly and takes pleasure in attaining it, we often say that he or she has a "passion" for it, a rather apt phrase. Using the example of Mr. Spock, Pinker notes that although Kirk's right-hand man was supposedly emotionless,

> he must have been driven by some motives and goals. Something must have kept Spock from spending his days calculating pi to a quadrillion digits

or memorizing the Manhattan telephone directory. Something must have impelled him to explore strange new worlds, to seek out new civilizations, and to boldly go where no man had been before. Presumably it was intellectual curiosity, a drive to set and solve problems, and solidarity with allies—emotions all. The emotions are mechanisms that set the brain's highest level goals. Once triggered by a propitious moment, an emotion triggers the cascade of subgoals and sub-subgoals that we call thinking and acting. Because the goals and means are woven into a multiply nested control structure of subgoals within subgoals within subgoals, no sharp line divides thinking from feeling, nor does thinking inevitably precede feeling or vice versa.[11]

Steven Pinker gives the example of fear, which is "triggered by a signal of impending harm like a predator, a cliff top, or a spoken threat. It lights up the short-term goal of fleeing, subduing, or deflecting the danger, and gives the goal high priority, which we experience as a sense of urgency."[12] Artificial intelligence experts, he notes, also concede that creating a functioning robot would require us to program in something resembling emotions "merely for them to know at every moment what to do next."[13]

A similar reason for not treating emotions as detrimental to cold reasoning processes is that they seem actively to aid in the formation of "good" decision-making, and may even be essential to it. In order to make sound, well-considered decisions, we first of all have to *care* about those decisions. This conclusion receives strong support in the work of neuroscientist Antonio Damasio and his colleagues. Damasio discovered that patients who have damage to their prefrontal cortex—the area of the brain that controls emotional responses—often make reckless decisions, even though they may otherwise have extensive intellectual capabilities.[14] He argues that this stems from the absence of emotions (such as fear) that would prevent normal individuals from acting in ways damaging to their social and professional lives. Put simply, they make bad decisions because they no longer have the capacity to care one way or another. As political scientist Jonathan Mercer relates,

> people without emotion may know they should be ethical, and may know they should be influenced by norms, and may know that they should not make disastrous financial decisions, but this knowledge is abstract and inert and does not weigh on their decisions. They do not care about themselves and others, and they neither try to avoid making mistakes nor are they capable of "learning" from their mistakes.[15]

Like Pinker and Damasio, Mercer sees emotion as *essential* to rationality, not a competitor with it.[16]

Whether emotions or cold cognitions "come first"—and thus whether a good theory of political reasoning ought to start with the material presented in this chapter or the previous one—is a debate almost as old as psychology itself. Yaacov Vertzberger is eclectic on this question, arguing that emotions "may cause cognition, or conversely cognition may cause emotions. They cause cognition where a prior experience triggers instant affective reactions before cold processes take place."[17] Robert Zajonc, on the other hand, was one of the first in recent times to argue that emotion may precede cold cognition, and many political psychologists now agree. Think for instance about what happens when you quite suddenly see someone standing directly in front of you or looking through a nearby window. If you weren't aware at all that the person was there—we commonly say that he or she has "crept up on you"—you immediately feel surprise or alarm, to the point where some of us will even cry out or shout. We experience fear or astonishment almost immediately, before the conscious mind has processed what is happening. But then, if the person is a friend or someone we know well, we process that information, and may be embarrassed at our own reaction. This is a simple example of emotion coming before conscious cognition or processing of information.

Again, however, our next step is as always to ask what relevance this has for the study of politics. We can best do this by briefly discussing two popular approaches that argue for the primacy of affect; both take the position that one cannot possibly think without feeling, and that feeling often comes first.

Affective Intelligence Theory

Building on insights from neuroscience—a topic which will be covered in more detail in the next chapter—George Marcus and his colleagues explicitly reject the popular view that we must first "think" before we can "feel."[18] They distinguish between two systems which they term the *disposition* and *surveillance* systems. The first deals with information that is routine. It evaluates incoming information according to the emotions that a particular stimulus elicits: in particular, a stimulus may evoke enthusiasm or aversion. While the first mechanism deals with common or habitual ways of thinking, the second deals with stimuli that are novel and unexpected. The dominant emotion dealt with in this second system is anxiety. As Redlawsk puts it:

> once aroused by something unexpected (read "dangerous") the surveillance system heightens awareness and prepares us to respond by elevating "anxiety" levels. This process is not driven by cognitive processing of the environment but by an emotional response to an unexpected stimulus.

The result is that in this aroused state learning is enhanced, since one needs to understand the nature of whatever threat has been encountered and is thus motivated to find out more about the stimulus.[19]

We are alerted to attend much more closely to the stimulus and rely less on habitual thought. In this way, the surveillance system promotes more "reasoned" thought.

Motivated Reasoning Theory

Milton Lodge and Charles Taber have been pioneers in developing a slightly different approach to understanding how emotion affects politics.[20] Although they agree with Marcus and his colleagues that affect should be regarded as prior to cold cognition, they approach the topic a little differently. They assume three things: (1) all political stimuli are affectively charged (the "hot cognition" hypothesis); (2) people keep in their heads an online, constantly updated "running tally" which includes their feelings about these stimuli; and (3) how a person "feels" generally affects the reception of stimuli as well. "The clear expectation is that most, if not all, citizens will be *biased reasoners*, finding it nearly impossible to evaluate any new information in an evenhanded way," Lodge and Taber say.[21]

These two perspectives may not be entirely complementary, as Redlawsk has suggested. In particular, they implicitly disagree about whether encountering a novel or unexpected situation is likely to lead to "better" decision-making. Under the Marcus model, evolutionary mechanisms have led to an ability to act instantaneously, before cold cognitive processes set in. This is expected to improve, not detract from, decision-making. In Lodge and Taber's approach, on the other hand, affect *biases* the interpretation of new information. As Redlawsk notes, Lodge and his colleagues "find people are more likely to stick to their guns, to support their prior beliefs, and thus allow affect to interfere with updating [of newly encountered information]."[22] Thus the first approach emphasizes the way that emotions help us learn, while the second stresses the ways in which emotions bias and distort that process.

How are Hot and Cold Cognition Linked?

Emotions have an "automatic" quality to them, and may sometimes reflect unconscious processes. As George Marcus puts it, "the idea that emotional processes occur outside of conscious awareness, which was initially treated with skepticism, is no longer much disputed."[23] More work needs to be done on the ways that specific cognitive processes in politics interact with emotion, however.

Although "hot cognitions" are not the primary focus of Khong's *Analogies At War*, he notes that analogical reasoning has an affective content as well as a purely cognitive one:[24]

> Thus, when [Secretary of State] Dean Rusk decided that the danger in Vietnam was analogous to that in Korea, the analogy might not only conjure up images of Chinese troops crossing the Yalu River, but also evoke negative feelings about inscrutable Chinese hordes.

He also felt "remorse about his failure to anticipate China's intervention in the Korean War," Khong points out.[25] We do not simply "match" the characteristics of a situation with a previous one in a detached way; frequently, we pick an analogy that has some strong emotional significance to us, as Korea did for both President Johnson and his secretary of state. Cognitive availability may thus be a function of hot processes as well as cold ones, but this has so far been a neglected area in political psychology.

Moreover, it is clear that emotions—especially fear—played a strong role in Johnson's Vietnam decision-making. One well-known fear that he mentioned often to his subordinates was the prospect that he might inadvertently set off World War III by bringing China into the war. "In the dark at night, I would lay awake picturing my boys flying around North Vietnam, asking myself an endless series of questions," Johnson told Doris Kearns Goodwin. "What if one of those targets you picked today triggers off Russia or China? What happens then?"[26] It is clear that this was based in part on the Korean analogy, but the comparison set off strong emotions in Johnson that inevitably affected policy-making. Blema Steinberg's analysis of U.S. decision-making on Vietnam also suggests that the emotions of shame and humiliation were very much behind the reasoning of both LBJ and his successor Nixon:

> Lyndon Johnson and Richard Nixon were two highly narcissistic individuals who suffered from painful feelings of shame and humiliation. It was these feelings, in the overall context of their narcissistic character structures, that played an important role in shaping their presidential decisions on Vietnam.[27]

While not everyone would agree with her psychoanalytic characterization of the two men, it seems beyond doubt that these emotions (and others) had an impact. Another of Johnson's well-documented fears was being "the first American president to lose a war."

One useful way of linking work on emotion with "cold" approaches such as schema theory may be to regard emotion as a kind of "cognitive short cut," as Fiske and Pavelchak suggest.[28] They argue that when someone appears to be a typical member of some category—for instance, a "typical Democrat" or a "typical Republican"—we react affectively not to that person's characteristics, but use our emotional reactions to the group category instead. Unless the person seems to be atypical in some noticeable way, we simply assign that person to the general category and ignore his or her particular characteristics. Cognitively this makes some sense, since as with other short cuts it puts less strain on our limited information-processing capabilities. Specific kinds of affect (happiness, sadness, anger, and so on) may also trigger particular information-processing styles.

This approach would seem to assume that affect is secondary, rather than primary, and this kind of approach has dominated the study of elite decision-making (including foreign policy decision-making). There is no reason, though, why the models developed by both the Marcus camp and the Lodge–Taber camp cannot be applied to international relations, just as they have become influential in approaching mass behavior. As Redlawsk notes:

> Where "political behavior" is usually focused on the mass behavior of citizens—often in terms of voting—the political psychology of emotion is often developed at a more individual level of analysis and therefore is broadly applicable to situations in which individuals must process information about political conditions, whether we talk about citizens evaluating candidates, or elites addressing beliefs about war and peace.[29]

The Negative Aspects of Emotion

While accepting that feeling is an integral part of human cognition, we should not of course lose sight of the fact that negative emotions clearly *can* have a damaging effect in politics and that emotion can contribute to highly irrational outcomes; emotion may be vital to human reasoning, but this does not mean that we will avoid all serious errors. We shall see many of these effects when we come to look at the negative aspects of nationalism and ethnic conflict, for instance, both of which are fuelled by powerful human emotions. Equally, some kinds of mood clearly damage the quality of decision-making. As Vertzberger notes, "depression produces rigid, narrowly focused information processing," especially extreme and overgeneralized assessments of the situation.[30] During his last days in office, Lyndon Johnson was clearly in a deeply depressed state, and this may have contributed to his closed-mindedness and unwillingness to listen to advice that ran counter to his Vietnam policies. The same seems to have been true of Richard Nixon during the scandal of Watergate.[31]

There is a greater tendency in the psychological study of international relations and foreign policy to treat emotion as a negative force than there is in the study of mass behaviors such as voting and public opinion, and there is some justification for this: it is hard to see the emotions that fuel ethnic hatred, genocide, apartheid, terrorism, and war between states as positive forces in the world. Nevertheless, the positive role of emotion in decision-making is beginning to be appreciated within the international relations branch of political psychology as well. Jonathan Mercer's work on trust provides a leading example of this kind of approach, as does Ralph White's work on empathy. The work of both of these scholars will be discussed in Chapter 16, and it is also consistent with the hypothesis that emotions can have a predominantly "good" effect on decision-making.

Can Emotions Be Measured?

As we noted earlier, the topic of emotion has often been equally ignored by devotees of both *Homo economicus* and *Homo psychologicus*, by rational choice theorists and advocates of cognitive psychological applications alike. The tendency to set affect aside has in part been a result of the difficulty of *measuring* emotional responses themselves, though. Supposing, for instance, you have just given your spouse or significant other a sweater for his or her birthday. He or she takes it out of its wrapping, holds it up and exclaims "just what I always wanted!" How do you know whether he or she really likes it, however? Your loved one may actually be delighted by the gift, of course. Alternatively, he or she may be rather disappointed, thinking "this isn't really my style" or "I wanted a new car." He or she may actively *hate* the sweater, but just claimed to like it because when we love someone, we usually try at all costs not to hurt their feelings.

Despite the simplicity of this example, there are a large number of different emotions potentially floating about here: mutual love, dislike of the sweater, liking the sweater, disapproval of one's partner's taste in clothes, the desire not to hurt the other's feelings, greed, disappointment, empathy, and so on. Despite the fact that the two individuals communicating the emotions are intimate friends accustomed to reading one another's emotional responses, neither can be absolutely sure which of several emotions the other is experiencing. If reading emotions in individual cases is this difficult, how can psychologists possibly measure people's emotions in an accurate way?

Conclusion

The most common approach to measuring emotional response has been to simply *ask* people what they are feeling. Analysts of mass behaviors have long made use of questionnaires and surveys in which individuals are asked to self-report their feelings towards some political stimulus or other. We have also long had more scientific ways of measuring emotional response, such as examining a subject's heart rate and perspiration levels using the same technology as lie detectors (though these techniques are far less widely used in political psychology). There are some problems with both of these techniques, of course: people may not be willing or able to describe their emotions with precision, and the use of older technologies to tap emotional responses involves ethical as well as financial issues, as well as being rather imprecise and unsuitable for some purposes. As we shall see in the next chapter, developments in neuroscience—most notably in brain imaging techniques such as MRI and fMRI—have made it easier than before to measure *directly* the emotions that individuals are experiencing, however. Moreover, political psychologists have begun to work with neuroscientists at an interdisciplinary level to utilize such techniques in their work. While this work is very new indeed and the results of the few studies done so far are extremely preliminary, in the next chapter we will examine and assess some of the latest research that has been done in this area.

Notes

1 This phrase was introduced by Robert Abelson in the early 1960s, and has become common in the literature on affect. See Robert Abelson, "Computer Simulation of 'Hot Cognitions,'" in Silvian Tomkins and Samuel Messick (eds.), *Computer Simulation of Personality: Frontier of Psychological Theory* (New York: Wiley, 1963).
2 Robert Zajonc, "Feeling and Thinking: Preferences Need No Inferences," *American Psychologist*, 35: 151–75, 1980, p.153.
3 Yuen Foong Khong, *Analogies At War: Korea, Munich, Dien Bien Phu, and the Vietnam Decisions of 1965* (Princeton, NJ: Princeton University Press, 1992), p.225.
4 David Redlawsk, "Feeling Politics: New Research into Emotion and Politics," in Redlawsk (ed.), *Feeling Politics: Emotion in Political Information Processing* (New York: Palgrave Macmillan, 2006), p.2.
5 Apart from Redlawsk's edited volume, see for instance Russell Neuman, George Marcus, Michael MacKuen, and Ann Crigler (eds.), *The Affect Effect: Dynamics of Emotion in Political Thinking and Behavior* (Chicago, IL: University of Chicago Press, 2007); Drew Westen, *The Political Brain: The Role of Emotion in Deciding the Fate of the Nation* (New York: Public Affairs, 2007); Ted Brader, *Campaigning For Hearts and Minds: How Emotional Appeals in Political Ads Work* (Chicago, IL: University of Chicago Press, 2006); George Marcus, *The* Sentimental *Citizen:*

   Emotion in Democratic Politics (University Park, PA: The Pennsylvania State University Press, 2002); and George Marcus, Russell Neuman, and Michael MacKuen, *Affective Intelligence and Political Judgment* (Chicago, IL: University of Chicago Press, 2000).

6 Redlawsk, "Feeling Politics," p.2.

7 Victor Ottati and Robert Wyer, "Affect and Political Judgment," in Shanto Iyengar and William McGuire, *Explorations in Political Psychology* (Durham, NC: Duke University Press, 1993).

8 With advances in neuroscience, it has become clear that depression is often the result of a deficiency of the chemical serotonin in the brain, something which is very often treated with a "synthetic serotonin re-uptake inhibitor" like Prozac and its many pharmacological cousins. This treatment was of course unavailable in Churchill's day.

9 See for instance George Marcus, *The* Sentimental *Citizen*.

10 Steven Pinker, *How The Mind Works* (New York: W.W. Norton, 1997), p.419.

11 Ibid., p.373. Spock's character is not necessarily contradictory, however, since as already noted one of his parents was human. While writing this book I was amazed to come across a whole book in my university library devoted solely to the psychology of *Star Trek*. See Robert Sekuler and Randolph Blake, *Star Trek on the Brain: Alien Minds, Human Minds* (New York: W.W. Freeman, 1998). The authors use examples from their book to teach neuroscience.

12 Pinker, *How the Mind Works*, p.374.

13 Ibid., p.374.

14 See Antonio Damasio, *Descartes' Error: Emotion, Reason, and the Human Brain* (New York: Putnam, 1994).

15 Jonathan Mercer, "Rationality and Psychology in International Politics," *International Organization*, 59: 77–106, 2005, p.93.

16 Ibid., p.94.

17 Yaacov Vertzberger, *The World In Their Minds: Information Processing, Cognition, and Perception in Foreign Policy Decisionmaking* (Stanford, CA: Stanford University Press, 1990), p.176.

18 Marcus, Neuman, and MacKuen, *Affective Intelligence and Political Judgment*, p.9.

19 Redlawsk, "Feeling Politics," p.4.

20 Milton Lodge and Charles Taber, "Three Steps Toward a Theory of Motivated Political Reasoning," in Arthur Lupia, Matthew McCubbins, and Samuel Popkin (eds.), *Elements of Reason* (New York: Cambridge University Press, 2000); Lodge and Taber, "The Automaticity of Affect for Political Leaders: Groups, and Issues: An Experimental Test of the Hot Cognition Hypothesis," *Political Psychology*, 26: 455–82, 2005; Taber and Lodge, "Motivated Skepticism in the Evaluation of Political Beliefs," *American Journal of Political Science*, 50: 755–69, 2006.

21 Lodge and Taber, "Three Steps Toward a Theory of Motivated Political Reasoning," p.184.

22 Redlawsk, "Feeling Politics," p.4.

23 George Marcus, "Emotions in Politics," *Annual Review of Political Science*, 3: 221–50, 2000, p.231.

24 Yuen Foong Khong, *Analogies At War: Korea, Munich, Dien Bien Phu and the Vietnam Decisions of 1965* (Princeton, NJ: Princeton University Press, 1992), pp.225–26.

25 Ibid., p.224.
26 Doris Kearns Goodwin, *Lyndon Johnson and the American Dream* (New York: St. Martin's Press, 1976), p.270.
27 Blema Steinberg, *Shame and Humiliation: Presidential Decision Making on Vietnam* (Pittsburgh, PA: University of Pittsburgh Press, 1996), p.7.
28 Susan Fiske and Mark Pavelchak, "Category-Based vs. Piecemeal-Based Affective Responses: Developments in Schema-Triggered Affect," in Richard Sorrentino and E. Tory Higgins (eds.), *Handbook of Motivation and Cognition* (New York: Guildford Press, 1986).
29 Redlawsk, "Feeling Politics," pp.5–6.
30 Vertzberger, *The World In Their Minds*, p.177.
31 Ibid., p.177.

Suggested Further Reading

David Redlawsk (ed.), *Feeling Politics: Emotion in Political Information Processing* (New York: Palgrave Macmillan, 2006).
Russell Neuman, George Marcus, Michael MacKuen, and Ann Crigler (eds.), *The Affect Effect: Dynamics of Emotion in Political Thinking and Behavior* (Chicago: University of Chicago Press, 2007).

Chapter 11

Biopolitics, Neuropolitics, and Genopolitics

During the last ten years or so, the terms "neuropolitics," "genopolitics," and "biopolitics" have begun to appear—or in the case of the latter, re-appear—in the vast literature which links psychology and politics. Neuropolitics and genopolitics are relatively new at the time of writing, and are still not as familiar to many political scientists as they ought to be. One thing I've tried to do throughout this book is to explain political psychology in a simple, accessible, and direct way. Writing about these topics in that fashion is admittedly rather hard to do, though, not least because *hardly anyone* is an expert in all the areas that these three general approaches or fields of study draw upon. In order to get a real handle on these subjects, you first of all need to be trained in political science, of course. But you also need to know about cognitive neuroscience, psychology, biology, physiology, primatology, ethology, and behavioral genetics as well! This is a pretty tall order, and I take my hat off to anyone who feels they're truly "expert" in all of these simultaneously (while retaining a healthy suspicion at the same time about anyone who makes this kind of claim).

Part of the problem, of course, goes back to the issues with which we started this book. On the whole, academia has traditionally rewarded those who specialize in narrowly defined areas which, by their very nature, are not interdisciplinary. As an undergraduate, you will probably take courses in a variety of areas. From one perspective, you are getting exposed to a broad range of topics. On the other hand, it can be hard to see how all of these "link up," and relatively few courses in universities today even try to do that for you. In other words, our appreciation of the woods tends to get lost in our fascination with particular trees. Writing a PhD thesis, moreover, usually involves a high degree of specialization within a single field, and both tenure and promotion within political science are hard to achieve without a similar, single-minded focus. Moreover, there is a great deal of bureaucratic resistance to incorporating genetic explanations (for instance) into the study of politics, and I have personally heard people who do this described in private as "loonies" or "crazies."[1] This kind of resistance is perhaps understandable, but it also inhibits the accumulation of learning and knowledge. And of course there is the problem of getting natural scientists to "do" politics. Salaries are generally higher in the natural sciences than they are in the social ones, so why go to the trouble and expense of working in a political science department when you can make much more money in a department of biology?

Fortunately, we *are* beginning to see more and more individuals trained in behavioral genetics or social neuroscience (for instance) working in political science departments. And an ever-bigger growth industry is the tendency of social scientists to collaborate with colleagues based in natural science departments, and to publish in natural science journals.[2] We are increasingly getting around the "expertise problem" by simply talking to (and working with) people in departments other than our own. And this tendency, of course, goes back to Harold Lasswell and Charles Merriam, both of whom (as we saw in earlier chapters) realized early on in the development of the subject this book covers that a full understanding of political behavior could not be acquired without training oneself in the materials traditionally covered only by non-political science departments.

As we shall see in the concluding chapter, these new perspectives also provide a handy way of combining our situationist and dispositionist approaches. Although in Chapter 11 we present neuroscience as an approach which is more dispositionist than situationist, in reality both neuropolitics and genopolitics *combine* dispositionist and situationist arguments to form a more rounded explanation of political attitudes and behavior. Neuropolitics and genopolitics may yet be formally (or informally) merged with one another to form a single approach—possibly with a new and different label that hasn't been coined yet—and indeed the terms are often used interchangeably. While they do in fact overlap in significant ways—and many researchers mix and match various elements of these complex topics—they should be logically distinguished from one another, and it's important that students get a good sense of this.[3]

While neuropolitics and genopolitics are relatively new additions to the political science *oeuvre*, biopolitics is a much older and more well-established approach which has undergone a major revival in recent years, and both neuropolitics and genopolitics are new approaches within the general label of biopolitics. Neuropolitics is the study of the role played by the human brain in politics, and is logically separate from genopolitics, which examines the genetic roots of political attitudes and behavior. The two are often linked, though, in the sense that genopolitical arguments often involve a theory of how the brain has evolved and thus become neuropolitical as well. Before we look at areas of overlap between biopolitics, neuropolitics, and genopolitics, of course, we first need to understand what these various terms mean. We'll take each in turn.

Biopolitics

Biopolitics is probably the easiest of the three to describe and understand. Setting aside its usage in postmodernism—where it has a rather different and specialized meaning—the term "biopolitical" in political psychology refers to approaches which examine the relationship between human biology and political behavior.[4] It is easily the oldest of the three approaches, first being used as a term in the 1920s and 1930s. Arguably, though, its use as a general approach can be traced much further back than this, to both Plato and Aristotle and certainly to the "state of nature" arguments of Thomas Hobbes and John Locke and Jean-Jacques Rousseau. The state of nature is a real or hypothetical condition employed by a number of thinkers, in which they imagined what life would be like if government did not exist and men and women were essentially left to their own devices. Hobbes famously concluded that life under such conditions would be "nasty, brutish, and short," while Locke and Rousseau both countered that the state of nature would in fact be a state of harmony in which everybody "got along" (to paraphrase Rodney King). Each of them justified their preferred form of government by these claims, but Hobbes in particular was making a biological (or biopolitical) argument about human nature. Human beings, he suggested, are born with certain predispositions and these "are" a certain way, regardless of what we might like to be the case.

For many years after World War II, biological explanations languished in political science, partly because state-of-nature-type explanations were regarded as unscientific by the 1950s and 1960s, an era in which *behavioralism* reigned supreme in political science. Not to be confused with the behaviorism that we examined in Chapter 3, this was a movement in political science which insisted that cumulative progress could only be made in attaining or accumulating knowledge about politics if the appropriate scientific (usually statistical) techniques were followed. The arguments of theorists like Hobbes and Locke were often deemed not to fulfill such criteria. Probably more important, though, was the almost automatic but ill-considered association which developed in many people's minds between the "Eugenics" movement, Nazism, and biological explanations of politics in general. As we saw earlier in this book, this movement had an impact not just on Germany—where pseudo-biological theories were used by Nazis to "justify" genocide—but in the United States of the 1920s and 1930s, where anti-immigration policies were drawn up in response to biological theories which claimed that immigration from Eastern Europe was somehow "poisoning the race."

The political fallout from Nazism and the Eugenics movement tended to tar *all* biological explanations with the same brush, regardless of their precise nature or scientific basis. Taken to their extreme, biological explanations of politics like eugenics can become highly deterministic, claiming that human behavior is fixed and that education or training is therefore effectively a waste of time. If human behavior is fixed and more or less predetermined, why bother with educating people and trying to make their lives better? While behaviorism (with its notion of the blank slate) reigned supreme in the rising and affluent America of the 1950s, biological explanations (which suggested that the slate was at least partially filled at birth) were never going to dominate psychology either. Since the late 1960s though, there have always been political scientists like Albert Somit who carried the torch for biopolitical approaches during a period where many others considered this odd or quaint. More recently, however, such approaches have been significantly revitalized by developments in cognitive neuroscience and evolutionary psychology, and most of all by advances in behavioral genetics. Moreover, political psychologists in particular have stressed that biological accounts need not be deterministic at all.[5] At the very least, they can be used as a supplement to situationist accounts which claim that your voting behavior (for instance) is entirely determined by your life circumstances. And at their best, they may provide better, independent accounts of behavior which rely on dispositionism rather than situationism. In many ways, neuropolitics and genopolitics are both revitalized versions of this older tradition, and we'll turn to each of these next.

Neuropolitics

Neuropolitics investigates the relationship between the human brain and politics, dealing with how each influences the other. How does the brain affect political behavior? And how, for that matter, does politics then affect our brains? This is of course a highly interdisciplinary subject, drawing on insights gleaned from political science, neuroscience, biology, and a number of the fields already mentioned above. Consider some of the classic questions that traditional political scientists ask. Where do our political attitudes come from? How do we judge candidates for political office? Are most of us racially biased, and how does race affect our political behavior? What role does emotion play in decision-making? Neuropolitics uses the methods of cognitive neuroscience (most notably, "neuroimaging" techniques) to investigate these issues in a way that traditional political scientists were never able to.

In late 2010, the British actor Colin Firth—best known to Americans for his starring (and stuttering) role in *The King's Speech*—guest-presented an episode of a radio program in England. During the broadcast, he casually and light-heartedly suggested that scientists should scan the brains of politicians—especially the brains of people who disagreed with him politically! He suggested that there might be differences in brain structure between those on the political left and those on the right (or what are termed "liberals" and "conservatives" in the U.S. context).

Firth probably did not expect anyone to actually do it, but psychologists at University College London took up his challenge. The result was an article published in the journal *Current Biology* the following year which credited the actor and his producer as "co-authors." The real work, of course, wasn't done by Firth but by Tom Feilden and Ryota Kanai of that university's Institute of Cognitive Neuroscience. To begin with, they scanned the brains of Alan Duncan, a member of the British Conservative Party, and Stephen Pound, representing the U.K. Labour Party, using fMRI (or functional magnetic resonance imaging) to map the brain structures of each. All of this was unusual enough, but the results themselves were even more surprising. Of course, there is little one can conclude in a social scientific sense from just two cases, so Rees and Kanai continued their research by adding ninety more subjects. But they found that Firth's intuition was correct. There are in fact differences in brain structure between those on the left and those on· the right, they discovered, so much so that after the researchers replicated the study on another sample of participants, they felt able to conclude that it is possible to *predict* someone's political preferences—with an astounding 72 percent accuracy—just by looking by looking at the structure of his or her brain. How is this possible? The authors argued that certain regions are "thicker" in Conservatives, while other regions are thicker in Labourites, allowing a researcher to predict with a great deal of confidence which one they are looking at. Just from the images on a computer screen.[6]

The invention of functional magnetic resonance imaging has played no small role in creating the new field of neuropolitics because it has given anyone interested in the political brain new tools to address questions that couldn't really be answered before. Of course, like anything else, fMRI results need to be used with care. In 2009, neuroscientist Craig Bennett and his colleague Abigail Baird put a dead salmon in their fMRI machine. Amazingly, this produced "evidence" of brain activity, as if the salmon was alive and thinking! This was actually just the kind of random "false positive" that is possible when this kind of technique is used, but Bennett and Baird did it in order to show how easy it is to misinterpret fMRI results. Bennett says that he's "so tired about hearing about 'the brain lighting up.' It makes it sound like you see lights in the head or something. That's not how the brain works." Many people, he argues, misunderstand what fMRI results actually mean.

> Those beautiful colorful maps . . . they're probability maps. They show the likelihood of activity happening in a given area, not *proof* of activity. According to our analysis, there's a higher likelihood of this region using more blood because we found more deoxygenated blood in this area. It's also correlational. Here's a time frame and the changes we'd expect, so we see which bits of brain correlate with that.[7]

In other words, while fMRI gives us a good indication of brain activity, it does so indirectly by estimating blood flow in the brain rather than "seeing" brain activity directly.

Some of the first studies in neuropolitics used fMRI techniques to find out whether there were differences in brain activity between political sophisticates and non-sophisticates (in other words, between people who knew a lot about politics and those who did not). Darren Schreiber and Marco Iacoboni asked subjects an array of questions while their subjects lay inside an fMRI machine.[8] It was a bit like a high-tech version of what Alex Trebek does on the TV show *Jeopardy*, since the categories involved a mixture of political and non-political subjects. The researchers found that the politically knowledgeable and the politically ignorant reacted in different ways to questions about U.S. national politics. The knowledgeable showed elevated levels of activity in regions of the brain associated with social cognition, while political novices showed diminished activity in those same areas. Other early experiments looked at how the brain responds to political candidates and their messages. The neuroscientists Jonas Kaplan, Joshua Freedman, and Marco Iacoboni of UCLA conducted experiments like these prior to the 2004 and 2008 presidential elections in the United States. At the same time—that is, just before the 2004 presidential election—Drew Westen and his colleagues at Emory University were independently conducting a very similar kind of experiment.[9] In both cases, the experiments used fMRI techniques to discover how voters respond to political images.

Kaplan, Freedman, and Iacoboni hooked up a Democratic voter called John Graham to an MRI machine and showed him images designed to evoke emotional responses, such as a Bush campaign commercial which used images from the events of September 11 and the (in)famous "daisy chain" commercial from Lyndon Johnson's 1964 presidential campaign. They subsequently followed this up with an imaging study of other Democratic and Republican voters looking at images of George W. Bush and John Kerry.[10] More recently, in 2007 (as the campaign for the 2008 election was in full swing) Iacoboni and his colleagues tested twenty subjects—ten men and ten women—who were self-declared swing voters, and showed them still and moving images of various candidates.[11] They also asked subjects to rate candidates on a traditional "feeling thermometer," from "very favorable" to "very unfavorable."

The results the neuroscientists obtained were interesting. For instance, in the 2007 study when men were shown the word "Republican," the amygdala and the insula—both areas associated with anxiety and disgust—activated quite noticeably, as they did to a lesser extent when both men and women viewed the word "Democrat." The experiment also confirmed the expectation that voters are divided in their emotions towards Hillary Clinton, but more unexpectedly they found that the divide on Clinton is as much within each party as it is between them. As Iacoboni and his colleagues note, voters who rated Mrs. Clinton unfavorably on a questionnaire (which subjects also had to fill out) appeared not entirely comfortable with their assessment. When viewing images of her, these voters exhibited significant activity in the anterior cingulate cortex, an emotional center of the brain that is aroused when a person feels compelled to act in two different ways but must choose one. It looked as if they were battling unacknowledged impulses to like Mrs. Clinton. John Edwards similarly provoked strong reactions. "When looking at pictures of Mr. Edwards, subjects who had rated him low on the thermometer scale showed activity in the insula, an area associated with disgust and other negative feelings," while "swing voters who did not give him low ratings, when looking at still photos of him, showed significant activation in areas of the brain containing mirror neurons—cells that are activated when people feel empathy. And that suggests these voters feel some connection to him."[12]

A few years earlier—that is, just before the 2004 presidential election—Drew Westen and his colleagues were independently working on a broadly similar project.[13] While the study by Kaplan and his colleagues investigated how partisans reacted to images of both their own party's candidate and those of the opposing parties, Westen and his colleagues looked at what goes on inside the brains of partisans who are presented with information that puts their candidate and the opposing one in a poor light. The experimenters first recruited fifteen strong Democrats and fifteen strong Republicans. While hooked up to an fMRI machine, the subjects were presented with contradictory statements (in reality, fabricated by the experimenters) supposedly made by both their favored and disliked candidates. In each case, the second supposed quote from a candidate clearly contradicted the first.

The experimenters hypothesized that those parts of the brain that deal with contradiction and negative affect would be activated, quickly removing the inconsistency in the case of their preferred candidate, and this was in fact what they found. Although they do not note the fact, this research is remarkable to the extent that, for the first time, it provides independent neurological evidence for the party identification model. Party ID, it will be recalled, is an affective or emotional tie to a particular political party, and its originators were much influenced by cognitive consistency theory. Westen and his colleagues' study similarly suggests that strong partisans "screen out" unfavorable information about their own candidate, and for the first time we can see something which at least looks like this process going on in brain scans.

The previous chapter noted that one of the most promising avenues for the measurement of emotion right now is coming from the field of neuro-science. Advances in our understanding of how the human brain works, spurred by significant advances in the technology used to observe its functions, have created the opportunity to increase our understanding of human perception and reasoning, especially our comprehension of the ways in which these are affected by emotion. That said, the study of neuropolitics is still in its infancy at the time of writing, so much so that there exist very few book-length introduc-tions to the topic written for political scientists.[14] There are of course plenty of textbooks aimed at neuroscientists themselves and their students, but as stu-dents of politics we face an immediate problem: we are unfamiliar with the extensive terminology used in the field. As John Ratey notes:

> The language used to describe the brain is, if anything, more opaque than any of the old psychoanalytic terminology, which was itself so obscure that only trained professionals could wade through the literature. Most people never even bother to learn such terminology, deeming that, like the language of the computer scientists of the early 1970s, it is better left to the nerds. If anyone should doubt it, a brief glance into a modern textbook on neurophysiology is all that is needed to make one want to run and hide.[15]

Nevertheless, appreciating the potential of neuroscience requires us to grapple with at least some of the terminology of the brain, since as we have already seen, this is central to an understanding of how this growing branch of cognitive science might throw light on a range of political behaviors.

The Human Brain 101

The human brain has evolved over millions of years. As Westen notes, "its creation was an elegant patchwork of circuits, one grafted onto the next, as the edifice grew larger and more complex."[16] Moving down from the outer layers of the brain to the spinal cord, the human brain is a kind of living "archeological" record of itself. First the brain stem developed—a highly primitive version of the brains we have today—allowing us to feel and think, and regulating basic drives such as hunger. After this, the cerebrum developed. "Further evolution led to structures higher up that are crucial to our experience of emotion," Westen notes. Among the most noteworthy of these structures is the amygdala, which "is involved in many emotional processes, from identifying and responding to emotional expressions in others, to attaching emotional significance to events, to creating the intensity of emotional experience, to generating and linking feelings of fear to experiences."[17]

The human brain as it exists now is in some ways like a Swiss army knife, where each of the components performs a specific task; in other respects, however, it is more like a separation of powers, where different functions are shared by different components rather than being wholly divided or parceled out. Westen compares the brain to a "federal system."[18] Certain areas— particularly those that developed first when the brain was in its primitive state—act as specialized centers for particular functions. The amygdala is particularly associated with fear and anger, for instance, while the insula is especially associated with disgust. Other regions, however, play a role in a variety of processes, which makes it difficult to generalize about them. As Westen notes, "no single structure has one function, and the more neuroscientists study the brain, the more we realize that every mental act of any consequence occurs through the activation and coordination of circuits throughout the brain, from the more primitive circuits of the brainstem to the more recently evolved circuits of the frontal lobes."[19]

On top of the cerebellum lies the cerebral cortex, and the area from just behind the eyes to the top of the head—known as the prefrontal cortex—is especially important in reasoning processes. The top and sides of the cerebral cortex are known as the dorsolateral prefrontal cortex. This is an area which, as Westen notes, "is always active when people are making conscious choices." This is a kind of "reasoning circuit," playing a role when people are weighing up the costs and benefits of particular actions.[20] In the language we have been using in this book, it involves primarily "cold" reasoning processes. Then there is the ventromedial prefrontal cortex, which is involved with emotions and emotional reasoning (what we have been calling "hot" cognition). This area also seems to act as a link between hot and cold processes.

When early doctors began to open up the human skull, they had little idea what role each part of the rather unattractive grey mass inside played in thought. Gradually, however, we began to learn how the human brain functions by observing what happens to an individual's behavior when he or she has undergone some sort of neurological damage.[21] In the previous chapter, we briefly described the work of Antonio Damasio, a neuroscientist whose work has had a particular impact on how political psychologists are starting to look at emotion. One of Damasio's most celebrated arguments relates to the *interdependence* of reason and emotion. This argument is based in large part on what happens to individuals who have damage to the area in and around the ventromedial prefrontal cortex, the region of the brain which we noted deals with the integration of reasoning and emotions. Damasio begins his book *Descartes' Error*, for instance, by telling the famous story of Phineas Gage.[22] Gage was a railroad construction foreman who met with a potentially fatal accident in 1848, when an explosion at his work site drove an iron rod through the front of his brain. Such was the force of the blast that the rod exited through the top of his head. To the disbelief of his workmates and his doctor, Gage not only survived the injury but appeared to have suffered minimal damage to his mental functions, even sitting up and relating the incident calmly and rationally to others right after it had occurred.

Phineas Gage appeared to make a full recovery, at least in a physical sense. But those who knew him noticed pronounced changes in his personality. "Gage was no longer Gage," as Damasio puts it. This "new" Gage was given to profanity, was impatient with others and would endlessly debate ideas and then drop them, none of which he had done before. He could no longer hold down a steady job. He seemed to have lost all interest in social conventions and ethical rules. He began making bad life choices, again a marked change from his previous behavior. Why did this happen? Using state-of-the-art imaging techniques and Gage's skull to reconstruct an image of his brain, Damasio argues that Gage had suffered damage to the ventromedial prefrontal cortex, an area "critical for normal decision-making."[23] Producing a range of similar cases, Damasio shows convincingly that "emotional" parts of the brain are essential to make sound, reasoned decisions, turning on its head the age-old assumption that emotion and reason are separate attributes or routes that can be taken in isolation from one another.

The Potential of fMRI and EEG

It would be nice if we could always precisely distinguish, using imaging, between different positive emotions (e.g. pride, love, empathy) and negative ones (e.g. disgust, hatred, fear), and to some extent—provided that such methodologies are used with care—we already can. The 2004 election study conducted by Kaplan and his colleagues attests to the fact that we are often able to do this. As Marco Iacoboni puts it, "there is evidence for some nice relationships between brain areas and emotions (amygdala and fear, insula and disgust), but there isn't a deterministic one-to-one mapping. Each activation should be interpreted in light of the experimental conditions in which the activation is observed."[24]

The reason for this again is that the human brain is in some ways like a Swiss army knife, but many of its functions are distributed across various regions. Referring to the amygdala, for instance, Ralph Adolphs argues that it is probable that a given structure participates in several processes, depending on the time at which its activity is sampled and on the details of the task and context. It is conceivable that the amygdala participates both in the initial, rapid evaluation of the emotional significance of stimuli, and in later assessment within a given context and goal.[25] Even though interpreting the results of brain imaging sometimes provokes disagreement among experts, it is fairly evident that brain imaging is superior in many ways to questionnaires. There are two main reasons for this. First of all, we cannot always trust what respondents in questionnaires tell us about the emotions they are experiencing (or other things they say about their political beliefs). According to political psychologist Shanto Iyengar, "academic research in political science into the effects of campaign advertising is 90 percent bogus, relying as it does on self-reported exposure to a multitude of disparate messages and images. Any efforts to isolate viewers' actual responses to ads—be they neurological, verbal or behavioral—is a step in the right direction."[26]

A great advantage of fMRI over self-report questionnaires is that respondents in a questionnaire may not be consciously *aware* of the emotions they are really experiencing, or may not be able to articulate these in a clear way. Iacoboni argues that "the nice thing about imaging is that it gives us information that we cannot get from verbal reports," not least because "there is plenty of evidence of dissociation between metarepresentation of cognitive states and the cognitive states themselves."[27] On the other hand, fMRI is still expensive to use. "In our center," Iacoboni notes, "machine time costs $600/hour, and this rate is pretty standard." Anyone who has had an MRI done in the United States and looked at the portion picked up by his or her insurance carrier—or, God forbid, had to pay the entire bill themselves—can attest to how expensive it is. This means that its use in political psychology is inevitably dependent on the researcher's ability to obtain large grants. The scenario with which we began this chapter is already technologically feasible, but the most prohibitive obstruction would be its cost. On the other hand, many neuroscientists would question whether a whole movie theater of subjects would be *necessary* to get the kind of data social scientists are interested in. The latter almost always prefer a large number of subjects for reasons of statistical reliability, but as Iacoboni notes, imaging specialists tend to look at this question differently:

> Even if one has unlimited financial resources, it is difficult (and probably not even so useful) to do studies encompassing hundreds of subjects. First

of all, fMRI generates tons of data even from one session in one subject. Studies with hundreds of subjects would produce serious data management issues. Second of all, it is not even clear whether one gets better information with more subjects. These days, typical sample sizes in imaging are between 15 and 25 subjects (it used to be less than that).

From the studies Iacoboni has done, his own impression is that "with fMRI one does not gain in signal-to-noise just by piling up subjects."[28] Not everyone agrees that small numbers of subjects are sufficient when addressing topics like voting behavior, however. As Dr. Jeffrey Bedwell—a clinical psychologist with experience in brain imaging at the University of Central Florida—notes, fMRI studies traditionally have not concerned themselves much with socioeconomic comparisons, for instance. However, political scientists know that it is essential to have a representative sample in order to draw broad conclusions about a wider population. It is not the case, Bedwell notes, that one brain is necessarily identical to another; the brain's precise development can potentially vary across gender, socioeconomic status, and age, for instance. The same kind of comparisons that are sought in traditional voting studies, he argues, are also needed when fMRI is the method of choice.[29]

For medical purposes, EEG (Electroencephalography) is conventionally used to detect general levels of brain activity. This technique is used, for instance, to detect interruptions in brain activity among patients who suffer from seizures. Potentially, this kind of device can be used to detect attentional mechanisms (whether, for instance, people are paying attention to political ads and other audio or visual stimuli). Unlike fMRI, however, it does not provide many details about the specific parts of the brain that are being activated, and hence can tell us little about the precise feelings people are experiencing. While it can tell us that a particular candidate is provoking emotional responses of some sort, it cannot tell us what *kind* of emotional response. As Iacoboni puts it, "the problem with EEG is that it does not give us enough spatial information to know exactly where the signal comes from, especially when it comes to emotions and reward, which are often linked to subcortical structures."[30] On the other hand, if one needs timing in the order of milliseconds, then EEG (Electroencephalography) is preferable to fMRI (the latter has sluggish temporal resolution in the order of seconds, not milliseconds).[31] EEG is also much cheaper than the latter, however, and this is its primary advantage. As long as its limits are appreciated, it can be used to do some interesting things, and new generations of political psychologists are beginning to do interesting things with it. As we shall see later in the work of Elizabeth Phelps on race, we can potentially use "eye-blink startle" measures as well in order to assess the presence or absence of racial bias or ingroup favoritism (see Chapter 15).

Many neuroscientists—including Iacoboni—are cautious about what we can expect imaging to add to our knowledge of politics. As Director of the Center for the Study of Brain, Mind, and Behavior at Princeton University, Jonathan Cohen notes that "brain imaging offers a fantastic opportunity to study how people respond to political information. But the results of such studies are often complex, and it is important to resist the temptation to read into them what we may wish to believe, before our conclusions have been adequately tested."[32] One limitation of current studies of political decision-making using brain imaging is that there is a certain indeterminacy about what exactly is going on inside the brains of those exposed to political images. We know a certain amount about the role played by various parts of the brain already, but that knowledge is far from complete. While neuroscientists can observe parts of the brain associated with emotional processing "lighting up," in some cases it is difficult to tell exactly *why* this is happening. For instance, in the study by Kaplan and his colleagues discussed earlier, the authors admit that some of their findings are consistent with a number of different hypotheses. For instance, they find evidence of activity in both the dorsolateral prefrontal cortex and the anterior cingulate cortex when voters look at images of the opposing candidate. It is not clear, though, whether this is happening because partisans are suppressing negative emotions in general because these are unpleasant, or suppressing positive feelings which they might harbor towards the opponent, or attempting to increase their negative feelings towards that opponent.[33]

Political scientists should also resist the temptation to use brain imaging or EEG for their own sake.[34] Like other methods, each is best thought of as simply one approach among many. There are times when the use of fMRI may be appropriate—again, it seems useful where we have reason to believe that self-reporting techniques are inadequate, for instance—but there are other occasions when better (but less "trendy") methodologies are available. There are also behavioral methods for going beyond self-reports, such as measuring reaction time to masked stimuli. Imaging may be able to provide us with moving images of the brain, but if we are interested in illustrating the link between thought and *behavior*—which is often the case in political psychology—there may be better strategies available. Given the high cost of imaging techniques in particular, we should always ask ourselves whether imaging will tell us something critical that we cannot just as well get somewhere else.

Neuropolitics is as much a *method* as it is a coherent body of theory; the neuroscientific approach is clearly dispositionist in the sense that it zeroes in on the characteristics of individuals. It is yet another perspective that assumes that it is the attributes of individuals—in this instance, their particular brain chemistries—that shape their behavior. As far as political scientists are concerned, there is no value added from political neuroscience unless what goes on in our heads actually makes a difference to how we act politically. On the one hand, neuroimaging might merely show us what changes take place in the brain when someone feels compelled to act against their own best judgment or values: an interesting thing in itself, but not something which really adds much to our explanation of behavior. As Dustin Tingley notes, "observing a pattern of brain activity 'x' alongside behavior 'z' does not necessarily give us a better understanding of why 'z' happened, or why departures from 'z' happened, in the context of the political questions we are interested in."[35] On the other hand, advocates of neuropolitics are united in their optimism that our understanding of political behavior is increasing. Brain imaging has the increasing potential to allow us to "see" ordinary people thinking about politics, and techniques such as EEG (while more limited in what they can tell us) are appropriate when we are simply interested in whether a political message is having some sort of resonance with the voter. So far neuroscientific advances have been employed almost exclusively to understand voting behavior, sophistication, and tolerance, and have been used in particular to investigate how the brain responds to racial outgroups (a literature we will discuss in Chapter 15). However, they have the potential to revolutionize how political scientists look at *all* cognitive processes, and not just those that have conventionally been regarded as dominated by hot cognitive processes.

Genopolitics

Last, but certainly not least, comes genopolitics, a term usually attributed to the political scientist James Fowler. As the name suggests, genopolitics is the study of the genetic basis of political attitudes and behavior, and while it is closely related to the field of neuropolitics—indeed, many of its advocates use both approaches simultaneously—its focus is more on our unique genes as humans and unique DNA as individuals than on brain scans or the use of neurological techniques. It's at the cutting-edge of the most interesting work being done by political psychologists today, and offers a chance for social scientists to collaborate with their natural science colleagues.[36] *The Chronicle of Higher Education* ran a feature on this topic in 2008, as did *The New York Times* the same year.[37] There are essentially two types of genetic argument in the study of politics, both of which qualify as genopolitical: those drawn from evolutionary psychology, which stress our *similarities* as a species, and those drawn from behavioral genetics, which emphasize our individuality and our *differences*.

The reader may recall that we briefly alluded to each approach in Chapter 1. In the first category, consider the arguments of Konrad Lorenz, an ethologist who wrote a famous book called *On Aggression*.[38] Lorenz was interested in probing our true nature, and he was rather pessimistic on this score. But he also developed a more interesting and less straightforward argument than Hobbes or Machiavelli. We often criticize others by saying "you're behaving like an animal," but Lorenz would see this statement as highly ironic, because in reality most animals are actually *better behaved* than us. With the possible exception of certain types of monkey, we are the only known vertebrate which kills its own kind (and perhaps the only one which takes pleasure in doing so). Murder or homicide seems to be almost uniquely human, as is suicide.

The old "nature versus nurture" debate offers us two competing explanations for this tendency. On the one hand, it could be that human beings are inherently aggressive or warlike, and that this can never be changed (a dispositionist claim). On the other hand, killing and war could be a learned behavior, a social practice that can be changed because it can be unlearned, perhaps through conditioning (a situationist argument). Lorenz argued the former position in *On Aggression*. He reached this conclusion by assuming that humans are animals who have evolved aggressive instincts for evolutionary purposes. At the same time, we are "nonlethal" creatures. To see what he means, consider the following. This might be a rather unsavory image, but imagine two naked men wrestling on the ground and trying to kill one another. One can pound the other's head into the ground, but let's assume that this is cheating, because the ground is being used to kill. You also can't use a gun or knife, since these are man-made weapons that don't exist in nature. Practically the only way that one man can kill the other without using the surroundings or a weapon, then, is by punching or strangling, both slow and inefficient means that probably won't be successful without an almighty and all-consuming struggle. When contrasted with lions or tigers, which of course have razor-sharp teeth, we are simply not *made* to kill, Lorenz argues.

At the same time, the technology of war has massively increased our ability to kill one other. We can now kill from thousands of miles away, from offices using unmanned "Predator" aircraft (commonly known as drones) or using missiles fired from the decks of ships. We never even need to see blood or suffering, unless we choose to do so. And of course since the 1940s the invention of nuclear weapons gives just a few people the capacity to destroy all of mankind. So technological innovations have made war more and more lethal. At the same time, *we have stayed the same*. And unlike (say) lions or tigers—which can kill very rapidly—we have never developed the evolutionary mechanisms which inhibit killing. As menacing as they look, lions (for instance) are quite restrained in the sense that they will only kill if they feel threatened or they need food. But humans have no such evolutionary "inhibitors." No such inhibitor was *needed* in a creature which is so ill-equipped by nature to kill, Lorenz argues. In this context, our intelligence, and especially our ability to dream up new and more inventive ways to kill, is a real curse. We are like no other species, in the sense that we kill over ideas and political differences, personal differences, and many other things not related to simple survival. Put very simply, it is as if we have placed a loaded gun in the hands of a child or a lunatic.[39]

Of course, one of the problems with evolutionary arguments is that they are difficult, and even impossible, to test, and others have generated contrasting arguments based on evolution that are equally convincing. The military psychologist Dave Grossman, for instance, argues in *On Killing* that we have evolved a predisposition *not* to kill, a position which in many ways jars with that of Lorenz.[40] Grossman makes the simple point that, for evolutionary purposes, it is beneficial for the species not to kill its own members (otherwise it would quickly die out). But this means that we need to be trained to kill, since it is not in our natures. To bolster this argument, he cites the example of "non-firers," soldiers who deliberately fire over the heads of the enemy during wars, or else don't fire their weapons at all. He cites evidence that non-firing in World War I and World War II used to be quite common, but that it has been far less so since the Vietnam War. In an argument that combines dispositionist with situationist positions, he argues that since the 1960s the U.S. Army has trained soldiers to kill far more effectively than it did, breaking down the natural resistance to killing with unrelenting behavioral conditioning.

Genetics 101

The upshot of all of this is that—for good or ill—many political scientists find evolutionary arguments of this first kind a bit too speculative to be considered "real science." For these reasons and others, many have turned to a second approach to genopolitics, drawn from modern behavioral genetics. Some readers may have heard of the Human Genome Project, a truly international and collaborative research program created back in the 1980s whose goal is to completely "map" human genes and DNA. Almost everyone has heard about "cloning" as well—the artificial manufacture of an identical copy of a human being, animal, or other living entity—and many political debates, works of science fiction, and Hollywood movies have focused on whether this is actually possible, and (if so) whether it is actually desirable in an ethical sense. Few of us, though, have more than a general sense derived mostly from these popular sources of what genetics really is and whether cloning actually goes on in real life. "Dolly the sheep" was the first animal to be cloned in 1996 by researchers at the University of Edinburgh in Scotland. Several other species have been cloned since, but never (as far as we know) human beings. As you might expect this whole area has been enormously controversial, and human cloning is banned in a number of countries.[41] Popular fear of the uses to which genetics can be and has been put, unfortunately, often clouds our understanding of what genetics is and what it can potentially offer us as a social science explanation.

It's important not to confuse genes with DNA (a distinction common enough in high school biology classes, but not conventionally drawn by political scientists). Every member of the human race has (almost) the same set of genes, and there are about 20,000 genes in all.[42] We share about 95.5 percent of our genes with other humans, and this is what gives broad evolutionary arguments their force (genetically, we are *nearly* "all the same"). But there is 4.5 percent left over, and the variation between humans comes from this small but vital difference. The 4.5 percent affects our physical appearance, for instance. While there is no "brown haired gene" or "blonde haired gene," there is a gene for hair color, and all of us have subtly different genetic versions that are ultimately what make us brown-haired, blonde, or something else. Of course, human behavior is a good bit more complex than this, because we all know that two brown-haired people selected at random may be entirely dissimilar otherwise (both physically and psychologically). Our DNA and chromosomes are what further subdivide us. We can think of DNA as a tiny subset of genes. DNA provides a kind of "instruction book" or set of instructions for replicating an exact copy of you as a person. Your DNA is what makes you uniquely *you* (this is why DNA tests are used by policemen and lawyers to prove whether a particular individual was present at a crime scene, for instance). The molecules of DNA in your cells are in turn organized in chromosomes. These chromosomes are then further grouped into short segments of DNA called genes. These relationships are depicted in Figure 11.1.

Fair enough, you might say. All very interesting, but I signed up for a course in political science. How does all of this affect political beliefs? How does it affect how I behave when I do political things? I can understand that the fact that I have brown or blonde or red hair is coded in my genes. But that's a physical thing, and politics is 100 percent the product of man-made ideas and more generally with socially constructed things that come from the environment around me. Or is it? Is this entirely true? Surely there's no "Democratic Party gene" or "Republican Party gene"? Surely there's no "liberal gene" or "conservative gene"? Well, yes and no. As we will see in what follows, the answers to these questions are complex but compelling.

Twin Studies and The Politics in Your DNA

When I was growing up in the North of England in the 1970s, my best friends were a pair of identical twins called Andrew and Peter (I'll use their

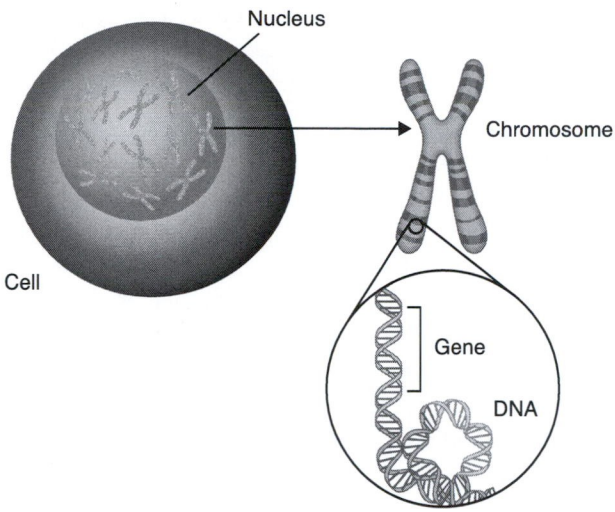

Figure 11.1 Genes, chromosomes, and DNA
Source: Shutterstock. (Compiled from Shutterstock images 47271088 & 110503349)

real names here, as they've given me permission to do that). I first met them in primary (grade) school, and while I don't remember meeting them for the first time—this was well over forty years ago, around about 1971—they both claim today that they remember meeting me (both have quite exceptional memories, something I've unfortunately not been blessed with). But I do know that most people who meet Andrew and Peter for the first time cannot tell them apart, and although I could tell the difference, it amused me a great deal as a child that many others (including their teachers) very often could not. Both Andrew and Peter are politically conservative as well, and readily concede that they tend to vote for the U.K. Conservative party. Their mother and father are fairly conservative politically, so they were brought up in an environment that was also quite conservative.

Like all "identicals," Andrew and Peter share 100 percent of their genetic DNA. In biological terms, this means that the egg they came from was fertilized with the same sperm, and the egg then split into two separate embryos (this type of twin is known technically as MZ, or "monozygotic"). Not everyone knows, though, that there is another kind of twin. In this type, two eggs are fertilized at the same time by different sperm (these twins are known as DZ, or "dizygotic"). I also just happen to know twins of this latter kind, whose names are Bill and Mary (again, they've given permission to use their real names). They are also English and were born a few years before me. While they may look very similar—indeed, many people often mistake them for one another—Bill and Mary are not identical genetically (like all DZs, they share about 50 percent of the same genetic DNA). Interestingly, Bill is left-leaning politically (he usually votes Labour), but Mary is not (she ordinarily votes Conservative).

Why talk about all this, and what could it possibly have to do with politics? Actually, a good deal, at least potentially. For geneticists—and for political scientists like James Fowler, John Hibbing, and Peter Hatemi, who do work in this area—the comparison between identical twins and non-identical ones offers a real opportunity to find out interesting things about the sources of our political preferences (and behavioral traits as well, such as whether we regularly show up to vote at national elections). More particularly, it offers a good chance to find out just *how much* impact your genetic inheritance has on your attitudes and behavior. What if we were to compare the attitudes of identical twins and non-identical ones and find that the former tend, on average, to be more similar (or closer together) ideologically than the latter? Again, the former share 100 percent DNA, while non-identicals share only 50 percent. First of all, of course, we need to get hold of a large database of different kinds of twins from somewhere that also includes data about their ideological views, but let's assume that we have done this. Now, if the identical twins tend to be more similar ideologically than non-identical ones, we will have good grounds for concluding that genes are at work in determining ideological preference. This is exactly what several of the twin studies have found.

Psychologists and behavior geneticists have been conducting twin studies since the mid-1980s, but it wasn't until 2005 that the first political science article using this technique appeared in the pages of the *American Political Science Review (APSR)*. John Alford, Carolyn Funk, and John Hibbing looked at a large database of MZ and DZ twins in just the way suggested above, and concluded that genetics influence the way in which we respond to the environment.[43] MZ twins *are* more alike ideologically than DZ twins, they find. While our genes don't determine which party we identify with—that bit is pretty much socially constructed, since there are different political parties in different countries—they do affect the ideological positions that we take, the authors conclude. Nevertheless, the "left–right" divide is identifiably part of political life everywhere (at various times and places), and the authors contend that there is a biological basis for this.

"Hang on a minute—not so fast!" critics have protested. The whole bio-politics or genopolitics approach remains controversial, and some critics like Evan Charney (a Duke University political scientist) have been especially vocal in denying that these studies are really showing what we think they are showing.[44] Twin studies are a simple idea, but if the situationist–dispositionist debate were this easy to resolve, wouldn't we have done it by now? I mentioned before that both Peter and Andrew grew up in a conservative environment, with parents who voted for the Conservative Party. Might it be that they are conservative simply because they grew up in a conservative household, and that this holds also for other identical twins (a conventional situationist proposition)? Might MZ twins just be treated more alike because they look alike? And might Bill and Mary have had less partisan or ideological parents, so that they were less influenced by household environment than Andrew and Peter (more situationism)? The designers of MZ versus DZ studies and those who utilize this research design are of course well aware of these problems, and they control for the effects of environment. In fact, twin studies are used because they provide a means of doing just that. By measuring the impact of environment as well as genetics, they allow us to compare how much of the variation can be attributed to genetics, how much to other dispositional variables, and how much to situational factors like the household environment.

At the same time, these issues are difficult to overcome entirely. To be 100 percent sure of Hibbing et al.'s findings, we would need to see how twins behave in different environments in order to conclude that genetics really do influence attitudes and behavior. As Doron Shultziner puts it:

> the closest possible method for testing the same genotype under different environments is investigating the case of twins who have been separated at an early stage of childhood and have been reared apart . . . a greater degree of trait similarity under these circumstances may suggest that the same genotype results in similar traits despite developing under unequal environments, assuming that the upbringing environments are indeed sufficiently dissimilar.[45]

Let's say that Andrew had been raised in Liverpool, England and Peter in Outer Borneo, and that we had a lot of other cases that we could add them to (two quite dissimilar environments, in other words). Sounds fair enough as a design, but the problem is that substantial databases of this sort are thinner on the ground, since twins are usually raised in the *same* environment to one another. Technically, we would also need to compare not just types of twins, but twins to *non-twins*. Many of these studies simply assume that if the role of genetics in behavior is more powerful for identical twins than it is for non-identical ones, it must also be powerful for unrelated "non-twins" (e.g. two typical members of the population chosen at random). But twin studies are of course only comparing identical twins to non-identical ones, not twins to the rest of the population. So technically all we can conclude from twin studies with 100 percent confidence is that identical twins are more alike in attitudes than are non-identical twins, and some might question whether we can extrapolate the results to the broader conclusion that genes exert a powerful impact on *everyone's* political behavior. At the same time, existing studies provide very few if any reasons for concluding that twins differ in their political behavior to non-twins.

Allford, Funk, and Hibbing's 2005 study provoked enormous controversy in the wider field. Many traditional scholars of voting behavior—as we will see in Chapter 12, a great many are died-in-the-wool situationists who were themselves "reared" on *The American Voter*—dismissed the result as absurd on its face. So genetics influence how we vote, and how we see politics in general? They had never heard of such a thing, and the techniques of Alford, Funk, and Hibbing were even less familiar to them. The notion that we are born with predispositions was alien to them, and even seemed crazy to some. Are people born as little conservatives and little liberals? How can this be? Others freaked out at the very notion of examining the genetics of twins, with its lurking overtones of Dr. Josef Mengele and *The Boys From Brazil*.[46] These people thought of eugenics and its horrors, and warned of biological determinism in social science. Others were somewhat convinced by the study, but countered with other points. It might be, for instance, that genetics can explain attitudes, but attitudes don't necessarily equal behavior. How about backing up the initial study with a study of actual political behavior, then?

A follow-up 2008 article by James Fowler, Laura Baker, and Christopher Dawes did just this. Focusing on the Los Angeles area, the authors wanted to use the twin research design to discover whether there was a relationship between genetics and voter turnout (as well as other forms of political behavior). To do this, they compared a registry of twins in LA to voter registration records in that city and to self-reported turnout.[47] They found that genes and environment both have a significant effect on variations in political behavior, but the biggest surprise for many political scientists—and even many political psychologists—was of course that there was any relationship *at all* between genes and voting! Scholars have also moved beyond this stage, looking for specific "candidate" genes that might be associated with political behaviors and attitudes.[48] It is fair to say that at the time of writing this issue has been difficult to pin down. But the hunt is still on.[49]

While it might be useful to know which particular genes (or more likely combinations of them) are linked to particular personalities, beliefs, and behaviors, given the still-limited state of our knowledge this may be a step too far right now, in terms of the highly complex relationships which exist between particular genes; it seems that behavior is often the product of the interaction of several genes together. There is certainly no single "gene for voting," for instance, and many political scientists would argue that particular genes or streams of DNA are primarily of interest in the natural sciences, or that political scientists "don't need to know" about this in specificity or depth. Perhaps the most important development, though, is the progress that has been made by Hibbing, Fowler, and others in breaking down resistance among situationists to the basic idea that there might be some genetic basis to beliefs and behavior (an uncontroversial claim in biology, but marginalized within political science as a field).

Most recently, Hibbing, Smith, and Alford have written an interesting and accessible book called *Predisposed* which examines the biology of political differences.[50] The kind of political fault lines that currently bedevil politics in Washington D.C. (and the seemingly endless debate over "Obamacare" in particular) are so enduring and hard to resolve because they are in fact biologically rooted, they claim. While it isn't the case that we are born with "liberal genes" or "conservative genes," we are born with a whole set of genes which *predispose* us towards one view or another (notice that the authors did not give the book the more forceful title "Predetermined," since they are only arguing that this is a matter of tendency rather than fate). We inherit from our parents not just hair color or eye color or other physical traits, but aspects of our personalities as well as genes which predispose us to particular political views and make it more likely that we'll be liberal or conservative (such as our views about human nature). Hibbing and his colleagues suggest that liberals and conservatives tend to cluster around other beliefs and attitudes that you might not think of initially as being "political," such as whether you like arugula (a kind of rock salad or cabbage leaf) or can't stand it, and whether or not you like to drink lattes and peruse *The New York Times* in Starbucks or prefer to swill Bud Lite at a NASCAR meeting. In fact, there is a whole neural architecture behind our ideological beliefs which sustains and supports them, making everything "hang together."

One "deep" factor which seems to affect political preferences, for example, is the simple perception of threat. Hibbing and his colleagues argue that liberals and conservatives appear to come pre-packaged with different attitudes toward threat. "Each of us is primed to respond physiologically and psychologically to certain categories of stimuli—just not to the same stimuli and not to the same degree," they argue. "Show a group of people the same stimulus and some will flatline while others will get a case of the vapors."[51] They cite the work of psychologist Joseph Vigil at the University of Florida, who finds that those on the political right (in America, conservatives or Republicans) are more likely to perceive an ambiguous signal or communication as threatening than are liberals. And overall, they note that "evidence exists that conservatives perceive disgusting images more unfavorably than do liberals, that they perceive threatening images slightly more unfavorably than do liberals, and that they perceive positive images more favorably than do liberals."[52] The research is still suggestive rather than definitive, but research conducted at the University of Nebraska by Hibbing and his colleagues suggests that skin-conductivity responses to threatening stimuli (like loud, unexpected noises) may be predictive of attitudes to things like war and capital punishment.

Conclusion

We noted in this chapter that neuropolitics is basically a dispositionist approach, in the sense that it begins from the assumption that individual differences lead to variations in behavior. If we believe in *neuroplasticity*—the capacity of our brains to be shaped by the outside world, or by the things to which we have been exposed—then any argument that starts with dispositions must also take account of how our brains are themselves molded and shaped by situations. Genopolitics, of course, starts from the same bio-political assumption. But it is hard to find any practitioners of either approach who are biological *determinists*; in other words, few (if any) advocates of these approaches argue that biology alone determines our attitudes and behavior. John Hibbing in particular explicitly argues that political behavior is the result of the *interaction* between dispositions and situations. This is an intriguing perspective and one which has a direct bearing on the themes of this book, so we'll come back to it at the very end when we discuss "The Future of Political Psychology." We have stressed also that neuropolitics and genopolitics are both biopolitical approaches and sometimes strongly reinforce one another. For instance the finding that liberals and conservatives have different brain structures can be used in support of the argument that many attitudes are "heritable." On the other hand, they are logically separate. As we'll see in the next chapter, neuropolitical perspectives often stress the centrality of emotion in voting choice, while many genopolitical approaches emphasize the extent to which many people's attitudes are already relatively fixed and are thus hard to sway.

We have now seen that there are different forms of both situationism and dispositionism. In the final section of the book we shall attempt what is admittedly a rather daunting task: bringing together a number of empirical areas which have been studied by political psychologists—a highly diverse group operating with a variety of theoretical mindsets and exhibiting a range of interests—under the rubric of the general organizing device we have been using. As we admitted at the beginning of the book, however, no conceptual framework is perfect, and the reader may sometimes encounter areas of ambiguity where a theory does not appear to fit into one category or another, or rather more commonly, where it seems to fit both simultaneously. This is to be expected, since relatively few theories emphasize psychological beliefs and personalities of actors to the wholesale exclusion of contexts, environments, and situations; equally, there are few theories that are purely situationist in character, saying absolutely nothing about the psychological makeup of political actors. In most areas of political psychology, as we shall see, research within a particular field has emphasized one or the other, with fashions changing over time.

Notes

1 It would be impolitic, of course, to identify the people I heard talking in these terms!

2 Peter Hatemi and Rose McDermott, "Introduction," p.6 in Hatemi and McDermott (eds.), *Man Is By Nature A Political Animal: Evolution, Biology, and Politics* (Chicago, IL: University of Chicago Press, 2011).

3 John Hibbing, "Ten Misconceptions Concerning Neurobiology and Politics," *Perspectives On Politics*, 11: 475–89, 2013. See Jonas Kaplan, Joshua Freedman, and Marco Iacoboni, "Us Versus Them: Political Attitudes and Party Affiliation Influence Neural Response to Faces of Presidential Candidates," *Neuropsychologica*, 45: 55–64, 2007; and Drew Westen, Pavel Blagov, Keith Harenski, Clint Kilts, and Stephan Hamann, "The Neural Basis of Motivated Reasoning: An fMRI Study of Emotional Constraints on Political Judgment During the US Presidential Election of 2004," *Journal of Cognitive Neuroscience*, 18: 1947–58, 2006. The latter study is also summarized in Drew Westen, *The Political Brain: The Role of Emotion in Deciding the Fate of the Nation* (New York: Public Affairs, 2007), especially pp.x–xv.

4 See for instance Albert Somit and Stephen Peterson, *Biology and Politics: The Cutting edge* (New York: Emerald Group Publishing Limited, 2011) and Robert Blank and Samuel Hines, *Biology and Political Science* (New York: Routledge, 2001).

5 See Hibbing, "Ten Misconceptions."

6 Ryota Kanai, Tom Feilden, Colin Firth, and Geraint Rees, "Political Orientations Are Correlated With Brain Structure in Young Adults," *Current Biology*, 21: 677–80, 2011. See also David Amodio, John Jost, Sarah Master, and Cindy Yee, "The Neurocognitive Correlates of Liberalism and Conservatism," *Nature Neuroscience* 10: 1246–47, 2007.

7 See Maggie Koerth-Baker, "What A Dead Fish Can Teach You About Neuroscience and Statistics," accessed at http://boingboing.net/2012/10/02/what-a-dead-fish-can-teach-you.html.

8 See Darren Schreiber and Marco Iacoboni, "Sophistication in Evaluating Political Questions: Neural Substrates and Functional Mechanisms," paper presented at the Political Methodology Annual Conference, Stanford, California, 2004; and Schreiber, "Political Cognition as Social Cognition: Are We All Political Sophisticates?", in Russell Neuman, George Marcus, Michael MacKuen, and Ann Crigler (eds.), *The Affect Effect: Dynamics of Emotion in Political Thinking and Behavior* (Chicago, IL: University of Chicago Press, 2007).

9 See Jonas Kaplan, Joshua Freedman, and Marco Iacoboni, "Us Versus Them" and John Tierney, "The 2004 Campaign: Using MRIs to See Politics On The Brain," *New York Times*, April 20, 2004. The author is indebted to Dr. Marco Iacoboni, Director of the Transcranial Magnetic Stimulation Laboratory at Ahmanson Lovelace Brain Mapping Center, UCLA and Dr. Jeffrey Bedwell of the Clinical Cognitive Neuroscience Laboratory at the University of Central Florida for

their assistance in answering the author's questions about the utility of different scanning techniques and their role in measuring emotion. Thanks also to David Pearl of Washington State University for stimulating my interest in the general topic of neuroscience and EEG in particular.

10 Marco Iacoboni, Joshua Freedman, and Jonas Kaplan, Op-Ed, "This Is Your Brain on Politics," *New York Times*, November 11, 2007.

11 Ibid.

12 Ibid.

13 See Westen, et al. "The Neural Basis of Motivated Reasoning" and Westen, *The Political Brain*.

14 The exceptions are George Marcus's excellent *The* Sentimental *Citizen: Emotion in Democratic Politics* (University Park, PA: The Pennsylvania State University Press, 2002), especially Chapters 3 and 4, and Westen's *The Political Brain*. Also important in this growing literature is the work of Darren Schreiber on political communication. See especially Schreiber, "Political Cognition as Social Cognition," "The Evolution of the Political Brain: An Agent-Based Model," paper presented at the annual meeting of the American Political Science Association, Philadelphia, 2006, and "Monkey See, Monkey Do: Mirror Neurons, Functional Brain Imaging, and Looking at Political Faces," paper presented at the annual meeting of the American Political Science Association, Washington, D.C., 2005; as well as Joel Weinberger and Drew Westen's work on subliminal political advertising. See Weinberger and Westen, "RATS, We Should Have Used Clinton: Subliminal Priming in Political Campaigns," paper presented at the International Society of Political Psychology Conference, Portland, OR, 2007. For discussions of the utility of neuroscience in understanding politics, see Rose McDermott, "The Feeling of Rationality: The Meaning of Neuroscientific Advances for Political Science," *Perspectives on Politics*, 2: 691–706, 2004; the special edition of *Political Psychology*, Volume 24, 2003 on neuroscience; Marcus, "The Psychology of Emotion and Politics," in David Sears, Leonie Huddy, and Robert Jervis (eds.), *Oxford Handbook of Political Psychology* (New York: Oxford University Press, 2003); and Dustin Tingley, "Neurological Imaging as Evidence in Political Science: A Review, Critique, and Guiding Assessment," *Social Science Information*, 45: 5–33, 2006.

15 John Ratey, *A User's Guide To The Brain: Perception, Attention, and the Four Theaters of the Brain* (New York: Vintage Books, 2001).

16 See Westen, *The Political Brain*, p.50.

17 Ibid., p.57.

18 Ibid., p.53.

19 Ibid., p.60.

20 Ibid., pp.60–61.

21 See for instance Oliver Sacks, *The Man Who Mistook His Wife For A Hat And Other Clinical Tales* (New York: Touchstone, 1998).

22 Antonio Damasio, *Descartes' Error: Emotion, Reason, and the Human Brain* (New York: Penguin, 1994).

23 Ibid., p.32.

24 Dr. Marco Iacoboni, communication with the author, December 7, 2007.

25 Ralph Adolphs, "Cognitive Neuroscience of Human Social Behavior," *Nature Reviews: Neuroscience*, 4: 165–78, 2003; Tingley, "Neurological Imaging as Evidence in Political Science," p.19.

26 Quoted in Tierney, "The 2004 Campaign."

27 Iacoboni, communication with the author.

28 Iacoboni, communication with the author.

29 Bedwell, conversation with the author, December 13, 2007.

30 Iacoboni, communication with the author.

31 Quoted in Tierney, "The 2004 Campaign."

32 Daniel Amen, "Getting Inside Their Heads . . . Really Inside," *Los Angeles Times*, December 5, 2007. For instance, Bedwell notes that the sophistication of brain imaging has not yet reached a level where confident predictions can be made about later Alzheimer's in any case. Bedwell, conversation with the author.

33 Kaplan, Freedman, and Iacoboni, "Us Versus Them," pp.60–61.

34 On this point, see also Darren Schreiber, "Race and Social Norms: An fMRI Study," paper presented at the International Society of Political Psychology Conference, Portland, OR, 2007.

35 Tingley, "Neurological Imaging as Evidence in Political Science," p.6.

36 James Fowler and Darren Schreiber, "Biology, Politics, and the Emerging Science of Human Nature," *Science*, 322: 912–914, 7 November 2008; see also Fowler and Christopher Dawes, "In Defense of Genopolitics," *American Political Science Review*, 107: 362–74, 2013.

37 Richard Monastersky, "The Body Politic: Biology May Shape Political Views," *Chronicle of Higher Education*, September 19, 2008; Emily Biuso, "Genopolitics," *The New York Times*, December 12, 2008.

38 Konrad Lorenz, *On Aggression* (New York: Harcourt Brace, 1966).

39 Ibid.

40 Dave Grossman, *On Killing: The Psychological Cost of Learning To Kill In War And Society* (Boston, MA: Little, Brown, 1995).

41 It is currently banned in the United Kingdom, for instance, but not in the United States.

42 This discussion draws closely on that provided at the website www.23andme.com/gen101/genes/, which provides a straightforward summary of the basics geared towards beginning students.

43 John Alford, Carolyn Funk, and John Hibbing, "Are Political Orientations Genetically Transmitted?," *American Political Science Review*, 99: 153–67, 2005. See also Peter Hatemi, John Hibbing, John Alford, Nicholas Martin, and Lindon Eaves, "Is There a 'Party' In Your Genes?," *Political Research Quarterly*, 62: 584–600, 2009; and Jaimie Settle, Christopher Dawes, and James H. Fowler, "The Heritability of Partisan Attachment," *Political Research Quarterly*, 62: 601–13, 2009.

44 Evan Charney, "Genes and Ideologies," *Perspectives on Politics*, 6: 299–319, 2008; Charney and William English, "Candidate Genes and Political Behavior," *American Political Science Review*, 106: 1–34, 2012. For an especially noteworthy response to Charney, see Rebecca Hannagan and Peter Hatemi, "The Threat of Genes: A Comment on Evan Charney's 'Genes and Ideologies'," *Perspectives on Politics*, 6: 329–35, 2008.

45 Doron Shultziner, "Genes and Politics: A New Explanation and Evaluation of Twin Study Results and Association Studies in Political Science," *Political Analysis*, 21: 350–67, 2013.

46 Originally a novel by Ira Levin, the film presents a fictionalized account of Simon Wiesenthal's hunt for the Nazi war criminal Josef Mengele. In both the book

and the film, Mengele is trying to clone "more Hitlers" genetically some time in the 1970s, having obtained a DNA sample from the Führer many years earlier. Interestingly, he realizes that he has to recreate the situational forces which shaped Adolf Hitler's life and made him what he became, as well as using Hitler's own genetic material. While the plot sounds a bit silly, the themes of the movie get to the very heart of the situationist–dispositionist debate.

47 James Fowler, Laura Baker, and Christopher Dawes, "Genetic Variation in Political Participation," *American Political Science Review*, 102: 233–48, 2008.
48 James Fowler and Christopher Dawes, "Two Genes Predict Voter Turnout," *Journal of Politics*, 70: 579–94, 2008.
49 Peter Hatemi et al., "Genome-Wide Analysis of Liberal and Conservative Attitudes," *Journal of Politics*, 73: 271–85, 2011.
50 John Hibbing, Kevin Smith, and John Alford, *Predisposed: Liberals, Conservatives, and the Biology of Political Differences* (New York: Routledge, 2014). See also Avi Tuschman, *Our Political Nature: The Evolutionary Origins of What Divides Us* (New York: Prometheus Books, 2013). Tuschman is an evolutionary anthropologist, and his argument is more focused on the evolutionary advantages of particular types of predisposition than that of Hibbing et al.
51 Hibbing et al., *Predisposed*, p.20.
52 Ibid., p.136.

Suggested Further Reading

Antonio Damasio, *Descartes' Error: Emotion, Reason, and the Human Brain* (New York: Putnam, 1994).

Peter Hatemi and Rose McDermott (eds.), *Man Is By Nature A Political Animal: Evolution, Biology, and Politics* (Chicago, IL: University of Chicago Press, 2011).

John Hibbing, Kevin Smith, and John Alford, *Predisposed: Liberals, Conservatives, and the Biology of Political Differences* (New York: Routledge, 2014).

Drew Westen, *The Political Brain: The Role of Emotion in Deciding the Fate of the Nation* (New York: Public Affairs, 2007).

Part III

Bringing the Two Together

Chapter 12

The Psychology of Voting Behavior

Some electoral campaign advertisements (or "ads") appeal to fear, like the now infamous 1964 "daisy chain ad" run by the Lyndon Johnson campaign, suggesting in rather unsubtle terms that we'd all soon be dead if his Republican rival Barry Goldwater became president. The 1988 "furlough" ad, promising that violent rapists would soon be running America's streets if Democrat Michael Dukakis was elected instead of Republican George H.W. Bush, had a similar objective (though this time the Republicans were the ones who used crude fearmongering). Others ads are more uplifting, inspiring hope and enthusiasm, like many of those run by the Obama campaign when he first ran for president in 2008 or Bill Clinton's "A Place Called Hope" ad in 1992. Ted Brader notes that we know remarkably little about the psychological processes which underlie successful advertising, but the short answer is that the most successful ones appeal to our emotions. What Brader calls "unimpassionated ads"—communications which simply convey information without trying to stir up people's passions—are very much the exception, because we know (even on an intuitive level, without even referring to political psychology) that emotionless ads generally don't work. Brader argues that "campaign ads affect voters by appealing to their emotions . . . campaign ads use symbolic images and evocative music to trigger an emotional response in viewers. By appealing to different emotions, ads can influence the participation and choices of viewers in distinct ways," Brader argues. "Enthusiasm appeals motivate voters to get involved and act on existing loyalties, while fear appeals provoke viewers to seek out new information and reconsider their choices," he adds.[1]

We have already seen Drew Westen's argument in *The Political Brain*, which has a similar theme about the centrality of emotion in voting. Reinforcing the claim that voting is emotionally based, moreover, is an increasing body of recent work which suggests that it is also rapid, instantaneous, and involves largely unconscious processes. Especially noteworthy in this regard is the work of Princeton psychologist Alexander Todorov.[2] His research suggests that we make extremely rapid judgments about candidates based upon their mere physical appearance (or what psychologists call "thin slice" information). More than half the time—in fact, up to 57 percent of the time in some of his results—subjects correctly "predict" the outcome of an election by simply assessing whether the candidates appear competent or not. This flies in the face of *Homo economicus* type explanations—in which a highly informed voter compares candidate positions on a variety of issues—and it is reinforced by many other studies which suggest that first impressions really do matter. What is most interesting is that participants in these experiments made judgments after only very brief exposure to the images (100–2000 ms), viewing pictures of politicians they were unfamiliar with. Michael Spezio and his colleagues have also shown that negative instant evaluations play as much of a role as positive ones in influencing voter choice, and they too stress the importance of instant evaluation via nonverbal cues.[3] With colleague Janine Willis, Todorov has found that the time of exposure to images does not matter in terms of how people assess a candidate, suggesting that the unconscious brain has already made up its mind about a candidate in a matter of milliseconds.[4] So much for issue positions.

One drawback of this type of research is that while it shows that we make rapid judgments about the competence (or otherwise) of others when we know nothing else about them, this still leaves the door open for snap judgments to be overridden, either when the candidates' traits are already known or by party identification (in other words, Todorov's approach works best when we literally know nothing about the person we are looking at). So while this might be exactly how we make judgments about candidates absent information about party or character traits (say, for instance, when people are making up their minds about two competing mayoral candidates, where neither has mentioned a party and little is known about either). But when we do have such information, snap judgments might be overridden or play much less of a role.

It's also clear that not all voters are swayed by emotional factors in general. Many seem to be unamenable to political messages and relatively *fixed* in their choices, either because they have strong party convictions, or ideological beliefs, or both. We have already encountered the work of Hibbing, Smith, and Alford in the previous chapter, which suggests that while our voting behavior is not fixed—again, it is not "predetermined"—we have powerful predispositions that make it hard for us to switch our allegiances, not least because there is a whole neural architecture beneath our political views which supports (and indeed, gives rise to) them. Changing your beliefs involves changing the whole architecture beneath. We have also seen research which suggests that even turning out to vote is "in the genes." As we shall see in this chapter, there is a long tradition of viewing the vote in the United States as composed of two rather unmoveable blocs. This regularity has long been assumed to come from situationist sources (like the income of the household we grew up in), but Hibbing et al. suggest that it has much deeper dispositionist roots. Various branches of psychology—most notably social and cognitive variations—have played a major role in the development of the study of voting behavior (or electoral choice, as it is sometimes referred to). As we shall see, the earliest work (heavily influenced by social psychology) was notably situationist in character, while later work (derived from economics, cognitive psychology, and work on affect and emotion) has been a bit more dispositionist. Much of the work on the application of schemas and other knowledge structures to politics has been done in the area of voting behavior. This is also a field in which the contrast between models of voting behavior based on economic and psychological assumptions is especially clear, and it is worth noting at the outset that the study of electoral choice today is still as much influenced by *Homo economicus* as it is *Homo psychologicus*.[5]

From Situationism to Dispositionism

The earliest models of voting behavior, such as the *index of political predisposition* (IPP) developed by Paul Lazarsfeld and Bernard Berelson, were almost completely situationist in character.[6] This approach claimed that voting could be predicted in advance with a high degree of accuracy simply by knowing the socioeconomic status, religion, residential, and other basic social characteristics of the voter. Voting was seen purely as a function of the social environment in which the voter existed. Moreover, the IPP approach viewed voters as essentially "passive" receptors of the situations in which they found themselves.

There was not much psychology in this early perspective, but in the 1960s voting behavior took a dispositionist turn, when a much revised version of this basic argument added an explicitly psychological variable: the *party identification* approach. This theory explicitly recognized that situation wasn't everything, and that voter choice is not just a matter of social or economic location. In their classic work *The American Voter*, Angus Campbell and his colleagues at the University of Michigan argued that most voters develop a long-term *emotional attachment* or disposition towards a particular political party during their formative or teenage years.[7] As we mature politically, we develop an affiliation to one party—often as a result of listening to our parents or neighbors talk about politics, or from some other aspect of the social environment—and that attachment tends to determine the way we vote for the rest of our lifetimes (unless something very dramatic happens to make us change our mind as is possible under the cognitive consistency theory). Voters develop their own individualized dispositions towards politics, albeit dispositions constrained by the makeup of the party system. The result is that the American electorate resembles two enormous blocs, one composed of Republican Party identifiers, the other of Democratic Party identifiers. This model was also imported to Britain by David Butler and his colleagues, who argued that the U.K. electorate similarly resembled two giant blocs composed of Conservative and Labour Party identifiers.[8]

One important thing to notice about party identifications is that they tend to be *highly stable* and resistant to change. Your party may lose a few elections, it may perform badly in government, or it may even adopt policy positions on some issues which you disagree with, but you will still support the party, because it's *your* party. One consequence of this is that for many people, the issues being discussed at the election do not matter nearly as much as party does. A strong party identifier, for instance, will tend to "screen out" or ignore altogether information about his or her party that is unfavorable, even where he or she disagrees with their party's representative on major policy issues. For example, many Republican voters and party members reportedly did not want Mitt Romney to be their party's presidential candidate in 2012. During the primaries, a number of (fairly conservative) "front runners" emerged, such as Texas Governor Rick Perry and Minnesota Congresswoman Michelle Bachman, only to drop back in the polls a week or two later. While Romney was the presumptive nominee very early on and was judged by far the most likely to beat Obama in the eventual presidential race, there seemed to be an "anybody but Romney" movement afoot in the primaries for a while. He ran to the right of the party, but had a history as a relatively liberal Governor of Massachusetts. However, there was very little possibility that strong Republican Party identifiers would vote against their party in 2012 because of Romney. This is because strong identifiers tend to screen out political information they dislike and engage in "selective perception"; in other words, they see what they want to and "hold their noses" at the polls if they happen to dislike the party choice.

One of *The American Voter*'s authors, Philip Converse, was a trained social psychologist, and the influence of that field as it existed in the 1950s and 1960s is readily apparent in the model. First of all, it emphasized social identification with reference groups. It also stressed the drive to maintain cognitive consistency.[9] The influence of cognitive consistency theory in particular should be pretty apparent to the reader, given what we already know about that approach from Chapter 9. As we saw in that chapter, people do not like to act in ways contrary to their own beliefs, or to hold incompatible beliefs, or to have their beliefs confronted with information that is incompatible with those beliefs. All of these conditions, the theory suggests, create a state of psychological discomfort. This is what Leon Festinger called "cognitive dissonance"[10] and manifests itself when a strong party identifier finds him-/herself at odds with his or her party on a key issue, such as abortion or civil rights, or may even dislike the presidential or vice-presidential candidate his or her party has nominated. The theory assumes that in the face of such dissonance, the voter becomes strongly motivated to bring things back into balance (what Festinger called "consonance"). This could be done by rationalizing away the issue disagreement or candidate choice as unimportant ("the Civil Rights Act won't change things around here," "the Supreme Court will decide the abortion issue anyway," and so on) or perhaps by adding some extra belief which reduces the dissonance. Finally, one could switch one's party allegiance altogether and so bring one's voting behavior more into line with one's choice of party, but the party identification model suggests that this is extremely unlikely given that it usually takes an earth-shattering event like war or depression to change a voter's allegiances.

Philip Converse became famous in particular for his argument that voters lack what is usually termed "attitude constraint."[11] Mass surveys conducted since the 1940s had found that ordinary voters in America were not that sophisticated; they possessed low levels of information about politics and paid only intermittent attention to what was going on in the political world. Converse noted in particular that very few possessed a worked out "ideology," as one might expect a political sophisticate to have; instead he argued that most people had attitudes "all over the place," as one of the author's teachers put it; they were liberal on some issues and conservative on others, and they often did not even fully understand what the terms "liberal" and "conservative" meant.

According to this model of voting behavior, for most people it does not usually matter who the candidates are or what positions they take on the issues of the day; people who identify with the Democratic Party will usually always vote for the Democratic Party's candidate, and Republican Party identifiers will normally always vote for the Republican candidate. A number of individuals sought the Democratic Party's presidential nomination in 2008, for instance, including Barack Obama, Hillary Clinton, and John Edwards. However, party identification theorists suggest that no matter which one of these got the nomination, Democratic Party identifiers would vote for him or her. Equally, no matter whether the Republican Party had chosen Mitt Romney, Rudy Giuliani, Fred Thompson, Mike Huckabee, John McCain, or someone else in 2008, Republican Party identifiers would vote for their party's candidate. For the majority of citizens, the act of voting is thus "habitual" or "instinctive." The average citizen is not that well informed about politics and does not spend his or her time dutifully scrutinizing the campaign proposals of the main political parties in deciding how to vote; rather the voter simply "short-cuts" the complex decision process by selecting that party towards which he or she has developed a long-term affinity since early adulthood.

There is another element of dispositionism in this theory as well. Since the Democratic Party for many years had the most identifiers within the American electorate, the Democrats would have won virtually every U.S. presidential election since the 1930s if party were all that mattered. Advocates of this approach, however, say that something like two-thirds of the electorate have stable party loyalties and always vote for their party at every election. One-third of the electorate, however, is composed of people who are only weakly attached to a political party or who are out-and-out independents. This one-third is made up of "switchers" or "swing voters," individuals who lack any stable party loyalty and hence are likely to change their minds as to which they support from one election to another. For this one-third, dispositions matter just as much as they do for the party identifiers, but these dispositions are far less stable and more changeable. This one-third is composed of individuals who make up their minds on the basis of the issues, and it is this segment of the voting population that in practice decides the result of the election. Voting behavior, according to the party identification model, is thus the result of the interaction between long-term (notably party attachment) and short-term dispositional forces (voter reactions to the issues). It also "portrayed candidate assessments as dominated by the more enduring forces of parties and issues," as Miller, Wattenberg, and Malanchuk note.[12]

The Rise of Issue Voting and *Homo Economicus*

To some extent the party identification model has gone out of fashion in recent years, in part because it has become progressively clear in the years since Campbell and his associates wrote that fewer voters nowadays *actually have* a strong and stable party affiliation. At the 1992 presidential election, for example, only about 29 percent strongly identified with either the Republicans or the Democrats, while 38 percent did in 1964, a drop of 9 percent (supposedly the proportion of identifiers has risen since then, but it depends how one measures it). Voters also seem to have become more ideologically and politically sophisticated since the 1960s. By the 1970s, these trends gave rise to an approach to explaining electoral choice that challenged the prevailing party identification orthodoxy: the *issue voting model*. This approach, moreover, was inspired in large part not by the assumptions of *Homo psychologicus*, but by those of *Homo economicus*.

In their book *The Changing American Voter*, Nie, Verba, and Petrocik argue that American voters are now a good deal more sophisticated than the party identification model gave them credit for.[13] The authors shared the same underlying approach or starting point as Campbell and his colleagues, in the sense that they concede that the party identification model accurately described the behavior of voters up until the late 1960s. But they argue that trends in electoral data necessitate a reassessment of the average voter's capabilities and behavior. The political environment surrounding the American voter changed dramatically during the 1960s, they argue. The ideological emphasis of Republican presidential candidate Barry Goldwater and the emergence of a range of "new issues" like civil rights, Vietnam, and Watergate, the growth of the mass media, and shifts in the nature of the electorate itself all produced major change. With regard to this last factor, a new generation of voters has entered the electorate which was and is disinclined to identify habitually with a particular political party.

Issue voting theorists argue that party loyalties are significantly declining as an influence on how people vote. They argue that in recent years we have seen a process of *dealignment* going on, a process by which voters are gradually losing their attachments to parties in general, and becoming independents instead. Between 1960 and 1993, the number of voters calling themselves "independents" rose from about 23 percent to 33 percent, and by 2011 it had risen as high as 40 percent according to one measure.[14] As the influence of party has gone down, issue voting supporters say, the importance of issues and candidate characteristics has increased. While previously most people simply voted for their party's candidate because it was "their party," nowadays they are a good deal more selective and sophisticated. The proportion of voters who do this, moreover, is much greater than the one-third described by Campbell and his colleagues, issue voting theorists contend, and may well be 50 percent or even more.

There are essentially two ways of voting on issues: *prospective* and *retrospective* issue voting. Voting prospectively is the more demanding of the two in terms of the knowledge and information it requires of the voter. In order to vote in this way, voters must: (1) look at the policies of the two parties and at the positions they take on the issues, (2) compare these two sets of policies, and (3) select that party which has the policy positions that look most like their own. So for example, if I am conservative on social issues, liberal on economic issues and conservative on foreign policy, I will want to choose the party that looks most like me on these things. In all likelihood no party platform will be a perfect match for my own preferences, but prospective voting simply requires that I select that party which comes closest to my own positions on the issues.

Retrospective issue voting is rather less demanding of the average citizen. Voters, V.O. Key argues in *The Responsible Electorate*, are not fools; they are rational in the sense that they reward incumbents for concrete achievements and punish them for their failures.[15] Voters are perfectly capable of looking backward at the previous few years and asking themselves how well the incumbent administration has performed. Economic performance is particularly salient for voters; generally speaking, if things are going well economically the government will be re-elected, and if things are going badly the administration will be removed from office. This kind of issue voting is relatively straightforward and easy to do. It does not demand that the voter be highly informed about politics and policy, or that he or she even knows a single policy of either party. All that is necessary is that the voter be aware of how well the president's party (for example) is performing. It may also be more "rational" to vote retrospectively on the issues than prospectively, since the informational costs are much lower. Weighing up party positions on the issues may also be actively inadvisable, since we know that politicians may break their promises. Given this fact, it makes little sense to pay much attention to what leaders say they will do during the electoral campaign; it makes a lot more sense to look at what they have actually done in the recent past.

How is it that both schools are able to claim that their model best explains empirical reality? Surely data from recent presidential elections can tell us who is right one way or another? Unfortunately this is far from being the case, for statistical data do not speak for themselves. The two rival approaches interpret the same data differently. The reason they are both simultaneously able to make a case for their own model is because both claim the weak party identifiers as their own. The party identification school argues that weak party identifiers nevertheless maintain a party affiliation, and that they ought to be classed as falling under the party identification category; issue voting supporters, on the other hand, treat those who say they have only a weak identification with party as independents prepared to vote on the basis of the issues and candidates. The party identification school argues that the so-called "decline" in party identification has been greatly exaggerated; between 1960 and 1988, the percentage of voters identifying with a party declined from 75 percent to 63 percent, but this is not an especially marked drop (the figure was 58 percent in the 2011 Gallup poll already cited, though). Some of the most recent work in voting behavior, it is worth noting, has restated the party identification position and attempted to refute the arguments of Nie, Verba, and Petrocik.[16]

The Impact of Hot and Cold Cognition

More recently, scholars of electoral choice have drawn upon the assumptions of cognitive psychology to create dispositionist approaches that do not rely on economistic or rational choice assumptions and/or see party identification in a more cognitive light. The party identification approach always assumed that electoral campaigns—and the messages put out by the candidates themselves—did not matter very much.[17] Voters would screen out most of the "noise" that results from campaigns, the approach suggested, since, as Simon and Garfunkel put it in their song "The Boxer," "a man hears what he wants to hear and disregards the rest." This was consistent, as we have noted, with the predictions of psychologists like Festinger. Recent work inspired by other cognitive and affective theories, however, has called this claim into doubt.[18]

In Chapter 9, we saw one application of this kind of approach to the study of how voters select candidates in presidential primaries, Samuel Popkin's theory of candidate appeal. This approach draws on both schema and attribution theory notions to explain how we decide whom to vote for in primaries and in other elections where we know relatively little about the candidates. Popkin argues that we base our decisions on only a handful of "knowns," and then use these to fill in missing information about the candidate (default values). In that way, we are able to reach a conclusion on how representative a candidate is of some ideal (or non-ideal) stereotype.[19]

Politicians continually try to evoke positive schemas in the minds of voters, even though they may do this only in an intuitive or folk psychological way. A good example is what we might call the "Kennedy schema." The ideal candidate for many voters is relatively young, politically moderate, highly intelligent, rhetorically gifted, and physically attractive, all attributes we nowadays associate with John F. Kennedy. The former Massachusetts senator was also a war hero, which is of course another attribute many voters find appealing. As a result, candidates for national office sometimes try to associate themselves with the Kennedy image and may even explicitly compare themselves to JFK. The most famous example came in the 1988 vice-presidential debate, when the Republican running mate Dan Quayle did just this, noting that he had as much political experience as John Kennedy when Kennedy ran for office. This led to one of the most famous put-downs in debating history, when Senator Lloyd Bentsen, the Democratic vice-presidential candidate, hit back with the following: "Senator, I served with Jack Kennedy. I knew Jack Kennedy. Jack Kennedy was a friend of mine. Senator, you're no Jack Kennedy."

Candidates are usually more subtle than this about trying to appear "Kennedyesque," however. Running for president in 1992, for instance, Bill Clinton's campaign team deliberately used photographic images of Clinton (as a young boy scout in the early 1960s) actually shaking hands with JFK. The discovery of this photograph was a godsend to his campaign, since it implicitly evoked the image and even suggested to some that Clinton was somehow "fated" to reach the same position Kennedy had. Interestingly, the Bush campaign in 2004 successfully deflated the challenge of John Forbes Kerry—a candidate superficially similar to John Kennedy in many ways, even down to his initials—by stressing at least two ways in which Kennedy and Kerry seemed to differ. The Republicans successfully portrayed Kerry as far more liberal than Kennedy had been, and also called into question his war record in various ways that the Kerry campaign seemed unwilling or unable to respond to.

Popkin is of course not the only scholar who has looked to cognitive psychology for clues to how ordinary people process political information; in fact, there is now a vast literature within voting behavior which does this. Kathleen McGraw summarizes that literature by distinguishing between (a) work that examines the ways in which people *structure* and store political information and (b) research that examines the cognitive *processes* that lead to a political judgment, response, or decision.[20] These two issues are of course closely related, for once we understand how people store political information in their heads, we are inevitably going to be interested in how that information is accessed and in the process by which this affects some sort of political outcome, such as a decision about whom to vote for.

In one of the earliest attempts in this first vein, Kinder and his colleagues as long ago as 1980 examined the ways in which voters assess presidential candidates by examining "presidential prototypes," schema-type stereotypes of the kind of attributes thought desirable in a person running for president. "An ideal president prototype . . . consists of the features that citizens believe best define an exemplary president," they note, adding that different individuals have different prototypes which emphasize different values as important.[21] The ideal president in particular is rated by Americans as honest, knowledgeable, open-minded, courageous, smart, and inspiring, to name only the most often cited qualities. "Some standards for appraisal of presidential candidates may be widely shared," but "some may be idiosyncratic, tied to the distinctive and conspicuous qualities of particular candidates."[22] Perhaps surprisingly, they find that their ideal prototype is a poor predictor of support for a candidate, except in the case of incumbent presidents, but that may be because voters seem not to use a single prototype to judge *all* candidates.

Questioning the timing of the 1980 study—the data for which were collected while an actual presidential campaign was going on—Arthur Miller and his colleagues come to rather different conclusions, arguing that "a presidential prototype, or schema, as we shall label it, can and will be evoked during the actual campaign period when people receive the appropriate stimuli to trigger these preexisting conditions."[23] Voters use a "few broad criteria, rather than specific information" to judge candidates—going beyond the information given, as described in Chapter 9—and the more politically sophisticated the voter, the "richer" the array of schemas, which then allows the voter to make more inferences than a less informed individual could.[24] Moreover, according to Miller and his colleagues voters *do* have a consistent schema "concerning what a president should be like, and judge real candidates according to how well they match the elements of these schemas."[25] Perhaps different attributes of this schema may be important at different elections, so that the "ideal candidate" varies with the times. For instance, amid the turmoil of 1968 the country was looking for a president who stressed stability and order, like Richard Nixon; in 1976, in the wake of Vietnam and Watergate, the ideal was a candidate with unimpeachable integrity, like Jimmy Carter; and by 1980 when the United States seemed to be suffering terminal economic and political decline, the country looked to a candidate like Ronald Reagan to restore "American power."

How Do We Decide Who to Vote For?

Work on the *process* side—how cognitive structures are used to evaluate candidates—has also been extensive. Think for a moment about the general theories of voting behavior we have described in this chapter, the IPP, party identification, and issue voting perspectives. None of them actually tells you *how* we decide who to vote for; each lists factors that "explain" the vote and claims some ability to predict electoral choice, but none of them actually tells you much (if anything at all) about the mental processes we go through during a campaign, or how we decide inside the voting booth itself. It is tempting to ascribe this absence of detail to the influence of behaviorism—which as we saw in Chapter 3 rejects any "introspective" examination of what goes on inside people's heads—but by the time the party identification model was developed, cognitive consistency theory had already largely supplanted Skinner's behaviorism. The established approaches described earlier on in this chapter, though, do treat the voter's decision processes as a "black box."[26]

Scholars of voting behavior have developed two main theories that deal with the process of assessing candidates: these are termed the *online* and *memory-based* perspectives. The online approach can best be explained by thinking of a movie you watched a while ago (say, two months ago) that you especially enjoyed. You can't now recall many of the scenes that you liked, but you know that you liked the movie. You rate it one of the best movies you've seen in the last year, but if asked to remember why, you can only relate a few details. Or imagine that you are watching a movie now. Perhaps you have had the experience of watching a movie that you liked initially, but then abandoned in the middle, never to be watched again. In my case, that happened with *Total Recall*, a film that I found philosophically interesting at the outset since it deals indirectly with perception, memory, and the subjective nature of reality, but half way through it degenerates into a standard action movie and became less interesting to me.[27] Today, though, my recall of the film's details is anything but "total." I can remember bits of what I liked and disliked, but not much; what sticks in my mind most is my *overall* assessment.

According to one popular approach, this is similar to the process by which we assess candidates.[28] According to the online theory, we keep a "running tally" or "judgment tally" which governs our impression of a particular candidate, just as we continuously update our assessment of how enjoyable a movie is. We constantly change the tally as new information becomes available, but we often forget the actual pieces of information that contributed to that impression, and we may not be able to recall what impressed us or "turned us off" a candidate when asked later on in an opinion poll. As Druckman and Miller put it:

> In sharp contrast to prior work, this model suggests that voters may have clear reasons for their votes and may be substantially affected by a campaign, even if they are unable to recite reasons for their votes or remember any campaign information. The reason is that voters keep a running evaluation of candidates; when they receive new information, they update their evaluations and then often forget the specific information because it is no longer needed. Thus, voters are able to retrieve the overall evaluation (which has been influenced by the campaigns), but not the information on which the evaluation is based.[29]

This is highly consistent with the *Homo psychologicus* approach, since it regards people as cognitive misers who simply retrieve the evaluations from memory but discard the bits of information used to construct them. So too, however, is a rival approach known as the *memory-based* perspective.[30]

This perspective differs markedly from the notion that campaign information is discarded in favor of online processing. The memory-based approach suggests that when political information is encountered, it is stored in long-term memory, depending on how salient it appears and on the limits of what we can store in our heads. As McGraw puts it:

> when a judgment is needed, the individual searches long-term memory for information and integrates the information that can be retrieved to compute the judgment. In the end, the opinion is a reflection of the information that can be retrieved from memory.[31]

On election day, we simply piece together what we can recall to create a composite judgment.

To see how the two approaches differ, consider for a moment assessments of Barack Obama as he ran for the presidency in 2008. As election day drew near, the online approach suggests that voters would keep in their heads a continually updated, running tally of how Obama had performed during the presidential campaign, a kind of mental scorecard which would also include other pieces of information that they had used to form assessments of him over the past year or two. For instance, a positive assessment of Obama that saw him as a dynamic, charismatic candidate might be updated with more negative information, such as the allegations made during the campaign that Obama's former preacher was supposedly "unAmerican." But on election day the voter might not necessarily even recall that piece of information even though it might impact the scorecard, or the negative information might have been supplanted in the tally by more positive, updated information in the voter's head. On the other hand, a memory-based assessment of Obama in 2008 would be more simple and straightforward; the voter would simply "add up" the positive and negative information he or she has about the candidate to form his or her assessment. Again, however, both approaches are highly cognitive in nature, since they both start from the assumption that there are limits to the amount of information that voters can and do store in their heads.

Conclusion: The Future of Election Research

In October 2006 a conference organized by the American National Election Studies (ANES) at Duke University on the psychology of voting concluded that voting behavior is best conceived of as the product of the interaction between both external (situational) factors and internal (dispositional) forces.[32] Recent work has focused on the cognitive and affective forces inside people's heads, on biological forces and the heredity of political attitudes and behaviors, and on the role of emotional or subconscious cues, but future research probably needs to do a better job of integrating this research with situationist factors such as movements in the national and international economy, the outbreak of major wars, the social pressures exerted by individuals in the voter's environment, and "one-off" events in the campaign itself that may radically alter our perceptions of the candidates. Some of our voting may be emotional and instinctive, and other patterns may come from predispositions in our biology. The next step will be to better examine how biology and other dispositional factors interact with one another.

Notes

1 Ted Brader, *Campaigning For Hearts and Minds: How Emotional Appeals in Political Ads Work* (Chicago, IL: University of Chicago Press, 2006).
2 See for instance Alexander Todorov, Anesu Mandisodza, Amir Goren, and Crystal Hall, "Inferences of Competence from Faces Predict Election Outcomes," *Science*, 308: 1623–26, 2005 and Christopher Olivola and Alexander Todorov, "Elected in 100 Milliseconds: Appearance-Based Trait Inferences and Voting," *Journal of Nonverbal Behavior*, 34: 83–119, 2010.
3 Michael Spezio, Antonio Rangel, Ramon Michael Alvarez, John O'Doherty, Kyle Mattes, Alexander Todorov, Hacklin Kim, and Ralph Adolphs, "A Neural Basis for the Effect of Candidate Appearance on Election Outcomes," *Social Cognitive and Affective Neuroscience*; 3(4): 344–52, 2008.
4 Janine Willis and Alexander Todorov, "First Impressions: Making Up Your Mind After a 100-Ms Exposure to a Face," *Psychological Science*, 17: 592–98, 2006.
5 The literature on this topic is now so substantial that it is impossible to do full justice to it here, but we shall concentrate on some of the main highlights.
6 See for instance Paul Lazarsfeld, Bernard Berelson, and Hazel Gaudet, *The People's Choice* (New York: Columbia University Press, 1948).
7 Angus Campbell, Philip Converse, Warren Miller, and Donald Stokes, *The American Voter* (New York: Wiley, 1960). This approach is sometimes known simply as the "Michigan School."
8 David Butler and Donald Stokes, *Political Change in Britain: Forces Shaping Electoral Choice* (New York: St. Martin's Press, 1969).
9 See the website of a 2006 Duke University conference on the psychology of voting at http://www.ssri.duke.edu/anes/voting.html.
10 Leon Festinger, *A Theory of Cognitive Dissonance* (Stanford, CA: Stanford University Press, 1957).
11 Philip Converse, "The Nature of Belief Systems in Mass Publics," in David Apter (ed.), *Ideology and Discontent* (New York: Free Press, 1964).
12 Arthur Miller, Martin Wattenberg, and Oksana Malanchuk, "Schematic Assessments of Presidential Candidates," *American Political Science Review*, 80: 521–40, 1986.
13 Norman Nie, Sidney Verba, and John Petrocik, *The Changing American Voter* (Cambridge, MA: Harvard University Press, 1976). See also Morris Fiorina, *Retrospective Voting in American National Elections* (London: Yale University Press, 1981).
14 See Gallup Politics website, "Record-High 40% of Americans Identify as Independents in '11," January 9, 2012, available at http://www.gallup.com/poll/151943/Record-High-Americans-Identify-Independents.aspx.
15 V.O. Key, *The Responsible Electorate* (Cambridge, MA: The Belknap Press, 1966).
16 See for instance Eric Smith, *The Unchanging American Voter* (Berkeley, CA: University of California Press, 1989); Warren Miller and Merrill Shanks, *The New American Voter* (London: Harvard University Press, 1996).
17 Milton Lodge, Patrick Stroh, and John Wahlke, "Black Box Models of Candidate Evaluation," *Political Behavior*, 12: 5–18, 1990.
18 See James Druckman and Joanne Miller, "The Political Psychology of Electoral Campaigns," *Political Psychology*, 25: 501–6, 2004 and the accompanying *Symposium* in that issue.

19 Samuel Popkin, "Decision Making in Presidential Primaries," in Shanto Iyengar and William McGuire (eds.), *Explorations in Political Psychology* (Durham, NC: Duke University Press, 1993).

20 Kathleen McGraw, "Contributions of the Cognitive Approach to Political Psychology," *Political Psychology*, 21: 805–27, 2000.

21 Donald Kinder, Mark Peters, Robert Abelson, and Susan Fiske, "Presidential Prototypes," *Political Behavior*, 2: 315–37, 1980, p.316.

22 Ibid., p.333.

23 Arthur Miller, Martin Wattenberg, and Oksana Malanchuk, "Schematic Assessments of Presidential Candidates," pp.523–24.

24 Ibid, p.524.

25 Ibid., p.535.

26 Lodge, Stroh, and Wahlke, "Black-Box Models of Candidate Evaluation."

27 The first part of the film is based on a short story by the late, great science fiction author Philip K. Dick called "We Can Remember It For You Wholesale."

28 Milton Lodge, Kathleen McGraw, and Patrick Stroh, "An Impression-Driven Model of Candidate Evaluation," *American Political Science Review*, 83: 399–419, 1989. See also Reid Hastie and Bernadette Park, "The Relationship between Memory and Judgment Depends on Whether the Task Is Memory-Based or On-Line," *Psychological Review*, 93: 258–68, 1986 and Howard Lavine, "On-Line Versus Memory-Based Process Models of Political Evaluation," in Kristen Monroe (ed.), *Political Psychology* (Mahwah, NJ: Lawrence Erlbaum, 2002).

29 Druckman and Miller, "The Political Psychology of Electoral Campaigns," p.502.

30 See for instance Stanley Feldman, "Answering Survey Questions: The Measurement and Meaning of Public Opinion," in Milton Lodge and Kathleen McGraw, *Political Judgment: Structure and Process* (Ann Arbor, MI: University of Michigan Press, 1995) and John Zaller, *The Nature and Origins of Mass Opinion* (New York: Cambridge University Press, 1992).

31 McGraw, "Contributions of the Cognitive Approach to Political Psychology," p.813.

32 See the conference website at http://www.ssri.duke.edu/anes/index.html.

Suggested Further Reading

Warren Miller and Merrill Shanks, *The New American Voter* (London: Harvard University Press, 1996).

Norman Nie, Sidney Verba, and John Petrocik, *The Changing American Voter* (Cambridge, MA: Harvard University Press, 1976).

Eric Smith, *The Unchanging American Voter* (Berkeley, CA: University of California Press, 1989).

Film

The Candidate (1972): Classic Hollywood depiction of a reluctant young candidate, played by Robert Redford, and the rise of the campaign machine.

Chapter 13

The Psychology of Political Communication, Persuasion, and the Mass Media

In one sense, the impact of mass media on politics is nothing new. Television played a role in American domestic and foreign policy on several occasions in the 1960s and 1970s, for instance, most notably during the JFK assassination, the Vietnam War and the Iran hostage crisis. What *is* new, arguably, is the growth of internet and advanced satellite communications and perhaps the degree of impact the media exerts. The 1960 presidential election debate between Richard Nixon and John F. Kennedy—where those who viewed the debate on television adjudged JFK the winner, while those who heard it on the radio thought it was a draw—is often seen as a turning point in American politics. Today, the instantaneous nature of TV and computer images that has accompanied these means that global news networks like CNN are able to transmit pictures around the world in real time. Images of "Tank Man" and Tiananmen Square in China in June 1989, and of the visually spectacular U.S. attacks on Baghdad during the Persian Gulf War in January 1991, are often said to have defined the mission of CNN as a news agency and made it a key player in the media business. The mass media also has the potential to "frame" domestic issues like the debate over the Affordable Care Act (commonly known as "Obamacare") as a "success" or a "failure."

Events like the Persian Gulf War have sparked a debate amongst academics and other observers about what is often referred to as the "CNN Effect." The CNN effect refers to the ability of global news networks not only to report what is happening, but supposedly to set the political agenda by actively shaping our awareness of what is important, thereby potentially affecting U.S. foreign policy in particular. Critics of this effect—now attributed to all satellite TV news outlets, not just CNN—allege that by transmitting emotive pictures of famines and other disasters thousands of miles away into people's living rooms, the global TV networks create unbearable pressure on politicians to "do something" about the situation. Sometimes this can lead to hasty and ill-thought-out foreign policies, they claim, because policy-makers are denied the time to reach rational or considered decisions. While in the past presidents would have several days to respond to a crisis, nowadays the instantaneous nature of TV images creates pressure for an instant response. Former United Nations Secretary General Boutros Boutros-Ghali once called CNN "the sixteenth member of the Security Council." He suggested that "the member states never take action on a problem unless the media take up the case. When the media gets involved, public opinion is aroused. Public emotion is so intense that United Nations work is undermined and constructive statesmanship is almost impossible."[1]

On the other hand, others claim that policy-makers and politicians play a more active role than this in the construction of what we take to be political reality. The "manufacturing consent" view, for instance—originally associated with the academic and activist Noam Chomsky, but more widely used in recent years—argues that decision-makers attempt to shape our perceptions of the world. The near monopoly of information on security issues that elites possess can be used to shape our perceptions of the world. After all, the media gets much of its news from the government itself. It encourages us to see what it sees. What, though, does political psychology have to say about alleged manipulation of reality by political elites? Does this really occur, and if so, how does it work? How do successful persuaders persuade?

The Influence of Lasswell—Again

It is no accident that Harold Lasswell, one of the founding fathers of political psychology whom we encountered in Chapter 2, was also one of the original scholars of political communication and a genuinely multidisciplinary figure. Through his classic 1920s study of "propaganda"—still examined today, even though that particular term is no longer nearly as fashionable as it once was— Lasswell realized that the popularity of a particular political message has much to do with its psychological reception in people's minds. Best known today to political scientists as a former president of the American Political Science Association (APSA) and most of all for his definition of politics as that thing which involves *who gets what, when, and how*,[2] Lasswell is equally well-known by students of communication for his definition of the latter as *who says what, in which channel, to whom, and with what effect*.[3]

Lasswell's "flow model of political communication," in which the communicator sends a message to a receiver through a medium to produce some effect, has had a major impact on the study of political persuasion. For instance, during an election campaign the sender is clearly the politician; the message might be a campaign ad; the medium is often television, mailed flyers, or nowadays the internet; the receiver or audience is the voter; and

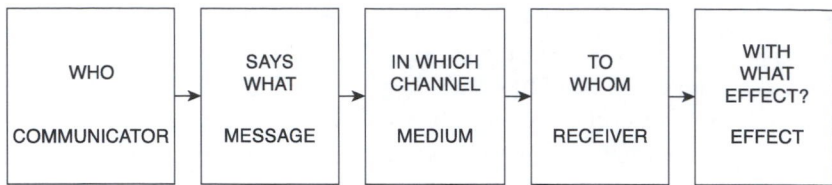

Figure 13.1 Harold Lasswell's model of communication

the effect can be a possible change in the vote. Some campaigns, such as the 1988 Bush–Dukakis presidential election, have turned on the effective use of campaign advertising by one candidate against the other. In this example, the infamous Willy Horton ad was the message which resonated with voters and may have turned many people "off" the Democrat Michael Dukakis.[4] Similarly, the Republican presidential candidate Mitt Romney was probably damaged during the 2012 electoral campaign by campaign ads which depicted him as an out-of-touch representative of the very wealthy, or "one percent" in the United States. The communicators (operatives working for the Democratic Party) seem to have been able to get the message ("Romney is not to be trusted") to stick with the receiver (the ordinary voter).

Earlier in his career, Lasswell had been preoccupied with the nature and effects of political propaganda. I have an especially vivid memory of one of my undergraduate professors, Anthony Arblaster, discussing the politics of Nazi Germany. At one point in a lecture hall many years ago, I recall him telling the class—in a typically pointed way—"people are capable of believing rubbish." How do they come to be convinced by notions like white supremacy or the "inferiority" of Jews, gypsies, or homosexuals? Part of the answer in the Nazi case, as we have seen in an earlier chapter, may relate to our marked propensity for obedience, our tendency to "do what we are told" when a valid authority figure tells us to do it. But that cannot be the whole of the story in the Nazi case. As far as we can tell, many people came to actively *believe* the Nazi political message. To restate Professor Arblaster's question, how do people come to believe in nonsense?

For Lasswell, the answer had to do with the effective use of political propaganda.[5] For him, propaganda was "the management of collective attitudes by the manipulation of significant symbols." He defined the notion of propaganda broadly, not necessarily reserving it for political messages that are deceptive or untrue, as others have done—in other words, he did not reserve the term for "nonsense." He saw propaganda as the effective communication of a political message from leaders to followers. It worked through fundamentally psychological mechanisms, moreover. "Not bombs nor bread," wrote

Lasswell, "but words, pictures, songs, parades, and many similar devices are the typical means of making propaganda." Lasswell was interested in the use of propaganda in both democracies and non-democracies, however, and he intended the use of that term in a broad sense, to embrace all political persuasion efforts by the state. The use of propaganda, he argued, worked via the manipulation and control of "symbols," subjective representations or perceptions of things. This was one of the first arguments in political science to stress the point that the subjective mattered far more than the objective. Propaganda, he argued, is the "management of collective attitudes by the manipulation of significant symbols." Because these symbols evoked a number of different associations, the role of the state in propaganda was to manipulate those associations in the desired way.[6]

Lasswell had an exceptionally long career within political science and the law, stretching from his time at the University of Chicago in the 1920s until his death from pneumonia in a New York City apartment in 1978. He was originally inspired to study propaganda by the influence of his mentor at Chicago, Charles Merriam. Merriam had been a propagandist in the U.S. government during World War I, and Lasswell wrote a PhD thesis under his supervision and inspiration called "Propaganda Technique in the World War," defended in 1927.[7] It was published as a book in the same year. He was later equally inspired by the political environment of the 1930s, which saw the rise of Adolf Hitler in Nazi Germany and that of Benito Mussolini in Fascist Italy. Both dictators depended to a large extent on the spread of their political propaganda as a source of popularity. Naturally enough, scholars began to ask with particular vigor what underlies the appeal of one political message or another. As Chief of the Experimental Division for the Study of War Time Communications at the Library of Congress, Lasswell apparently studied Nazi propaganda films in order to better understand the psychological mechanisms on which communication is based. Leni Riefenstahl's film *Triumph of the Will* (1935), for instance, is one of the best-known examples of such propaganda, featuring close-ups of Adolf Hitler and an audience almost "hypnotized" by his charisma, as well as an especially memorable image of a member of Hitler Youth banging on a booming drum (a musical technique also used to rouse enthusiasm for NFL football teams and U.S. political candidates today). Hitler—who was apparently impressed by the British use of propaganda during World War I—asked Riefenstahl to create a film that would glorify the Nazi state. The effect was to create a strange and almost primitive union between Hitler and his followers, elevating the Nazi party and its control of Germany.

In part because of the negative connotations of the term "propaganda" itself—due in no small part to its association with the Nazis and World War II, and with dictatorship in general—the study of that phenomenon is no longer as popular as it was in Lasswell's day. Words like "propaganda" and "indoctrination," as Deborah Stone puts it, represent "persuasion's ugly face," and they are often contrasted with the notion of "rational deliberation" which is supposedly the norm in democratic societies.[8] "Each view of persuasion has its own language," she notes. "'Information' in one is 'propaganda' in the other. Information 'enlightens' and 'liberates'; propaganda 'beknights' and 'enslaves'. 'Education' in one view is 'brainwashing' in the other. 'Learning' in one is 'compliance' in the other."[9] Members of political parties who wish to discredit the other team will often use terms like propaganda to describe the rival message.

Given the modern association of propaganda with indoctrination or intentional manipulation, many scholars today prefer the more neutral term "political communication," or sometimes "public diplomacy." The study of the political psychology of communication remains a thriving enterprise, with scholars like Dennis Chong, Donald Kinder, Ann Crigler, Jamie Druckman, Shanto Iyengar, Doris Graber, and Russell Von Neuman continuing the broad traditions which Lasswell began early in the twentieth century. Others who do not consider themselves political scientists, such as George Lakoff, are similarly interested in the cognitive and emotional mechanisms that underlie effective political communication. The modern study of this topic focuses on *agenda setting*, *framing*, and *priming*, and it is to these topics that we turn next. We will then conclude with an analysis of the impact that emotional appeals can have on voters during election campaigns.

Agenda Setting

Bernard Cohen once observed—in a phrase that has often been repeated by the writers of textbooks like this one—that the press "may not be successful much of the time in telling people what to think, but it is stunningly successful in telling its readers what to think about." From the early 1970s, the emphasis on agenda construction—how and why some issues get on the political agenda, while others do not—began to replace the focus on propaganda and persuasion. Maxwell McCombs and Donald Shaw found in a now famous study of the 1968 presidential election (conducted in Chapel Hill, North Carolina that year, but not published until 1972) that the issues that voters considered important tended to closely track those emphasized and discussed in the local and national press, suggesting that the media had a powerful role in setting the agenda. Through their access to those media, moreover, politicians could in turn influence what voters thought was important as well.[10] While this approach may not appear very psychological, a key mechanism through which news stories "stuck" in people's minds was *accessibility*. The reader may recall Daniel Kahneman and Amos Tversky's claim in an earlier chapter that the accessibility of information in the mind is a function of either recency or vividness or both. Through the focus on and repetition of particular stories, some issues became accessible in people's minds, and they tended therefore to view those issues as salient.[11]

Agenda setting often involves the successful leaking or "planting" of stories in the media by policy-makers. There is some evidence that lower level officials from the first (George H.W.) Bush administration originally urged media outlets like CNN to cover the Somali famine of 1991, for example, and many ordinary Americans came to understand the reasons why American forces would be committed as a result to *Operation Restore Hope*. In other words, foreign policy elites set the agenda, telling the news agencies what to cover. Most of us would not object to this kind of agenda setting, since it's in the aid of a good cause. What, though, if it were to be used to get the mass public to believe something that wasn't true, either because the elites were mistaken or because they wanted to deliberately misrepresent reality?

One of the most successful efforts at agenda setting in recent years is the (George W.) Bush administration's successful presentation of the case for war in Iraq in 2003, using the justification that Saddam Hussein allegedly possessed "weapons of mass destruction" (WMD). On September 8, 2002, the conservative journalist Judith Miller and her fellow *New York Times* colleague Michael Gordon reported a story claiming that the Iraqi regime had tried to acquire a number of "aluminum tubes" from Africa. The tubes, the piece claimed, were only suitable for use in the production of atomic weapons:

> In the last 14 months, Iraq has sought to buy thousands of specially designed aluminum tubes, which American officials believe were intended as components of centrifuges to enrich uranium. American officials said several efforts to arrange the shipment of the aluminum tubes were blocked or intercepted but declined to say, citing the sensitivity of the intelligence, where they came from or how they were stopped. The diameter, thickness and other technical specifications of the aluminum tubes had persuaded American intelligence experts that they were meant for Iraq's nuclear program, officials said, and that the latest attempt to ship the material had taken place in recent months.[12]

The source of stories like these appears to have been the now discredited Iraqi exile Ahmad Chalabi (who had not lived in Iraq since the age of 12) and individuals within the Vice President's own office. Soon after Gordon and Miller's article was published, National Security Adviser Condoleezza Rice, Secretary of State Colin Powell, and Secretary of Defense Donald Rumsfeld all made TV appearances pointing to the story as "evidence" of their claim that Iraq was an imminent threat to the United States. On the same day the article was published, Vice President Dick Cheney triumphantly cited the story in an interview with the late Tim Russert on the Sunday morning NBC talk show *Meet the Press*, thus "closing the circle":

CHENEY: . . . He [Saddam] is now is trying, through his illicit procurement network, to acquire the equipment he needs to be able to enrich uranium to make the bombs.

MR. RUSSERT: Aluminum tubes.

CHENEY: Specifically aluminum tubes. There's a story in *The New York Times* this morning—this is—I don't—and I want to attribute *The Times*. I don't want to talk about, obviously, specific intelligence sources, but it's now public that, in fact, he has been seeking to acquire, and we have been able to intercept and prevent him from acquiring through this particular channel, the kinds of tubes that are necessary to build a centrifuge. And the centrifuge is required to take low-grade uranium and enhance it into highly enriched uranium, which is what you have to have in order to build a bomb. This is a technology he was working on back, say, before the Gulf War. And one of the reasons it's of concern, Tim, is, you know, we know about a particular shipment. We've intercepted that. We don't know what else—what other avenues he may be taking out there, what he may have already acquired. We do know he's had four years without any inspections at all in Iraq to develop that capability.[13]

The New York Times was a clever choice. Since the newspaper has a reputation for being ideologically liberal, using a journalist who worked for that outlet to put out the story convinced many on the political left that it must be true. Cheney in particular was especially adept at planting stories in the media and making it look as if the information on which these were based was *not* coming from the government. Having placed the stories, when they appeared in print he would later use them as supposedly "independent corroboration" of what he was saying. But all along, the stories were only saying what he—or someone else—had told them to say. This attempt was also highly successful, as judged by U.S. public opinion polls. In 2003, 53 percent of Americans believed Saddam Hussein was personally involved in 9/11 according to a CBS/*New York Times* poll, and the number was still an astounding 33 percent as recently as 2007. Although the WMD claim was based on faulty intelligence, many Americans even today—though thankfully, not a majority anymore—continue to believe that WMD were found in Iraq. A September 2011 PIPA survey conducted by the University of Maryland, for instance, found that 47 percent of Americans believe that Iraq either had WMD or a major WMD program, and 16 percent actually believe that the United States found WMD in Iraq, some seven or eight years after it had become publicly known that no such weapons existed. Apparently the message really stuck, because some people even repeat it in 2014, more than a decade after the invasion.

How does the successful manipulation of the agenda translate into government policy, then? John Kingdon's influential model of agenda setting—while more concerned with the making of public policy itself, as opposed to political psychology—nevertheless implies a significant psychological component. The focus of his best-known book, *Agendas, Alternatives, and Public Policies*, is not so much on the "pictures in people's heads" as it is on how and why particular public policies become the law of the land.[14] Kingdon argues that policies make it through the process when at least two of his "streams"— which he labels *the problem stream*, *the proposal stream*, and *the political stream*— come together simultaneously to create a "window of opportunity." The three streams operate in largely independent fashion, although the actors in each may overlap a bit:

- *The problem stream* is probably the most cognitive, because it refers to the process of problem definition. At any time, there are many problems competing for a decision-maker's attention, and only some will rise to the top.
- *The proposal stream* has a strong cognitive dimension as well. While the first stream deals with problems, this one deals with solutions. Which policy proposals are generated and debated as viable solutions to the problems? Viability is determined by things like technical feasibility, compatibility with existing political values, and economic cost.
- *The political stream* is the least amenable to manipulation, as it consists of factors which are mostly "givens" in the short term. This stream involves historical and political factors that influence agendas such as the political climate or mood in the country. Politics in the United States often seems to move alternately through liberal and conservative waves, and it can be hard to push through major increases in domestic spending during the latter (for instance).

Successful agenda setting requires that at least two of these streams coincide, and the likelihood of this happening is greatest if all three come together at an opportune time. Put in the terms we have been using in this book, we can see successful agenda setting and its translation into actual policies as a function of the *dispositions* of the decision-makers and the *situational* forces with which they must contend.

Framing

Kingdon's model raises some interesting questions for the political psychologist. How exactly do problems come to be *seen* as problems? How do both elites and ordinary people decide what are the most *serious* issues to address? And how does an issue or policy solution come to have public appeal? Political phenomena do not "speak for themselves." We often rely on politicians and media pundits to interpret them for us, and this is arguably where *framing* becomes critical. While there is some disagreement in the literature as to exactly how frames should be defined, we can probably best think of them as broad psychological interpretations which locate smaller events within a bigger picture or pattern (much like a picture frame encloses a photograph or painting). They are a form of cognitive short cut or heuristic. Like any short cut, frames simplify the world and make it comprehensible, rendering something understandable which would otherwise appear confusing or overwhelming. For this reason, frames are often described as a form of schema or script (recall for Chapter 9 that schema "fit" smaller events into bigger mental categories. "Ahah," we unconsciously tell ourselves, "*this* is an instance of *that*"). Many who stress the role of framing in political persuasion trace the origins of their work to that of the sociologist Erving Goffman, especially his book *Frame Analysis* (originally published in 1974)[15] and to research on cognitive scripts by Roger Schank and Robert Abelson.[16]

There are often a number of *alternative* frames available for understanding an event or process. As Dennis Chong and Jamie Druckman note, "the major premise of framing theory is that an issue can be viewed from a variety of perspectives and be construed as having implications for multiple values or considerations." But this is not the end of the story, of course. "Framing refers to the process by which people develop a *particular* conceptualization of an issue or reorient their thinking about an issue."[17] We just presented the WMD example as an instance of successful agenda setting, but from a frame theory perspective that case was nested within a much larger frame. There were also choices to be made as to how we should frame the overall policy response to September 11, 2001. After 9/11, the response to the terrorist attacks on New York City and Washington D.C. was successfully framed as a matter of "foreign policy" or "external security," instead of a matter of domestic "law and order." Had the issues not already been framed this way, it is hard to imagine an attempt to put Iraq (and its potential invasion) on the agenda being as successful as it was. In this sense, the "Iraq threat" might be regarded as a smaller frame within a much larger one.

Frames can deal with larger definitions and interpretations like these which set the whole context of policy-making, or they may deal with the effects of relatively small changes in the way an issue is presented. One simple form of framing discovered by Daniel Kahneman and Amos Tversky in the 1970s shows how people may either favor (or oppose) an identical option, based on the way that choice is posed (or "framed") to the decision-maker. Prospect theory (discussed in more depth in Chapter 17) is based on this research. To provide an interesting political example, Sniderman and Theriault found that when Americans were asked if they favored allowing a hate group to hold a rally in their home town, only 45 percent did when the question was prefaced with the phrase "Given the risk of violence . . ." However, that number rose dramatically to a decisive 85 percent when the question was prefaced with "Given the importance of free speech . . ." instead. The first version is framing the issue as one of "public order," while the second is framing it as a question of "civil rights."[18]

Shanto Iyengar is usually credited with introducing the idea of the "frame" to the psychological study of political communication,[19] but in a folklore sense frames have proved to be of interest to political operatives running campaigns as well. This makes some sense, since if frames are so critical, the possibility exists that politicians and other partisans might *deliberately manipulate* framing to favor one political party or the other. This is what the Republican Party campaign specialist Frank Luntz has been trying to do for many years. Deliberately trying to shift American politics in the opposite direction, however, is the work of the cognitive scientist and Democratic Party campaigner George Lakoff. Lakoff has popularized his ideas about framing in books like *Don't Think of An Elephant!* and *The Political Mind*, but his major work thus far within academia has been *Moral Politics*.[20] Lakoff uses the concept of framing in a very broad way, and he often cites the example of taxes to illustrate his argument. Nobody especially likes paying taxes, but most of us agree to do so because government provides us with certain services we like (access to education, for instance, or protection from crime or a terrorist attack). If you want to cut taxes, it makes sense to come up with a frame which calls to mind the discomfort most of us experience when forking over a portion of our paycheck. George W. Bush, for instance, often talked of "tax relief." For Lakoff, this was a skillful political move because it evokes all sorts of other ideas:

> For the term "tax relief" to be meaningful, taxes have to be defined in a frame in which they are a financial loss: money earned by taxpayers and rightly belonging to them, but taken from taxpayers by the government. In addition, there has to be a metaphor in place in which Financial Loss is Pain, and Pain has to be in a frame in which Affliction Causes Pain. Then—and only then—does adding "tax" to "relief" give rise to the metaphor Taxation is Affliction.[21]

In other words, there are hidden frames and metaphors within our brains that skillfully created slogans and concepts can tap into. The essence of persuasion for Lakoff is language, and once Democrats themselves began unwittingly using the term "tax relief," Lakoff argues, the debate was effectively over. Another phrase which was often used later on by conservative thinkers—this time in arguing for *not repealing* the Bush tax cuts—was that of "class warfare." In the run-up to the 2012 presidential election, many Republicans argued that the Bush administration's tax cuts needed to be left in place in order to reward individual innovation and promote job creation by "the wealth creators." Thinking about "class warfare" evokes unfavorable connotations for most Americans. It makes us think of economic resentment, pitched battles in the streets and perhaps 1960s-style riots. Most Americans do not instinctively feel themselves to be members of an economic "class" either, which suggests a European (and therefore almost un-American) mindset. By framing the issue of tax this way, Republicans hoped to win the debate by influencing the frame most Americans used to understand the issue.

For liberals or progressives to win the political debate, on the other hand, it follows that they too need to use language and metaphors which tap into the American psyche in some fundamental way and play upon favorable associations instead of unpleasant ones. Drew Westen has argued, for instance, that Democrats might be better off referring to taxes as "a membership fee," which evokes a frame more favorable to the notion of taxation by suggesting that we get something in return for our taxes and that paying taxes is just like paying to be a member of a club (something we do voluntarily, if we join a club at all). We usually agree that in order to be members of a club, we ought to pay something towards the upkeep of the club. If we get benefits in return, we ought to pay our fair share. Indeed, by 2012 there were clear signs that the Obama administration—without actually using "the membership fee" phrase itself—were trying to frame the issue as one of basic fairness rather than class resentment.

Of particular interest with regard to "hidden frames" is Nicholas Winter's book *Dangerous Frames*.[22] Both race and gender play a very overt and divisive role in American politics, but Winter is interested in the hidden ways in which these work, underneath the surface of things. Earlier books, like Tali Mendelberg's *The Race Card*, had suggested that race plays an almost subliminal role in American politics. Winter takes up the same theme, showing how a vast array of issues that don't seem related to either race or gender nevertheless *become* related to them, as politicians manipulate our perceptions of reality. What Winter calls "group implication" "occurs when a subtly crafted issue frame shapes an issue to match the structure of a cognitively accessible race or gender schema. The issue is then mapped analogically to the race or gender schema, and feelings about race or about gender are transferred back to the issue, influencing evaluation of the issue."[23] Using schema theory, analogical reasoning theory, and framing theory, Winter shows how unrelated issues get mapped onto the "race schema" and the "gender schema." Issues which mention "crime" and "cities" a lot tend to invoke the racial schema, for instance, and Winter shows how framing has influenced debates about welfare and Social Security. He also argues that the manner in which health care reform was framed in the 1990s divided Americans along gender lines, even though Clinton's health care reforms really had nothing at all to do with gender.

Priming

Related to both agenda setting and framing is the concept of *priming*. In psychology, priming usually refers to a process in which one idea triggers one or more associated ones in the human mind, often outside of conscious awareness. Unfortunately, the term priming is often used in different ways by political scientists, communication theorists, and cognitive psychologists. Some see priming as very similar if not identical to framing.[24] Others (often political communication specialists) view the two ideas as somewhat different, for reasons we won't go into here. But it is worth noting that in political psychology priming has a common meaning, where it refers to the tendency to weight some matters more heavily in one's evaluation of a candidate because those matters have been given weight in the media. As Severin and Tankard put it, media priming is "the process in which the media attend to some issues and not others and thereby alter the standards by which people evaluate election candidates."[25] For instance, if the media tend to focus on foreign policy, the president's foreign policy performance will tend to play a disproportionate role in the voter's evaluation of his time in office. Or if the media focus on education, the voters will tend to judge the candidate by his performance in education policy, and so on. Priming, in other words, can affect the criteria that people use to judge a candidate's performance.

Isn't this plain old agenda setting again? On the face of it, yes; but priming effects go deeper than agenda setting. While the former determines the issues that voters attend to, the latter affects the way that candidates are evaluated too, and various studies have demonstrated powerful media effects that go beyond agenda setting. In 1982, Iyengar, Peters, and Kinder first identified this added dimension as the "priming effect."[26] Like framing, the theory is based on the assumption that people do not have extensive knowledge about politics and don't take all the information into account when making decisions; instead, they just "satisfice."

It is easy to see how both agenda setting and priming might have considerable political effects. For instance, in 2012 many voters preferred Barack Obama on economic policy, while many others thought Mitt Romney would do the best job on foreign policy. If the mass media have an overall tendency to focus on economic policy, according to priming theory this will benefit Obama; on the other hand, a focus on foreign policy will benefit Romney. As with framing, politicians may sometimes deliberately use the priming device themselves to try to improve the public's assessment of them, as Jacobs and Shapiro argue in their study of John F. Kennedy's 1960 presidential campaign.[27] The original focus of priming was on how voters make decisions, but Jacobs and Shapiro argue that a candidate who has at least some basic familiarity with the technique of priming has incentives to use this to his or her benefit, which "changes the analytic focus from unintentional priming to intentional priming, namely, the deliberate strategies that candidates pursue to influence voters." Candidates can deliberately set out to "hit" issues in debates. Priming can be an effective campaign strategy for presidential candidates, the authors suggest, by the carefully calculated exploitation of public opinion on policy issues to influence voters' standards for assessing the candidates' attributes. In this study, the authors focus on the 1960 election because innovative public opinion surveys were incorporated into Kennedy's campaign strategy, polls that enabled him to shape his image through position taking. We are almost back in the place where Lasswell left us, with the intentional manipulation of minds.

Again, priming has been applied to the way race is viewed in America, in what is usually termed "racial priming."[28] In one noteworthy study, Valentino, Hutchings, and White find that:

> the language of government spending and taxation has become racially "coded," such that its invocation in political appeals primes racial considerations even in the absence of racial imagery. More powerful effects emerge, however, when the imagery in political ads links blacks to the narrator's comments about undeserving groups. Ads that visually compare the interests of whites and blacks are slightly less powerful racial primes. Furthermore, none of the cues we manipulate prime individualism, egalitarianism, or partisan identification. We also find that racial priming is mediated by the accessibility of race in memory, not the self-reported importance of group representation. Finally, counter-stereotypic black cues suppress racial priming, while violating positive stereotypes of whites has, if anything, a positive racial priming effect.[29]

Emotion and Persuasion

Much work on framing and priming suggests that it may be that both really matter in persuading people. In Lakoff's theory, it is language and the way that it literally hard-wires our brains with meaning that persuades (or fails to). But what if the emotions that a communication inspires matter as much or more than its cognitive content? The real appeal of Riefenstahl's *Triumph of the Will*, for instance, may well have been the simple feelings of intense patriotism and national pride it inspired in Germans of that era and the sense that they had been "wronged" by the international community after World War I, as much as the actual cognitive content of Hitler's speeches. We have already dealt with the use of emotion in voting in Chapters 10 and 12, suggesting that the way that elites evoke emotion may be critical to explaining how people make electoral choices, so a briefer treatment is in order here. But consider the argument made by Ted Brader in his book *Campaigning For Hearts and Minds*.[30] Brader draws upon the "Affective Intelligence" model we discussed earlier in this book, showing how the emotions of enthusiasm and fear are used to influence and persuade voters. On the enthusiasm side, the makers of campaign ads often try to persuade voters with "feel good" ads designed to associate their candidate with pleasing stimuli. A classic example is the "Morning in America" series of TV ads that promoted Ronald Reagan in 1984. On the other hand, fear is also frequently employed to great effect, as in the 1964 Lyndon Johnson "Daisy Chain" ad which was so controversial that it ran only once, or the 2004 Republican ad against John Kerry which showed America's enemies as a "pack of wolves" waiting to pounce on the Democratic Party's alleged weakness.

There may also be a strong behavioral or operant conditioning element to political persuasion. Advertisers have long understood that consumers can be prompted to purchase a good or service if the reward normally attached to something can somehow be *transferred* to something unrelated. For instance, when he left academia and moved into the world of advertising, John B. Watson was supposedly instrumental in getting printed and television ads to portray beautiful or sophisticated men and women smoking, so that the "reward" one gets from looking at an attractive or "cool" person could become associated with cigarettes.

Conclusion

Which view is correct? Do elites manipulate the messages we see and hear, or do spontaneous images drive popular pressure to "do something" about the things we see going on in other parts of the world? It's probably a mixture of the two, as far as we can tell. The British political scientist Piers Robinson has attempted to reconcile the "manufacturing consent" approach with the "CNN Effect" one by specifying the conditions under which each seems to apply.[31] Maybe each theory works well under some circumstances but not others, and Robinson argues that the key factor is *the presence of uncertainty*. When elites know what they want to do, they will generally go ahead and do it. Under these kinds of conditions—where they have relative certainty, or think that they do—the "manufacturing consent" approach seems to work well, as in the Iraq case. Here policy-makers will use the mass media to mobilize public opinion in favor of a chosen foreign policy. On the other hand, the "CNN Effect" approach seems to work best where policy-makers don't know whether or how to respond.

A growing literature eschews an "either–or" approach to the CNN/manufacturing consent debate and tries to integrate them with one another. Viewing politics as a "contest," Gadi Wolfsfeld articulates five principles of political communication, which outline the ways in which politicians and the mass media influence one another:

- Political power can usually be translated into power over the news media.
- When authorities lose control over the political environment they also lose control over the news.
- There is no such thing as objective journalism.
- The media are dedicated more than anything else to telling a good story.
- The most important effects of the news media on citizens tend to be unintentional and unnoticed.[32]

The powerful have most control over the news cycle, he suggests, and they do use techniques like agenda setting and framing. But there are times when they lose the ability to shape and mold the news (this often happens during wartime, for instance, or major scandals). Elites may start off with the ability to "manage" the news, but they can easily lose this.

Notes

1 Larry Minear, Colin Scott, and Thomas G. Weiss, *The News Media, Civil War, and Humanitarian Action* (Boulder, CO: Lynne Rienner Publishers, 1996), p.4.
2 Harold Lasswell, *Politics: Who Gets What, When, How* (New York: Peter Smith, 1990, originally published 1936).
3 Harold Lasswell, "The Structure and Function of Communication in Society," in Lyman Bryson (ed.), *Religion and Civilian Series: The Communication of Ideas* (New York: Cooper Square, 1964).

4 Ann Crigler, "Introduction: Making Sense of Politics, Constructing Political Messages and Meanings," p.3, in Crigler (ed.), *The Psychology of Political Communication* (Ann Arbor, MI: University of Michigan Press, 1996).

5 William Ascher and Barbara Hirschfelder-Ascher, *Revitalizing Political Psychology: The Legacy of Harold D. Lasswell* (Mahwah, NJ: Lawrence Erlbaum, 2005), p.40.

6 See Gabriel Almond, *Harold Dwight Lasswell, 1902–1978: A Biographical Memoir* (Washington, D.C.: National Academy of Sciences, 1987).

7 Harold Lasswell, *Propaganda Technique in the World War* (New York: Peter Smith, 1938). The title is a refreshing (and depressing) reminder that, at this point, there had been only one "World War."

8 Deborah Stone, *Policy Paradox: The Art of Political Decision Making* (New York: W.W. Norton, 1988), p.305.

9 Ibid., p.306.

10 Maxwell McCombs and Donald Shaw, "The Agenda-Setting Function of Mass Media," *Public Opinion Quarterly* 36: 176–87, 1972.

11 See also Shanto Iyengar and Donald Kinder, *News That Matters: Television and Public Opinion* (Chicago, IL: University of Chicago Press, 1987).

12 Michael Gordon and Judith Miller, "Threats and Responses: The Iraqis; US says Hussein Intensifies Quest for A-Bomb Parts," *The New York Times*, September 8, 2002.

13 Dick Cheney, Interview with Tim Russert on *Meet the Press*, September 8, 2002, transcript available at https://www.mtholyoke.edu/acad/intrel/bush/meet.htm.

14 John Kingdon, *Agendas, Alternatives, and Public Policies*, second edition (New York: HarperCollins, 1997).

15 Erving Goffmann, *Frame Analysis: An Essay on the Organization of Experience* (Cambridge, MA: Harvard University Press, 1974).

16 Roger Schank and Robert Abelson, *Scripts, Plans, Goals, and Understanding* (Hillsdale, NJ: Lawrence Erlbaum, 1977).

17 Dennis Chong and James Druckman, "Framing Theory," *Annual Review of Political Science*, 10: 103–26, 2007, p.104. See also Dennis Chong and James Druckman, "Dynamics of Mass Communication Effects Research," in Holli Semetko and Margaret Scammell (eds.), *The SAGE Handbook of Political Communication* (London: Sage Publications, 2012).

18 Paul Sniderman and Sean Theriault, "The Structure of Political Argument and the Logic of Issue Framing," in Willem Saris and Paul Sniderman (eds.), *Studies in Public Opinion: Attitudes, Nonattitudes, Measurement Error, and Change* (Princeton, NJ: Princeton University Press, 2004).

19 Shanto Iyengar, *Is Anyone Responsible? How Television Frames Political Issues* (Chicago, IL: University of Chicago Press, 1991).

20 George Lakoff, *Don't Think of an Elephant! Know Your Values and Frame the Debate* (White River Junction, VT: Chelsea Green Publishing, 2004), *The Political Mind: A Cognitive Scientist's Guide to Your Brain and Its Politics* (New York: Penguin Books, 2009), and *Moral Politics: What Conservatives Know That Liberals Don't* (Chicago, IL: University of Chicago Press, 1996).

21 Lakoff, *The Political Mind*, p.236.

22 Nicholas Winter, *Dangerous Frames: How Ideas About Race and Gender Shape Public Opinion* (Chicago, IL: University of Chicago Press, 2008).

23 Ibid., p.31. *The Race Card* is discussed in greater detail in Chapter 15.
24 Chong and Druckman, "Dynamics of Mass Communication Effects Research," p.115.
25 Werner Severin and James Tankard, *Communication Theories: Origins, Methods, and Uses in the Mass Media* (New York: Longman, 1997).
26 Shanto Iyengar, Mark Peters, and Donald Kinder, "Experimental Demonstrations of the 'Not-so-Minimal' Consequences of Television News Programs," *American Political Science Review*, 76: 848–58, 1982.
27 Lawrence Jacobs and Robert Shapiro, "Issues, Candidate Image, and Priming," *American Political Science Review*, 83: 527–40, 1994.
28 Tali Mendelberg, "Racial Priming Revived," *Perspectives on Politics*, 6: 109–23, 2008.
29 Nicholas Valentino, Nicholas Hutchings, and Ismael White, "Cues that Matter: How Political Ads Prime Racial Attitudes During Campaigns," *American Political Science Review*, 96: 75–90, 2002.
30 Ted Brader, *Campaigning For Hearts and Minds: How Emotional Appeals in Political Ads Work* (Chicago, IL: University of Chicago Press, 2006).
31 Piers Robinson, *The CNN Effect: The Myth of News, Foreign Policy and Intervention* (New York: Routledge, 2002).
32 Gadi Wolfsfeld, *Making Sense of Media and Politics: Five Principles in Political Communication* (New York: Routledge, 2011).

Suggested Further Reading

Ann Crigler (ed.), *The Psychology of Political Communication* (Ann Arbor, MI: University of Michigan Press, 1996).
George Lakoff, *The Political Mind: A Cognitive Scientist's Guide to Your Brain and its Politics* (New York: Penguin Books, 2009).
Wayne Le Cheminant and John Parrish, *Manipulating Democracy: Democratic Theory, Political Psychology, and Mass Media* (New York: Routledge, 2010).
Brian Schaffner and Patrick Sellers, *Winning with Words: The Origins and Impact of Political Framing* (New York: Routledge, 2009).
Nicholas Winter, *Dangerous Frames: How Ideas About Race and Gender Shape Public Opinion* (Chicago, IL: University of Chicago Press, 2008).
Gadi Wolfsfeld, *Making Sense of Media and Politics: Five Principles in Political Communication* (New York: Routledge, 2011).

Chapter 14

The Psychology of Nationalism, Ethnic Conflict, and Genocide

"Why, over the past century, have good people repeatedly ignored mass murder and genocide?," Paul Slovic asks.[1] Why do we so often turn a "blind eye to murder"?[2] It's a simple question, but one that's hard to give a simple answer to. Perhaps it has much to do with the famous "bystander effect," which has been replicated numerous times by psychologists. Inspired originally by a horrific attack on a young woman called Catherine "Kitty" Genovese in New York in 1964, social psychologists have repeatedly investigated the conditions under which one individual will assist another in distress or danger, finding that *most* people are all too willing to just walk past someone who seems to be suffering.

Suppose, for instance, you suddenly hear a woman screaming in the street. It is about 3am, and something about the woman's screams seems very real and desperate. You move away from your late-night television and gaze out of your apartment window. You see a woman being attacked. An apparently deranged man is chasing her. He catches up to her and stabs her repeatedly with a knife as she falls. You can't believe what you are seeing, but you also notice that other people are watching as well. You see that a few people are standing on their fire escapes, and still more people are sticking their heads out of windows watching the scene unfold. You have a telephone in your apartment. Should you call the police? You debate this for a while, but then—perhaps to your own surprise—you find yourself going back to the TV show. After all, so many people saw what happened that *someone* must have already called the cops. You feel disturbed at what you saw, sure, but you don't actually do anything. It takes you a while to get to sleep that night, but you convince yourself that someone must have helped that unfortunate woman.

This seems to have been (very roughly) what happened in the Genovese case, where nobody picked up the phone until it was too late—she died of her wounds—although ironically the whole bystander aspect (and especially how many witnesses there really were) may have been greatly exaggerated by a cub reporter working for *The New York Times*. Nevertheless, it inspired numerous experimental replications designed to test where and when bystanders will intervene. Many of my students have told me stories of other cases where bystanders "walked on by," and there was a chilling reminder of the effect in the streets of Woolwich in southeast London on May 22, 2013. A young British Army soldier called Lee Rigby was walking down the street near his military barracks when he was attacked and killed in broad daylight by two men. Both killers were Islamic extremists and were British-born sons of Nigerian immigrants, and both are at the time of writing being tried in the British courts. Amazingly, video cameras captured numerous people simply walking past the scene with their shopping, seemingly oblivious to the victim and to the fact that they were passing a dangerous, ranting man holding a meat cleaver with his hands soaked in blood (though at least one heroic woman tried to comfort the unconscious soldier Lee, and one actually confronted the killers).

John Darley and Bibb Latané's work in the 1960s was directly inspired by their reading of the Genovese incident, in which "thirty-eight witnesses" (it was claimed at the time) failed to come to the aid of a young woman being murdered outside their windows.[3] The behavior of the bystanders provoked outrage back in 1964, and there were public calls for all thirty-eight to be arrested (or worse). Common sense suggests that out of thirty-eight people, at least one should have had the "moral fiber" to at least pick up the phone and call 911.

Paradoxically, however, Darley and Latané found that it was precisely *because* there were so many people watching or listening to what had happened that no one came to Genovese's aid. The task of responding to her plight was shared by a large number of people—a factor Darley and Latané call *the diffusion of responsibility*—and everyone seems to have assumed that someone else would do something.[4] Setting out to test this hypothesis—which they originally hammered out at an all-night party at which the topic of Genovese was being discussed—Darley and Latané set up an experiment which, like much other social psychological research of the time, involved a large measure of deception.

Rather cleverly, they led students to believe that they were involved in group discussions about personal problems, such as the difficulty of adapting to university life.[5] These naive subjects were led to believe that they were talking to other students sitting in separate cubicles via an intercom, but in reality they were listening to tape recordings of other students acting out roles in the "discussion." Sometimes the subjects were told that they were involved in one-to-one discussions with only a single person, sometimes there were supposedly three people involved, sometimes four, and so on, but in all cases they were actually only listening to pre-recorded tapes. The first recording, moreover, was always the same: it was the voice of a student that tells of the stress he is undergoing at university and the fact that he suffers from epileptic fits. In reality, this was of course a student acting out the part (interestingly the voice was that of Richard Nisbett, then a graduate student at Columbia University and in later life a leading situationist and attribution theorist).[6]

After a short while, the voice of the student on tape would begin to sound frantic and incoherent, as Nisbett convincingly played out the part of someone having an epileptic seizure. Of the subjects involved in the one-to-one condition—that is, where the naive subject thought that he or she was the only person around who could help—an impressive 85 percent reported the seizure immediately and sought help. However, when the subject was led to believe that he was in a discussion with five other people, only 31 percent sought the assistance of the experimenter. Quite simply, the presence of others had socially inhibited the subjects in the latter condition from acting to assist the person supposedly in distress.

A few years later, Darley and Batson conducted an even more fascinating experiment by using divinity students to test the theory of the bystander effect, again using a classic piece of deception.[7] In this study, the students were given the task of preparing a sermon on the parable of the "Good Samaritan," in which a kindly stranger passing by helps feed and clothe an injured man he has found in the street. There seems to have been a good deal of deliberate irony involved here on the experimenters' part, but they also rather neatly stacked the deck against their own hypothesis by using individuals with a presumably strong religious disposition as subjects. Could these individuals be placed in a situation where they "forgot" these values and where the demands of the situation effectively took over? What if the students were asked to prepare a sermon on this parable and hence were primed to have it in their minds as they confront an "injured man" in real life? This is exactly what Darley and Batson did, but they added a complicating situational factor: time pressure.

"Don't be late" is one of the simplest rules of social etiquette there is, but on an intuitive level most people imagine that it is not as powerful in its effects as moral beliefs or values are. But this expectation was confounded in the study. Some students were given strict time limits to complete the sermon, while others were told they had plenty of time to do the work. The experimenters further arranged for all of the subjects to pass by an "injured" person (in reality, of course, an actor playing the role). Against most people's expectations but not of course their own, they found that social pressure proved more important than dispositions when the student was in a hurry to complete the work, but that dispositions were more important for those with time on their hands. By and large, only the latter proved to be "Good Samaritans." Sixty-three percent of those in the "low hurry" condition offered help, as opposed to only 10 percent of those in the "high hurry" condition.[8]

The bystander effect becomes more intense and acute when we regard victims as "the other" (that is, as fundamentally different to ourselves or "alien"), and when this happens it may override helping behavior even when you are the *only* witness to an incident. Psychologist Mark Levine came up with a simple but ingenious experimental variation on the classic bystander experiment which illustrates the role of identity in bystander intervention and works rather well in a British context.[9] Many people who grow up in the North of England, as I did—mainly but not exclusively males—come to identify very early on with a particular football team (or soccer team, as most Americans put it). From the age of four or five, it becomes a powerful identity, often taken from one's parents or other close relatives, and this often persists through life, as powerful (or even more so) than religious allegiances. The former Liverpool manager Bill Shankley summed up the view in this region of England when he said that "football's not a matter of life and death; it's *more important* than that."

Liverpool and Manchester United are bitter rivals in the English Premier League, and Levine had the clever idea of using this in a field experimental context. He had a confederate or actor deliberately slip up on a rain-soaked concrete floor in front of various bystanders, but he varied the clothing worn by the actor. In one condition he wore a Manchester United shirt, and in another condition a Liverpool shirt. Using self-declared Manchester United fans as his subjects, Levine and his colleagues found that bystanders came to the aid of the actor 80 percent of the time when he was wearing a Manchester United shirt, but only 40 percent of the time when he was wearing a Liverpool shirt. We will have more to say about ingroups and outgroups in a moment, but it is clear from the experiment that participants were a lot more willing to help someone they viewed as being part of their own social grouping.

The bystander effect—and a kind of diffusion of responsibility to act between states or world leaders during a genocide—may indeed play a role in non-intervention. But the answer to why we often just stand by in the face of suffering, Paul Slovic thinks, may also have to do quite simply with the way human beings think. When we are confronted by a single case of suffering which is humanized—say, the case of an African child who is starving—it activates the emotional parts of our brain. We come to empathize, to "feel" her suffering. But when we are given a statistic—so many millions dead due to genocide or starvation—it fails to activate these instinctive reactions. Numbers are neutral and impersonal, and when we hear statistics, the prefrontal cortex knows that this is wrong and that we should help, but it doesn't make us *feel* bad in the same way as a single well-publicized case. Our neural circuitry is not set up to fully appreciate what a million or a billion even means, or would look like. And because genocide by its nature involves the death of large numbers of people rather than a single case, it fails to "register" in our minds in the same way. But Small, Loewenstein and Slovic found that if you give people information about an identifiable victim who is starving or ill together with statistical data about similar cases, overall donations actually *decline* (a rather irrational outcome). They also discovered that if you *tell them* about the inconsistent levels of sympathy that identifiable and statistical victims evoke—the "identifiable victim effect," to use a term employed by the researchers—people become like Ebenezer Scrooge, reducing their giving to identifiable victims but not increasing their giving to statistical victims.[10]

Thus if we want to increase sympathy for the victims of genocide, we should "appeal to the heart not the head." An even more fundamental puzzle, of course, is why people commit genocide in the first place. This is a question to which we will turn in a moment, but first we need to put genocide in the broader context of nationalism and ethnic conflict.

Nationalism and Ethnic Conflict

The explosion in nationalism and ethnic conflict that we have observed since the early 1990s has led to renewed interest in these topics as matters for academic study, and a few book-length treatments of the psychological dimensions of this topic are now available.[11] Of course, nationalism and ethnic conflict are not new phenomena, and the idea of nationalism dates at least as far back as the French Revolution of 1789. Writing in 1966, Walker Connor noted that national and ethnic unrest was then present in places as diverse and far-flung as Canada, Guyana, India, Uganda, the Sudan, Burma, Yugoslavia, Cyprus, Rwanda, the United Kingdom, and Iraq.[12] It is fair to say, however, that the severity of issues was obscured by the intensity of the Cold War; nationalistic and ethnic struggles were commonly viewed almost solely through the lens of the struggle between Communism and capitalism, the Vietnam War being only the most obvious and prominent case in point.

Despite the prevalence of the idea of the "nation state," most states today do not contain only one nation or ethnic group, and there is often no neat territorial coincidence between "nations" and "states," the governmental bodies that rule over nations. The United Kingdom, for instance, is a multinational state, composed of England, Scotland, Wales, and Northern Ireland. Iraq, as any reader of today's newspaper headlines knows, has for many years been composed of Kurds, Shiites, and Sunnis, and those who identify themselves as Kurds are spread across Northern Iraq and parts of Turkey. The fact that nations do not always equal states often gives rise to secessionist or irredentist movements, which seek to unify a nation under a single state and body of territory.

Recent decades have seen particularly bloody ethnic conflicts in places like Yugoslavia, Rwanda, and the Sudan, three of the places Connor alluded to back in the mid-1960s as hotspots of unrest. In April 1994 Rwandan President Habyarimana was killed and Hutu extremists seized control of the government. Over the next 100 days, about 8,000 Rwandans a day were butchered. This was the fastest rate of mass killings in the twentieth century. Some 800,000 people—roughly 10 per cent of the population—were murdered. Ninety percent of the victims were Tutsis—*men, women, and children.* Since 2003, a similar scenario has played out in the Darfur region of the Sudan. The Janjaweed are an armed, extremist Arab militia that has committed genocide in Darfur, and so far this group has killed what some estimate to be several hundred thousand people from rival, non-Arab Sudanese groups. The Janjaweed are in league with government, and both UN and African Union troops have tried in vain to bring the parties together in a lasting peace.

Definitions of nationalism and ethnicity, like other social scientific concepts, are always the subject of dispute; nevertheless, it is relatively easier to arrive at a consensual definition for these notions than it is (say) for terrorism. It is tempting to use Potter Stewart's famous definition of pornography— namely, "I know it when I see it"—but as social scientists we require at least a good working definition of the thing we are trying to explain. Joshua Searle-White's definition is especially useful because it brings out the extent to which nationalism is a *psychological* factor, something that exists primarily in our heads:

> Nationalism, in its broadest definition . . . is simply a sense of identification with a group of people who share a common history, language, territory, culture, or some combination of these. Nationalism may or may not explicitly be a movement to create an independent state for a national group, although, because self-determination is privileged in the world today, the nation-state (an independent country that is populated primarily by one national group) is a particular goal of many nationalist movements.[13]

This point was also brought out perfectly by Sir Ernest Barker:

> The self-consciousness of nations is a product of the nineteenth century. This is a matter of the first importance. Nations were already there; they

had indeed been there for centuries. But it is not the things which are simply "there" that matter in human life. What really and finally matters is the thing which is apprehended as an idea, and, as an idea, is vested with emotion until it becomes a cause and a spring of action. In the world of action apprehended ideas are alone electrical; and a nation must be an idea as well as a fact before it can become a dynamic force.[14]

Similarly, most collections of studies on nationalism today emphasize the degree to which nationalism is something socially constructed.[15] Given that nationalism is primarily a psychological thing—much as party identification in Western democracies is—what theories exist which might explain the social cohesion which holds nations together and creates a sense of "nationhood?" And what can political psychology tell us about the causes of conflict between rival ethnic forces? In past chapters we have already suggested some paradigms that might provide partial answers to some of these questions, most notably the authoritarian personality theory and the work of Stanley Milgram. We will begin by looking at five approaches that have been used to explain nationalism in recent years: *realistic group conflict theory*; *social identity theory*; *social dominance theory*; *the psychoanalytic approach*; and *the biopolitical approach*.[16] The first two approaches are unambiguously situationist, while the last three are primarily dispositionist in nature. As we shall see in the next chapter, moreover, they can also be used to explain other forms of identity and group conflict.

Five Approaches to Explaining Nationalism

Realistic Group Conflict Theory

This approach deals with "us versus them" thinking—or the distinction between what social psychologists call "ingroups" and "outgroups"—and it suggests quite simply that conflict develops where one group has a realistic, "rational" reason to compete with or fight another. In the early 1950s, the social psychologist Muzafer Sherif conducted an interesting field experiment at Robbers' Cave, Oklahoma. Sherif took twenty-two schoolboys—none of whom knew one another before the experiment—to a summer camp, dividing them at random into two groups as soon as they arrived. Each group was then segregated from the other for about a week—the groups were assigned cabins some distance away from one another, so minimizing the possibility of social interaction—by which time each group had developed its own leaders, identity, and culture. Sherif then threw the two groups into a series of competitive activities and games. Hostility quickly emerged between the two groups, to the point where they could not engage in noncompetitive activities without insulting and even fighting one another.

The reader will readily appreciate how favorable to situationism this finding was. Like Zimbardo later on, Sherif made sure that his subjects were normal, well adjusted individuals with no psychological abnormalities, and then randomly assigned them to two groups, thus pre-empting the argument that might be later raised that the dispositions of his subjects were to blame for their competitive behavior. Despite the fact that (unlike nations) the groups were not divided along ethnic or other ties, their mere categorization into separate, randomly assigned groupings was enough to create hostility when the two groups were brought together. Moreover, the results Sherif obtained should not be that surprising to anyone who has ever played soccer, baseball, American football, or other competitive team sports at an organized level, or indeed to anyone who has been a spectator at games like these. Active hatred can sometimes develop between two teams—say the "Pittsburgh Steelers" and the "Baltimore Ravens," or "Manchester United" and "Arsenal"—despite the fact that they are not divided along any evident racial, socioeconomic, religious, or other category.[17]

Of course, we can always dismiss such observations as indicative of a basic human disposition, such as the "competitive instinct," and this may indeed be a valid criticism. But such conflicts seem to occur in some circumstances and not in others, casting doubt on the idea of competition as some sort of innate quality. It is clear, moreover, how this kind of theory might explain the long-standing conflict between the Palestinians and the Israelis, for example, since they are competing over the same piece of territory, which each claims as its own. What, though, if we could show that hostility, prejudice, and discrimination can occur between groups even in the absence of any actual competition between them? What if we could show that this kind of hostility can occur even when the two groups have no contact or interaction whatsoever with one another? This is precisely what advocates of the second theory we discuss below have found.

Social Identity Theory

Underlying the "soccer shirts" experiment that we described earlier is social identity theory. This is another situationist approach, and it has become perhaps the most common way of understanding the psychology of nationalism—offering insights into both the social and political cohesion that holds nations together, and the processes that bring groups into conflict.[18] Like the first perspective, this one also revolves around the distinction between ingroups and outgroups. Going beyond Sherif's approach, though, British social psychologist Henri Tajfel and his colleagues found—much against their initial expectations—that hostility towards outgroups and favoritism towards one's own can occur in the absence of any interaction between them, and in the absence of any "reasonable" or "rational" differences between the groups. Social identity theory suggests, in other words, that conflict can occur where the ingroup has absolutely *nothing* to gain from competing with the outgroup.[19]

Like Sherif, Tajfel used complete strangers as his subjects, and also randomly assigned them into groups for similar reasons. In his experiments, Tajfel also deliberately divided his subjects along quite absurd and theoretically meaningless lines, such as their musical preferences. As Waller relates,

> in the most famous series of studies, participants were asked to express their opinions about indistinguishable abstract paintings by artists they had never heard of and were then randomly assigned to a group that preferred either the "Paul Klee style" or the "Wassily Kandinsky style."[20]

Having divided his subjects using these arbitrary classifications, the two groups were never allowed to come into contact with one another. To Tajfel's own surprise, however, members of each group still displayed a marked favoritism towards their own ingroup and an equally pronounced hostility to the outgroup. This *minimal group paradigm*, as it is called, had been used initially simply as a baseline for further experimentation, and Tajfel himself apparently expected no Robbers' Cave-type group effects to occur in this condition; instead, what Tajfel and his colleague John Turner found was that "trivial, ad hoc intergroup categorization leads to in-group favoritism and discrimination against the out-group." Faced with the task of allocating financial resources between the two groups, for instance, the ingroup chose to penalize the outgroup rather than receive more money itself: "relatively less was given to the out-group, even when giving more would not have affected the amounts for the in-group."[21]

While Tajfel's model was initially purely cognitive, he felt that there had to be some other motivation for the individual's strong identification with the ingroup. Tajfel found this motivational factor in the idea of self-esteem. Identification with a group—especially where the group has a high status or believes itself to have this advantage—allows the individual member to enhance his or her self-esteem. It is this basic motivational need that leads us to favor members of our ingroup and to disparage or discriminate against members of the outgroup.

In an interesting analysis, Joshua Searle-White utilizes this theory to try to understand the phenomenon of nationalism from a social psychological angle.[22]

Searle-White teaches courses in the psychology of nationalism in which he recreates Tajfel's minimal group paradigm, successfully showing his students in a very direct and first-hand way how competing identities can be constructed out of very little (he actually divides his classes up into random categories with meaningless labels). Searle-White acknowledges that individuals have many identities, and that these differing identities can serve some purposes equally well. Nevertheless, *national* identities serve several particularly useful purposes in the modern era, he argues. Social identity theory suggests that feeling that one's nation is superior serves a basic human need for self-esteem. To this Searle-White adds a number of points of his own: the idea that "our cause is just" fulfills another basic human need in all of us, for instance. Sometimes this is paired with a sense of victimhood that enhances the feeling that we are right and seems to justify retribution and revenge. Finally, national identity helps us to find meaning in our lives.[23]

Social identity theory has been criticized as an overly simplistic explanation of nationalism, however, and some have highlighted the problems it faces as an account of political phenomena in general. Alan Finlayson, for instance, contends that nationalist groups differ in kind from other groups observed in the laboratory or even in naturalistic settings, not least because national groupings arouse passions of a depth rarely found in other social arrangements. He insists:

> We cannot simply take the findings of social psychological research into groups and transfer them to the study of nations . . . nations are not just any group with which people identify, but a particular kind of recently invented mass political force fundamentally related to the modern state form.[24]

Beyond Finlayson's "uniqueness" argument, Leonie Huddy highlights several other (more general) problems involved in the application of social identity theory to politics. Many of these have to do with the fact that as a primarily situationist theory, social identity theory may underestimate the extent to which identities are created by human beings, and can therefore be changed by them (in other words, dispositionism is important as well).

Not all groups come into conflict with one another, Huddy notes, something which a general theory like Tajfel's is ill equipped to explain. Another problem is that "individuals vary in the degree to which they identify with a group," Huddy notes.[25] Moreover, while identities at one time used to be quite fixed—one was born into a religion or economic status and "that was it"—identities today are often a matter of choice. One can change one's nation, for example, and many individuals do. One can even change one's gender, something considered physically impossible only a few decades ago. "It is important to understand what turns a weak or nonexistent identity into something that can motivate ethnic hatred," Huddy notes. "But this process would be difficult to understand if all we examined were the very weak identities that arise in the minimal intergroup situation, or the very powerful identities that characterize ethnic or national conflicts."[26] In addition to group attachments, as we shall note later, various psychological processes— such as dehumanization of the "other"—seem absolutely critical to forging ethnic hatred, for example, but social identity theory is largely silent on these processes. There is some evidence, moreover, that personality differences may affect the degree to which individuals take on a group identity (and by extension, a national identity).

Social Dominance Theory

The analysis of nationalism and other forms of group conflict has also been carried out through the relatively "new" social dominance approach, which is especially associated with Jim Sidanius and his colleagues.[27] This theory is heavily influenced by evolutionary psychology. Put most simply, the approach "views society as inherently oppressive and group oppression to be the 'normal,' default condition of human relations."[28] Sidanius argues that:

> most forms of oppression including racism, ethnocentricism (including the oppression of religious minorities such as Jews), sexism, nationalism, and classism and as well as a number of other social attitudes, human drives, and social institutions function, in part, to help establish and maintain the integrity of this group-based, hierarchical structure.[29]

All societies are to some extent hierarchically based, supporters of the theory note, and within every society there is at least one dominant group and at least one subordinate group. As Monroe, Hankin, and Van Vechten put it, "the social dominance orientation is a fundamental desire to view one's own group as positive and occupying higher social statuses than other relevant groups."[30] An orientation toward social domination serves as a legitimizing ideology for the inequality, oppression, and discrimination that occur within all hierarchically organized systems. Like Milgram, Sidanius sees such hierarchies as emerging naturally because such societies have a competitive evolutionary advantage over those that are not organized this way, and like Milgram he also focuses on the dark side of this evolutionary "fact." Discrimination, even in the most subtle forms, is a basic fact of daily life within such systems. But unlike in social identity theory, *outgroup favoritism* or deference also frequently occurs, especially among lower status groups who defer to higher status ones (Sidanius gives "Uncle Tomming" by blacks towards whites during the era of racial segregation in the United States as the clearest example in recent times).[31] Lower-status groups may also underachieve due to lower social expectations placed upon them, a form of "self-handicapping."[32]

Although this theory notes the importance of both situational and individual level forces, it is often seen as rather more dispositionist than it really is. Sidanius and his colleagues note that models such as social identity theory fail to account for individual differences in the degree of discrimination and prejudice against "the other" among people who have the same structural relationships to "the other."[33] Sidanius also frequently notes that the belief-based concept of *social dominance orientation* (or SDO) is central to his theory. This refers to the extent to which individuals actually desire to dominate others. And yet while he has shown that SDO is something which can vary across gender, for instance, with males exhibiting higher levels than females,[34] the theory more often homes in on competitive social groups rather than individuals (and what they do or do not think). He and his colleagues point out that social context, socialization, and social roles play a leading role in their theory, all factors that lead us in a situationist direction once we have gotten past the evolutionary roots of the perspective.

As currently constituted, social dominance theory can be vague and confusing, however, and seems at times to incorporate a mishmash of dispositionist and situationist factors that make the theory difficult to falsify. Nevertheless, the finding that outgroup *favoritism* is not only possible but frequently occurs within social hierarchies is at the very least a significant caveat to social identity theory, for instance. The fact that human beings across a variety of cultures tend to organize themselves within hierarchical structures is difficult to deny as well.

The Psychoanalytic Approach

A more clearly dispositionist approach to nationalism is provided by our old friend psychoanalytic theory, which (as in the study of terrorism) refuses to go away within political psychology. Sigmund Freud talked about "the narcissism of minor differences"—the tendency for conflicts to occur with people who not only live close to us but are also remarkably like us.[35] This has a certain resonance when one looks at the Arab–Israeli conflict or the conflict between Protestants and Catholics in Northern Ireland, since these are obvious examples of neighbors who often seem somewhat indistinguishable to outsiders. Freud also specifically argued that aggression was a basic and innate human drive, as we have seen already, albeit one which society socializes us to repress.

Beyond this, Freud had little to say about the psychology of nationalism, and as in other areas it has been left to his followers to expand upon his ideas. Among those who have adapted these ideas to nationalism and ethnic conflict, probably the best known have been Vamik Volkan and his colleagues. In *The Need To Have Enemies and Allies*, Volkan starts from the classic Freudian idea of "splitting." In our early development, we tend to split the world into "good" and "bad," externalizing or projecting those aspects of ourselves we dislike or find unacceptable onto others. Thus, when we condemn our enemies, we are really condemning not just them but the things which we dislike in *ourselves*. We are projecting the unwanted aspects of ourselves outwards onto the external world. Thus enemies serve a highly valuable but subconscious purpose. The anger and rage we feel towards them rid us of the anger and rage we unknowingly feel towards ourselves.[36]

Volkan and his followers may well be correct that there is something going on at the subconscious level in all international conflicts of which we are not aware. On the other hand, arguments about the subconscious are notoriously difficult to verify and/or falsify. While neuroscience is steadily accumulating evidence that shows that the subconscious does in fact exist, we still do not have the capability to test complex theories like these (through fMRI techniques we can see whether an individual is experiencing disgust, but not whether this is really *self-disgust*, for instance). Additionally, as Searle-White notes, there are problems involved in simply "jumping" from the individual level to that of the group. Groups, as we have seen already, carry their own dynamics, and are not simply aggregations of individuals.[37] Indeed, Dusan Kecmanovic—himself the author of a book on this topic—goes so far as to claim that there is no psychological theory of nationalism, in part because "nationalism is primarily a social phenomenon, and a psychological approach is not considered the best way to explain a social occurrence."[38]

This may be pushing the argument too far, but there are certainly well-known problems in moving from observations noted in clinical practice to broader conclusions about social behavior. This is where social psychological theories, designed to account for *aggregate* behaviors, arguably become more useful.

Biopolitical Approaches

One popular biological explanation for nationalism and ethnic conflict—and indeed, for all kinds of human conflict—is the simple idea that natural selection has imbued human beings with an innately aggressive instinct (as we saw in Chapter 11, evolutionary theory represents one approach to biopolitics, but not the only one).[39] This is rather plausible, since in the days before humans got their sustenance from supermarkets, they had to kill to get food. Most of us are not aggressive all the time, however, so even if this argument is accurate, it begs the question of what situations bring out this instinct. Some commentators speak of *the* biopolitical approach to politics, a Darwinian perspective in which evolution has caused us to think and act in ways that are predictable, at least within a range. In fact, though, such a unified view of evolutionary theory is illusory. While evolutionary psychologists, ethologists, and biologists may share the view that we are genetically "hard-wired" in some way by evolutionary processes—equally rejecting Skinner's notion of the blank slate—they disagree on the critical issue of just what the hard-wiring consists of.

Contrast, for example, Richard Dawkins' well-known bestseller *The Selfish Gene* with Mary Clark's *In Search of Human Nature*. Dawkins sees a world in which human beings evolved the ability to act through self-interest:

> a predominant quality to be expected in a successful gene is ruthless selfishness. This gene selfishness will usually give rise to selfishness in individual behavior . . . there are special circumstances in which a gene can achieve its own selfish goals best by fostering a limited form of altruism at the level of individual animals. "Special" and "limited" are important words in that last sentence. Much as we might wish to believe otherwise, universal love and the welfare of the species as a whole are concepts that simply do not make evolutionary sense.[40]

As Clark describes Dawkins' theory, "'selfish genes' do not allow for love, for empathy, for being virtuous. Those are evolutionary no-no's; they just aren't efficient. They decrease one's fitness to survive."[41] But it is difficult indeed to explain the many altruistic actions we do observe in the real world—the activities of rescuers such as Raoul Wallenberg and Per Anger, for instance—if this is really how we are "wired" genetically. "I cannot see how we could have evolved at all if we were constructed this way," Clark argues. "Indeed, I cannot see how any social mammals—the other primates, dolphins, elephants—ever came into being following such rules of natural selection for behavior."[42] In particular, such a view fails to explain not only altruistic and empathetic behavior in social life, but why we experience feelings of love and grief and why we come together in groups at all. Instead of being shaped by "selfish genes," we are genetically predisposed or hard-wired to *help* other human beings, Clark argues. In order for a species to continue to propagate itself, it would certainly help enormously if that species were predisposed to aid other members.

J. Philippe Rushton, on the other hand, argues that we can explain both altruism towards our own ethnic groups and hostility towards others using "genetic similarity theory," the theory that we tend to favor those who are genetically similar to us.[43] This kind of limited altruism evolved for evolutionary purposes, since it tends to replicate our own genes. We tend to marry those who are ethnically similar to ourselves, for instance, as well as similar in age, education, attitudes, and even personality.[44] Analyses like these are highly reductionist, however; though he disavows a purely genetic analysis of politics, Rushton seems to view political attitudes as subconscious rationalizations for genetic interests, a suggestion which leaves out a great deal.[45] This kind of analysis does not really specify the mechanisms by which genetic impulses become translated into political action, and also has difficulty explaining hostility towards those who *do not* share our genetic makeup. Beyond stating that "ethnic nationalism, xenophobia and genocide can become the 'dark side' of altruism," Rushton does not explain why genetics would lead to outgroup hostility or the *depth* of such feelings.[46]

An even more fundamental problem in attributing nationalism to evolutionary processes, however, is that we cannot be sure just *what* has been "hard-wired" into us, since it is difficult to disentangle innate or biological factors from learned social behaviors; and even if we could specify exactly the nature of our genetic hard-wiring, we would then face the problem of explaining how these evolutionary factors interact with social and political forces (since as we have seen already, no one argues that biology alone accounts for everything). Even more telling, a real problem for any theory that suggests that intense nationalistic conflict is in some sense "innate" is that it seems *more* likely that we are hard-wired to come to one another's aid, as Clark's work suggests, though as we have seen, various social pressures can interfere with this process. The sources of conflict, in other words, might be found someplace other than simple human biology. This is a problem not just for out-and-out biopolitical theories that suggest that discrimination and prejudice are in a sense "integral" to human beings, but is also a problem for approaches like social dominance theory which propose that the mere existence of hierarchy is sufficient to produce oppression and exploitation.

The Psychology of Genocide

We began this chapter by suggesting a couple of psychological explanations for the relative tolerance of "bystander publics" to the incidence of genocide elsewhere. Why, though, does genocide even occur in the first place? As Kristen Monroe and her colleagues suggest, social identity theory is especially troubling because it "suggests that genocide and racism may in fact be extreme manifestations of normal group identification and behavior."[47]

Nevertheless, general situational theories like social identity cannot by themselves explain why national and ethnic identities sometimes "morph" into more extreme behaviors, as James Waller suggests:

> Social categorization, and its role in us–them thinking, does not lead us to hate all out-groups. Social exclusion, let alone mass killing and genocide, is not an inevitable consequence of social categorization. Social categorization does remind us, however, that, once identified with a group, we find it easy to exaggerate differences between our group and others, enhancing in-group cooperation and effectiveness, and—frequently—intensifying antagonism with other groups.[48]

What all of this indicates is that we cannot fully explain nationalism and ethnic conflict using theories that outline the mere existence of "us versus them" thinking alone. This is probably a necessary condition for conflict to take place, but it is often not sufficient for this outcome to occur. Clearly, what is needed in the analysis of nationalism and ethnic conflict is a better understanding of how "us versus them" situational dynamics interact with dispositional factors such as personality and beliefs to produce extreme behaviors, and there is currently very little research that does this.

The "sudden" nature of many genocidal events also exposes another weakness of the theories we have examined in this chapter. The events in Yugoslavia in the early 1990s provide a case in point. Serbs, Bosnians, and Croats—ethnic groups which had lived together in seeming harmony for many years—suddenly not only went to war, but began attempting to destroy one another on a massive scale. In the West, where the terms "Serb" and "Bosnian" were assumed to be outdated labels of relevance only in a history test about World War I, the genocide in Yugoslavia was initially met with stunned incredulity. The events in Rwanda in 1994 also took many unawares, although mass killings had been occurring there intermittently for a number of years at regular intervals. But since none of the theories we have looked at in this chapter really deals with *change*—all the theories are to varying degrees rather static—they arguably provide only partial explanations for sudden acts of genocidal activity.

What exactly *is* genocide? As Monroe notes, "genocide refers to the deliberate and systematic destruction of people, not because of individual acts or culpability but because of their birth in a national, ethnic, racial or religious group."[49] We have already seen various explanations for the Nazi Holocaust in this book, but what might explain genocide—the most extreme form of ethnic conflict—in general? As Monroe points out:

> two explanations are frequently offered. The first stresses group disparities in political-economic situations and the desire of the dominant group to use

its power to obtain better living conditions, more land, and the material wealth held by an ethnic minority.

This offers a kind of *Homo economicus* approach or realistic group conflict account—"a glimmer of rationality," as Monroe puts it—and hence makes some sort of sense to us. The second kind of explanation does not, however. "In contrast to such rational explanations, we find genocide explained through ancient hatred festering in the body politic, hatreds that remain inherently unresolvable through moderate forms of political negotiation because of their primordial force and passion." Unfortunately, both kinds of explanation are deficient, Monroe notes, not least because both competition over scarce resources and ancient hatreds exist in many places where events do not boil over into genocide.[50]

Monroe suggests a more sophisticated, multilevel, layered explanation for genocide. She argues that various factors must be present—many of them situational, but others more dispositional—for genocides to occur. First of all, there must obviously be existing ethnic divisions or a "pluralistic" society. This is a *facilitating condition* or a necessary condition, but it is not of course a sufficient one. At a second level, then, these divisions are overlaid by specific contextual or situational factors (economic distress, political instability, war, or revolution are notable examples). These serve to divide the society against itself, so that it may temporarily or permanently "dissolve" into conflictual elements along the existing ethnic fault lines. This is a vital step in the process, but it still does not necessarily lead to the slaughter of members of one group by another. At the third level, the various groups must come to develop a cognitive perception of their neighbors as "the other." Scapegoating and stereotyping must occur, providing a victim on whose shoulders blame for the uncomfortable external condition can be heaped. The scapegoat, moreover, must eventually be dehumanized in a way that makes it possible for the dominant group to feel morally justified in committing horrendous atrocities against the subordinate one.

The first level or prerequisite is clear enough. Almost by definition, genocides do not occur *within* genuinely heterogeneous societies where ethnic fault lines aren't present to serve as dividers, although genocides may occur between such groups. Moreover, "genocide is greatly facilitated when such long-standing inequalities in political participation overlap accentuated economic and social cleavages and when there is a history of conflict between the groups."[51]

The second level involves the appearance of destabilizing economic and political conditions "that threaten the social order," Monroe notes.[52] In *Balkan Tragedy*, Susan Woodward offers us an excellent account of the breakup of Yugoslavia that focuses on this second type of explanation.[53] As recently as the late 1970s, Yugoslavia had been feted as the wave of the future, and its economic system was widely regarded as an ideal marriage of the socialist- and market-based systems by many liberal political economists.[54] It also survived the death of its "strongman" Marshal Tito, whom many observers regarded as having played an essential role in Yugoslavia's economic and political development as a state. After the Cold War, however, Yugoslavia rapidly disintegrated into its older constituent "parts" (it had been constructed by the victorious Allies after World War I, much as Iraq was). How are we to explain this sudden event?

Many international observers rapidly resorted to the "ancient hatreds" argument. British Prime Minister John Major, for instance, told the House of Commons that the genocide took place because of:

> the collapse of the Soviet Union and of the discipline that that exerted over the ancient hatreds in the old Yugoslavia. Once that discipline had disappeared, those ancient hatreds reappeared and we began to see their consequences when the fighting occurred.[55]

However, this exaggerated the degree of control the Soviets had exerted over the non-aligned Yugoslavia, ignored the fact that Serbs, Croats, Bosnians, and others had coexisted in reasonable harmony within the same national space for many years, and also downplayed the fact that the state had survived the demise of a figure who had supposedly been holding its various ethnic components together by force.[56] Eschewing the kind of views then popular, Susan Woodward provided a conspicuously economic explanation for what happened. Economic distress—more specifically, dismantling the existing economic arrangements and plunging too far and too fast into the icy waters of the global market system—what Woodward calls "a shock-therapy program of economic reform"—had created tensions which pulled this relatively new state apart at the seams.[57] Similarly, land shortages created in part by an influx of Tutsis created economic instability in Rwanda, laying the groundwork or potential for the horrors which followed.[58]

Of course, these broad situational conditions—while critical forces which always seem to be present in such cases—are not by themselves enough to lead to genocide. It is conceivable in the Yugoslavian case, for instance, that the various parties might have separated peacefully—much as the former Czechoslovakia did—or that the factions might have gone to war but avoided the full-scale genocide that occurred. Logically then, there has to be a further step or series of steps, Monroe notes. This is where insights from psychology become most useful to us, and where cultural and individual perceptions and dispositions become critical.

As Monroe suggests, the first step within this psychological level is that some kind of legitimizing ideology frequently emerges to justify the slaughter that is to occur. Often this justification takes a dubious "scientific" form. "Ironically, the doctrine of biological determinism serves as a justification for genocide and genocide is frequently equated with a holy crusade to free the body politic of diseased tissue," Monroe notes. "Thus genocide becomes a scientific prevention of contamination by agents of 'racial pollution' who are viewed as parasites and bacteria causing sickness, deterioration, and death in the host peoples they supposedly infect."[59] *Demonization* of the minority group, the perception that it is a threat and a feeling of racial or religious superiority all follow from commitment to such a radical ideology.[60]

The next step is that we undergo *a shift in our perception of ourselves* in relation to others. Evidence drawn by Monroe from Christopher Browning's work on Nazi Battalion 101 suggests that social etiquette and the desire not to "lose face" in front of one's colleagues become more important than the lives of "the other" under these conditions.[61] We may also come to see ourselves as "having no choice" but to act the way we do. A third psychological change is that we may convince ourselves that we are acting through a kind of "twisted compassion." We may begin to think of ourselves as moral beings, putting "the other" out of their misery; in particular, some members of Battalion 101 saw it as a *moral* act to kill children, since once their parents had been executed their lives would become unbearable anyway. Last—and this is perhaps the "master" shift which precedes all the others—*dehumanization and distancing* occur. Distancing does not necessarily refer to physical distance—the kind of distance which kept Eichmann away from those he was in effect killing—but to the psychological and emotional distance perpetrators create in their heads from their victims, who come to be blamed for their own fate.[62]

Dehumanization is the tendency to perceive others as being something less than human, and hence undeserving of the moral respect we ordinarily accord to other human beings. The great irony is that we often humanize things which are not human—including computers and pets—but we dehumanize some people who *are* objectively human. The psychologists Lasana Harris and Susan Fiske have been especially prominent in examining this phenomenon in recent years, and they posit that it probably underlies all atrocities, including torture, racial prejudice, and genocide:

> People spontaneously fail to consider another person's mind if that person elicits predominantly disgust, a phenomenon we characterize as dehumanized perception. Perceivers moreover view these targets as less typically human, unfamiliar, dissimilar, unintelligent, inarticulate, cold, incompetent, and having more ups and downs in life; perceivers

describe it as more difficult to infer the content of their minds and personality, and perceivers do not use mental state verbs when describing dehumanized targets' daily life. Specifically, participants spontaneously think about the minds of dehumanized targets less often than the minds of other social targets. Moreover, these human-perception dimensions correlate with parts of the brain implicated in disgust, conflict resolution, and attention.[63]

Conclusion

Going back to the topic of neuroscience discussed earlier, it may be that there are changes in the human brain that occur when—for instance—neighbors kill people they have known for years, as frequently happens in genocides.[64] As Dave Grossman notes in regard to killing on the battlefield:

> when a man is frightened, he literally stops thinking with his forebrain (that is, with the mind of a human being) and begins to think with the midbrain (that is, with the portion of his brain that is essentially indistinguishable from that of an animal).[65]

While fear is not the only psychological emotion we experience when killing another member of our own species—in fact, the primary emotion in normal human beings when confronted with the prospect of killing seems to be a *resistance* to doing so, as Grossman notes—it would be interesting to learn whether something similar happens in those who commit genocidal acts. It is plausible to suppose that the more primitive parts of the brain are activated when individuals engage in genocidal behaviors, but not much research exists on this question.

Apart from the points Monroe makes, as we noted in Chapter 4 the human propensity towards obedience—even where there is no "draconian" authority standing over us ensuring that we comply—may be a powerful contributing factor to the occurrence of genocide; since genocides require large numbers of people to kill similarly large numbers of victims, genocide would probably not be possible were it not for some basic human tendency to obey authority. Interestingly, moreover, Milgram was able to elicit a high degree of obedience in his subjects even *without* dehumanizing the "victim"; indeed, as Waller notes, the jovial-looking, likeable actor who pretended to receive shocks was remarkably "personalized," something which leads us to expect that obedience in natural political settings might be even higher.[66]

Equally important is the nature of the authority *itself*. To Monroe's otherwise very comprehensive overview we should probably add the *transformative potential of leaders* and other individual agents as critical variables. While both Adolf Hitler and Slobodan Milosevic, for instance, capitalized upon social and political conditions beyond their control, both also played an instrumental role in *shaping* the course of events in Europe during two different genocides. Although Hitler of course never faced justice for his actions, Milosevic did, and no social scientist has seriously suggested that he was not at least partly responsible for the genocide in Yugoslavia. Similarly, in Rwanda Hutu leaders played an integral role in creating discriminatory practices which disadvantaged Tutsis at many levels, and in the Darfur region of Sudan the ongoing genocide has been encouraged by the country's leaders. On top of malevolent leadership and the propensity of large numbers of people to go along with what they are told (*à la* Milgram), what they think they are supposed to do (Zimbardo), and things they know or suspect are wrong (Janis and Asch), it is not surprising that genocide—when these factors are combined with broad situational factors such as economic distress, "us versus them" thinking, dehumanization and demonization of the other, ideological indoctrination, and the profound power of social etiquette and other forces—is such a common and repetitive feature of human history.

Notes

1 Paul Slovic, "'If I Look at the Mass I Will Never Act': Psychic Numbing and Genocide," *Judgment and Decision Making*, 2(2): 79–95, April 2007.

2 This phrase is Tom Bower's. See Bower, *Blind Eye To Murder* (Boston, MA: Little, Brown, 1995).

3 Bibb Latané and John Darley, *The Unresponsive Bystander: Why Doesn't He Help?* (Englewood Cliffs, NJ: Prentice-Hall, 1970).

4 John Darley and Bibb Latané, "Bystander Intervention in Emergencies: Diffusion of Responsibility," *Journal of Personality and Social Psychology*, 8: 377–83, 1968.

5 Darley and Latané, "Bystander Intervention in Emergencies."

6 See Morton Hunt, *The Story of Psychology*, updated and revised edition (New York: Anchor Books, 2007), pp.483–84.

7 John Darley and Daniel Batson, "From Jerusalem to Jericho: A Study of Situational and Dispositional Variables in Helping Behavior," *Journal of Personality and Social Psychology*, 27: 100–8, 1973.

8 Ibid., p.105.

9 Mark Levine, Amy Prosser, David Evans, and Stephen Reicher, "Identity and Emergency Intervention: How Social Group Membership and Inclusiveness of Group Boundaries Shapes Helping Behavior," *Personality and Social Psychology Bulletin*, 31, 443–53, 2005.

10 Deborah Small, George Lowenstein, and Paul Slovic, "Sympathy and Callousness: The Impact of Deliberative Thought on Donations to Identifiable and Statistical Victims," *Organizational Behavior and Human Decision Processes*, 102: 143–53, 2007, p.1.

11 One of the earliest studies of this kind was Leonard Doob's *Patriotism and Nationalism: Their Psychological Foundations* (New Haven and London: Yale University Press, 1964), which drew heavily on the language of S–R behaviorism. More recently, we have seen the appearance of Dusan Kecmanovic, *The Mass Psychology of Ethnonationalism* (New York and London: Plenum Press, 1996) and Joshua Searle-White, *The Psychology of Nationalism* (New York and Basingstoke: Palgrave, 2002).

12 See Walker Connor, *Ethnonationalism: The Quest For Understanding* (Princeton, NJ: Princeton University Press, 1994), p.4.

13 Searle-White, *The Psychology of Nationalism*, p.3.

14 Quoted in Connor, *Ethnonationalism*, p.4.

15 Anthony Smith (ed.), *Theories of Nationalism*, second edition (New York: Holmes and Meier, 1983).

16 See James Sidanius, "The Psychology of Group Conflict and the Dynamics of Oppression: A Social Dominance Perspective," in Shanto Iyengar and William McGuire, *Explorations in Political Psychology* (Durham, NC: Duke University Press, 1993).

17 The (now rare) exception to this in British soccer is teams which *have* historically been divided along religious lines. This is still the case somewhat with Rangers FC and Celtic FC, two teams from the Scottish city of Glasgow which traditionally represent Protestants and Catholics respectively, though the strength of this division has weakened considerably. The city of Liverpool in England was also once divided along similar religious lines between Liverpool FC and Everton FC, though this is no longer the case today. It should also be noted that until the last ten years, British soccer was far less racially integrated than it is today. British soccer has now been "globalized" to the point where each of the teams (in the top divisions, at least) is exceptionally mixed racially and ethnically, with each including a large number of non-U.K. players.

18 See the excellent summary of this in James Waller, *Becoming Evil: How Ordinary People Commit Genocide and Mass Killing* (New York: Oxford University Press, 2002), pp.238–44, from which I have drawn freely here.

19 See Henri Tajfel and John Turner, "The Social Identity Theory of Intergroup Behavior," in John Jost and Jim Sidanius (eds.), *Political Psychology: Key Readings* (New York and Hove: Psychology Press, 2004); this can also be found in S. Worchel and L.W. Austin (eds.), *Psychology of Intergroup Relations* (Chicago, IL: Nelson-Hall, 1986); Tajfel, "Experiments in Intergroup Discrimination," *Scientific American*, 223: 96–102, 1970; Tajfel, *Human Groups and Social Categories* (Cambridge: Cambridge University Press, 1981); Tajfel, *Social Identity and Intergroup Relations* (Cambridge: Cambridge University Press, 1982).

20 Waller, *Becoming Evil*, p.241.

21 Tajfel and Turner, "The Social Identity Theory of Intergroup Behavior," p.282.

22 Searle-White, *The Psychology of Nationalism*.

23 Ibid., pp.87–100.

24 Alan Finlayson, "Psychology, Psychoanalysis and Theories of Nationalism," *Nations and Nationalism*, 4: 145–62, 1998. The "uniqueness" critique can also be leveled at other theories as well, such as realistic group conflict theory and social dominance theory.

25 Leonie Huddy, "From Social to Political Identity: A Critical Examination of Social Identity Theory," *Political Psychology*, 22: 127–56, 2001.

26 Ibid., p.137.
27 See for instance James Sidanius and Felicia Pratto, "The Inevitability of Oppression and the Dynamics of Social Dominance," in Paul Sniderman and Philip Tetlock (eds.), *Prejudice and Politics in American Society* (Stanford, CA: Stanford University Press, 1991); Sidanius, "The Psychology of Group Conflict and the Dynamics of Oppression: A Social Dominance Perspective"; James Sidanius, Felicia Pratto, Colette van Laar, and Shana Levi, "Social Dominance Theory: Its Agenda and Method," *Political Psychology*, 25: 845–80, 2004.
28 Sidanius, "The Psychology of Group Conflict and the Dynamics of Oppression," p.217.
29 Ibid., p.214.
30 Kristen Monroe, James Hankin, and Renee Van Vechten, "The Psychological Foundations of Identity Politics," *Annual Review of Political Science*, 3: 419–47, 2000, p.431.
31 Sidanius, "The Psychology of Group Conflict and the Dynamics of Oppression," p.202.
32 Ibid., p.204.
33 Sidanius et al., "Social Dominance Theory," p.846.
34 Sidanius, "The Psychology of Group Conflict and the Dynamics of Oppression," p.210.
35 Sigmund Freud, *Civilization and Its Discontents* (New York: W.W. Norton, 1961), p.61.
36 Vamik Volkan, *The Need To Have Enemies and Allies: From Clinical Practice to International Relationships* (Northvale, NJ: J. Aronson, 1988). See also Volkan, *Bloodlines: From Ethnic Pride To Ethnic Terrorism* (New York: Farrar, Strauss and Giroux, 1997) and Finlayson, "Psychology, Psychoanalysis and Theories of Nationalism."
37 Searle-White, *The Psychology of Nationalism*, p.41.
38 Dusan Kecmanovic, "Review of Joshua Searle-White, *The Psychology of Nationalism*," *Nations and Nationalism*, 9: 459–61, 2003.
39 See for instance Konrad Lorenz, *On Aggression* (New York: Harcourt Brace, 1966).
40 Richard Dawkins, *The Selfish Gene*, 30th anniversary edition (New York: Oxford University Press, 2006), p.2.
41 Mary Clark, *In Search of Human Nature* (New York: Routledge, 2002), p.55.
42 Ibid.
43 J. Philippe Rushton, "Ethnic Nationalism, Evolutionary Psychology and Genetic Similarity Theory," *Nations and Nationalism*, 11: 489–507, 2005.
44 Ibid., p.495.
45 Ibid., p.501.
46 Ibid., p.503.
47 Monroe, Hankin, and Van Vechten, p.436.
48 Waller, *Becoming Evil*, p.243.
49 Kristen Monroe, "Review Essay: The Psychology of Genocide," *Ethics & International Affairs*, 9: 215–39, 1995, p.216.
50 Ibid., pp.215–16.
51 Ibid., p.218.
52 Ibid., p.218.
53 Susan Woodward, *Balkan Tragedy: Chaos and Dissolution After The Cold War* (Washington, D.C.: Brookings Institution, 1995).

54 See, for instance, Charles Lindblom, *Politics and Markets: The World's Political Economic Systems* (New York: Basic Books, 1977).

55 Cited in Noel Malcolm, *Bosnia: A Short History* (London: Macmillan, 1994), p.xx.

56 Note, though, that Walker Connor had mentioned Yugoslavia as a site of ethnic unrest as long ago as the mid-1960s (see the beginning of this chapter).

57 Woodward, *Balkan Tragedy*, p.1.

58 Philip Gourevitch, *We Wish To Inform You That Tomorrow We Will Be Killed With Our Families: Stories From Rwanda* (New York: Picador, 1998), p.73.

59 Ibid., p.220. Richard Lerner in his book *Final Solutions: Biology, Prejudice, and Genocide* (University Park, PA: Pennsylvania State Press, 1992) details the ways in which biological arguments were used to justify the Holocaust. It is little wonder that biopolitical arguments were out of fashion for many years after World War II, since for a long time these evoked images of Nazism.

60 The dehumanizing notion of Tutsis as "cockroaches," with all the highly negative connotations attached to this label, is similar.

61 Christopher Browning, *Ordinary Men: Reserve Police Battalion 101 and the Final Solution in Poland* (New York: HarperCollins, 1992).

62 Monroe, "Review Essay: The Psychology of Genocide," p.236.

63 Lasana Harris and Susan Fiske, "Dehumanized Perception: A Psychological Means to Facilitate Atrocities Torture and Genocide?," *Journal of Psychology*, 219: 175–81, 2011. See also Harris and Fiske "Social Neuroscience Evidence for Dehumanised Perception," *European Review of Social Psychology* 20: 192–231 2009.

64 See Waller, *Becoming Evil*, p.244.

65 Dave Grossman, *On Killing: The Psychological Cost of Learning To Kill In War And Society* (Boston, MA: Little, Brown, 1995).

66 Waller, *Becoming Evil*, p.249.

Suggested Further Reading

Joshua Searle-White, *The Psychology of Nationalism* (New York and Basingstoke: Palgrave, 2002).

James Waller, *Becoming Evil: How Ordinary People Commit Genocide and Mass Killing* (New York: Oxford University Press, 2002).

Films

Ghosts of Rwanda (2005): Exceptionally moving PBS documentary film. There is a website for the program at http://www.pbs.org/wgbh/pages/frontline/shows/ghosts/.

Hotel Rwanda (2004): Award-winning Hollywood movie directed by Terry George.

Scream Bloody Murder (2008): CNN Special documentary about mass killing presented by Christiane Amanpour, highlighting individuals who stood up against genocidal governments.

Chapter 15

The Psychology of Racism and Political Intolerance

Jane Elliott is a retired schoolteacher today, but in 1968 she created a now famous exercise in the small town of Riceville, Iowa usually known simply as the "blue eyes–brown eyes" experiment.[1] Elliott first conducted the experiment just after Martin Luther King's assassination, and by deliberate design it had much to say about the psychology of racial and ethnic differences and most of all how easy it is to create artificial "ingroups" and "outgroups." She had attempted to explain what racism was like to the children, but she could see that her all-white class did not really understand what racism was or what it felt like to judge someone on the basis of his or her skin color. So she did something rather remarkable, even radical: she decided to segregate her class based on their eye color. Designating blue-eyed children as "superior"—with deliberate arbitrariness and absurdity—Elliott then began to "discriminate" against the brown-eyed kids, giving the blue-eyed children special privileges and making the brown-eyed ones sit at the back of the class. Brown-eyed kids were not allowed to use the water fountain or to play with blue-eyed children.

Elliott also broke down the resistance of the brown-eyed children to what was happening by making up a pseudo-scientific theory claiming that blue-eyed children were inherently more intelligent (echoing Nazi claims of Aryan superiority, as well as white supremacy groups in the United States).[2] The superiority notion quickly became a self-fulfilling prophecy, as the blue-eyed kids began to perform better in class and the brown-eyed kids started to perform poorly (even those who had obtained high grades before). The blue-eyed kids also began to actually *believe* that they were better. The next day, she reversed the social order of things, making the brown-eyed kids the superior class, but according to Elliott the effect was much more muted now. Both sets of children now knew what racial discrimination felt like, and although Elliott's actions were the subject of much controversy, she became a national celebrity and effective anti-racism campaigner for many years. The inventive but emotionally draining exercise is now often used in diversity training, and has been repeated many times across the world.

In a racial sense the United States has unquestionably become more egalitarian since the time Elliott first conducted this experiment, if we measure egalitarianism as *expressed* attitudes; opinion poll after opinion poll shows that it has simply become socially unacceptable to express racist attitudes, especially since the civil rights revolution ushered in by Lyndon Johnson and Martin Luther King during the 1960s. New norms appear to have developed which discourage open racial prejudice or the making of crude distinctions based on race. On the other hand, simply because we *wish* to be "non-racist" it does not necessarily follow that we can easily eradicate any and all racial feelings or stereotypes we might harbor overnight. What if (for instance) favoring one's racial ingroup over outgroups is an ingrained part of being human, or perhaps has some "hard-wired" or genetic basis in the way we have evolved over thousands of years? What if racism and prejudice towards one's ingroup is even favored by evolution, and exists within us because of this?

While there are still major limitations on what techniques like neuro-imaging can objectively "prove" in a scientific sense—even relatively advanced fMRI-based studies are often open to competing interpretations—a growing number of neuroscientists in recent years have become interested in what goes on in the human brain when we view individuals of a racial grouping which is not our own (when we're looking at an outgroup, in other words). Neuroscientists who are interested in race most often study "deep" or implicit attitudes by showing subjects in an fMRI machine photographs of members of their own race as well as pictures of members of other racial groups, comparing the results to see whether there is any systematic variation in the way that various parts of the brain react to each. Since we now have a reasonably good idea what some regions of the brain "do" as opposed to other areas, such comparisons can be instructive.

Elizabeth Phelps, a psychologist based at New York University, is an especially noteworthy pioneer of such approaches. In a now classic 2000 study, by placing electrodes on the heads of her subjects, Phelps showed that eye-blink startle—a reflex which is set off by loud noises or the sudden appearance of something in front of us—is stronger for white people looking at images of a black person than it is for whites looking at other whites (or black people looking at other blacks).[3] Many of us prefer to believe that we have no racial bias, and when asked to self-report racial basis, the results are rather different from Phelps's findings.

If you are in a slightly fearful state, Phelps notes, the eye-blink startle will be more magnified than it is when you are relaxed. The amygdala, as we have seen in previous chapters, is implicated in fear or disgust. The fusiform face area is a part of the brain which activates when we look at faces. This technique may not be entirely accurate as a test of racial bias, since it may simply indicate that the amygdala activates when we see faces we are not familiar with. This reflects the debate going on now between what is called the "perceptual expertise" view and the "social cognitive" one. For the first camp the tendency of white people to be startled when they see black faces is due to a lack of exposure to the latter, and can be changed when people do gain such exposure. For instance, the author of this book was brought up in a region of the North of England where there were very few black people, and in fact very few people of any color other than white, and so I did not regularly interact with non-whites before I moved to the United States in my early twenties. It seems likely that my amygdala would "fire up" more when I did not interact with black people than it does now, now that I am accustomed to people of another race. On the other hand, supporters of the "social cognitive" view state that being startled—especially where a strong amygdala response is shown—is indicative of a hard-wired phenomenon, showing the continuing presence of racial prejudice in people's minds. As impressive as fMRI and other new methods are, then, one thing they cannot do is adjudicate between rival theories of *why* the amygdala often activates when we look at faces of another race, and this remains an open debate.

In a recent review of the literature on this topic, Phelps shows that a number of brain regions have been consistently implicated in a large number of neuroimaging studies about race.[4] As already noted the amygdala features in a large number of these studies, and may indicate racial bias even among those who are strongly motivated not to feel or show any. Phelps and her colleagues believe that the anterior cingulate cortex (ACC) plays a key role here. Like the amygdala, it also shows activation in many neurological studies of race, leading researchers to conclude that it may play a role in regulating feelings of prejudice among those who really want to be non-prejudiced. Phelps's research suggests that most people show an initial racial bias, but that this is often then regulated or modified by the ACC. Other research suggests that while many of us may exhibit initial racial bias, there is nothing inevitable about such biases, and they can be eradicated by repeated exposure to members of other races. In other words, situational factors can change our existing dispositions.

Studying Prejudice

Not surprisingly, political psychologists have long been interested in the roots of racial prejudice. What is it that makes apparently reasonable, normal, psychologically healthy individuals discriminate—either overtly or covertly—against someone else or an entire group, based on nothing more than the fact that this person or group happens to possess a skin color different from their own? This is one of the great puzzles of social and political psychology—not to say social science as a whole—and it is unsurprising that many have sought to address the causes of this widespread phenomenon.

As Susan Fiske notes, a great deal of the research that has been done on racism, prejudice, and discrimination has come out of the United States. "Centuries of dramatically heterogeneous immigration into one nation may have brought ethnic issues to the surface sooner in the USA than elsewhere," Fiske suggests. She notes, though, that many of the theories that have been used to account for racism are just as applicable to prejudice in European politics as they are to the American case.[5] In fact, most of the theories we shall look at in this chapter can be applied to any region of the world where significant racial and ethnic differences exist within a particular state.

A dizzying number of psychological theories have been proposed to try to explain racism and the development of racial tensions, and we cannot possibly do justice to all of them here. We can, however, certainly sketch their broad details. We have met some of these theories already in previous chapters, and so will pass over them more quickly here (while making it clear, of course, how they can be applied to racism as opposed to other things). Since intergroup conflict takes many forms, the general theories we examined in the previous chapter can also be utilized to explain racial discrimination. Additionally, there exist more specific theories that have been developed to explain racism and prejudice in an exclusively U.S. context. Fiske notes that all of these theories can be divided into what she calls individual-level and contextual-level theories, and broadly speaking these can be thought of as alternative terms for our dispositionist and situationist approaches.[6] Like other political phenomena we have discussed, racism may be the product of the beliefs or personalities of particular individuals, or it may result from situational factors that encourage or somehow otherwise fashion racist behavior.

What Explains Racism?

Authoritarian Personality Theory

Our discussion in Chapter 4 has probably left you with the impression that the "authoritarian personality" died in the 1960s, felled like a great tree by the powerful situationist axe of Stanley Milgram and others. But in recent years the theory has made a comeback, principally through the work of Bob Altemeyer.[7] Altemeyer retains the basis of the "old" authoritarian personality theory associated with Theodore Adorno and his colleagues, but has sought to make it less vague. Originally the theory highlighted nine personality traits that were supposed to characterize right-wing authoritarians, but Altemeyer jettisoned some of these and boiled the theory down to three "attitudinal clusters": authoritarian submission (meaning a strong tendency to submit to authority), authoritarian aggression (hostility towards outgroups) and conventionalism (denoting conformity with social norms and an unwillingness to challenge "the way things are"). Altemeyer labeled this revised approach *right-wing authoritarianism* (RWA) and has developed an RWA scale designed to measure the degree to which a given individual conforms to this characterization.

For Altemeyer, racism is best thought of quite simply as an attribute of this personality category. RWAs exhibit a high degree of prejudice towards outgroups of all kinds, including African-Americans and homosexuals. Right-wing authoritarians:

> have plenty of "kick" in them. They are hostile toward so many minorities, they seem to be equal opportunity bigots. But they do not usually realize they are relatively egocentric. Nor do they want to find out . . . They are relatively ready to help the government persecute almost any group you can think of—including themselves![8]

In the movie *Dirty Harry*, for instance, fictional policeman Harry Callahan's colleagues describe him this way. Harry's old partner, Frank De Georgio, tells his new partner "that's one thing about our Harry, he doesn't play any favorites. Harry hates everybody." An extensive series of racial epithets follow in the movie, but if Dirty Harry really "hates everybody" he would be just the kind of "equal opportunity racist" Altemeyer has in mind, although in the follow-up film (*Magnum Force*) it becomes clear that he is not in fact racist (he has an Asian girlfriend and a black partner in that film, for instance, script moves which may have been designed to defuse criticism of the racial overtones in the original film).

In Altemeyer's RWA theory we see another example of the point made in Chapter 1 about the distinction between situationism and dispositionism. Surely people become racist because of the environments and situations they find themselves in, not because they were that way at birth. In this sense, we noted, most theories are "situationist" at root, because people have to get their dispositions from somewhere (the exception being evolutionary theories, which argue that we are born with at least some *innate* dispositions rather than being "blank slates"). Altemeyer argues that RWAs probably learn their authoritarian beliefs in childhood—as, he suggests, do non-RWAs—but the differences lie in the fact that non-RWAs are more self-aware and come to moderate their early beliefs with experience, while RWAs do not.[9] Again however, this is a dispositionist theory in the sense that while authoritarian beliefs are learned, RWAs form *dispositions* which are in turn difficult to change and may persist throughout their lives. While the more distant cause of their behavior may have to do with situational factors, the immediate, or proximate cause is dispositional.

While Altemeyer's theory is now well known and has gained some adherents, it has not been as widely accepted as other approaches. Apart from some of the standard criticisms we have raised about simple personality theories already, it also poses the question of why entire regions—presumably populated by people with a variety of personality types—express especially racist sentiments and/or practice discrimination. A classic example would be the "Jim Crow" system of racial segregation which existed in the old South of the United States.

Social Dominance Theory

As we saw in the previous chapter, Jim Sidanius is especially prominent in arguing for the social dominance theory of intergroup relations.[10] Unlike the previous approach, this is a general theory of intergroup relations, and as such it can be used to understand various kinds of conflict other than the nationalistic variety. Individuals who exhibit a high social dominance orientation (SDO) view their group as "different"—that is, superior to others—and actively want their group to dominate society. As we have seen already, though the theory is more complex than the preceding one, it is at its root *personality-based*; more specifically, it distinguishes individuals by reference to their preference for a high or low SDO. As mentioned before, according to the theory, low-status individuals can also buy into the "hierarchy-legitimating myths" of a society to such a degree that they come to favor the high-status outgroup[11] Sidanius provides "Uncle Tomming" by blacks towards whites during the era of racial segregation in the United States as the clearest example in recent times, a tradition of deference by blacks towards whites.[12]

Advocates of this approach have devoted considerable attention to racism in particular. According to Felicia Pratto and her colleagues, SDO is strongly related to anti-black racism, and a prejudice against minority groups in general.[13] They argue that "the ideology of anti-Black racism has been instantiated in personal acts of discrimination, but also in institutional discrimination against African-Americans by banks, public transit authorities, schools, churches, marriage laws, and the penal system."[14] The theory says little about where the "legitimating myths" come from or what their nature is beyond the claim that it is perpetuated by the dominant ingroup or hierarchy, and its advocates claim that it matters little where this ideology comes from or what specific form it takes.[15] The theory therefore has little to say about the individual psychological mechanisms that promote racist thinking, although its non-specific nature allows it to be applied to a range of intergroup conflict situations.

Schema Theory/Stereotyping

An especially popular approach in recent years within the dispositionist camp has been to trace racism to the way in which the human mind categorizes information. One common reaction students have to hearing about schema theory is to ask whether it can be applied to racial stereotypes. And the answer I always give as a teacher is "indeed it can, and indeed it has been." From a schema theory perspective, it is possible that racial stereotyping arises in part from people's basic need to *simplify reality* and put people and things into categories. As Fiske and Taylor noted in their classic book *Social Cognition* in 1984, "the view of stereotypes simply as part of the normal cognitive process applied to people has become widespread. It contrasts sharply with the traditional view of stereotypes as an irrational isolated phenomenon."[16] Negative schemas of minority groups or racial stereotypes seem to occur in part because people draw *illusory correlations* between individuals and the wider group of which they are seen to be a part. As Fiske and Taylor note:

> majority-group members have relatively few contacts with minority-group members, and negative behaviors are also relatively infrequent. It may be that members of the majority group make an illusory correlation between two rare events and infer that minority-group members are more likely to engage in negative behaviors.[17]

For instance, imagine that you are a white college student from a rural area renting an apartment from a Pakistani landlord in Leeds, England. Pakistanis form a significant racial minority in the United Kingdom, but tend to live mostly in major cities in the North and Midlands, such as Birmingham, Manchester, and Leeds. And let us imagine that a leak develops in your roof. To your surprise, the landlord never responds to your phone calls and letters asking him to fix it, and you develop a strong dislike of him as a result. You find him an unpleasant person generally, and decide to move out as soon as possible. In such a situation, especially if you have no Pakistani friends and have had little or no contact with other Pakistanis, you may be particularly likely to draw a connection (or illusory correlation) between this one individual and Pakistanis as a group. You may even find yourself using racial slurs against all Pakistanis, though you would not ordinarily have thought of yourself as prejudiced. Since this kind of cognitive approach sometimes also assumes that we are all "naive scientists," one might be tempted in this case to draw a dubious conclusion from a single case.

It is not inevitable that racist feelings towards all Pakistanis would occur in the example given, however; if we have known a large number of landlords and had a similar experience with most of them, we might assign this individual to our "landlord schema" instead of a "Pakistani schema."[18] In that case, the incident might result in a feeling of prejudice against all landlords instead. Schema theory suggests, then, that racism is not inevitable; it depends on the schema invoked, and on the repertoire of schemas a particular individual possesses. It is this element of variation that makes this theoretical position fundamentally dispositionist.

Stereotyping and its role in prejudice has been studied since at least the early 1930s,[19] and much of the earliest work argued in classic Freudian or psychoanalytical fashion that racism was a form of projection in which psychologically flawed individuals offloaded their feelings of inadequacy onto others. The true leader in studying this phenomenon, however, was the famous social psychologist Gordon Allport, whose book *The Nature of Prejudice* (first published in 1954) has continued to influence the field long after his death.[20] Allport treated prejudice as "an antipathy based on faulty and inflexible generalization. It may be felt or expressed. It may be directed toward a group or an individual of that group."[21] When Allport wrote, racial stereotyping tended to be condemned as a kind of personality defect, but he was the first to argue the somewhat disturbing point that racism may arise from processes which reflect the "normal" workings of human cognition. "The human mind must think with the aid of categories," Allport insisted. "Once formed, categories are the basis for normal prejudgment. We cannot possibly avoid this process. Orderly living depends upon it."[22] On the one hand he was instrumental in developing the cognitive approach to prejudice, but Allport also advocated the old-fashioned view of prejudice as "fundamentally irrational hatred, born of ignorance and the ego-defensive maneuvers of people with weak personality structures," as Dovidio and his colleagues point out.[23] He also stressed the role of emotional and motivational factors in prejudice, something that has enabled generations of scholars to take different points of departure from his work.

Later researchers have built upon the *cognitive* dimension of Allport's analysis in particular, although they have of course sometimes deviated from his arguments.[24] Allport assumed, as have others, that the presence of stereotypes *inevitably* leads to prejudiced attitudes.[25] The example we gave above regarding Pakistani landlords in Great Britain, for instance, suggests that just having a stereotype in our heads—whether of Pakistanis, landlords, or both—inevitably leads to prejudice. The work of Patricia Devine suggests that this is not the case, however, since stereotyping does not *necessarily* lead to prejudice or discriminatory views. Interestingly, she finds that prejudiced *and* unprejudiced individuals possess racial stereotypes, but that nonprejudiced people mentally *suppress* these stereotypes, while the prejudiced do not.[26] This might explain, or at least throw some light upon, the ambivalent ideas many people have towards race.

Although this is admittedly an anecdotal application of Devine's work, consider for a moment the views of the man who probably did most within American government to end discrimination towards African-Americans, Lyndon Johnson. While LBJ grasped the necessity for the Civil Rights Act of 1964 as a moral issue, he also frequently referred to black people as "niggers" in private (on one occasion, in front of Roger Wilkins, a black historian and journalist then working as Assistant Attorney General). This suggests that Johnson—coming from the "old South," where racial discrimination had been a way of life for him—may have come to suppress racial stereotypes in his head much of the time, but that such thoughts were so instinctive that they often just "popped out" in his private speech patterns. Russell Fazio and his colleagues suggest that Devine's model only applies to some individuals, on the other hand.[27] There are indeed individuals who possess negative stereotypes but suppress them, they find, as well as individuals who appear to have no qualms about negative feelings towards black people, but there are also individuals who appear to possess no negative stereotypes of African-Americans at all. Fazio and his colleagues label this group the "truly nonprejudiced."[28]

Jon Hurwitz and Mark Peffley note that racial stereotypes have enormously important consequences, since they influence public attitudes towards crime and the punitive nature of many anti-crime policies.[29] Equally, however, they note that people do not *always* rely on stereotypes, and they draw on the cognitive literature to examine where and when white stereotypes of African-Americans affect perceptions and policies. Noting that people do sometimes rely upon stereotypes or schemas—a form of "'top-down' processing" which is relatively easy to do since it requires minimal cognitive effort—they add that on other occasions we process information in a "bottom-up" style; in other words, people do sometimes engage in the effort of processing the information at hand on its own merits.[30]

In the case of racial stereotypes, people rely upon these when the stereotypes seem to "fit" the situation, and in particular where there is no attenuating information which would lead someone to treat a case "bottom up," or on its own merits. As Hurwitz and Peffley put it:

> when the attributes of the individual target easily fit the global category, stereotypes are convenient and powerful heuristics. When individuating

information clearly contradicts the stereotype, however (such as when an African-American criminal is described as making a serious effort to reform himself) the group image becomes less relevant.[31]

They find for instance that when whites are asked to estimate the probability that a given black male committed a crime, they are more likely to see the black person as "guilty" when given no further information about him (so that cognitively most people "fit" him into the broader social stereotype) than they are when told that the black person is a model member of society (so that people apply the individuating information instead of the stereotype). As we shall see, some interesting support indirectly confirming this argument has come from some of the work which uses fMRI techniques to measure racial attitudes and responses.

Affective/Neuropolitical Approaches

Treating prejudice in the cognitive tradition—that is, as a "normal" aspect of how human beings reason—may seem odd to you, and in an example like this the "naive science" of prejudiced individuals is plainly very naive indeed. A more telling problem with the standard cognitive approach, however, is that by itself it is incomplete, not least because racism obviously implies more than this kind of cold categorization (a common criticism of many early cognitive approaches which we discussed in Chapter 9). Racial prejudice also obviously involves strongly *emotional* processes as well as mere categorization.[32] A large and growing body of work within social psychology has recently examined the emotional bases of stereotyping and prejudice, as well as the ways in which these factors might interact with cold cognitive ones.[33] Although much of her work previously focused on the cold cognitive aspects of social behavior, political and social psychologist Susan Fiske (for instance) has more recently come to focus on the "hot" or emotional side of this topic. In a metaanalysis of fifty years of studies on racial prejudice and bias (co-authored with her colleagues Cara Talaska and Shelly Chaiken), Fiske found that emotions are better predictors of behavior than negative stereotypes and other beliefs; indeed, emotional prejudices predict discriminatory behaviors with far more accuracy than the latter, she and her colleagues discover:[34]

> The central role of emotions and the diminished role of beliefs suggest that people may recruit beliefs as a post-hoc justification for their own emotion-driven behavior. A person has an aversion response (disgust), avoids sitting next to a racial outgroup member on the subway, notices the behavior, and justifies it. More seriously, an employer responds with

pride to an ingroup candidate and with ambivalence (pity, resentment) or even contempt to an outgroup candidate, and the employment results are clear.[35]

Fiske and her associates concede, however, that it is difficult to measure emotions scientifically. The study of racism is one of those areas of political psychology where we might expect the methods of neuroscience to bring particular dividends, however, not least because (a) racism is increasingly being characterized as a primarily emotional response, (b) fMRI techniques are particularly suited to the measuring of emotions, and (c) some approaches—for instance, the symbolic racism perspective we shall examine later in this chapter—argue that racism has simply "gone underground" since the 1960s. If we cannot expect people to tell us honestly what they think about racial questions face-to-face, in questionnaires, or over the phone, perhaps neural imaging can be used to reveal our conscious and unconscious emotions about the topic. There is a sense that many of the standard approaches to racism "black box" the individual, focusing on overt attitudes as measured by survey data rather than looking at the mental processes through which decisions about race are made.

In fact, imaging has already produced some preliminary results of substantial interest concerning the ways in which we view social outgroups. Lasana Harris and Susan Fiske have shown that people respond with disgust when viewing photographs of such groups, for instance, and their work is especially interesting because it suggests that we can effectively "see" processes like dehumanization at work in the human brain.[36] In their study, subjects were shown a large number of photographs of different social groups (including Olympic athletes and drug addicts), as well as images of objects (including the Space Shuttle and an overflowing toilet) designed to elicit the emotions of pride, envy, pity, or disgust.

A pretest was conducted in order to determine which emotion best "matched" each photograph. Using imaging, the authors then compared activity in the medial prefrontal cortex (mPFC) of the brain to determine whether the students accurately chose the correct emotion illustrated by the picture. The mPFC is activated only when we engage in social cognition, such as when we think about ourselves or other human beings. When viewing a picture representing people who were regarded as "disgusting"—in this case, drug addicts and the homeless—though, no significant mPFC brain activity was recorded; only the amygdala—one of the most "primitive" parts of the brain, often associated (as we saw in Chapter 11) with fear or disgust—was activated. This suggests that while individuals may recognize at a conscious level that they are looking at pictures of human beings, unconsciously our brains process images of extreme social outgroups as if we are looking at unpleasant inanimate objects like an overflowing toilet. Harris and Fiske infer that the absence of mPFC activity while viewing pictures of extreme outgroups shows that "people dehumanize these groups, not perceiving them as human to the same extent that they perceive in-groups or moderate outgroups as fully human."[37]

This work is broadly consistent with other neuroscientific work which has been done specifically on emotional prejudice and race. The results of Allen Hart and his colleagues "are consistent with the notion that the amygdala might be sensitive to learned racial stereotypes or participate in their development."[38] In an especially interesting comparative study, Elizabeth Phelps and her colleagues showed white subjects faces of both known and unknown black individuals. When the white subjects viewed unknown black faces, strong amygdala activity suggested "an unconscious negative anti-Black or pro-White evaluation."[39] However, when the subjects were shown faces of familiar and generally well-regarded black faces—such as images of Martin Luther King, Muhammad Ali, and Denzel Washington—little or no amygdala activity occurred. This suggests strong independent support for Hurwitz and Peffley's conclusion that people use individuating information when confronted with individuals who contradict the common social stereotype, but resort to that stereotype when no compensating individuating information is provided.

Matthew Lieberman and his colleagues, moreover, find that negative stereotypes of African-Americans are shared by blacks *themselves*. Using both white and black subjects, they find that greater amygdala activity occurs in both races when shown images of (unknown) black faces.[40] While the possibility exists that both races are responding simply to the novelty of the faces—something which can also cause the amygdala to become activated— Lieberman and his colleagues argue that this is probably the result of learned social stereotypes. "Although no single study can conclusively address this issue, the present study suggests that the amygdala activity typically associated with race-related processing may be a reflection of culturally learned negative associations regarding African-American individuals."[41] This conclusion receives independent support in the work of Sniderman and Piazza, who also find using survey data that many blacks *share* the negative views of whites.[42]

As Ralph Adolphs notes, "the role of the amygdala in processing information about race is still unclear," and much work remains to be done in this area.[43] Other regions of the brain are activated as well when making judgments about race, as practically all the work done to this point illustrates, and all the caveats about fMRI techniques as a measure of political phenomena already discussed apply here. Ongoing work by political scientist Darren

Schreiber in this area, moreover, suggests just how complex this area of investigation is.[44] Nevertheless, promising new avenues of research are being opened up as this book goes to press.

Situationist Theories

As noted above, dispositionist theories—particularly personality theories— do not seem especially suited to explaining why entire groups or regions would express racist sentiments and/or practice discrimination, so situationist theories of racism have been just as popular in accounting for racial prejudices as dispositionist ones, if not more so. Of these, two approaches (both of which we have seen already) seem especially noteworthy; however, the literature has highlighted notable problems with each.

As we saw in the previous chapter, *realistic conflict theory* has been used to try to account for ethnic conflict, but it has also been employed in the effort to explain racism within a single society. As we saw in the last chapter with our discussion of the "Robbers' Cave" experiment, this approach treats conflict between groups (racial or otherwise) as revolving around the competition for scarce resources. It also treats politics as a *zero-sum game*: this is a situation in which by definition what one side wins, the other loses. As with children on a see-saw, when one side goes up the other must come down (and vice versa). This is a situationist theory in the sense that where one is located within the group structure of society largely determines one's outlook. Drawing on Herbert Blumer's early work on the importance of group position, Lawrence Bobo has applied this to the analysis of racism. In his best-known article from this perspective, Bobo focuses on white opposition to busing in the United States.[45] He argues that for realistic conflict theory to "work" as a theory of racial conflict, busing and other affirmative action measures need not represent an immediate or *objective* threat to the interests of whites; all that is necessary is that whites and blacks perceive their interests as being in conflict with one another. Taking the position that previous definitions of interests have been too restrictive, Bobo argues that "racial attitudes reflect the existing economic, social, and political relationships between black and white Americans, in other words, the *real* features of group relations and conflict" (my italics).[46]

There are some problems with this approach as applied to racism, however. First of all, it is not so clear that race relations in many countries actually do represent a zero-sum game in the sense of a real competition over scarce resources. In a land of abundant economic resources such as the United States, for example, the conflict appears far more symbolic than real, a criticism which helped lead to the formation of the *symbolic racism* school in the United States (discussed below). Moreover, reconceptualizing interests as something subjective—as Bobo does—may tear the heart out of realistic conflict theory, since racial conflicts may be patently "unrealistic." Secondly, as noted in the previous chapter, Henri Tajfel and his colleagues have shown that it is not necessary for there to be real or meaningful conflicts over resources for ingroup bias or favoritism to occur.

Social identity theory, also described in Chapter 14, can readily be applied to the study of racism as well. While there are different approaches to this theory, the reader will recall that in Henri Tajfel's model individuals are strongly motivated to identify with the ingroup because this bolsters self-esteem. For this reason, we try to identify with high-status groups, and it is this basic motivational need that leads us to favor members of our ingroup and to discriminate against members of the outgroup. This favoritism can occur wholly in the absence of any "rational" justification which would make it more understandable to others, since mere categorization itself—even into meaningless, artificially created categories—can produce ingroup favoritism and discrimination against outgroups. This kind of theory would appear to explain racial hostility well, since racial differences—though only skin-deep—are well understood by all members of a society in which such cleavages exist and are immediately identifiable. Moreover, since many individuals even in a multi-ethnic state may have only minor contact with racial outgroups, this situation seems to meet the conditions of the "minimal group paradigm."[47]

James Gibson has seriously questioned the applicability of group identity as an explanation for racial conflict and intolerance, however.[48] He selects South Africa during the apartheid era as an "easiest-case-to-prove" for Tajfel and Turner's theoretical claims. Gibson notes with plausibility that if social identity theory is ever to be useful for understanding group relations, it is in countries like South Africa, where group identities and differences are quite salient, and have not only been socially constructed and manipulated over long periods of time, but where they were also rigidly codified within the laws of the apartheid state.[49] Somewhat surprisingly, he finds that "most aspects of group identities are unrelated to interracial tolerance. For instance, blacks and whites more strongly attached to their ingroup are no less tolerant of people of the opposite race. Being able to identify a group with which one negatively associates does not predict levels of interracial tolerance."

Put more simply, just by knowing that an individual favors their own racial group—in this case, white or black—does not make them correspondingly likely to *disfavor* the other group. Using a variety of measures, Gibson concludes that it would be "difficult indeed" to conclude from his data that social identity theory explains levels of tolerance between blacks and whites.[50] While Gibson concedes that his results may be an artifact of the timing of his study—South Africa is currently in a state of flux—it is likely that cross-cutting cleavages (for instance, the rise of a black middle class) may be reducing the impact of racial group identities in the country. Put differently, it is not people's proximity to their ingroup that allows them to tolerate people of other races, but an increase in the diversity of society that appears to encourage tolerance.

Are Americans Still Racist?

The theories we have discussed to this point have broad applicability, both in the sense that most are general theories of intergroup conflict (not simply theories of why racism occurs, per se) and in the geographical sense that they may readily be applied to countries other than the United States. Some theories are more uniquely "American," however, in that they focus on explaining racism within a U.S. context rather than attempting to explain its existence as a wider phenomenon. Two such theories are the *symbolic racism* and *principled conservatism* approaches.

Symbolic or "New" Racism

This approach to understanding racism is particularly associated with David Sears and his colleagues, and it focuses in particular on negative affect among whites towards blacks.[51] Looking at the beliefs of ordinary Americans and the ways in which these have changed over the years with regard to race, Sears and others argue that racism as a set of beliefs has in a sense "gone underground" in the United States. Because it is no longer socially acceptable to express overtly racist views, racism has changed in subtle ways that are often not recognized. As Sniderman and his colleagues summarize it, according to this position:

> Racial prejudice is now regarded as undesirable, so people favor disguised, indirect ways to express it. They will not say that they are opposed to blacks getting help from government because they are black; they will instead say they are opposed because blacks are not making a genuine effort to solve their own problems—the kind of effort everyone should make.[52]

The racism which persists is not of course the racism of the "old" American South, segregation, Jim Crow, and former Alabama Governor George Wallace, but it is racism of a rather more covert sort. The new, symbolic racism combines anti-black affect with traditional American values, according to this view. Two fairly recent works which provide especially strong support for the view that American politics is still racially charged—and that politicians still use race, but in a more subtle way that they used to—are Tesler and Sears's *Obama's Race* and Tali Mendelberg's earlier *The Race Card*.

Mendelberg agrees with the "symbolic racist" position that it is simply no longer acceptable to overtly use race, but she argues that it has gone underground as a technique rather than disappearing.[53] She cites George H.W. Bush's use of the Willy Horton/furlough story during the 1988 presidential campaign as a prime example of this practice, since its real purpose was not only to suggest that Michael Dukakis was "soft on crime" (she argues) but also to create fear among white Americans about black people and to capitalize on racial stereotypes of African-Americans as "criminals." Often voters are not even aware that these almost subliminal messages are being sent, but politicians still routinely "play the race card," and usually get away with it. Issues like "welfare" and "crime" are used to manipulate white voters, addressing race only indirectly. She concludes that in the end such techniques will cease to be effective, though, when their true purpose is made public and voters understand how they are being manipulated.

Equally controversial—and also coming directly from the symbolic racist camp—is Michael Tesler and David Sears's *Obama's Race*.[54] Many liberal commentators rejoiced at the election of America's first-ever black president in 2008. Many also see this as a portent that something fundamental has changed, and that the United States can no longer truly be characterized as "racist." But Tesler and Sears think that reaching this conclusion would be a major mistake. The authors contend that the presidential election of 2008 was in fact the most racially polarized in America's history. Republicans knew that they could not attack Obama directly on his race, so they found other ways to suggest that he was "alien" and not "one of us" (such as calling into question the president's birth certificate and suggesting that he was a Muslim). But Democrats engaged in the racial game too, they argue. Determined to right historical wrongs, "racial liberals" found in Obama a vessel for doing just this, and Obama received huge support in the primaries despite the fact that he wasn't that different ideologically to his white rival, Hillary Clinton. People's racial beliefs, moreover, predict their views towards a whole host of Obama's policies, even those that have absolutely nothing to do with race (like health care reform). In short, whether you support his policies—and even whether you like his dog, Bo— depends on how "racially conservative" or "racially liberal" you are, Tesler and Sears conclude.

Principled Conservatism

If David Sears has been the chief standard bearer for the symbolic racism approach, Paul Sniderman and his colleagues have been especially important advocates of a rival approach, sometimes termed the "principled objection" or "politics-as-usual" model. Sniderman and his colleagues argue that opposition to affirmative action policies such as busing does not in and of itself demonstrate "racism."[55] While they do not dispute the idea that racism is still prevalent, opposition to affirmative action more likely represents opposition to the racial policies liberals have pursued since the days of Lyndon Johnson. As Jeremy Wood notes, to prove their symbolic racism thesis Kinder and Sears "must show that negative affect toward blacks has a role in motivating many whites' opposition to liberal racial policies." Supporters of the symbolic racism view believe that this is in fact the case; opponents like Sniderman believe that by and large it is not. The whole debate thus hinges on questions of motivation.[56] As already noted, supporters of this view are also troubled by the apparently non-falsifiable nature of the symbolic racism approach. If people are reluctant to express their racist views openly, how can we know whether, deep down, they are racist or not?

Tolerance and Intolerance

Another (somewhat related but rather broader) way of looking at the issue of how people treat outgroups is to examine levels of general political tolerance within a society. As with other issues, the study of this topic within political science has been especially well developed in the United States, though a growing number of cross-national comparisons exist. The basic pattern that researchers have uncovered repeatedly across time is that while most Americans express support for political tolerance *in the abstract*, when confronted with actual cases which involve individuals who are perceived as violating conventional norms, many Americans are somewhat less tolerant.[57] In order to measure tolerance, it obviously will not do to examine our attitudes towards groups that we like; the essence of tolerance resides in a willingness to live alongside individuals and ideas of whom we disapprove. This kind of definition derives from Voltaire's famous statement, "I detest your views, but am prepared to die for your right to express them." While a tolerant individual need not go this far—this might be described as a form of extreme tolerance—he or she should be able to at least "put up" with political ideas and behaviors that sharply differ from his or her own.

The classic study on this topic was conducted by the sociologist Samuel Stouffer in 1954, the results from which were related in his book *Communism, Conformity, and Civil Liberties*.[58] In the summer of 1954, Stouffer and his assistants polled a representative sample of the American population to find out how tolerant the average U.S. citizen was, and specifically how the average American viewed nonconformist behavior (especially attitudes towards Communists). The results he obtained would make him famous, since as John Sullivan, James Piereson, and George Marcus note, his findings were "disturbing" to many:

> Substantial majorities said that an admitted communist should not be permitted to speak publicly, or to teach in high schools or colleges, or, indeed, to work as a clerk in a store. Majorities also agreed that communists should have their citizenship revoked, that books written by communists should be taken out of public libraries, that the government should have the authority to tap personal telephone conversations to acquire evidence against communists, and that admitted communists should be thrown in jail.[59]

Most respondents were intolerant of socialists and atheists as well, though not to the same degree as in the case of Communists. Stouffer's study was conducted during the McCarthy era, a period in which the average American was supposedly less tolerant than in previous or later eras. This would lead us to expect that people in the United States are more tolerant now. To what extent is this actually the case, however?

The answer to this question is not as clear-cut as it might appear, since it depends to a considerable extent on how one measures tolerance. In a study which has become almost as well known as Stouffer's original one, Sullivan, Piereson, and Marcus set out in the early 1980s to examine what, if anything, had changed in the intervening period, and their conclusion was essentially "not much."[60] They argue that while people felt less threatened by Communists by the early 1980s than they had in the early 1950s—so that more people were prepared to grant basic civil liberties to them—most Americans were *not* more tolerant, since the focus had simply shifted to other groups. In other words, the context or primary targets of intolerance had changed, but not the degree of intolerance. In order to measure intolerance, they argue, we must logically focus on studying those who say they dislike a particular group, and in order not to prejudge the issue, they allowed respondents to select their own "least liked" groups rather than simply focusing on Communists. When we do this, they find, levels of tolerance have not appreciably changed since the Stouffer study.

Paul Sniderman and his colleagues come to a quite different conclusion, on the other hand.[61] They consider the Sullivan study "imaginative, but possibly misleading."[62] The main reason they give is that while it is obvious why one would want to study the tolerance of individuals towards groups that they dislike—it is easy to "tolerate" groups that we identify with—measuring tolerance and intolerance this way probably underestimates just how tolerant most Americans have become. For instance, it is surely not the case that the only people who can be regarded as "tolerant" towards African-Americans are those who say that they *dislike* African-Americans. We should also include those who are merely indifferent to black people, and even those who say they like black Americans, Sniderman and his colleagues stress.[63] Again, determining the degree of tolerance that exists within a society is dependent on how one *measures* tolerance, though it has to be said that the paradigm proposed by Sullivan and his colleagues remains the conventional wisdom in the study of this topic.

In the wake of 9/11, what evidence exists that Muslims have become the "new Communists"? While as one might expect there is evidence of some intolerance towards Muslims since 9/11 (and indeed, before that date), it does not at present compare with the hostility towards Communists which Stouffer found in the 1950s. While we cannot directly compare the data since the question wordings between the two periods differ markedly, we are not observing the kind of generalized levels of hostility towards Muslims that were captured with regard to Communists by Stouffer. Data indicate that negative views of Muslims have varied widely across different opinion polls since 9/11, which seems to indicate the absence of clear or solid preferences on this issue. Moreover, when Muslim Americans were polled in a May 2007 Pew Research Center study, as many Muslims reported being the beneficiary of positive support from non-Muslims as reported being the *victim* of discrimination or intolerance because of their faith: 33 percent reported being either treated with suspicion, called offensive names, singled out by police or physically attacked or threatened, but 32 percent (almost the same figure) said that someone had expressed support for them. Moreover, in the same survey self-reported acts of intolerance towards African-Americans were notably higher than those for Muslim Americans (46 percent reported being subject to at least one of the measures of intolerance noted above).[64]

The difference may be at least partially attributable to differing elite behavior in the 1950s and 2000s. James Gibson contends that much of the intolerance of the McCarthyite era may have been driven by elites rather than ordinary Americans.[65] In the 1950s, it was very common for foreign policy elites in the United States to portray Communism as an undifferentiated menace— "a commie is a commie"—while since 9/11 the Bush administration has repeatedly differentiated moderate Muslims from extreme Islamists, or those who are often misleadingly labeled as "fundamentalists."[66] If, as V.O. Key thought, the voice of the people is "but an echo chamber," then the relatively high levels of intolerance observed towards Communists witnessed in the 1950s and relatively low levels towards Muslims seen now may both simply reflect the kind of messages being conveyed by elites.

The reaction of ordinary Americans to 9/11 also shows, perhaps, how difficult it is to sustain a purely situationist position on the issue of tolerance. It is not the mere existence of an "objective" threat that feeds intolerance of outgroups, but our *perceptions* of the nature of that threat; to go back to the analogy used in Chapter 1, different individuals vary in the degree to which they believe that "the building is on fire," and hence differ in their willingness to countenance taking civil liberties away from Muslim Americans and other groups. Nevertheless, it cannot be denied that there is *some* evidence of intolerance in the United States towards Muslims, or what some refer to as "Islamophobia." A Cornell University poll conducted in 2004 found, for example, that 27 percent of American respondents believed that Muslims should be required to register their whereabouts with the federal government, 26 percent said that mosques should be placed under close surveillance, 22 percent believed that federal agencies should target individuals from Islamic or Middle Eastern background, and 29 percent agreed that Muslim civic associations should be infiltrated by federal agents to keep watch on their activities. Moreover, 44 percent of those polled believed that at least one of these restrictions should be placed on the civil liberties of Muslim Americans.[67] While these numbers do not come close to the sizeable majority who would deny Communists the right to speak in Stouffer's study,[68] these are still disturbing figures in a developed democracy. Erik Nisbet and his colleagues find that political conservatives and those who express strong support for Christian religious values are a good deal more likely to support restricting the civil liberties of Muslims than are other groups.[69]

Conclusion

From Stouffer on, most of the literature on political tolerance has been dispositionist. The studies by both Stouffer (rigidity, authoritarianism, optimism) and Sullivan and his colleagues (psychological insecurity, dogmatism, lack of trust) found that tolerance was associated with certain enduring personality characteristics, for instance. George Marcus, John Sullivan, and their colleagues have recently continued this tradition with an analysis of the factors that affect our decision-making about tolerance judgments in their book *With Malice Toward Some*.[70] Their perspective focuses on the role of emotion in decision-making and is similarly dispositionist in the sense that it stresses the ways in which people may respond differently to the same informational environment around them. "We use the term *individual differences* to denote the idea that people may differ in how they make tolerance judgments and in how they process contemporary information," Marcus and his associates note. "People differ in the predispositions and standing decisions they hold, and these standing decisions may then affect the extent to which they are tolerant or intolerant."[71] For instance, people vary in their levels of political knowledge and expertise, how and to what extent they process new information, and so on. Decisions about tolerance, they argue, are ultimately the result of a mixture of factors: long-standing predispositions learned early on in life, beliefs about democratic values, and specific information about the case in hand.

Notes

1 William Peters, *A Class Divided* (Garden City, NY: Doubleday, 1971).
2 In one recreation of the experiment by Elliott many years later using grown adults—conducted for a BBC series broadcast in 2001 and called *Five Steps To Tyranny*—one adult came to believe in her "inferior" role so intensely that she was literally reduced to tears.
3 Elizabeth Phelps, Kevin O'Connor, William Cunningham, Sumie Funuyama, Christopher Gatenby, John Gore, and Mahzarin Banaji, "Performance on Indirect Measures of Race Evaluation Predicts Amygdala Activation," *Journal of Cognitive Neuroscience*, 12: 729–38, 2000.
4 Jennifer Kubota, Mahzarin Banji, and Elizabeth Phelps, "The Neuroscience of Race," *Nature Neuroscience*, 15: 940–48, 2012.
5 Susan Fiske, "Stereotyping, Prejudice, and Discrimination at the Seam Between the Centuries: Evolution, Culture, Mind, and the Brain," *European Journal of Social Psychology*, 30: 299–322, 2000, p.302.
6 Ibid.
7 Bob Altemeyer, *Right-Wing Authoritarianism* (Winnipeg: University of Manitoba Press, 1981). See also his *Enemies of Freedom: Understanding Right-Wing Authoritarianism* (San Francisco, CA: Jossey-Bass, 1988) and *The Authoritarian Specter* (Cambridge, MA: Harvard University Press, 1996). For a summary of the "old" approach see Roger Brown, "The Authoritarian Personality and the Organization of Attitudes," and on the newer one see Bob Altemeyer, "The Other 'Authoritarian Personality'," both in John Jost and Jim Sidanius (eds.), *Political Psychology: Key Readings* (New York: Psychology Press, 2004).
8 Altemeyer, "The Other 'Authoritarian Personality'," p.87.
9 Altemeyer, "Reducing Prejudice in Right-Wing Authoritarians," in Mark Zanna and James Olson (eds.), *The Psychology of Prejudice*, volume 7 (Hillsdale, NJ: Lawrence Erlbaum, 1994).
10 Jim Sidanius and Felicia Pratto, *Social Dominance: An Intergroup Theory of Social Hierarchy and Oppression* (New York: Cambridge University Press, 1999).
11 Felicia Pratto, Jim Sidanius, Lisa Stallworth, and Bertram Malle, "Social Dominance Orientation: A Personality Variable Predicting Social and Political Attitudes," *Journal of Personality and Social Psychology*, 67: 741–63, 1994, p.741.
12 James Sidanius, "The Psychology of Group Conflict and the Dynamics of Oppression: A Social Dominance Perspective," in Shanto Iyengar and William McGuir, *Explorations in Political Psychology* (Durham, NC: Duke University Press, 1993), p.202.

13 Felicia Pratto et al., "Social Dominance Orientation: A Personality Variable Predicting Social and Political Attitudes"; see also Jim Sidanius, Erik Devereaux, and Felicia Pratto, "A Comparison of Symbolic Racism Theory and Social Dominance Theory as Explanations for Racial Policy Attitudes," *Journal of Social Psychology*, 132: 377–95, 1992.

14 Pratto et al., "Social Dominance Orientation," p.741.

15 Ibid., p.742.

16 Susan Fiske and Shelley Taylor, *Social Cognition* (Reading, MA: Addison-Wesley, 1984), p.166.

17 Ibid., p.265. See also David Hamilton and Robert Gifford, "Illusory Correlation in Interpersonal Perception: A Cognitive Basis of Stereotypic Judgments," *Journal of Experimental Social Psychology*, 12: 392–407, 1976.

18 Fiske and Taylor, *Social Cognition*, p.166.

19 See Daniel Katz and Kenneth Braly, "Racial Stereotypes of 100 College Students," *Journal of Abnormal and Social Psychology*, 28: 280–90, 1933.

20 Gordon Allport, *The Nature of Prejudice* (Reading, MA: Addison-Wesley, 1954).

21 Ibid., p.9.

22 Ibid., p.20.

23 John Dovidio, Peter Glick, and Laurie Rudman (eds.), *On The Nature of Prejudice: Fifty Years After Allport* (Malden, MA: Blackwell, 2005), pp.1–2.

24 For a good summary, see Susan Fiske, "Social Cognition and the Normality of Prejudgment," in Dovidio et al. (eds.), *On The Nature of Prejudice*.

25 Allport, *The Nature of Prejudice*.

26 Patricia Devine, "Stereotypes and Prejudice: Their Automatic and Controlled Components," *Journal of Personality and Social Psychology*, 56: 5–18, 1989.

27 Russell Fazio, Joni Jackson, Bridget Dunton, and Carol Williams, "Variability in Automatic Activation as an Unobtrusive Measure of Racial Attitudes: A Bona Fide Pipeline?," *Journal of Personality and Social Psychology*, 69: 1013–27, 1995.

28 Ibid., p.1025.

29 Jon Hurwitz and Mark Peffley, "Public Perceptions of Race and Crime: The Role of Racial Stereotypes," *American Journal of Political Science*, 41: 375–401, 1997.

30 Ibid.

31 Ibid., p.381.

32 Molly Tapias, Jack Glaser, Dacher Keltner, Kristen Vasquez, and Thomas Wickens, "Emotion and Prejudice: Specific Emotions Towards Outgroups," *Group Processes & Intergroup Relations*, 10: 27–39, 2007.

33 See for instance Diane Mackie and David Hamilton (eds.), *Affect, Cognition, and Stereotyping: Interactive Processes in Group Perception* (San Diego, CA: Academic Press, 1993); Mackie and Eliot Smith (eds.), *From Prejudice to Intergroup Emotions: Differentiated Reactions To Social Groups* (Philadelphia, PA: Psychology Press, 2002).

34 Cara Talaska, Susan Fiske, and Shelly Chaiken, "Legitimating Racial Discrimination: A Meta-Analysis of the Racial Attitude-Behavior Literature Shows That Emotions, Not Beliefs, Best Predict Discrimination," *Social Justice Research: Social Power in Action* (in press). The author thanks Susan Fiske for providing a copy of this article.

35 Ibid.

36 Lasana Harris and Susan Fiske, "Dehumanizing the Lowest of the Low: NeuroImaging Responses to Extreme Outgroups," *Psychological Science*, 17: 847–53, 2006; see also Harris and Fiske, "Social Groups that Elicit Disgust Are

Differentially Processed in MPFC," *Social Cognitive and Affective Neuroscience*, 2: 45–51, 2007.

37 Harris and Fiske, "Dehumanizing the Lowest of the Low," p.849.

38 Allen Hart, Paul Whalen, Lisa Shin, Sean McInerney, Hakan Fischer, and Scott Rauch, "Differential Response in the Human Amygdala to Racial Outgroup vs Ingroup Face Stimuli," *Neuroreport*, 11: 2351–55, 2000, p.2354.

39 Elizabeth Phelps, Kevin O'Connor, William Cunningham, Sumie Funuyama, Christopher Gatenby, John Gore, and Mahzarin Banaji, "Performance on Indirect Measures of Race Evaluation Predicts Amygdala Activation," *Journal of Cognitive Neuroscience*, 12: 729–38, 2000, p.731.

40 Matthew Lieberman, Ahmad Hariri, Johanna Jarcho, Naomi Eisenberger, and Susan Bookheimer, "An fMRI Investigation of Race-Related Amygdala Activity in African-American and Caucasian American Individuals," *Nature: Neuroscience*, 8: 720–22, 2005.

41 Ibid., p.722.

42 Paul Sniderman and Thomas Piazza, *The Scar of Race* (Cambridge, MA: Harvard University Press, 1993).

43 Ralph Adolphs, "Cognitive Neuroscience of Human Social Behavior," *Nature Reviews: Neuroscience*, 4: 165–78, 2003, p.169.

44 Darren Schreiber, "Race and Social Norms: An fMRI Study," paper presented at the International Society of Political Psychology Conference, Portland, OR, 2007.

45 Lawrence Bobo, "Whites' Opposition to Busing: Symbolic Racism or Realistic Group Conflict?," *Journal of Personality and Social Psychology*, 45: 1196–210, 1983; see also Bobo and Mia Tuan, *Prejudice in Politics: Group Position, Public Opinion, and the Wisconsin Treaty Rights Dispute* (Cambridge, MA: Harvard University Press, 2006).

46 Ibid., p.1198.

47 Henri Tajfel, *Human Groups and Social Categories* (Cambridge: Cambridge University Press, 1981); Tajfel, *Social Identity and Intergroup Relations* (Cambridge: Cambridge University Press, 1982).

48 James Gibson, "Do Strong Group Identities Fuel Intolerance? Evidence from the South African Case," *Political Psychology*, 27: 665–705, 2006.

49 Ibid., p.667.

50 Ibid., p.684.

51 Donald Kinder and David Sears, "Prejudice and Politics: Symbolic Racism versus Racial Threats to the Good Life," *Journal of Personality and Social Psychology*, 40: 414–31, 1981; David Sears and P.J. Henry, "Over Thirty Years Later: A Contemporary Look at Symbolic Racism and its Critics," *Advances in Experimental Social Psychology*, 37: 95–150, 2005; David Sears, Coletle van Laar, Mary Carillo, and Rick Kosterman, "Is it Really Racism? The Origins of White Americans' Opposition to Race Targeted Policies," *Public Opinion Quarterly*, 61: 16–53, 1997.

52 Paul Sniderman, Thomas Piazza, Philip Tetlock, and Ann Kendrick, "The New Racism," *American Journal of Political Science*, 35: 423–47, 1991, p.424.

53 Tali Mendelberg, *The Race Card: Campaign Strategy, Implicit Messages, and the Norm of Equality* (Princeton, NJ: Princeton University Press, 2001).

54 Michael Tesler and David Sears, *Obama's Race: The 2008 Election and the Dream of a Post-Racial America* (Chicago, IL: University of Chicago Press, 2011).

55 Paul Sniderman et al., "The New Racism."

56 Jeremy Wood, "Is 'Symbolic Racism' Racism? A Review Informed by Intergroup Behavior," *Political Psychology*, 15: 673–86, 1994, p.677.
57 George Marcus, John Sullivan, Elizabeth Theiss-Morse, and Sandra Wood, *With Malice Toward Some: How People Make Civil Liberties Judgments* (New York: Cambridge University Press, 1995), p.8.
58 Samuel Stouffer, *Communism, Conformity, and Civil Liberties: A Cross Section of the Nation Speaks its Mind* (New York: Doubleday, 1955).
59 John Sullivan, James Piereson, and George Marcus, *Political Tolerance and American Democracy* (Chicago: University of Chicago Press, 1982), p.28.
60 Ibid.
61 Paul Sniderman, Richard Brody, and Philip Tetlock, *Reasoning and Choice: Explorations in Political Psychology* (New York: Cambridge University Press, 1991).
62 Ibid., p.220.
63 Ibid., pp.134–36.
64 See *Muslim Americans: Middle Class and Mostly Mainstream*, Pew Research Center, May 22, 2007, p.38, available online at http://pewresearch.org/assets/pdf/muslim-americans.pdf.
65 James Gibson, "Political Intolerance and Political Repression During the McCarthy Red Scare," *American Political Science Review*, 82: 511–29, 1988.
66 Bernard Lewis, *The Crisis of Islam: Holy War and Unholy Terror* (New York: Random House, 2003), p.xv.
67 See Erik Nisbet and James Shanahan, "MSRG Special Report: Restrictions on Civil Liberties, Views of Islam, and Muslim Americans," December 2004, available online at http://www.eriknisbet.com/pdfs/report1a.
68 Only 27 percent of Stouffer's respondents believed that Communists should be permitted the liberty to do this.
69 Erik Nisbet, Ronald Ostman, and James Shanahan, "Shaping the Islamic Threat: The Influence of Ideology, Religiosity, and Media Use on Public Opinion Toward Islam and Muslim Americans," in Abdulkader Sinno (ed.), *Muslims in Western Politics* (Bloomington, IN: University of Indiana Press, 2008).
70 Marcus et al., *With Malice Toward Some*.
71 Ibid., p.23.

Suggested Further Reading

Tali Mendelberg, *The Race Card: Campaign Strategy, Implicit Messages, and the Norm of Equality* (Princeton, NJ: Princeton University Press, 2001).
William Peters, *A Class Divided* (Garden City, NY: Doubleday, 1971).
Paul Sniderman and Thomas Piazza, *The Scar of Race* (Cambridge, MA: Harvard University Press, 1993).
Michael Tesler and David Sears, *Obama's Race: The 2008 Election and the Dream of a Post-Racial America* (Chicago, IL: University of Chicago Press, 2011).

Film

Five Steps to Tyranny (2001): First-rate BBC documentary which makes good use of various psychological experiments discussed in this book, including Jane Elliott's "blue eyes—brown eyes" exercise. Available via YouTube.

Chapter 16

The Psychology of Terrorism

The psychological study of terrorism, it is fair to say, remains very much in its infancy. As Rex Hudson notes:

> In contrast with political scientists and sociologists, who are interested in the political and social contexts of terrorist groups, the relatively few psychologists who study terrorism are primarily interested in the micro-level of the individual terrorist or terrorist group. The psychological approach is concerned with the study of terrorists per se, their recruitment and induction into terrorist groups, their personalities, beliefs, attitudes, motivations, and careers as terrorists.[1]

As we shall see in this chapter, this topic also throws our distinction between dispositionist and situationist theories into sharp relief. For many years, researchers have looked in vain for what John Horgan terms "the terrorist personality."[2] However, after many years of reliance on theories that emphasize the "peculiarity" or "psychological abnormality" of terrorists, it is now rather more fashionable to view terrorism the way a situationist like Stanley Milgram would view genocide; that is, as predominantly a product of the environmental circumstances surrounding the individual, rather than of the personal attributes of the terrorist.

Most analysts today think there is no single terrorist personality. Moreover, there is a growing consensus around the argument that political extremists in general are in many ways "normal" (that is, not insane), although they are obviously heavily driven by an ideology which "justifies" their actions. After reviewing the older dispositionist literature and approaches such as frustration–aggression and narcissism–aggression theory, we shall examine more cutting edge approaches such as the process model of John Horgan, which takes a more situationist approach but also blends the dispositions of the individual into the analysis. Reinforcing this with what we know about suicide terrorism, we shall conclude that terrorism is such a complex phenomenon that it cannot be traced to either dispositionist or situationist factors alone, but that a satisfactory explanation of the phenomenon must incorporate both.

What is Terrorism?

As a concept, "terrorism" is notoriously loaded with value judgments, so much so that the phrase "one person's terrorist is another's freedom fighter" has almost become a cliché. A useful starting point is the definition given by the celebrated expert on terrorism, Brian Jenkins:

> What sets terrorism apart from other violence is this: terrorism consists of acts carried out in a dramatic way to attract publicity and create an atmosphere of alarm that goes far beyond the actual victims. Indeed, the identity of the victims is often secondary or irrelevant to the terrorists who aim their violence at the people watching. This distinction between actual victims and a target audience is the hallmark of terrorism and separates it from other modes of armed conflict. Terrorism is theater.[3]

Terrorism differs from mass killing or genocide in that the latter focus on killing an entire group, while terrorism focuses on killing only a few to influence a much wider audience. Hitler and the Nazis sought to exterminate the Jews, just as the Hutus later sought to kill all Tutsis in Rwanda. Similarly, in most murders the intended victim is usually the actual target. This is certainly not true of terrorism, however, in which the true target is the wider population. Terrorists are attempting to communicate a *message* to some broader group of individuals, and in that sense those whom they kill are incidental to their cause.

When analysts have attempted to understand the actions of terrorists using psychological models, they have traditionally drawn upon a variety of psychoanalytic theories. Frustration–aggression theory, narcissistic rage theory, and other psychoanalytically rooted explanations have frequently been offered to explain why people become terrorists.[4] The work of terrorism expert Jerrold Post, for instance, has especially contributed to this literature.[5] All of these approaches, as we shall see in this chapter, are strongly dispositionist in character.

Frustration–Aggression Theory

One dispositionist theory that has long been popular in explaining terrorism—and political violence in general—is frustration–aggression theory. First developed by John Dollard and his colleagues in their book *Frustration and Aggression* in the late 1930s, this approach is simple and straightforward.[6] It argues that aggression occurs when an individual's goals are frustrated or blocked. Dollard argues, moreover, that frustration always leads to aggression, and aggression is always the result of frustration. Applied to terrorism, the terrorist act is a form of "displacement," an argument which wears its Freudian or psychoanalytic roots on its sleeve. Imagine that you have just lost your job. You are in a bad mood, and you come home and kick the family dog. The dog has done nothing to deserve this unkind fate, but your aggression is displaced onto the unfortunate animal. In similar fashion, the theory suggests, terrorism is aggression displaced onto another object. The abnormal personalities of terrorists stemming from their personal frustration with their own lives, it is argued, lead them to engage in acts of extreme violence against others.

Frustration of one's goals does seem to play an obvious role in terrorist activity, especially where the political makeup of the state allows no other outlet for "normal" political activity. Moreover, there is some support for this approach in the literature. A famous study of terrorists in 1981 in what was then West Germany, for instance, found that many of the subjects had experienced personal difficulties in their earlier life. About one-quarter, the study found, had lost a parent in their childhood years. It is plausible to assume that losing a parent creates resentment or a sense of inadequacy which needs some sort of outlet. Since most children have two living parents, being a child with only one might be one way in which frustration towards the outside world develops. Nevertheless, there are difficulties involved when moving from the individual level, the level at which frustration–aggression theory operates, to the social or group one. This is because—as we saw in Chapter 6—groups are not simply *aggregations* of individuals; frequently, the group dynamic exerts its own impact on behavior, altering the decisions that an individual might make alone. This is also a problem that besets the next two approaches we will examine here.

Narcissism–Aggression Theory

The term "narcissist" comes from the Greek legend of Narcissus, a beautiful youth who is said to have fallen in love with his own reflected image. There is probably a little bit of narcissism—or at least vanity—in all of us, since it plays a role in maintaining self-esteem. Some scholars, however—most notably Richard Pearlstein in his *The Mind of the Political Terrorist*, John Crayton, and Jerrold Post—have suggested that narcissism in its extreme form provides a plausible explanation for terrorist activity.[7] The narcissist is deeply convinced of his or her own importance and significance in the world. Unfortunately for such individuals, their exalted self-image is very often not shared by others. According to this theory, this can produce *narcissistic rage* and aggression. As Hudson puts it:

> Basically, if primary narcissism in the form of the "grandiose self" is not neutralized by reality testing, the grandiose self produces individuals who are sociopathic, arrogant, and lacking in regard for others. Similarly, if the psychological form of the "idealized parental ego" is not neutralized by reality testing, it can produce a condition of helpless defeatism, and narcissistic defeat can lead to reactions of rage and a wish to destroy the source of narcissistic injury.[8]

Again, there is some evidence to support this claim. The 1981 West German study sparked interest in this theory, since in addition to the findings already noted, supporters of the narcissistic rage theory found evidence that many of the terrorists had experienced major setbacks in their personal lives (for instance, performing poorly at school). Analysts like Post conclude that terrorism results from the rage and damage to self-esteem that such failure induces.

Psychoanalytic/Freudian Accounts

While the previous two theories are derived from psychoanalytic roots, other (rather "purer") forms of this approach have been offered in the literature as explanations of terrorism. As we have already seen in previous chapters, Freud argued that humans are motivated by a variety of factors of which they are often unaware themselves (they are "unconscious"). These desires are often repressed because they are socially unacceptable. One of these is the *Oedipal complex*, a stage of psychosexual development which Freud identified in childhood where the child comes to see the father as an adversary and competitor for the mother's love. When this conflict is not successfully resolved, it can lead to various problems in later life.

In his analysis of the terrorists Hans-Joachim Klein and Carlos the Jackal, Konrad Kellen argues that conscious or unconscious hatred of the father led each to rebel against authority or "father figures," ultimately by violence. Less consciously, their turn to terrorism was merely the externalization into public life of this private struggle (an argument which recalls in some ways Lasswell's famous characterization of the "political personality" in general).[9] Other followers of Freud such as Eric Erikson have developed "negative identity" theory, in which unresolved personal struggles and the failure to integrate one's personality lead to profound psychological difficulties in later life. Jeanne Knutson applies this approach in her analysis of a Croatian terrorist who, in Hudson's words:

> was disappointed by the failure of his aspiration to attain a university education, and as a result assumed a negative identity by becoming a terrorist. Negative identity involves a vindictive rejection of the role regarded as desirable and proper by an individual's family and community.[10]

This approach sounds like frustration–aggression theory, and there is a point at which these various (very similar) theories blend into one another.

Problems With These Theories

As appealing as they may seem initially, there are various problems with all of these theories as explanations of terrorist activity, and in recent years the value of psychoanalytic and other personality-based approaches to understanding the psychology of terrorism has increasingly been called into question.[11] One issue already noted relates to the questionable "leap" that must be made when moving from the analysis of particular individuals to the level of the group. Another issue relates to the fact that all of the above theories have pretty much fallen out of favor within the broader study of psychology. If they are no longer considered credible by many psychologists, why does their use persist within the study of terrorism and social science generally? While we should not automatically question their value on this ground alone—after all, the fate of academic theories rises and falls over time—there are still other, more practical reasons why many who study the psychology of terrorism have become discontented with these approaches.

The first has to do with the problem of *psychological reductionism* we have encountered before in work such as that of James David Barber: the temptation to reduce complex social and political phenomena to oversimplified psychological formulae. Advocates of all of these theories may themselves be academic victims of what supporters of attribution theory (as we saw in Chapter 9) term the *fundamental attribution error*. Readers will recall that this involves the tendency to overestimate the extent to which the behavior of the "other"—in this case, terrorists—is shaped by their dispositions rather than the circumstances they face.

A second problem common to all these theories is that they strongly suggest that terrorists are somehow mentally "abnormal." These theories assume that "abnormal acts" are necessarily carried out by "abnormal individuals." Like an increasing number of terrorist experts, however, Horgan and others strongly reject a mental disorder approach; though we lack sufficient access to real terrorists to make reliable diagnoses, what evidence we have suggests that most terrorists are psychologically normal and certainly not insane. Horgan argues that while psychoanalytic approaches uniformly stress the role of psychopathy in shaping the personality of terrorists, "there is poor evidence for the principle that psychopathy is an element of the psychology of terrorist organizations."[12] Similarly, Andrew Silke suggests that writers who claim that terrorists are in some way psychologically "abnormal" have usually had the least amount of contact with actual terrorists, while those who argue the opposite tend to have had considerable interaction with terrorists.[13] This makes sense when we think about it; since terrorist organizations rely on a high degree of organization, secrecy, and self-discipline, they appear to weed out insane individuals who might jeopardize these requirements.

Third—in related vein to the second problem—the evidence that a single "terrorist personality" exists must be regarded as exceptionally weak. Horgan regards the methodological approaches of those who claim to have uncovered such a single personality as "pitiful."[14] What studies there have been on this issue come to different conclusions (e.g. the West German study), and much research has found that terrorists in fact display no special character traits that distinguish them consistently from "ordinary" members of the population. The competing diagnoses and results that emerged from that study in and of themselves seem to undermine the claims made by the various theories. On the other hand, we do have evidence that many terrorists frequently find it difficult to kill and that their victims are incidental to the ends they are attempting to pursue.

A fourth problem—which is perhaps clearest in the case of narcissism–aggression theory—is that they may be victims of what social scientists call the "fallacy of composition." This is the failure to study the broader population in which a group is situated, and a tendency to obsess on the characteristics of the group itself. Narcissism, for instance, is probably rather common within the general population, but not all narcissists adopt the lifestyle of the terrorist, by any means. Rex Hudson, for instance, notes that many of the traits attributed to terrorists as causes of their activities are also present within the general population.[15] Narcissists seem especially unlikely to become suicide terrorists, for one thing. Hudson also questions whether terrorism is really the result of narcissistic rage stemming from personal failure, noting that the theory "appears to be contradicted by the increasing number of terrorists who are well-educated professionals, such as chemists, engineers, and physicists."[16] This is also a major problem for other theories which argue that terrorism is the externalization of frustration in one's personal life, such as frustration–aggression theory. Clearly, something else must be at work in the process of becoming a terrorist that goes beyond any simple personality trait.

Finally, the obsession with personality downplays what is arguably the most powerful terrorist motivation: ideology. What all terrorists share is a commitment to some political goal, be it religious, nationalistic, or economic in nature. The beliefs of individual terrorists may be far more important than the so far rather fruitless search for a single terrorist personality. A focus on beliefs, moreover, is dispositionist in nature—this is a criticism from *within* the dispositionist camp, not outside it—and so perhaps what is wrong with the existing literature is not its focus on the individual per se, but a focus on the wrong attributes of that individual. We will expand on this point in a moment.

Situational Factors

After an atrocity like the destruction of the World Trade Center in New York City on September 11, 2001, the Madrid train bombing on March 11, 2004, or the London Underground bombings on July 7, 2005, there is a natural and very human tendency to believe that the perpetrators of such acts must be insane or "unhinged" in some way; surely no one who is psychologically similar to the rest of us—no one whom a psychiatrist could plausibly diagnose as "sane"—could bring themselves to be responsible for such an action? Such a view of terrorism is reinforced by television images of finger-wagging fanatics such as Osama Bin Laden whose cause seems incomprehensible to many Westerners, and by images of individuals such as "Unabomber" Theodore Kaczynski, whose unkempt appearance, lifestyle, and actions suggested that he was suffering from mental abnormalities. Equally, we are often quite surprised by images of terrorists who look like perfectly normal, average members of society. Timothy McVeigh, for instance, played a key role in the Oklahoma City bombing of 1995—for which he was later executed—but media images showed McVeigh to be a clean-cut, smiling "boy next door," the very opposite of Kaczynski. It is tempting to conclude, as noted above, that highly abnormal actions must be committed by highly abnormal individuals. But there are various reasons to cast doubt on this conclusion beyond those we have already discussed.

One reason is that the literature on *other* forms of political extremism that we have discussed in earlier chapters—especially that on the psychology of genocide—suggests that situational forces can compel us to behave in ways contrary to our own professed values. "Ordinary" or "banal" men such as Adolf Eichmann were responsible for appalling atrocities. If psychologically normal individuals are quite capable of committing such actions, it should come as no surprise that equally normal individuals might be capable of committing similarly outrageous atrocities in the name of some ideological cause, given the right social inducements. Those who committed the outrages at Abu Ghraib were similarly normal in a psychological sense, as were the subjects in the

Stanford experiment. Philip Zimbardo's analysis of the psychology of evil in *The Lucifer Effect*, though not an analysis of terrorism itself, does suggest that there is an exceptionally thin line between right and wrong, a line that most of us are capable of crossing far more readily than we usually assume.

A second reason to push the analysis towards situationism is that we have some evidence that many terrorists feel that they *have no choice* but to commit terrorist acts. They feel trapped, in other words, by the situation they face, and compelled to resort to political violence to achieve their objectives. Taylor and Quayle found in interviews with actual terrorists that what they all have in common is that they see themselves as acting in self-defense against an enemy,[17] and that they commonly feel that violence is "an inevitable response" to that external threat.[18] Of course, such individuals may have fallen prey to the opposite side of the fundamental attribution error: overestimating the extent to which one's own actions derive from the demands of the situation. Nevertheless, it is plausible to argue that in at least some circumstances, there *are* few alternatives available. In repressive political systems in particular, terrorism may in fact be the sole course of action available to those who seek change. The ruthless suppression of human rights in Saudi Arabia, for instance, leaves no practical outlet for dissent but political violence. As Fareed Zakaria asks, who is there for young people to admire in Saudi Arabia today? A corrupt, bloated monarchy that has squandered the nation's oil wealth, or someone who has given up everything—including a massive family fortune—for his vision? In a profoundly repressive society, hero figures are in short supply, but for many young radicals Bin Laden constitutes a far more appealing role model—and his methods seem more attractive—than anything else on offer.[19]

Bjorgo provides a long list of situational factors which have been identified as "root causes" of terrorism:[20]

- Lack of democracy, civil liberties, and the rule of law
- Failed or weak states
- Rapid modernization
- Extremist ideologies of a secular or religious nature
- Historical antecedents of political violence, civil wars, revolutions, dictatorships, or occupation
- Hegemony and inequality of power
- Illegitimate or corrupt governments
- Powerful external actors upholding illegitimate governments
- Repression by foreign occupation or by colonial powers
- The experience of discrimination on the basis of ethnic or religious origins
- Failure or unwillingness by the state to integrate dissident groups or emerging social classes

- The experience of social injustice
- The presence of charismatic ideological leaders
- Triggering events.

Inevitably, some of these factors probably have more impact than others. Just as dispositions cannot be the whole story about terrorist activity, moreover, so situational explanations can only explain so much. Taking economic factors as an example, it is clear that situational factors alone are insufficient to explain why people resort to terrorist activity. It has often been noted that Wahabbi radicalism—an especially austere form of Islamism to which Bin Laden subscribed—for instance, is strongest in the oil-rich state of Saudi Arabia. If poverty is the leading cause of terrorism, why have the United States and other Western states not been attacked by individuals from impoverished sub-Saharan Africa? As Zakaria notes:

> in fact the breeding grounds of terror have been places that have seen the greatest influxes of wealth over the last thirty years. Of the nineteen hijackers on the four planes used in the September 11 attacks, fifteen were from Saudi Arabia, the world's largest petroleum exporter. It is unlikely that poverty was at the heart of their anger.[21]

While some terrorist groups harbor grievances that are economic in nature, that is certainly not the case with al-Qaeda, whose concerns are obviously more religious and political than they are economic. Moreover, why do only *some* individuals who face harsh situations respond to these in violent fashion, while others seem to accept them as an inevitable part of their fate?

Also, while all terrorist organizations have grievances that they use to justify and legitimize the use of political violence, it is true that terrorist groups frequently change those grievances over time. As Horgan puts it:

> We know that terrorism can be, and often is, based on imagined or "virtual grievances", and whatever perceived "real" grievances are identified as having existed at one time or another, terrorist organizations can be remarkably adept at changing the identity and nature of such grievances, all the while presenting them in a positive light when frequently attached to other publicized plights.[22]

The grievances listed by Osama Bin Laden provide a case in point. While his videotaped statements originally and rather prominently claimed that the presence of U.S. troops in Saudi Arabia was an insult to Islam, the withdrawal of those troops did not lead to any appreciable change in al-Qaeda's public positions or strategies; it simply produced an emphasis on the organization's other grievances against the United States. The broader point is that terrorist groups are not simply passive bodies that emerge in response to some situational factor in the environment; they frequently change and adapt even as an original grievance diminishes.

Horgan's Process Model

The earlier points about the weaknesses of existing dispositionist theories and the problems of equally simplistic situationist arguments have prompted John Horgan to begin to develop an approach that recognizes the contributions of both camps, a framework he calls the *process model*. We need to understand *both* the situations that provide the general preconditions for terrorism *and* the dispositions that make particular individuals susceptible to react to these situations by joining terrorist groups, he argues.

For Horgan, the kind of situational forces listed above are merely *preconditions* for the emergence of terrorist activity; in other words, they are necessary but not sufficient for terrorism to occur. For this to happen, these general factors have to interact with certain dispositions already present in the individual. "It can be misleading to attempt to identify the presence of unifying catalysts events as unambiguous 'push' factors," he notes. "It might be more useful to attempt to examine how and why specific people are individually affected and experience those events in ways that act as a catalyst towards increased involvement."[23]

Horgan admits that finding what these individual-level factors are is a difficult task, and that we lack sufficient research on some aspects of the terrorist recruitment process to give definitive answers to this question. Nevertheless, he suggests that the process of becoming a terrorist is typically an *incremental* one—involving a series of small steps—and that a number of factors are probably critical to the process. These include: the individual's susceptibility to the positive rewards that membership of a terrorist group brings (membership of Hamas, for instance, is socially prestigious, and suicide bombers in the West Bank attain greater status after death); membership in a group of this kind brings the comfort of community and ideological solidarity with like-minded individuals; respect for "role models" such as Abdullah Azzam or Bin Laden may lead Islamic radicals to take the step into terrorist activity; social pressure from the community and even positive conscription may play a role; and approval from a significant other, particularly a wife or husband, may have an impact. Determining what makes particular individuals more susceptible than others is difficult, Horgan notes, but an individual's existing beliefs, socialization, life experiences, and sense of dissatisfaction with life and ability to imagine alternatives all probably play a role. Clearly, however, we need far more appreciation than we currently possess of the group dynamics and social forces that lead particular individuals to take the individual-level decision to join a terrorist organization, and more understanding of what makes some individuals take this route rather than others. Our ability to answer these questions, sadly, remains rather primitive.

The "Mystery" of Suicide Terrorism

Suicide terrorism may be defined relatively simply, though broad and narrow definitions already exist in the literature. "Suicide terrorism includes a diversity of violent actions perpetrated by people who are aware that the odds they will return alive are close to zero," Ami Pedahzur notes in quite a broad definition.[24] Assaf Moghadam more restrictively defines it "as an operational method in which the very success of the attack is dependent upon the death of the perpetrator," noting that "such a definition excludes from the present discussion all attacks in which the perpetrator had a high likelihood, yet no certainty, of dying in the course of the attack."[25] Since the second meaning is the more conventional one, we will adopt it here, though the basic issues will remain the same in any case.

Although the tactic itself is very old indeed, the practice of suicide *bombing* is more recent, and is generally agreed to have taken off in the early 1980s, especially after the 1983 bombing of the U.S. embassy and its marine barracks in Beirut. Like the systematic study of the broader topic of terrorism, the study of suicide terrorism is really only beginning to get off the ground, but we have seen a number of books come out in recent years that address this topic from at least a partially psychological angle.[26] In the last few years a slew of documentaries have appeared on this topic as well, with titles like *The Cult of the Suicide Bomber*, *Inside The Mind of a Suicide Bomber*, and *Suicide Killers*, all attempting (albeit with varying degrees of success) to probe the central causes behind the phenomenon.

Robert Pape disputes the notion that there is any inherent connection between suicide terrorism and radical Islamism, a connection that many people have instinctively drawn after 9/11. Though al-Quaeda is of course one of the groups which has and continues to practice suicide terror tactics, Pape—who has compiled a database of suicide terror attacks from 1980 to 2003, a total of 315 attacks in all—notes that most suicide attacks (at least historically speaking) have been secular in inspiration rather than religious:

> The data show that there is little connection between suicide terrorism and Islamic fundamentalism, or any one of the world's religions. In fact,

the leading instigators of suicide attacks are the Tamil-Tigers in Sri Lanka, a Marxist-Leninist group whose members are from Hindu families but are adamantly opposed to religion . . . Rather, what nearly all suicide terrorist attacks have in common is a specific secular and strategic goal; to compel modern democracies to withdraw military forces from territory that the terrorists consider to be their homeland. Religion is rarely the root cause, although it is often used as a tool by terrorist organizations in recruiting and in other efforts in service of the broader strategic objective.[27]

How, though, are we to explain such a widespread practice? The phenomenon of suicide terrorism poses a "mystery" for practically all the psychological perspectives we have examined in this book. Killing oneself in order to further a cause seems outside the bounds even of "bounded rationality," but it poses difficulties for two perspectives in particular. First of all, those biopolitical perspectives that emphasize what Richard Dawkins famously referred to as "the selfish gene"—an approach which we discussed in Chapters 11 and 14—find it especially difficult to account for suicide terrorism. Rushton subscribes to "genetic similarity theory"—the theory that altruism towards others of a similar genetic makeup has evolved to help replicate the gene pool—and argues that "people have evolved a 'cognitive module' for altruistic self-sacrifice that benefits their gene pool. In an ultimate rather than proximate sense, suicide bombing can be viewed as a strategy to increase inclusive fitness."[28] Why would the evolutionary impulse to propagate one's genes lead to a decision to destroy one's *own* genetic makeup, however? And since the primary purpose of such techniques is to send a political message to the adversary, how does the killing of others help spread one's gene pool?

The renowned terrorism expert Martha Crenshaw has suggested that much terrorist behavior can be interpreted as a rational, instrumental response to the situation faced and is made explicable by cost–benefit analysis.[29] Nevertheless, suicide terrorism presents a profound challenge to *Homo economicus* or rational choice, for why would a rational, utility-maximizing individual choose to destroy his or her own life? Mohammed Hafez, for instance, has noted the profound limitations of rationalist explanations in accounting for this phenomenon.[30] On the one hand, he notes, one can construct perfectly plausible, believable reasons why bodies like al-Qaeda and the Tamil Tigers would utilize such techniques—suicide attacks constitute relatively inexpensive "smart bombs," for instance—but all of these explanations work at the *organizational* level. They provide "rational" reasons why an organization would want its members to commit such acts. On the other hand, they do not explain why particular *individuals* would want to do this. Indeed, classic rational actor models suggest that individuals will choose to "free ride" if they can derive the same benefits from not doing something as they would from acting. As we noted early in this book, the *Homo economicus* approach stresses the position that individuals select that option that maximizes benefits relative to costs. Organizational benefits are not enough; the personal benefits to the suicide must be seen to outweigh the costs of "martyrdom."

One way out of this conundrum is to assume that the individual believes that his or her life will not actually "end," but that there will be *heavenly rewards* for the action that ultimately outweigh the costs. This of course only works for those who hold such beliefs, and as we have noted already, most suicide terrorists do not. On the other hand, this seems to work for radical Islamists, but it calls into question the whole utility of the term "rationality." We preserve the shell of instrumental rationality, but in a way that renders *anything* rational that an individual happens to believe. Thus Hitler's slaughter of the Jews would be regarded as "rational" in this instrumental sense because it served his belief system; to his way of thinking, the benefits far outweighed the costs. This merely raises the question of how a supposedly rational individual could come to assess costs and benefits in such a bizarre way, something only *Homo psychologicus* can tell us much about.

Another way out of the problem, Hafez notes, is to transfer the benefits onto *family members*: financial benefits and social prestige for one's family, plus one's own status as a martyr after one's death, are defined as benefits, so that benefits can outweigh costs through this alternative route instead. But for one thing this ignores the significant costs imposed on the martyr's family after the suicide attack. Family members are frequently interrogated and even arrested afterwards. As Hafez notes, however, for Islamic bombers the motivation for suicide must be "pure"; suicides motivated by financial considerations or fame after death are regarded as suicide, plain and simple, and punishable by eternal damnation.

An even more telling critique, though, is the one we have adopted all along in this book: there is simply no compelling evidence that suggests that people make detailed cost–benefit calculations of this kind in any sphere of political behavior, a fact which rational choice theorists of the "let's-assume-as-if" variety readily concede. It seems far more likely, as Hafez notes, that cultural, symbolic, and religious explanations account for this form of behavior or that the practical desire to remove foreign military forces (emphasized by Pape) is most critical. Assuming that people *do* make such cost–benefit calculations merely poses the issue of how individuals come to hold the beliefs that drive their reasoning. Moreover, realistic cognitive and affective theories, based on the ways that we know human beings *actually* reason, seem far more likely to yield useable insights.

If neither of these approaches seems useful in accounting for suicide terrorism, what *does* explain the phenomenon? As with terrorism in general, we probably need to avoid simplistic dispositionist explanations which attribute all suicidal terrorist behavior to psychopathy or other personality traits, especially theories which have been found wanting within the larger literature on terrorism. In this regard Assaf Moghadam has devised what is probably the best—that is, most inclusive and comprehensive—framework for understanding suicide terrorism to date.[31] In order to satisfactorily explain suicide terrorism, we require a "multi-causal approach," Moghadam maintains, since any suicide attack is the result of variables at three levels: the *individual level*, the *organizational level*, and the *environmental level*.[32]

The first level corresponds to dispositional factors, the second to immediate situational factors, and the third to more distant sociocultural, economic, and political situational forces. Beginning with the individual level, Moghadam argues that most suicide bombers are likely to have a variety of motives for their actions. While he notes that some commentators have stressed the psychopathy of suicide bombers—in an approach similar to those with which we began this chapter, Vamik Volkan, for instance, contends that humiliation in early life leads to the development of "abnormal" personalities[33]—Moghadam sides with the more general consensus in the literature and notes in particular that many suicide bombers are motivated by the emotion of *revenge* (often after having lost a loved one or deriving from a sense of outrage at societal injustices). This is especially the case with both Chechen and Palestinian suicide bombers. In religious cases, the motive of reward in the afterlife can be important, but not of course in the secular circumstances which Pape has noted are actually more common. Often, a broader sense of duty is the motivating factor. As Hafez has noted, suicide bombing may derive from "a duty to one's own values, family, friends, community, or religion. Failure to act, consequently, is perceived as betrayal of one's ideals, loved ones, country, God, or sense of manhood."[34]

Such motives and perceptions, of course, have to come from somewhere, and it seems rather obvious in the case of suicide bombing that they derive from broader situational circumstances. As Moghadam notes, "terrorist acts are rarely carried out by individuals acting on their own, but by individuals who are members of organizations, groups, or cells attached to a larger network."[35] The suicide bomber needs technical expertise, financial aid, social support, assistance with planning, and so on. The immediate organizational level is also important because as we have seen already, organizational and individual motives can and do differ. Organizations and their leaders may feel that the costs of suicide tactics are low, or may adopt such approaches because others have failed, because they enhance the power and visibility of the organization, or perhaps most of all because suicide attacks are highly reported events within international media such as CNN, drawing global attention to a group's cause.[36]

Finally, the environmental level provides the general conditions that give rise to terrorism, including that of the suicide variety (see the list by Tore Bjorgo above for a sense of the sheer range of such factors). As Moghadam notes, the force of particular historical, economic, social, and political forces will obviously vary according to the situation, but there is a tendency to overestimate the impact of simple economic factors as already noted. A similar point can be made about the political context. We should recognize that just as not all poor nations produce legions of terrorists, so "not all societies under occupation have produced suicide bombers, or else we would need to add Tibetans, Kosovars, Cambodians and other occupied and recently occupied groups to the growing list of suicide bombers."[37] Cultural and religious forces may also act to prevent suicide bombing, something which is underappreciated by most commentators. Buddhist monks in South Vietnam famously protested the oppressive regime of No Dinh Diem by burning themselves to death, a symbolic protest that self-consciously avoided causing the deaths of others. Nevertheless, it is clear that in many other cases, the religious and political context does directly give rise to societal conflict and has eventually led to suicide terrorism, as in the West Bank and Chechnya. Common to all regions or nations in which suicide bombing is practiced, Moghadam notes, is a "culture of martyrdom," a set of societal mores which either allows or encourages the taking of one's own life as in some way noble, fearless, or heroic. As with the dispositional factors, however, it is clear that situational forces on their own cannot account for suicide terrorism, and Moghadam's great contribution is to show that suicide terrorism results from the *interaction* of both.

Conclusion

There is now a general consensus that terrorists—even those who take their own lives for their cause—are psychologically normal individuals rather than psychopaths;[38] moreover, the prominence of psychoanalytical approaches within terrorist studies renders the latter something of an anachronism within contemporary social science, both because these theories stress the idea of terrorist "abnormality" and because they have been widely criticized elsewhere on both conceptual and methodological grounds.[39] As Silke notes, "after 30 years of research all that psychologists can safely say of terrorists is that their outstanding characteristic is their normality."[40] Logically, however, the next step is to apply models previously utilized to understand the behavior of normal individuals in order to understand terrorist behavior. So far, this has not really been attempted in the established literature. As Martha Crenshaw notes, "cognitive psychology and the use of information-processing frameworks can provide rich insights into political behavior, including terrorism."[41] There is still plenty of room to apply the insights of *Homo psychologicus*, in other words, to the study of the psychology of terrorism.

Notes

1 Rex Hudson, *The Sociology and Psychology of Terrorism: Who Becomes a Terrorist And Why?* A report prepared under an interagency agreement by the Federal Research Division, Library of Congress (Washington, D.C.: The Division, 1999), p.17.
2 John Horgan, "The Search for The Terrorist Personality," in Andrew Silke (ed.), *Terrorists, Victims and Society: Psychological Perspectives on Terrorism and Its Consequences* (Chichester, U.K.: Jon Wiley, 2003).
3 See http://www.csmonitor.com/specials/terrorism/lite/expert.html.
4 For overviews of these approaches, see for instance Andrew Silke, "Cheshire-Cat Logic: The Recurring Theme of Terrorist Abnormality in Psychological Research," *Psychology, Crime and Law*, 4: 51–69, 1998 and Hudson, *The Sociology and Psychology of Terrorism*.
5 See for instance Jerrold Post, "Terrorist Psycho-Logic: Terrorist Behavior as a Product of Psychological Forces," in Walter Reich (ed.), *Origins of Terrorism: Psychologies, Ideologies, Theologies, States Of Mind* (New York: Cambridge University Press, 1990) and *Leaders and Their Followers in a Dangerous World: The Psychology of Political Behavior* (New York: Cornell University Press, 2004). Post now maintains that terrorists are psychologically "normal," while also insisting that most terrorists share narcissistic characteristics.
6 John Dollard, Leonard Doob, Neal Miller, O.H. Mowrer, and Robert Sears, *Frustration and Aggression* (New Haven, CT: Institute of Human Relations, 1939). This theory is also often attributed to Leonard Berkowitz, "Some Aspects of Observed Aggression," *Journal of Personality and Social Psychology*, 12; 359–69, 1965 and to Ted Robert Gurr, *Why Men Rebel* (Princeton, NJ: Princeton University Press, 1970).
7 Richard Pearlstein, *The Mind of the Political Terrorist* (Wilmington, DE: SR Books, 1991).
8 Hudson, *The Sociology and Psychology of Terrorism*, p.17.
9 Konrad Kellen, *On Terrorists and Terrorism* (Santa Monica, CA: Rand Corporation, 1982).
10 Hudson, *The Sociology and Psychology of Terrorism*, p.17.
11 Of recent notable work in this area, see in particular Silke (ed.), *Terrorists, Victims and Society*, Fathali Moghaddam and Anthony Marsella (eds.), *Understanding Terrorism: Psychosocial Roots, Consequences, and Interventions* (Washington, D.C.: American Psychological Association, 2004) and John Horgan, *The Psychology of Terrorism* (London: Taylor & Francis, 2005).
12 Horgan, "The Search for The Terrorist Personality," p.7.
13 Andrew Silke, "Becoming a Terrorist," in Silke, (ed.), *Terrorists, Victims and Society*, p.32.
14 Horgan, "The Search for The Terrorist Personality," p.10.

15 Hudson, *The Sociology and Psychology of Terrorism*, p.27.
16 Ibid.
17 Maxwell Taylor and Ethel Quayle, *Terrorist Lives* (London and Washington, D.C.: Brasseys, 1994).
18 Ibid., p.90.
19 Fareed Zakaria, *The Future of Freedom: Illiberal Democracy at Home and Abroad* (New York: W.W. Norton, 1993).
20 Tore Bjorgo (ed.), *Root Causes of Terrorism* (Oslo: Norwegian Institute of International Affairs, 2003), quoted in Horgan, *The Psychology of Terrorism*, p.83.
21 Zakaria, *The Future of Freedom*, p.137.
22 Horgan, *The Psychology of Terrorism*, p.84.
23 Ibid., p.88.
24 Ami Pedahzur, *Suicide Terrorism* (Malden, MA: Polity Press, 2005), p.8.
25 Assaf Moghadam, "The Roots of Suicide Terrorism: A Multi-Causal Approach," in Ami Pedahzur (ed.), *Root Causes of Suicide Terrorism: The Globalization of Martyrdom* (New York: Routledge, 2006), p.82.
26 See for instance Pedahzur, *Suicide Terrorism*; Robert Pape, *Dying To Win: The Strategic Logic of Suicide Terrorism* (New York: Random House, 2005); Mia Bloom, *Dying to Kill: The Allure of Suicide Terror* (New York: Columbia University Press, 2005); Diego Gambetta (ed.), *Making Sense of Suicide Missions* (New York: Oxford University Press, 2005); Pedahzur, *Root Causes of Suicide Terrorism*.
27 Pape, *Dying To Win*, p.4.
28 J. Philippe Rushton, "Ethnic Nationalism, Evolutionary Psychology and Genetic Similarity Theory," *Nations and Nationalism*, 11: 489–507, 2005, p.501.
29 Martha Crenshaw, "The Logic of Terrorism: Terrorist Behavior as a Product of Strategic Choice," in Reich (ed.), *Origins of Terrorism*.
30 Mohammed Hafez, "Dying To Be Martyrs: The Symbolic Dimension of Suicide Terrorism," in Pedahzur, *Root Causes of Suicide Terrorism*, pp.56–60.
31 Moghadam, "The Roots of Suicide Terrorism."
32 Ibid., p.83.
33 Vamik Volkan, "September 11 and Societal Aggression," *Group Analysis*, 35: 456–83, 2002.
34 Mohammed Hafez, *Manufacturing Human Bombs: The Making of Palestinian Suicide Bombers* (Washington, D.C.: United States Institute of Peace, 2005).
35 Moghadam, "The Roots of Suicide Terrorism," p.93.
36 Ibid., pp.93–96.
37 Ibid., p.97.
38 Martha Crenshaw, "The Causes of Terrorism," *Comparative Politics*, 13: 379–99, 1981; see also Silke, "Becoming a Terrorist."
39 On this point, see Maxwell Taylor, *The Terrorist* (New York: Brasseys, 1988), p.140.
40 Andrew Silke, "An Introduction To Terrorism Research," in Silke (ed.), *Research on Terrorism: Trends, Achievements and Failures* (London: Frank Cass, 2004), p.1.
41 Martha Crenshaw, "Questions to be Answered, Research to be Done, Knowledge to be Applied," in Reich (ed.), *Origins of Terrorism*, p.259. For an attempt to do this in the case of hostage taking, see David Patrick Houghton, "Explaining the Origins of the Iran Hostage Crisis: A Cognitive Perspective," *Terrorism and Political Violence*, 18: 259–79, 2006.

Suggested Further Reading

John Horgan, *The Psychology of Terrorism* (London: Taylor & Francis, 2005).

Louise Richardson, *What Terrorists Want: Understanding the Enemy, Containing the Threat* (New York: Random House, 2006).

Andrew Silke (ed.), *Terrorists, Victims and Society: Psychological Perspectives on Terrorism and Its Consequences* (Chichester, U.K.: Jon Wiley, 2003).

Film

Soldiers in the Army of God (HBO, 2000): Examines domestic terrorism in the United States in the context of anti-abortion protests.

Chapter 17

The Psychology of International Security

It would be fair to say that the development of the study of international security and the broader study of international relations has been hampered by a common neglect of psychological factors. As James Goldgeier notes:

> A major impediment to the development of adequate explanation and prediction in the study of international relations and foreign policy is the failure by many academics in the field to treat seriously the role of psychological factors in individual decision making and intergroup relations. Work in both of these areas has demonstrated the prevalence of systematic biases due to cognitive limitations and emotional needs. Key puzzles will remain unresolved without incorporating these insights into our analytical frameworks.[1]

Studying the psychological aspects of IR is integral to the study of the subject, not least because of the limits of situational explanations.[2] It is not of course the case that international relations as a field has ignored psychology altogether. We have already seen (under different headings and chapters) some of the work that has been done on the psychology of foreign policy decision-making, including work on belief systems and analogical reasoning. This chapter will examine in a rather more detailed way some of the classic work that has been done in the field of international politics from a psychological angle, including the work of Robert Jervis and Richard Ned Lebow. We shall also look at an illustrative selection of some of the most innovative work being done on the psychology of IR by four increasingly prominent younger authors—Jacques Hymans, Rose McDermott, Jonathan Mercer and Dominic Johnson—and conclude with a look at Ralph White's work on empathy, a useful corrective to what in Chapter 9 we described as *the fundamental attribution error*.

Mercer and McDermott's contributions in particular draw on attribution theory. This approach—which will provide a useful hinge for this chapter, not least because it focuses on both situational and dispositional factors—suggests that while academic observers of international relations have relied *too much* on situationism to explain behavior, practitioners or policy-makers have relied on it *too little*. In other words, while most IR theorists have generally ignored the psychological dispositions of actors—usually because they consider such explanations too "messy" and/or that they would rob their models of predictive value—most policy-makers underrate the importance of situations and the ways in which these can compel an adversary to undertake actions and express positions that *do not* reflect their underlying dispositions, values, or preferences.

The Situationism of International Relations Theory

Many of the established approaches to international relations work at the systemic level of analysis. While this is not the place to provide a comprehensive account of all of the various theories themselves—doing this would take, and has taken, a textbook in its own right[3]—it is certainly true to say that neorealism, neoliberalism, world systems theory, dependency theory, and Alexander Wendt's version of constructivism all operate at this level. In the terms that we have been using in this book, all the established theories of IR represent especially strident versions of a *situationist* approach. This is especially true for neorealism, which is particularly associated with its creator Kenneth Waltz. We will use neorealism here as an illustration because in many ways it represents an example of what might be termed "hyper-situationism," though many of the same points could be made of the other theories mentioned above. Describing what neorealism constitutes should also make it clear what is meant by a "systemic level" approach to international politics.

Neorealists argue, to put it bluntly, that "situation is everything"; the individual characteristics of the state—including the characteristics of its leaders, its domestic political situation, whether it is a democracy or dictatorship, and so on—matter very little in determining what happens in international politics. Instead, they focus on the character of the international system.[4] Quite simply, the principal determinant of a state's behavior in the international system is *where it is located* within that system. For instance, neorealism contends that all superpowers are essentially alike in the sense that they tend to behave in the same way, as do all middle-range powers and all weak powers. This might not seem like such a radical claim to make, but it has some radical implications when you think about it. For one thing, the idea that "superpowers are superpowers" implies that the Cold War would still have occurred if, say, the two great powers after World War II had been the United States and France, or the United States and Canada. According to neorealists, the same intense rivalry between the two powers would be expected had the ideological competition between the U.S.A. and the Soviet Union never existed, because international politics is ultimately not about ideas but the struggle for security.

For neorealists, what matters most if we want to explain what happens in international politics is not the domestic makeup of states or the individual psychological characteristics of those who lead them ("a state is a state," as they see it, and all states have similar objectives), but *how many powers* there are in the system. They distinguish between bipolar and multipolar systems in particular; that is, between systems in which only two powers predominate and more than two (say three, four, or five) exert influence. According to advocates of this theory such as John Mearsheimer, a multipolar system is actively dangerous and prone to produce conflict between states, while a bipolar system is comparatively stable and far less likely to lead to war. For this reason, Mearsheimer predicted back in 1990 that we would "soon miss the Cold War," since the presence of only two great powers in the system during that era supposedly led to international stability.[5]

You may find Waltz's theory convincing or you may not. The larger point we wish to make here, however, is that Waltz's theory—and again, this applies to any theory of international politics working at this vague situationist level—requires some sort of account of how states *know* what roles they are supposed to play in the international system. Stanley Milgram (for instance) generated a theory which explained precisely why people obey situational pressures, but Waltz offers no corresponding theory as to how and why states follow the "signals" that the international system is sending, as many critics of Waltz's theory have noted. Systemic theories of international politics commonly invoke some version of *Homo economicus*—the argument that a state perceives the world rationally and accurately, and therefore realizes that it is, say, a middle-range power that must not act as a superpower does. Waltz denies that he makes any such assumption, merely asserting that states that fail to recognize their "proper roles" in life decline or die out (interestingly, an argument which itself invokes Darwinism and evolutionary psychology). "Notice that the theory requires no assumptions of rationality or of constancy of will on the part of all of the actors. The theory says simply that some do relatively well, others will emulate them or fall by the wayside," Waltz argues.[6] Other systemic-level theories more commonly rely on the claim that states *are* rational actors, though (the neoliberalism of Robert Keohane, for instance, explicitly makes this assumption). This rational choice approach accepts the possibility that a state and its leaders may actively *misperceive* the nature of the situation they face, and similarly Waltz's evolutionary argument also implicitly allows for states to misperceive the situation. Once this point is conceded, however, we are back to square one, since we are left wondering what psychological factors cause a state and its leaders to do this.

Situationism in international relations takes a variety of other forms as well, as Martin Hollis and Steve Smith suggest,[7] for *anything* above the level of the individual dispositions is situational. We can conceive of these different kinds of approach as akin to a Russian doll, in which opening up one structure gives rise to a smaller one. When we open up the international system, we find states. When we open up the state, we find bureaucracies. Opening up bureaucracies, we find groups, another situational level. It is only when we consider the contents of groups that we confront individuals and dispositions, however. Moving from the international system down the ladder of analysis to less general forms of situation that shape behavior, other situationist theories include those that focus on the societal environment, such as the democratic peace thesis, and those that deal more immediately with the ways that organizational and bureaucratic constraints shape and limit foreign policy behavior. Within the latter category, the work of Graham Allison has been especially influential, particularly his now classic work with Philip Zelikow, *Essence of Decision*.[8] And as we have already seen, group pressures constitute yet another situational level.

Like Waltz, Allison and Zelikow explain the behavior of leaders situationally and dispense with psychological considerations, but there most similarities end. In their approach—commonly referred to in the literature as the *bureaucratic politics theory*—the behavior of decision-makers is mostly (though not exclusively) determined by parochial positions within the bureaucracy. The aphorism "where you stand depends on where you sit," variously attributed to Rufus Miles and Don Price, captures this position especially well. According to this, the views of those who occupy bureaucratic positions are significantly colored by the organizational outlook and mission of the bodies they work for. Secretaries of state tend to argue for negotiation and diplomacy, for instance, because this is what the State Department "does"; defense secretaries tend to argue for conventional military solutions; meanwhile, representatives of the CIA tend to advocate covert operations.

Unfortunately, this aspect of Allison and Zelikow's model has not fared well in recent years, not least because it neglects the force of existing beliefs, personalities, and other values.[9] When Colin Powell was chairman of the Joint Chiefs during the first Persian Gulf War, he was the last holdout *against* U.S. military intervention, while Secretary of State Dean Rusk was very much *for* escalating American military involvement in Vietnam; in both cases, their philosophical positions were highly inconsistent with their bureaucratic roles. As a variety of critics have noted, bureaucratic position or "situation" is a far less accurate predictor of foreign policy views than are the existing dispositions of leaders. The approach clearly works sometimes—as when Colin Powell quietly opposed the 2003 invasion of Iraq, arguing for continued diplomacy—but when it does seem to "explain" behavior, it often seems to do so only by coincidence or happenstance, not because the theory "works" as such. To the extent that we can tell, Powell would have had strong reservations about the war *regardless* of the bureaucratic position he occupied.

Misperceptions, Cold and Hot

As Brian Ripley notes, a number of classic works compete for the title of "seminal work" in the psychological study of international politics and foreign policy.[10] The first attempt to apply the insights of psychology to international relations was Snyder, Bruck, and Sapin's *Foreign Policy Decision-Making*, which first introduced the notion that individuals play an important role in shaping foreign policy decisions.[11] Another classic work that appeared some years later was Joseph de Rivera's *The Psychological Dimension of Foreign Policy*, which applied some of the insights of social psychology to foreign policy analysis.[12] Important though these initial efforts were, however, the scholar who has arguably done most to convince international relations scholars to incorporate the insights of psychology into their work has been Robert Jervis.

In his path-breaking book, *Perception and Misperception in International Politics*—first published in the mid-1970s—Robert Jervis thrust psychology onto the center stage of international relations. Drawing primarily on cognitive consistency theory, Jervis placed the analytical emphasis on leaders and their characteristics. Beginning with a compelling argument that strongly suggested that situationist arguments were by themselves insufficient to explain the decisions that leaders reach—and hence what "goes on" in international politics—Jervis examined the ways in which political leaders commonly misinterpret the signals that other leaders intend to send and other ways in which our existing dispositions affect our decision-making.

As we have seen already, human beings have a tendency to interpret evidence in a way that comports with existing beliefs, and to disregard information which does not. As Jervis puts it:

> This means not only that when a statesman has developed a certain image of another country he will maintain that view in the face of large amounts of discrepant information, but also that the general expectations and rules entertained by the statesman about the links between other states' situations and characteristics on the one hand and their foreign

policy intentions on the other influence the images of others that we will come to hold. Thus western statesmen will be quicker to see another state as aggressive if a dictator has just come to power in it than if it is a stable democracy.[13]

Jervis provides a large number of examples in which prior beliefs affected the perceptions of the actors. Prior expectations, he notes, critically affect what we "see." For example, during World War II British aircraft bombed their own battleship (the *Sheffield*) by mistake.[14] The reason was that they were expecting to be confronted by the German ship *Bismarck*, which was actually what they were looking for. Ironically, the two ships did not even resemble one another and the flight crews were quite familiar with the British ship, but the expectation proved powerful enough to result in a disastrous misperception (the same psychological phenomenon is undoubtedly behind the many "friendly fire" incidents witnessed during the first Persian Gulf War and in the 2003 U.S. war in Iraq). Jervis also highlights the importance of analogical reasoning and the ways in which leaders may "overlearn" the lessons of an event such as the 1938 Munich conference, the seminal event in the appeasement of Adolf Hitler prior to World War II. "The only thing as important for a nation as its revolution is its last major war," Jervis notes.[15]

Another important study published only a few years after Jervis's seminal work was Richard Ned Lebow's *Between Peace and War*.[16] While not discounting the role played by cold cognitive processes, Lebow argues that an equal or perhaps greater role in generating misperceptions is played by hot, motivated, or emotional factors, such as wishful thinking, guilt, shame, and anxiety. He examines twenty-six crises—situations which escalated into war and cases where war seemed likely but was averted—spanning a period of seventy years. He focuses in particular on Fashoda (1898), the July crisis (1914), Munich (1938), Korea (1950), the Sino–Indian dispute (1962), and the Cuban missile crisis from the same year. Balancing the theoretical drive of the political scientist with the historian's nuanced instinct for detail, Lebow highlights the cognitive and motivational forces that inhibit policy learning, and he uses the case studies to develop a typology of different crisis types. One way in which war can occur, for instance, is through a "justification of hostility" type of crisis, where a leader challenged domestically initiates war in order to mobilize support at home. As Lebow puts it:

justification of hostility crises are unique in that leaders of the initiating action make a decision for war *before* the crisis commences. The purpose of the crisis is not to force an accommodation but to provide a *casus belli* for war. Initiators of such crises invariably attempt to make their adversary appear responsible for the war. By doing so they attempt to mobilize support for themselves, both at home and abroad and to undercut support for their adversary.[17]

Some Recent Innovations

We have already seen some of the innovative work that has been done within the psychological study of foreign policy decision-making in the areas of cognition, personality, group behavior, and leadership in general, and the reader is referred back to Chapters 6–10 in particular. Summarizing all of the other notable work done in this area would be an impossibility, but instead of attempting this I will examine four recent areas of innovation—on the psychology of nuclear proliferation, risk-taking, deterrence, and evolutionary psychology as a cause of war respectively—which in the author's view have been especially significant, concluding with some rather older insights about the psychology of international relations which have recently received renewed attention.

The Psychology of Nuclear Proliferation

One of the leading concerns of policy-makers in the post-Cold War era has been the concern that so-called "rogue states" and terrorist groups might acquire and then use nuclear weapons. North Korea (which by most accounts already possesses nuclear weapons) and Iran have been countries of particular concern for Western policy-makers, especially in the United States. Until recently, however, much of the literature on nuclear proliferation has been largely normative—"we should prevent state A from developing a nuclear capacity"—or technical in nature. What explains why some states decide to "go nuclear" while others do not, though? Clearly, situationism alone cannot explain this puzzle, since a large variety of states have access to nuclear technology, but only relatively few choose to go nuclear. The answer, then, must have something to do with the *dispositions* of states and their leaders. In a highly innovative use of the psychological literature on international relations, Jacques Hymans has produced an interesting theory that seeks to explain the puzzle in these terms.[18]

To explain why some states go nuclear while others do not, Hymans develops the useful idea of *national identity conceptions* (NICs). We have already seen how social identity theory can be used to explain conflicts between groups; the NIC, however, is not a shared or social conception of identity but an idiosyncratic, individual-level factor that varies by leader. In other words, different leaders within the same state can hold markedly different conceptions about their own nation. More specifically, a leader's NIC refers to "his or her sense of what the nation naturally stands for and of how high it naturally stands in comparison to others."[19] Taking this further, Hymans distinguishes between conceptions of *solidarity* and *status*. Within the first dimension—while all leaders tend to see their own state in "us versus them" terms—some see this in black-and-white or oppositional terms, while others adopt what Hymans calls a more "transcendent" identity. This is another way of saying that some leaders sense a kind of common humanity or destiny with others, while others do not. Within the second dimension, meanwhile, some leaders see their own state as superior to, or the equal of, other states, while others view their states as "below" or subordinate to others in status.[20] Putting these two dimensions together yields a two-by-two table (see Table 17.1).[21]

Hymans hypothesizes that nuclear proliferation will occur solely under the leadership of "oppositional nationalists," where a stark us-versus-them conception is combined with the perception of state superiority. To test this theory, he examines four cases, two of which (France and India) took the decision to go nuclear and two of which (Australia and Argentina) decided after much deliberation against doing this. Before 1972, Australia had set out develop a nuclear weapons program under its then Prime Minister John Gorton, characterized by Hymans as an "oppositional nationalist." When Gough Whitlam took over in 1972, however, he reversed his predecessor's nuclear strategy, a decision which Hymans traces to Whitlam's lesser concern about Chinese intentions in general, and more specifically to his psychological beliefs as a "sportsmanlike subaltern."[22]

No theoretical framework can explain everything, of course, and it is possible that some cases that Hymans does not examine might not "fit" the argument. Nevertheless, as Robert Jervis notes, this argument:

> gains much of its power from showing that it was not "France" that chose nuclear weapons and "Australia" that did not, but rather that leaders in these countries fell into different places in his four-fold table developed from the two dimensions, and that the fact—often an accidental fact— of who was in power at key points determined what the country would do. This is not to deny that the country's situation and shared intellectual and cultural characteristics shape national policy, but only that there is almost always room for individual choice.[23]

One of the most pressing issues in the latter years of the George W. Bush administration was a deep concern that Iran was developing a nuclear capability. Iranian President Mahmoud Ahmadinejad has said that "we will not retreat even one iota from our nuclear rights . . . today Iran is a nuclear country

Table 17.1 Solidarity and status dimensions

Solidarity dimensions	Us and them (nested)	Us against them
Status dimensions		
We are naturally their equals if not their superiors	Sportsmanlike nationalist	Oppositional nationalist
We are naturally below them	Sportsmanlike subaltern	Oppositional subaltern

Source: Jacques Hymans, The Psychology of Nuclear Proliferation: Identity, Emotions, and Foreign Policy (New York: Cambridge University Press, 2006), p.25

and nuclear knowledge and nuclear science is in the brains of our scientists."[24] It is interesting, therefore, to consider how Hymans' theory might be applied to that case, and Ted Reynolds has examined this question in an interesting paper.[25] He acknowledges that Hymans' model becomes difficult to use "when considering cases of proliferation where the decision-making process is diffused or data regarding the psychological profile of the leader is unavailable or obscured as a result of the closed nature of the state apparatus," also noting that the approach is difficult to apply to non-state actors such as al-Qaeda and other terrorist organizations. Reynolds notes that Kim Il Sung and Kim Jong Il of North Korea both appear to be oppositional nationalists when one examines their public statements, as does Ahmadinejad, though it is unclear in the first case whether the statements are intended as mere propaganda and whether Ahmadinejad is in control of nuclear policy in the second instance. Nevertheless, to the extent that North Korean and Iranian leaders genuinely exhibit the characteristics of oppositional nationalism as opposed to the other three categorizations, the model predicts that their nuclear programs will grow and expand. The approach of Hymans also adds something new and interesting to our understanding of nationalism—an understanding of the role of leaders and their individualized conceptions of national identity, a topic that we examined in Chapter 14 and mostly conceive of at a group or social level.

The Psychology of Risk-Taking

When do leaders take risks in international politics? Is it a matter of personality—with some more prone to "roll the dice" than others—or is it primarily a matter of the nature of the situation the leader faces? Or is it instead a matter of how one construes or perceives the situation one faces? Rose McDermott has pioneered the application of prospect theory to international relations, which provides one rather interesting answer. In essence, prospect theory—developed in the late 1970s by Daniel Kahneman and Amos

Tversky—suggests that the manner in which a problem is *framed* has a decisive impact on the attractiveness of various options that foreign policy decision-makers consider.[26] Specifically, whether we regard ourselves as operating in a "domain of gains" or a "domain of losses" determines the degree to which we will be prepared to take a risk. If we perceive ourselves as being in a loss-making situation, we are far more likely to take risks than we are if we think we are making gains. Individuals will be *risk averse* (that is, will avoid risky options) when dealing with gains, but they will be *risk acceptant* when dealing with losses.

Another way of putting this is to imagine yourself in a casino, let's say The Palms in Las Vegas. Let's imagine also that you've had a good night at Blackjack or Texas Hold 'Em, and your pockets are full of chips that you are looking forward to converting into cash. The theory suggests that you are in a domain of gains—you are winning, in other words—and so you are unlikely to take reckless risks with the chips. For instance, you are unlikely to put the whole lot down on a single roll of the roulette wheel, when you know quite well that your chances of doubling or tripling your winnings are quite slim (though the casino, of course, would love it if you did). Put in terms of Kahneman and Tversky's theory, you will be *risk averse*.

Now imagine the opposite scenario. You have had a lousy night at the tables, and you are down to your last few chips. Aside from the free drinks the waitress is serving you, you're getting very little enjoyment out of the evening and are deeply regretting walking through the door. You are, as the theory would have it, in a domain of losses, and you recognize this all too clearly. Under these conditions, you are also likely to put everything you have on a high-risk option that promises high returns if you win but where it is correspondingly less likely that you *will* win. You are *risk acceptant*, in the terms of prospect theory, and now you are quite likely to risk everything you have on a single turn of the wheel. After all, you have a chance to recoup from the casino a fair bit of what you've lost.

As Robert Jervis puts it:

> people are loss-averse in the sense that losses loom larger than the corresponding gains. Losing ten dollars, for example, annoys us more than gaining ten dollars gratifies us . . . more than the hope of gains, the specter of losses activates, energizes and drives actors, producing great (and often misguided) efforts that risk—and frequently lead to—greater losses.[27]

In her book *Risk-Taking in International Politics*, Rose McDermott applies this theory to a variety of cases in foreign policy decision-making, such as the disastrous Iran hostage rescue mission of 1980, decisions about whether to admit the Shah of Iran to the United States, the U-2 crisis, and the Suez crisis.[28]

In the hostage rescue mission case, for instance, McDermott argues that President Jimmy Carter perceived himself (not unreasonably) as being in a domain of losses by March/April of 1980, and this made him more risk acceptant than he would otherwise have been. Carter's personal popularity was in free fall, he had just lost two presidential primaries to Senator Edward Kennedy and negotiations to get the hostages out by peaceful means seemed to have run aground. "By the time of the rescue mission," McDermott argues:

> Carter was a leader ready to take a gamble to return things to the status quo, with the hostages safely at home, national pride and international honor restored, and his political fortunes turned upward . . . in terms of prospect theory, he was a man operating in the domain of losses.[29]

Similarly, Barbara Farnham argues that prospect theory throws considerable light on Franklin Roosevelt's decision-making during the Munich crisis of the late 1930s.[30]

Like any theory of political behavior, prospect theory has some drawbacks.[31] Perhaps risk-taking is primarily a matter of personality rather than perception of the situation, for instance.[32] It may also be that the perception of loss does not automatically lead to risk-taking in complex, real-world decision-making. Like Hymans' theory of nuclear proliferation, it is difficult to test in some cases as well. Because what matters in the theory is not the "objective" situation, but how the individual decision-maker *construes* that situation—this is what makes the theory dispositionist—we cannot know for sure in at least some instances whether gain or loss was what was perceived, but must infer this from the available information. We must also infer from that information available in a given case how risky a decision-maker perceived the various choices to have been. But this is a problem that confronts *any* theory that seeks to reconstruct the mindsets and dispositions of decision-makers. Moreover, McDermott argues that we can ascertain all the information we need in this case, since it seems fairly apparent that Carter saw himself operating in a domain of loss by March 1980 and that he saw the rescue mission as the riskiest of the options available.

The Psychology of Deterrence

As we have seen already, one place where the visions provided by *Homo economicus* and *Homo psychologicus* clash most clearly is in the study of voting behavior. But there is an area where the difference of perspective they provide arguably matters even more, because it has to do with matters of life and death: deterrence theory. As Ned Lebow and Janice Stein note, the rational actor version of deterrence theory (on which a lot of international security theorizing is based) is flawed because it relies upon assumptions which—as we have seen repeatedly in this book—human beings *depart from* in practice, for both cold cognitive and emotional reasons. The films *Doctor Strangelove* and *Fail-Safe*, both released not long after (and in large part inspired by) the Cuban missile crisis of October 1962, imagine ways in which human error might have led to a U.S. nuclear attack against the Soviet Union and then all-out nuclear war. In books like *We All Lost The Cold War*, however, Lebow and Stein critique the very assumptions on which rational deterrence theory rests, assumptions which are supposed to prevent conventional or nuclear war between superpowers through the simple operation of rational self-interest.[33]

Rational deterrence theory essentially assumes, as Lebow and Stein put it, that all leaders are "risk-prone gain maximizers"; in other words, rational self-interest dictates that all leaders will attempt to expand their territory at the expense of others, but that (equally) they will be constrained from doing so when the costs outweigh the benefits. As Christopher Achen and Duncan Snidal put it:

> if a country knows that it is likely to lose a long nasty war in the process, it will probably not seek to press its claims against a rival. The trick is to learn the likelihood that the rival country will fight—and if it fights, how likely it is to win.[34]

It is thus vitally important that a state convinces its rivals that it will fight, and that it is more than capable of defeating those rivals. Some believe in this rational actor view so strongly that they *advocate* nuclear proliferation, encouraging states like Germany and Japan to acquire nuclear weapons, for instance.[35] The logic of analysts like John Mearsheimer, who strongly advocates this position, is that rational deterrence is so compelling that it would lead to greater peace and stability in the world.

This theory is flawed, first of all, because not all leaders are "risk-prone gain maximizers." Lebow and Stein argue that *some* leaders are—they give Hitler and Stalin as examples—but that this is relatively uncommon in international politics.[36] As we saw in the previous section, moreover, risk propensity can vary with a leader's perception of the situation. Calling into question how "rational" the deliberations of policy-makers are, moreover, they highlight cases in which leaders did act in a risk-prone, gain-maximizing way, but then entirely failed to weigh up the costs and benefits in the way that *Homo economicus* approaches suggest that they do. "Empirical analyses of deterrence failures have identified cases in which leaders calculated in accordance with the expectations of deterrence theories but acted contrary to their predictions," they note. "These leaders estimated the expected costs of war as very high, the probability of winning as low, and the probability that the defender would retaliate as virtually certain. Yet, they chose to challenge deterrence."[37] They give the Japanese attack on the United States in 1941 and Egyptian leader Anwar Sadat's attack on Israel in 1973 as examples. The strong implication of Lebow and Stein's approach is that deterrence theory not only fails to account for the ways that real-world leaders behave, but that it is *positively dangerous* for our own leaders to rely on such a theory.

In a fascinating contribution to the literature, Jonathan Mercer also uses psychological theory to critique deterrence theory in an entirely novel way.[38] In Chapter 9 we described attribution theory, and noted the prevalence of what the social psychologist Lee Ross called "The fundamental attribution error." This refers to the human tendency, replicated in a large number of psychological studies, to attribute the cause of someone else's behavior to their dispositions. When we see someone perform an act of kindness, we tend to assume that the person performing the act did so because he or she *is* kind. But this ignores the effects that situation can have on behavior. For instance, seeing someone appear somber (or even crying) at a funeral should not lead us to assume that he or she is a somber person, because the social situation demands that we appear this way (even if we didn't much care for the deceased). Social etiquette suggests that it is appropriate to "look sad" in such situations, even if what we're actually thinking of is the food and drink that often follows.

Mercer uses these insights to generate a new (and rather counter-intuitive) approach to reputation that runs directly counter to deterrence theory. The latter, as we have seen, suggests that it is critical for a state to send out the "right signals" if deterrence is to operate properly; if one's rival doubts that one is credibly prepared to fight, for instance, it may well attack, rational deterrence theory suggests. It is certainly true, moreover, that at least some leaders *do* worry about a reputation for resolve. Lyndon Johnson, for instance, worried that if he backed down over Vietnam and let the South fall to Ho Chi Minh and the Communists, this would irreparably damage the reputation and standing of the United States among both our enemies and our allies. The former, he reasoned, would be emboldened by our failure to act, while the latter (notably the Europeans) would begin to fear that America's commitments to them weren't worth the paper they were written on. If we didn't stand up to the Communists in Vietnam, we would not be able to deter the spread of global Communism because no one would take us seriously anymore. We would be dismissed as a "paper tiger." Other U.S. presidents, from Truman to Ford, seem to have shared this concern.

Jonathan Mercer argues that these kinds of concerns—which frequently lead to huge losses in blood and treasure—are often entirely misplaced, however, and his reasoning is relatively simple. Using attribution theory's insights, he argues that it is impossible—or at least very difficult—for enemy leaders to get a reputation for "lacking resolve."[39] Because the fundamental attribution error (in which we attribute a rival or enemy's behavior to dispositional causes) is so common, even behavior that is benign or non-aggressive tends to be ignored, and even when it is not we simply maintain the negative image by attributing the behavior to situational causes (as John Foster Dulles did when he dismissed signs of a desire to move towards détente on the part of the Soviets). We tend to attribute the behavior of our allies, on the other hand, to situational factors; just as enemies find it hard to get a reputation for not having resolve, allies have the opposite problem.[40] Allies, according to the theory, have a hard time getting a reputation for possessing resolve because when we view allies as acting out of necessity—from the "demands of the situation," as it were—we find it difficult to give them credit for having a disposition towards *being* resolute. For instance, many observers in the United States rightly or wrongly attributed Saudi Arabia's support for the first Persian Gulf War as stemming from the situation; faced with Saddam Hussein's invasion of Kuwait in 1990s, the Saudis (and other Gulf states who supported the war) feared they might become the Iraqi dictator's next victim.

Evolutionary Psychology and the Road to War

The reader may recall Stanley Milgram's argument from Chapter 4 about the roots of human obedience. Milgram argued that we probably have a built-in, hard-wired tendency to obey authority, and he based this claim partly on evolutionary psychology. Evolutionary psychology—a form of genopolitical argument, as we saw earlier—is an increasingly popular approach which argues that certain psychological traits—especially those which are not culturally unique but occur across time and space—probably developed through natural selection. "Evolved" adaptations developed as a way to solve recurrent problems that human beings faced in ancestral environments, according to this view. Just as evolutionary biology has argued that many physical aspects of the human body developed in order to address recurring challenges that beset human beings long ago, many evolutionary psychologists utilize the same kind of argument about the brain and human decision-making. Perhaps human behavior is itself the product of evolutionary adaptation, and perhaps the array of cognitive biases to which *Homo psychologicus* inevitably falls prey are built-in too.

During the last ten years, we have begun to see scholars of international security apply this kind of argument to their work. Dominic Johnson, for instance—a scholar trained in both evolutionary biology and political science—employs evolutionary psychology to try to understand a variety of phenomena in international relations. In his book *Overconfidence and War: The Havoc and Glory of Positive Illusions*, for example, Johnson examines the psychological roots of hubris, a tendency to overestimate our own power and capabilities. From the *Homo economicus* perspective we discussed in Chapter 2, why nations go to war at all is a real puzzle. Wars generally occur when each side believes it is likely to win, but if they were truly rational, states would accurately assess their own power and thus agree not to fight. And yet states fight anyway. This is because human beings have developed an evolutionary bias towards overconfidence, Johnson argues.[41] This cognitive bias is called "positive illusions." We believe in our own virtue and in our ability to control events. This bias may have been favored by natural selection because it conferred various advantages on our ancestors, and thus maximized our chances of survival. For instance, overconfidence gives us the capacity to "bluff" our way out of a conflict, and supreme self-belief (through the mechanism of the self-fulfilling prophecy) may also improve our fighting abilities. And yet in the modern world the consequences of this evolutionary legacy can be truly deadly, as changes in the technology of warfare have far outpaced man's primitive ancestral makeup. "Humans are fish out of water," Johnson argues, "Modern life is far removed from our 'natural' environment of evolutionary adaptation."[42] Our brains evolved when we were hunter-gatherers, but today overconfidence is a major liability, as positive illusions can easily escalate into enormously damaging and costly wars.

Similarly, Kenneth Payne's *The Psychology of Strategy: Exploring Rationality in the Vietnam War* convincingly demonstrates that although strategic studies have often given short shrift to psychology—preferring the well-known "rational actor" approach, on the whole—evolutionary and emotional psychology can explain a lot of behaviors which rational choice theory simply cannot. Payne examines how leaders decide what they wish to achieve through war and how they try to accomplish it. Using the example of Vietnam and the Nixon and Johnson administrations, he shows how wrong our understanding of conflict, war, and violence often is. Payne examines in particular the way in which cognitive biases and short cuts distort our decision-making, focusing especially on emotion and unconscious mental processing.[43]

Empathy: The Antidote to Attribution Error and Other Things

Mercer's work in particular suggests that policy-makers often underrate the role played by the situation in determining behavior (ironically, just the opposite problem to that generally exhibited by IR theorists). This is also—from a somewhat different angle of approach—the conclusion of Ralph White's classic work on *empathy*. As White often explains, empathy is very different from sympathy, or at least each represents an opposite point along a continuum. The latter implies active approval, while the former simply entails putting oneself in the shoes of another in order to better understand his or her motives. Empathy, White notes, is "defined as a realistic understanding of the thoughts and feelings of others," while sympathy is "defined in accordance with its Greek derivation, as *feeling with* others—being happy because they are or unhappy because they are—which often implies doing what one can to help them. Empathy is primarily cognitive, in the language of psychology; sympathy is affective."[44]

Empathy is important because it is, in White's phrase, "the *great* corrective for all forms of war-promoting misperception."[45] It is also a potential corrective to the fundamental attribution error, since it forces the decision-maker to appreciate the situation that the adversary is confronting. White's work helped pioneer a rich tradition of work in the study of international relations on empathy, perception, and misperception which continues today.[46]

While obviously a laudable goal for policy-makers to pursue, however, it is especially difficult to achieve under some circumstances. It is patently easier to achieve in retrospect than it is at the time, for instance, and an example from Errol Morris's outstanding documentary film of Robert McNamara's life, *The Fog of War*—America's escalation of the Vietnam War—illustrates another significant problem: one has to know the adversary sufficiently well to put oneself in their shoes. By McNamara's own admission, this was not the case with Vietnam. Lyndon Johnson and the principals in the Tuesday Lunch Group had little familiarity with the history of Vietnamese–Chinese relations; if they had, McNamara notes, they would have been far less likely to see the North Vietnamese as a mere satellite of the Chinese. Greater familiarity with the nationalist aspects of Ho Chi Minh's thinking—as opposed to his Communist beliefs, which were fairly well understood—might equally well have discouraged a tendency to see North Vietnam as a mere puppet of the Soviets. Sadly, those who did have the capacity to empathize with Ho were largely marginalized and regarded, in James Thomson's phrase, as "troublemakers."[47] Equally, most members of the Carter administration found it difficult to empathize with the students who seized the U.S. embassy in Tehran in 1979, the act that precipitated the Iran hostage crisis.

Simply stated, a major problem for Jimmy Carter and his advisers in 1979—even more so than for Johnson's entourage in 1965—was that very little was known about the Ayatollah Khomeini and the movement he represented at the time. Members of the Carter administration, including its own Middle Eastern specialists, struggled to make sense of the Ayatollah's actions. The threat posed by radical Islamism—or what, for want of a better phrase, has become widely but rather misleadingly known as "Islamic fundamentalism"—represented uncharted territory at the time. Lacking any cognitive compass with which to make sense of the Iranian radical, President Carter himself (quite understandably but non-empathetically) often dismissed the Ayatollah's actions as irrational and even insane during the early days of the hostage crisis. U.S. decision-makers also did not fully appreciate the importance of history in the Middle East, and in particular the impact that the memory of 1953—the year in which the CIA helped depose the democratically elected leader Mohammed Mossadegh—continued to have on Iranian thinking.

Conclusion

Nevertheless, empathy with one's adversary is possible to achieve when decision-makers consciously and deliberately make an effort to place themselves in the shoes of that adversary, and the policy-makers "know" the opponent well enough for realistic empathy to be possible. The success of *The Fog of War* has brought the importance of empathy with one's adversary as a means of conflict resolution renewed attention in international relations and foreign policy, a theme echoed in McNamara's book *Wilson's Ghost*, co-authored with James Blight, and in the book by James Blight and Janet Lang that accompanies the film.[48] The film features a notably successful case of empathizing: John Kennedy's handling of the Cuban missile crisis. What got us out of the Cuban missile crisis and pulled us back from the brink—apart from "sheer dumb luck," to use Dean Acheson's memorable phrase—was JFK's ability to empathize with Khrushchev, McNamara argues. Spurred on by U.S. Ambassador to the Soviet Union Llewellyn "Tommy" Thompson, Kennedy was able to successfully place himself in the shoes of the adversary and thus avert nuclear disaster. Thompson realized that Khrushchev almost certainly knew several days into the crisis that he had made a serious miscalculation in placing missiles in Cuba, and that he would be looking for some sort of face-saving way out of the crisis; successful resolution of the situation would therefore require a negotiated solution from which both sides could claim some sort of "victory."

Notes

1 James Goldgeier, "Psychology and Security," *Security Studies*, 6: 137–66, 1997.
2 Ole Holsti, "The Political Psychology of International Politics: More than A Luxury," *Political Psychology*, 10: 495–500, 1989. "Structural" is a more common

term than "situational" in the study of IR, but it covers the same phenomenon, although as we shall see situationism covers more than the structure of the international system.

3 See for instance Scott Burchill, Richard Devetak, Andrew Linklater, Matthew Paterson, Christian Reús-Smit, and Jacqui True, *Theories of International Relations*, second edition (New York: Palgrave, 2001) and Paul Viotti and Mark Kauppi, *International Relations Theory: Realism, Pluralism, Globalism, and Beyond*, third edition (New York: Prentice Hall, 1998).

4 Kenneth Waltz, *Theory of International Politics* (Reading, MA: Addison Wesley, 1979). For an excellent article which contrasts the neorealist and psychological perspectives towards international relations, see Brian Ripley, "Psychology, Foreign Policy, and International Relations Theory," *Political Psychology*, 14: 403–16, 1993.

5 John Mearsheimer, "Back To The Future: Instability in Europe After the Cold War," *International Security*, 15: 5–56, 1990; for a shorter and more readable version, see his "Why We Will Soon Miss The Cold War," *Atlantic Monthly*, 266: 35–50, 1990.

6 Waltz, *Theory of International Politics*, p.118; see also the various contributions to Robert Keohane (ed.), *Neorealism and its Critics* (New York: Columbia University Press, 1986).

7 Martin Hollis and Steve Smith, *Explaining and Understanding International Relations* (New York: Oxford University Press, 1990).

8 Graham Allison and Philip Zelikow, *Essence of Decision: Explaining the Cuban Missile Crisis*, second edition (New York: Longman, 1999).

9 See for instance David Patrick Houghton, "Essence of Excision: A Critique of the New Version of Essence of Decision," *Security Studies*, 10: 162–91, 2000.

10 Ripley, "Psychology, Foreign Policy and International Relations Theory," p.405.

11 Richard Snyder, H.W. Bruck, and Burton Sapin (eds.), *Foreign Policy Decision-Making: An Approach To The Study of International Politics* (New York: Free Press, 1962).

12 Joseph de Rivera, *The Psychological Dimension of Foreign Policy* (Columbus, OH: Charles Merrill, 1968).

13 Robert Jervis, *Perception and Misperception in International Politics* (Princeton, NJ: Princeton University Press, 1976) p.146.

14 Ibid., p.92.

15 Ibid., p.266.

16 Richard Ned Lebow, *Between Peace and War: The Nature of International Crisis* (Baltimore, MD: The Johns Hopkins University Press, 1981).

17 Ibid., p.25.

18 Jacques Hymans, *The Psychology of Nuclear Proliferation: Identity, Emotions, and Foreign Policy* (New York: Cambridge University Press, 2006).

19 Ibid., p.21.

20 Ibid., pp.21–25.

21 Ibid., p.25.

22 Ibid., pp.62–63.

23 Robert Jervis, "Review of *The Psychology of Nuclear Proliferation*," *Political Psychology*, 28: 269–72, 2007.

24 *Reuters*, "Iran Says More UN Steps Won't Stop Its Nuclear Work," June 3, 2007.

25 Ted Reynolds, "Understanding Nuclear Weapons Proliferation," unpublished manuscript.

26 Daniel Kahneman and Amos Tversky, "Prospect Theory: An Analysis of Decision Under Risk," *Econometrica*, 47: 263–91, 1979.

27 Robert Jervis, "Political Implications of Loss Aversion," *Political Psychology*, 13: 187–204, 1992, p.187.

28 Rose McDermott, *Risk-Taking in International Politics: Prospect Theory in American Foreign Policy* (Ann Arbor, MI: University of Michigan Press, 1998); see also McDermott, "Prospect Theory in Political Science: Gains and Losses from the First Decade," *Political Psychology*, 29: 289–312, 2004.

29 Rose McDermott, "Prospect Theory in International Relations: The Iranian Hostage Rescue Mission," *Political Psychology*, 13: 237–63, 1992, pp.241–42.

30 Barbara Farnham, *Roosevelt and the Munich Crisis: A Study of Political Decision-Making* (Princeton, NJ: Princeton University Press, 1997).

31 For assessments of the strengths and weaknesses of prospect theory generally, see Jervis, "Political Implications of Loss Aversion," Jack Levy, "Prospect Theory and International Relations: Theoretical Applications and Analytical Problems," *Political Psychology*, 13, 283–310, 1992, and Eldar Shafir, "Prospect Theory and Political Analysis: A Psychological Perspective," *Political Psychology*, 13, 311–22, 1992. The McDermott, Jervis, Levy, and Shafir articles are all part of a special edition of *Political Psychology* devoted to prospect theory.

32 On this point, see for instance Yaacov Vertzberger, *Risk Taking and Decision Making: Foreign Military Intervention Decisions* (Stanford, CA: Stanford University Press, 1998), p.30.

33 Richard Ned Lebow and Janice Gross Stein, *We All Lost The Cold War* (Princeton, NJ: Princeton University Press, 1994); see also Richard Herrmann, "Image Theory and Strategic Interaction in International Relations," pp.300–3, in David Sears, Leonie Huddy, and Robert Jervis (eds.), *Oxford Handbook of Political Psychology* (New York: Oxford University Press, 2003).

34 Christopher Achen and Duncan Snidal, "Rational Deterrence Theory and Comparative Case Studies," *World Politics*, 41: 143–69, 1989, p.149.

35 John Mearsheimer, "Why We Will Soon Miss The Cold War."

36 Richard Ned Lebow and Janice Gross Stein, "Rational Deterrence Theory: I Think, Therefore I Deter," *World Politics*, 41: 208–24, 1989.

37 Ibid., p.211.

38 Jonathan Mercer, *Reputation and International Politics* (Ithaca, NY: Cornell University Press, 1996).

39 Ibid., p.213.

40 Ibid., p.214.

41 Dominic Johnson *Overconfidence and War: The Havoc and Glory of Positive Illusions* (Cambridge, MA: Harvard University Press, 2004). See also Dominic Johnson and James Fowler, "The Evolution of Overconfidence," *Nature*, 477: 317–20, 2011.

42 Johnson, *Overconfidence and War*, p.15.

43 Kenneth Payne *The Psychology of Strategy: Exploring Rationality in the Vietnam War* (London: Hurst, 2013).

44 Ralph White, "Empathizing With the Soviet Government," in White (ed.), *Psychology and the Prevention of Nuclear War: A Book of Readings* (New York: New York University Press, 1986), p.82.
45 Ralph White, *Fearful Warriors: A Psychological Profile of U.S.–Soviet Relations* (New York: Free Press, 1984), p.160; see also James Blight and Janet Lang, *The Fog of War: Lessons from the Life of Robert S. McNamara* (New York: Rowman & Littlefield, 2005), p.28.
46 Apart from works already cited, see for instance Ralph White, *Nobody Wanted War: Misperception in Vietnam and Other Wars* (Garden City, NY: Doubleday, 1968); Robert Jervis, "Hypotheses on Misperception," *World Politics*, 20(3): 454–79, 1968; Jervis, *Perception and Misperception in International Politics*; Jack Levy, "Misperception and the Causes of War: Theoretical Linkages and Analytical Problems," *World Politics*, 36: 76–99, 1983; Yaacov Vertzberger, *The World In Their Minds: Information Processing, Cognition, and Perception in Foreign Policy Decisionmaking* (Stanford, CA: Stanford University Press, 1990), especially Chapter 1; and the edition of *Peace and Conflict* on empathy and Ralph White, including Richard Wagner, "The Earliest Pioneer: Ralph K. White," *Peace and Conflict*, 10: 313–15, 2004; M.G. Wessells, M.D. Roe, and S. McKay, "Pioneers in Peace Psychology: Ralph K. White," *Peace and Conflict*, 10: 317–34, 2004; M.B. Smith, "Realistic Empathy: A Key to Sensible International Relations," *Peace and Conflict*, 10: 335–39, 2004; James Blight and Janet Lang, "Lesson Number One: 'Empathize With Your Enemy'," *Peace and Conflict*, 10: 349–68, 2004; and Ralph White, "Misperception and War," *Peace and Conflict*, 10: 399–409, 2004.
47 See Robert McNamara and James Blight, *Wilson's Ghost: Reducing the Risk of Conflict, Killing and Catastrophe in the 21st Century* (New York: Public Affairs, 2001), pp.64–73; Blight and Lang, *The Fog of War*, pp.27–57.
48 Blight and Lang, *The Fog of War*; McNamara and Blight, *Wilson's Ghost*.

Suggested Further Reading

James Goldgeier, "Psychology and Security," *Security Studies*, 6: 137–66, 1997.
Jacques Hymans, *The Psychology of Nuclear Proliferation: Identity, Emotions, and Foreign Policy* (New York: Cambridge University Press, 2006).
Kenneth Payne, *The Psychology of Strategy: Exploring Rationality in the Vietnam War* (London: Hurst, 2013).
Brian Ripley, "Psychology, Foreign Policy, and International Relations Theory," *Political Psychology*, 14: 403–16, 1993.

Film

The Fog of War: Eleven Lessons from the Life of Robert S. McNamara (2003): Superb, award-winning documentary which really brings history to life and argues for the use of empathy in international relations.

Chapter 18

The Future of Political Psychology

Since this book first appeared in 2008, the fast pace of change in the field of political psychology has already necessitated an updated assessment of where we are going. In particular, the new recognition gained within the field of economics—that many of the theories presented in this book not only exist but may better explain human behavior than *Homo economicus* does—is changing that field quite dramatically. The award of the Nobel Prize in Economics to Daniel Kahneman in 2002—even though he is a distinguished psychologist by training, who says that he has never even taken a class in economics—is but one portent of that. A new field of *behavioral economics* has emerged in a discipline long-dominated by the old Enlightenment view of reason and "Rational Man," as has a field of *neuroeconomics*.

We are often slow to embrace change in political science. In the 1980s, for instance, just as political scientists were discovering the ideas of Michel Foucault, he was often dismissed as rather *passé* within French philosophy. It would be a tragedy if political scientists continued to embrace rational choice so warmly, just as economists were looking around for something that better explained real behavior. There is as yet no counterpart to behavioral economics there, or what might be called "behavioral politics." But the time is arguably ripe for such a shift. There has long been a recognition of the significance of "bounded rationality" in the study of both foreign policy decision-making and voting behavior, although political science as a wider field has largely failed to integrate these approaches into a concerted attack upon the Rational Actor model. Why? In part, analysts have preferred to cling to the simplifying but non-empirical and anti-behavioral assumptions that traditional *Homo economicus* provides, allowing political behavior to be modeled in a comforting but ultimately misleading way. Perhaps, though, the time has come for political science to follow the lead of economics and take psychology more seriously. We need a fresh approach to the study of politics, based perhaps on the integration of some of the approaches covered in this book, into a single "cognitive neuroscience of politics" or "behavioral politics."

It would be ironic indeed if political scientists were to cling stubbornly to an economic model which economists themselves are increasingly abandoning and see as increasingly anachronistic. But a major problem with the version of *Homo psychologicus* that we have presented in this book—and outlined in Chapter 2—may well be that it is not nearly radical enough. It is based on the model of "bounded rationality" developed by people like Herbert Simon and dominant for decades within cognitive psychology, but it is nevertheless an "imperfectionist" model. In other words, at its philosophical core it is really an amendment to an approach to decision-making which we now know to be basically incorrect. In other words, it tries to be a more "realistic" version of *Homo economicus*, but it is still based on amendments to the latter's (faulty) basic assumptions. And therein may lie the problem. Great minds like Plato, Descartes, and even Freud based their arguments on the idea of the "Rational Man" fighting against the demon of emotion. Plato in particular famously described emotion as being like an unruly horse, constantly pulling the rational and reasoning "charioteer" where he didn't want to go. The human mind, as we stressed earlier, is capable of amazing things, but it does not follow that it is capable of readily understanding itself, or that we have done so accurately through our own history. Indeed, we may have fundamentally misunderstood how our own brains work, at least until now.

Emotional Brains, Homo Neurobiologicus and Shifting Paradigms

If we now know the *Homo economicus* approach to have been wholly wrong—and not just in need of revision—then what should replace it? Fortunately, the seeds of a replacement have already emerged within neuroscience and the study of emotion. The artificial "wall" between the latter and cognition is being broken down. As we have already seen, Antonio Damasio showed in *Descartes' Error* that emotion is *essential* to human reasoning, and not at all some sort of inhibition to it as the classical thinkers believed. A new approach might be based, for instance, on Daniel Kahneman's distinction in his book *Thinking Fast and Slow* about "System 1" and "System 2"-type thinking.[1] System 1 works very fast, and we are often unconscious of it; it is intuitive, effortless, and based on emotional impulses. System 2, on the other hand, is slow and deliberative. It is more laborious and cognitive. We are conscious of choosing between alternatives when we use System 2, and we make an effort to choose between them. Most decision-making, however, is of the System 1 variety; in other words, it is entirely unconscious. As Joseph LeDoux has argued, emotional, unconscious processing is by far the most common.[2] This undoubtedly explains why a good batter in baseball is able to hit a fastball, even though the conscious brain doesn't have enough time to process the information coming at it, or why a good quarterback knows just where to throw the ball in a split second when everything is chaos around him and the pocket is collapsing.[3]

Thomas Kuhn's most famous work, and the one in which he presents his celebrated "theory about theories," was *The Structure of Scientific Revolutions*, originally published in 1962.[4] Simply stated, the book challenged the so-called "common sense" idea that science is a purely rational process that is also cumulative. We often assume that the history of science is marked by a steady progression to more and more knowledge about the natural world, in which truth accumulates as we find out more and more about that world. But Kuhn showed that this is not how science actually works. His argument was that science was not a steady accumulation of knowledge. Instead, it was "a series of peaceful interludes punctuated by intellectually violent revolutions." And in those revolutions, he wrote, "one conceptual world view is replaced by another."

According to Kuhn, what he calls "normal science" is characterized by the existence of a dominant *paradigm*, a general "world view" that unites scientists under a set of common assumptions, sets the standards of what questions are legitimate to study, and lays down rules as to how they should be studied. Kuhn argues that natural science has nearly always been characterized by the existence of a single, dominant paradigm that has performed the functions just mentioned. For instance, Ptolemy had the theory that the sun revolves around the earth, and Ptolemaic scientists worked within this paradigm, never challenging the fundamental assumption that the earth is at the center of everything. But of course there are always things in any paradigm that the dominant view cannot explain. These are *anomalies*, findings which the theory cannot explain. At particular times in history, Kuhn says, the anomalies have mounted up to the point where people start to doubt their fundamental assumptions about the world. If this happens, it creates a "crisis" in the paradigm. If there is a meaningful alternative to the old view, this then ushers in a period of what Kuhn calls "revolutionary science." A revolutionary figure appears, like a Lavoisier or an Einstein, who champions a whole new way of looking at things and ushers in a "paradigm shift." Albert Einstein's theory of relativity, for instance, challenged Isaac Newton's conception of physics by showing that Newton's laws of gravity were only applicable on earth.

In short, real science looks nothing like the image we get in textbooks of a "steady progression towards truth." Instead, what we see is the replacement of one supposed truth with another (and one which is often completely incompatible with the previous truth). Now Kuhn, it should be noted, warned that his approach should not be used to try to understand the social sciences. The natural sciences are often characterized by the existence of a single paradigm. Kuhn regarded social science as an immature "pre-science," characterized by *a variety* of paradigms existing simultaneously. This has not stopped social scientists using his theory for their own purposes, though, as Kuhn has influenced not only scientists but also economists, historians, sociologists, philosophers, and political scientists.

There are certainly some problems with transferring Kuhn's approach wholesale from the natural sciences to the social. Scientific discoveries or "Eureka!" moments presaging the emergence of a dominant paradigm are common enough in the natural sciences, but they are mostly lacking in (say) political science, which has always been dominated by competing paradigms which co-exist somewhat uneasily. International relations theory is a good example, where the list of extant theories is now so long that they can hardly be covered in a single course. Nevertheless, we are beginning to see a number of different areas of political psychology coalesce behind the neuroscientific approach. If there is not yet a single dominant paradigm within political psychology, the signs are there already that it might be at least the dominant approach among several in the future.

Cognitive scientists are beginning to uncover the neurobiological bases of many of the behaviors discussed in this book. For instance:

- *Psychobiography:* genopolitics potentially offers us an alternative explanation for Woodrow Wilson's stubborn willfulness and refusal to reconsider his options. Although this must be speculative, it is possible that the young Woodrow simply inherited this genetic trait from Joseph Wilson. Rather than the latter humiliating him, perhaps he simply passed along his own unyielding and unbending personality traits? It is at least worth considering this possibility.
- *Analogical reasoning:* a part of the brain called the anterior cingulate cortex (or ACC) allows us to learn from the past. When something happens that pleases us, the ACC releases the pleasure-giving neurotransmitter dopamine. When something goes wrong that is unpredicted, however, the brain generates a signal known as "error-related negativity." Learning by analogy, discussed in Chapter 9, seems to involve this chemical process.[5]
- *Behavioral conditioning:* in Chapter 3, we began our analysis of situationism by looking at the experiments of John Watson and B.F. Skinner. How was the latter, for instance, able to train pigeons to perform relatively complex tasks? Reinforcement seems to involve the same neurological process as analogical reasoning. The dopamine-delivering qualities of the ACC can be

manipulated to condition monkeys to perform certain behaviors or to refrain from others.[6]

- *Empathy*: in the previous chapter we discussed the capacity of leaders to empathize with one another's situation, as when John Kennedy put himself "in the shoes" of Nikita Khruschchev in October 1962. But how is it that we pull off this formidable feat? During the 1980s, a neurobiologist called Vittorio Gallese discovered the existence of what are now called "mirror neurons" in monkeys. As the usual story goes, Gallese was eating an ice cream, and the brain activity of the monkey—which was attached to a machine by wires in its skull—went haywire, even though the monkey was perfectly still and performing no physical activity itself. This story is probably a fiction created for the sake of dinner parties and speeches—the process of discovery was apparently a good bit more lengthy and drawn-out than that—but we now know that something very similar happens in human beings when, for example, we watch lovers kiss in a movie or we are watching a gardener dig on TV. The same mirror neurons "fire" that would activate if we were actually performing those same actions ourselves. Although we still do not fully understand this phenomenon, it appears to be the neurobiological basis of empathy.[7]

Choosing Between Dispositionism and Situationism?

Regardless of whether political neuroscience really is the wave of the future, of course, it is up to the student to make up his or her own mind about the relative merits of our two "meta-approaches," *situationism* and *dispositionism*. What follows is merely a suggestive and personal view of how one might reconcile the two, and students and teachers who genuinely want to make up their own minds wholly independently of the author are of course welcome to skip the rest of this final chapter. Since the material that we have come to call "political psychology" has rarely been categorized consistently by most of its practitioners in the way we have done in this book, we are in some ways on our own in coming to conclusions on this issue. We are not *entirely* alone, however, since various political scientists (especially those in international relations) and psychologists (especially those influenced by attribution theory and social psychology generally) have reflected upon this issue in depth.

Some of you will already have made up your minds on the central issue of what contributes most to the causes of human behavior, the situation or the individual. Indeed, the author sincerely *hopes* that you have at least reached some tentative answer to this question already, since the entire book is designed to prompt you to do this. Some of you may even have become rather "partisan" on this issue by now. Whatever you have concluded, however, you should take into account some of the following as you finish this book.

First of all, in Part III it has to be said that *we have not consistently seen situationism or dispositionism emerge as the clear "winner"* across the limited range of empirical cases we have examined in this final section. The reader may have noticed that there is no *consistently* pro-disposition or pro-situation bias across the five empirical areas—terrorism, nationalism and ethnic conflict, race and tolerance, voting behavior, and international relations—we have examined. Although no attempt has been made to summarize everything written on each topic, an effort has been made to summarize current preferences and biases among scholars working within a particular subtopic as a whole.

What is perhaps most interesting is that scholars appear to be pulling in fundamentally different directions across the cases. In the psychological study of terrorism, analysts began by looking for a "terrorist personality," but have almost uniformly turned away from what has been recognized as a fruitless search and are starting to favor approaches that stress the importance of situation. In the study of nationalism and conflict, both types of theory have predominated, but genocide in particular seems best explained by a mixture of dispositional and situational factors. When we came to look at both racism and intolerance and the study of voting behavior, on the other hand, we saw that the dispositions of individuals have traditionally been given more emphasis than situational forces. In international relations theory, on the other hand, situationism has been the dominant approach to explaining the actions of states, and psychological dispositions—while studied extensively—are rarely treated as a comprehensive approach in their own right. IR scholars have seemed not to know what to do with psychology, since it questions many assumptions made by popular models and "muddies" the search for parsimonious theories.

Second, and in related vein, the preceding point seems to suggest that *the importance of situationism/dispositionism varies with the situation, and that both matter a great deal*. On the one hand, there does appear to be a number of circumstances in which the environment or context surrounding the individual has been shown, at least under laboratory or experimental conditions, to exert a powerful impact on behavior. Many of these involve what Morton Hunt refers to in his popular history of the study of psychology as "closed cases" (issues that are no longer much studied because they involve findings which have been replicated so many times).[8]

The ability of the situation to override moral values is especially clear in experiments like those of Milgram, and Darley and Latane, and since we are almost never free of social pressures of some sort—unless, like "Unabomber" Ted Kaczynski, we choose to live like a hermit—one might expect that situations reign supreme under most or all conditions. On the other hand, there are areas in which the "determining force" of situations has probably been greatly overemphasized. In international relations theory in particular, as we saw in the previous chapter, leaders have too often been seen as responding "rationally" to supposedly unambiguous cues provided by the informational environment, and political psychology has failed to develop its own theory of international relations (or, at least, a theory which is *recognized* and accepted by other scholars in the field as being a theory of international relations). We have also seen a variety of circumstances where people's dispositions do play a more critical role than the situation they find themselves in. And even in classic experiments like that of Milgram, one can argue that there is a very significant proportion of human behavior that he is simply not explaining.

Just as we ignore situationism at our peril, so too is it folly to ignore the power of dispositions in politics. As John Hibbing notes in an especially perceptive essay, we have long underestimated the power of human biology in shaping behavior and just as long overstated the force of situations.[9] That is especially true in the field of voting behavior, where situationism has reigned supreme for almost as long as anyone can remember, and only now are we beginning to see biological theories about political attitudes and behavior. But people like Hibbing, we should note, are not saying that "biology is everything." In biology itself, issues like the "situationist–dispositionist" debate are simply no longer debated, and the nature versus nurture debate is old hat. As a field, its practitioners have long ago realized that there is both a situationist and a dispositionist dimension to human behavior, and that this is simply not an "either–or" proposition. Psychology as a field is also starting to accept that both genetics and the environment matter. There is, as Hibbing suggests, no reason why political science should be any different in the twenty-first century.

Notes

1 Daniel Kahneman, *Thinking Fast and Slow* (New York: Farrar, Straus and Giroux, 2011).
2 Joseph LeDoux, *The Emotional Brain: The Mysterious Underpinnings of Emotional Life* (New York: Simon & Schuster, 1998).
3 Jonah Lehrer, *How We Decide* (New York: Houghton Mifflin, 2009).
4 Thomas Kuhn, *The Structure of Scientific Revolutions,* second edition (Chicago, IL: University of Chicago Press, 1970).
5 Lehrer, *How We Decide*, pp.38–39.
6 Ibid, pp.34–41.
7 Marco Iacoboni, *Mirroring People* (New York: Farrar, Strus and Giroux, 2008), pp.3–12.
8 Morton Hunt, *The Story of Psychology*, updated and revised edition (New York: Anchor Books, 2007).
9 John Hibbing, "Ten Misconceptions Concerning Neurobiology and Politics," *Perspectives On Politics*, 11: 475–89, 201.

Index